Table of Contents

Point to and say the numeral. Ask the child to count and color the bird at the top of the page. Then ask him or her to count and circle one bird at the bottom.

Counting 1

Count and color **1**.

Count and circle **1**.

Ask the child to count and color one item in each group.

Showing 1

Count and color **1** in each group.

Point to and say the numeral. Ask the child to count and color the gingerbread houses at the top of the page. Then ask him or her to count and circle two gingerbread men at the bottom.

Counting 2

Count and color **2**.

Count and circle **2**.

Ask the child to count and color two items in each group.

Showing 2

Count and color **2** in each group.

Point to and say the numeral. Ask the child to count and color the shells at the top of the page. Then ask him or her to count and circle three shells at the bottom.

Counting 3

Count and color **3**.

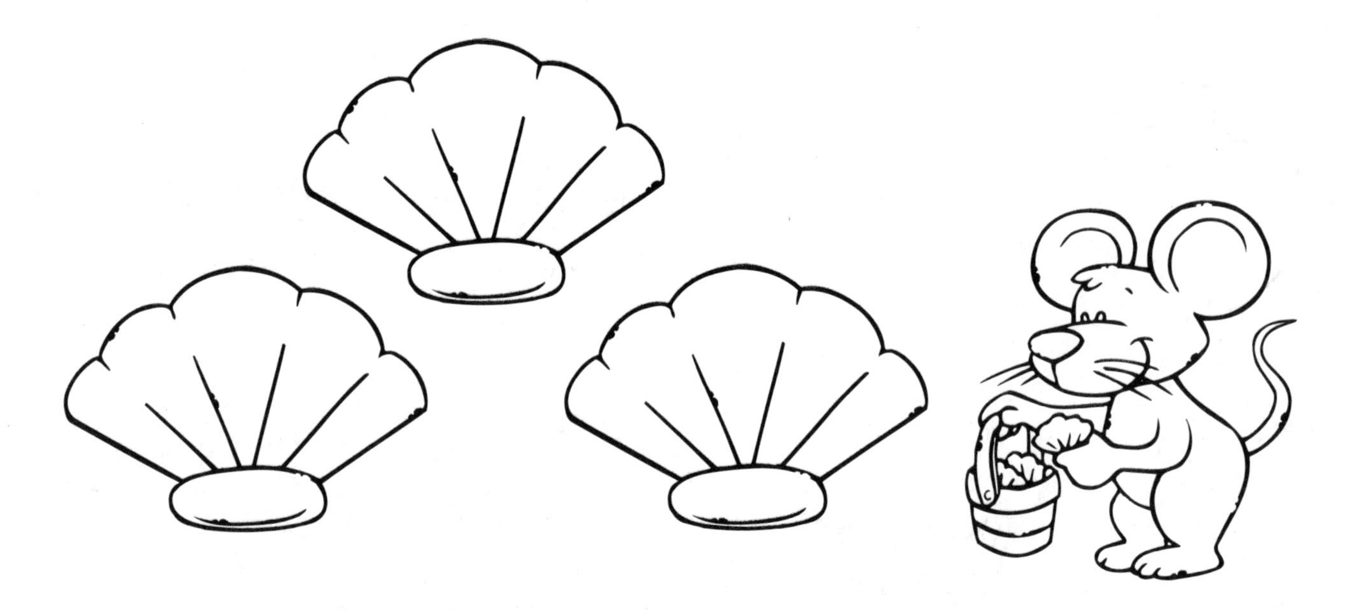

Count and circle **3**.

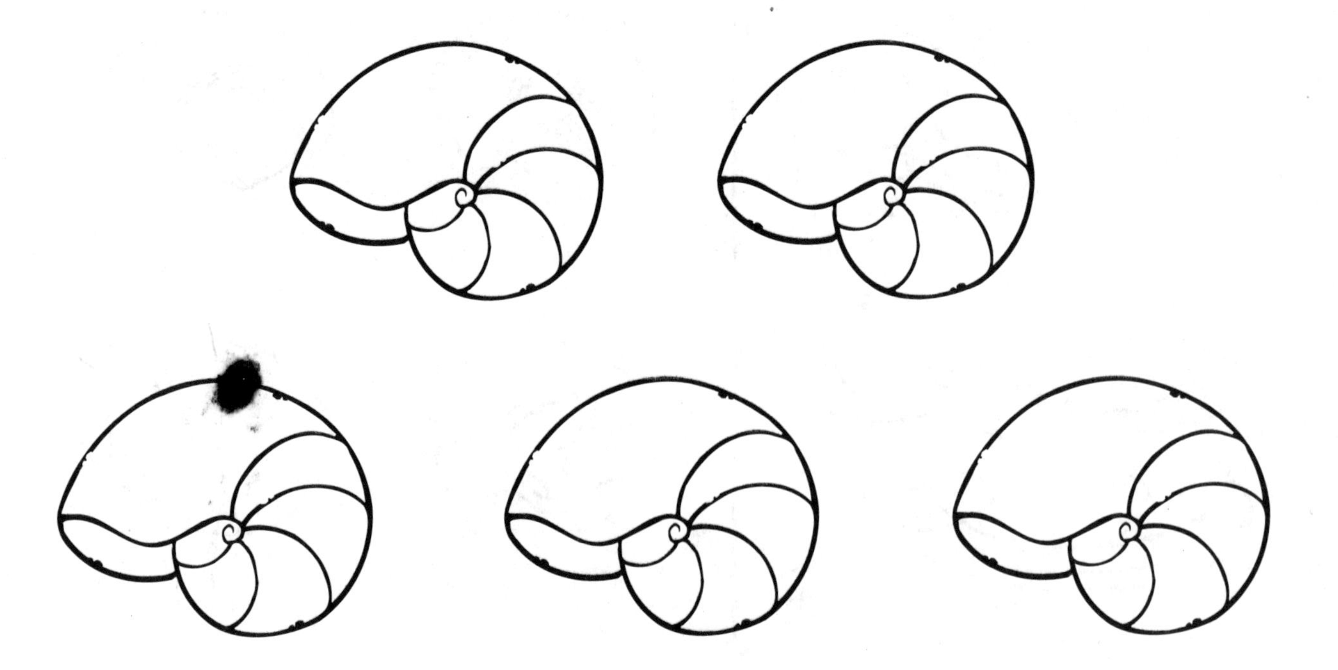

Ask the child to count and color three items in each group.

Showing 3

Count and color **3** in each group.

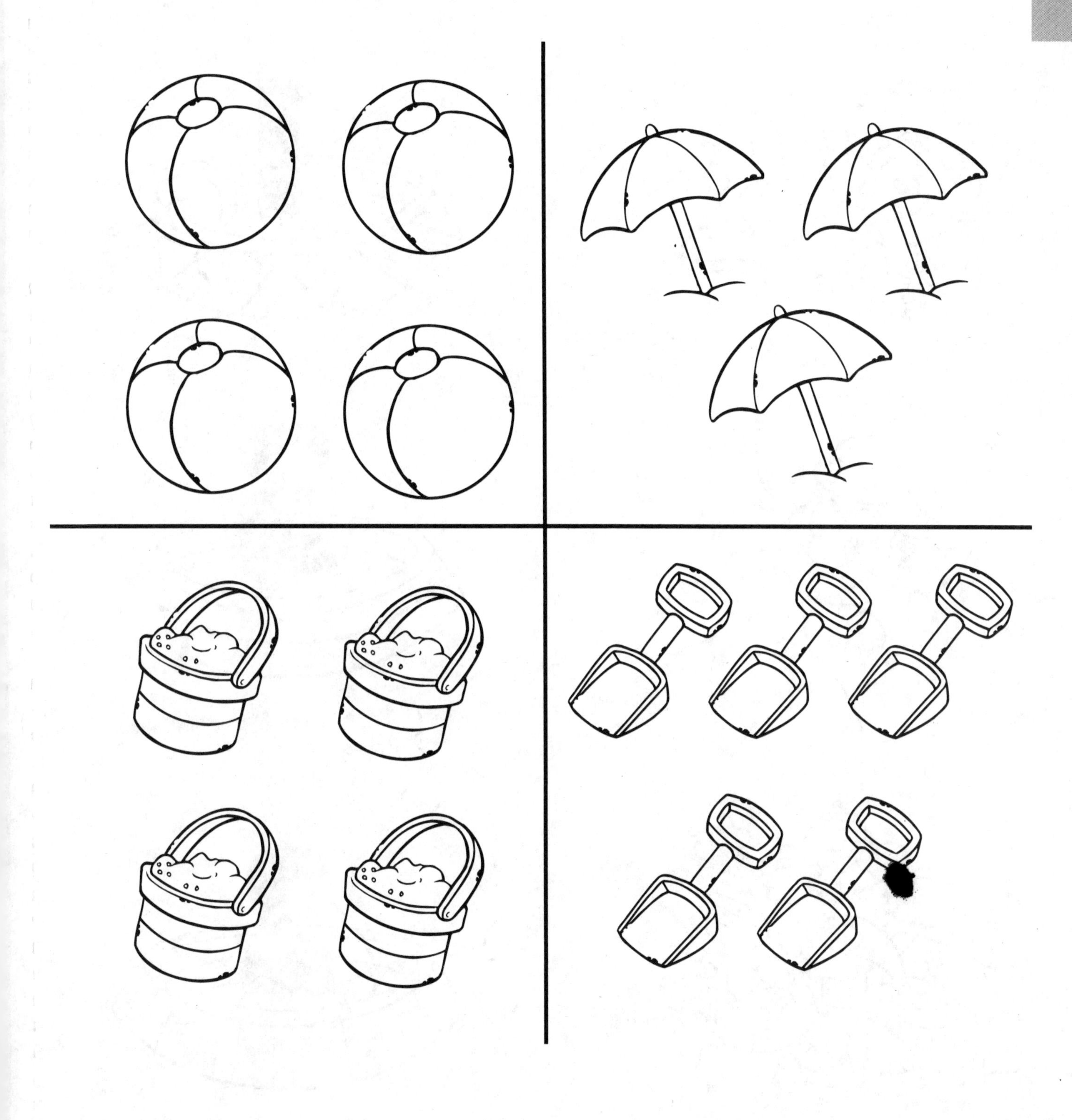

Ask the child to count the number of clowns in each group. Then have him or her draw a line to the number that shows how many there are.

Circus Fun

Draw a line to the correct number.

Understanding numbers; matching groups of objects and numerals 1-3

Ask the child to count the number of instruments in each group. Then have him or her circle the number that shows how many there are.

Music Fun

Circle the correct number.

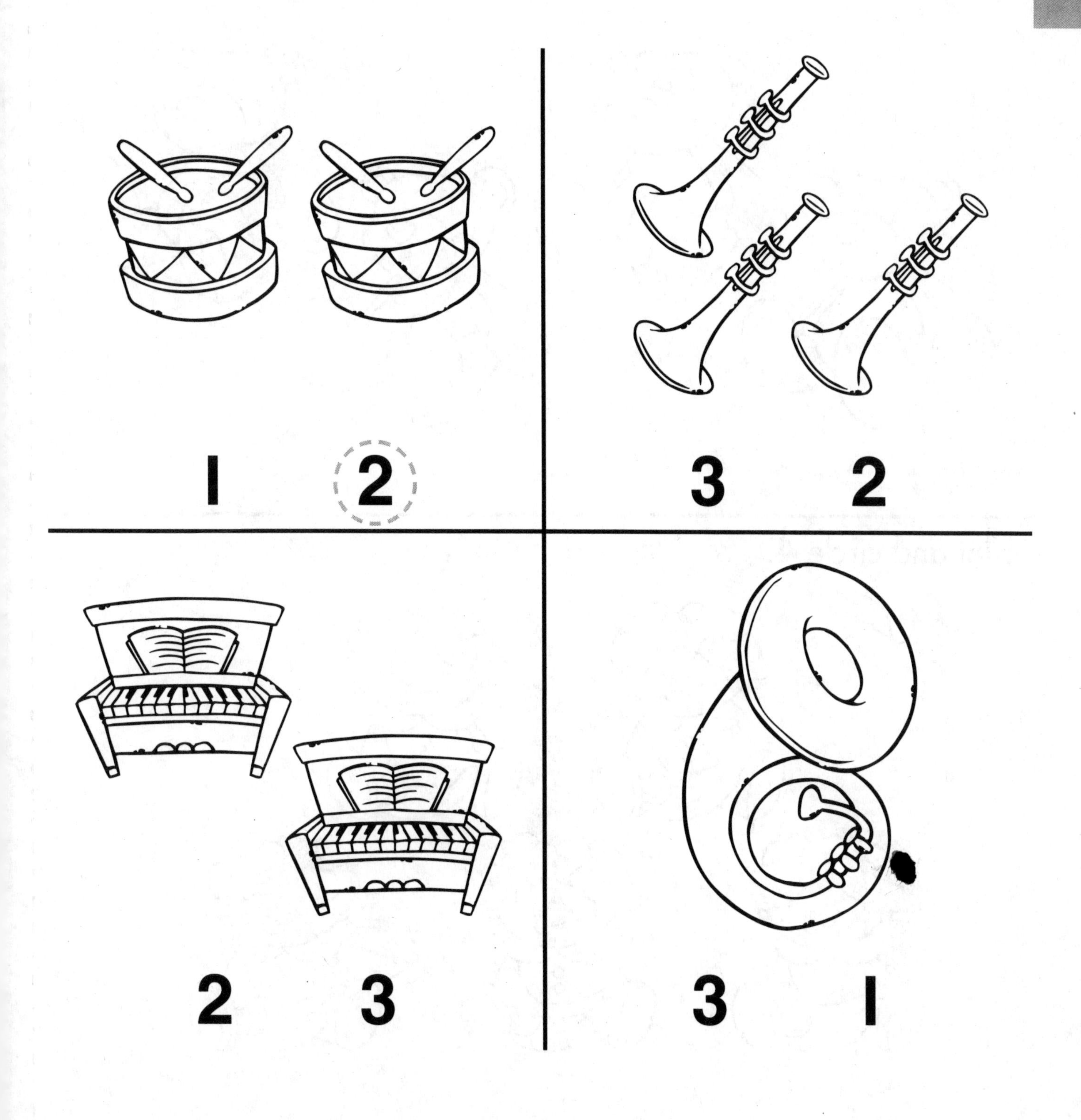

Point to and say the numeral. Ask the child to count and color the bears at the top of the page. Then ask him or her to count and circle four dolls at the bottom.

Counting 4

Count and color **4**.

Count and circle **4**.

Understanding numbers: identifying a set of four

Ask the child to count and color four items in each group.

Showing 4

Count and color **4** in each group.

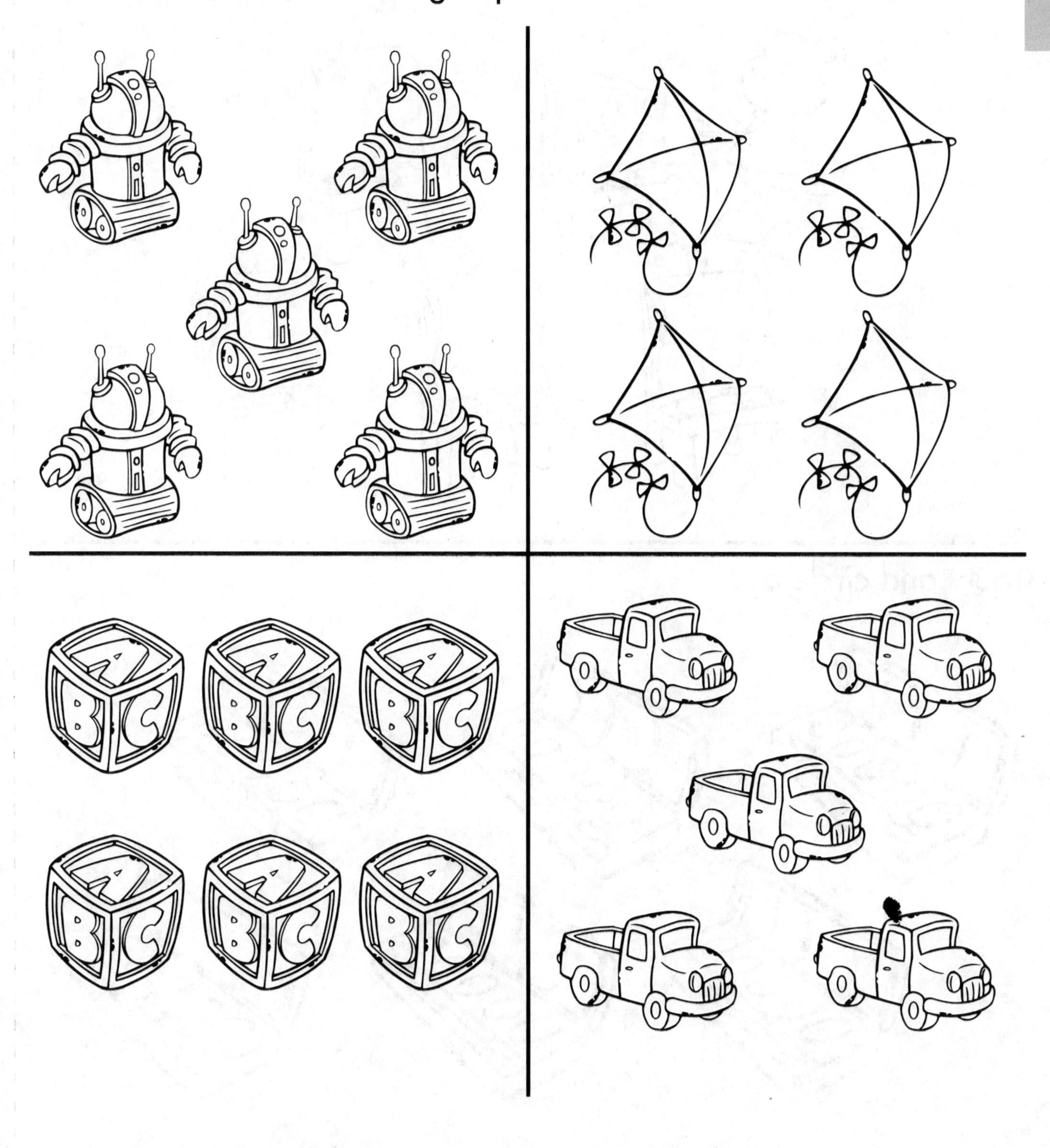

Point to and say the numeral. Ask the child to count and color the easels at the top of the page. Then ask him or her to count and circle five paint trays at the bottom.

Counting 5

Count and color **5**.

Count and circle **5**.

Ask the child to count and color five items in each group.

Showing 5

Count and color **5** in each group.

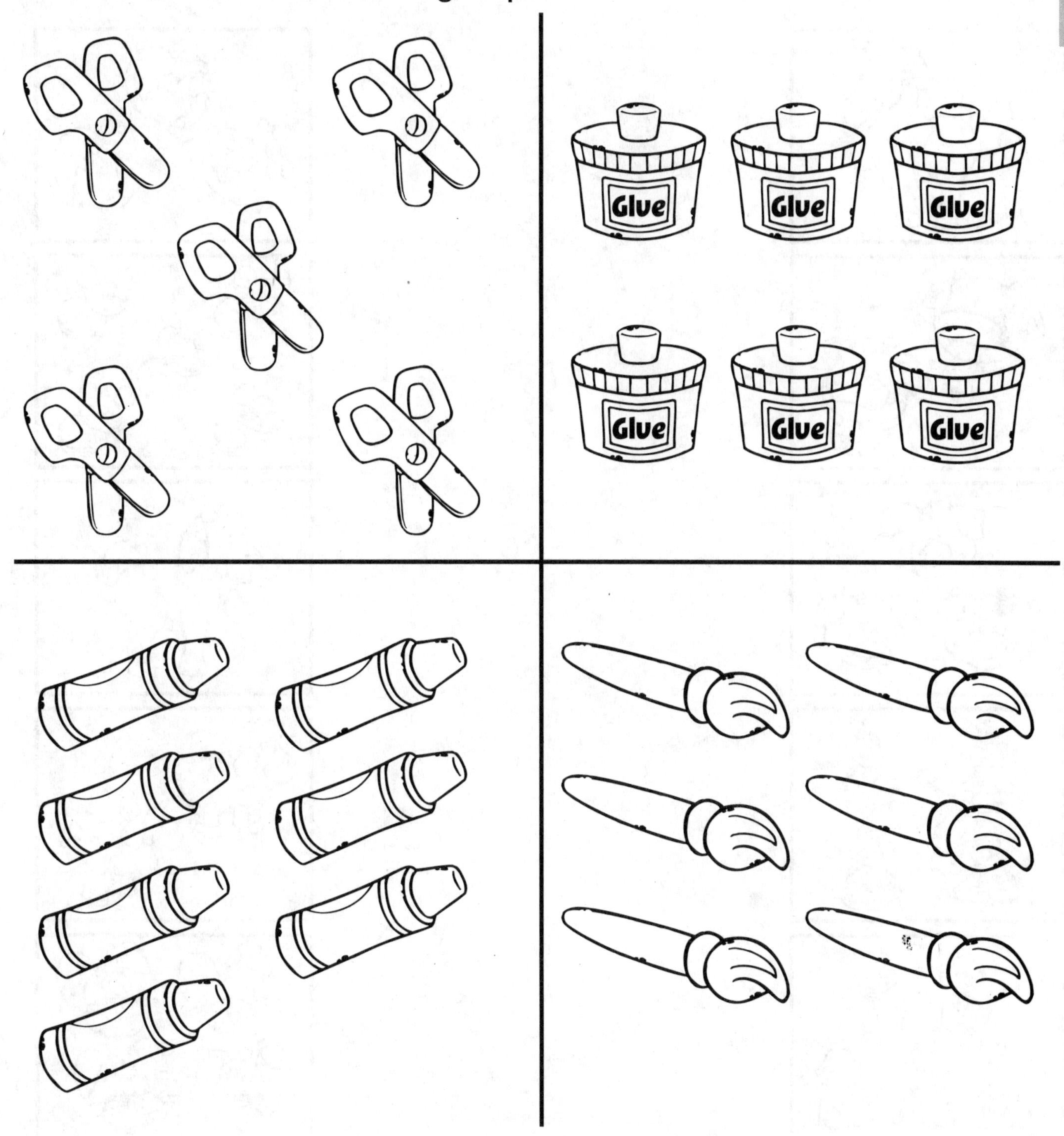

Ask the child to count the number of animals in each box. Then have him or her draw a line between the groups with the same number.

On the Farm

Match.

Ask the child to read the numeral at the beginning of each row. Then have him or her color that number of animals in the row.

At the Zoo

Color the correct number.

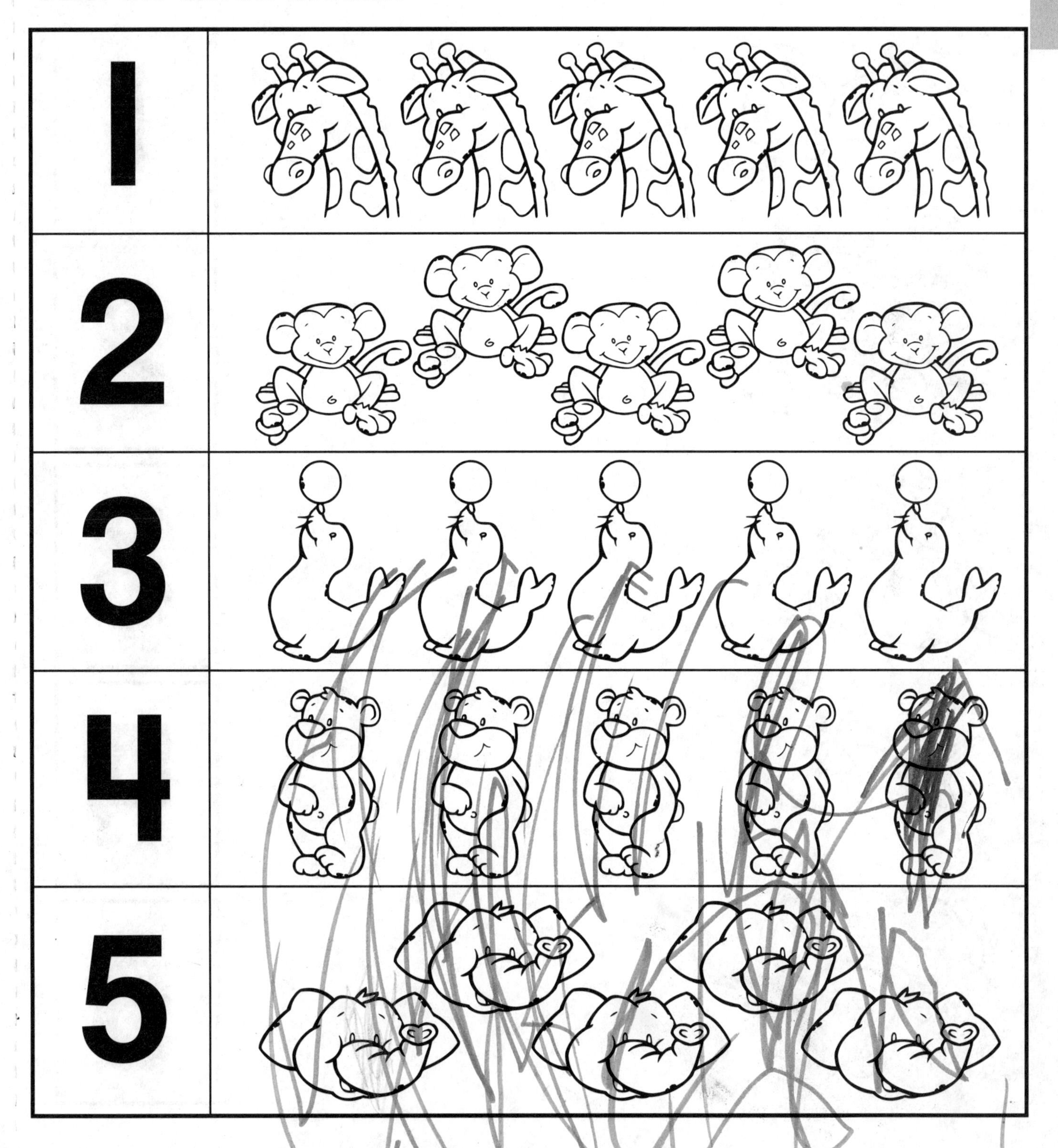

Ask the child to count the fish in each group. Then have him or her draw a line to the matching numeral on the right.

Gone Fishing

Match.

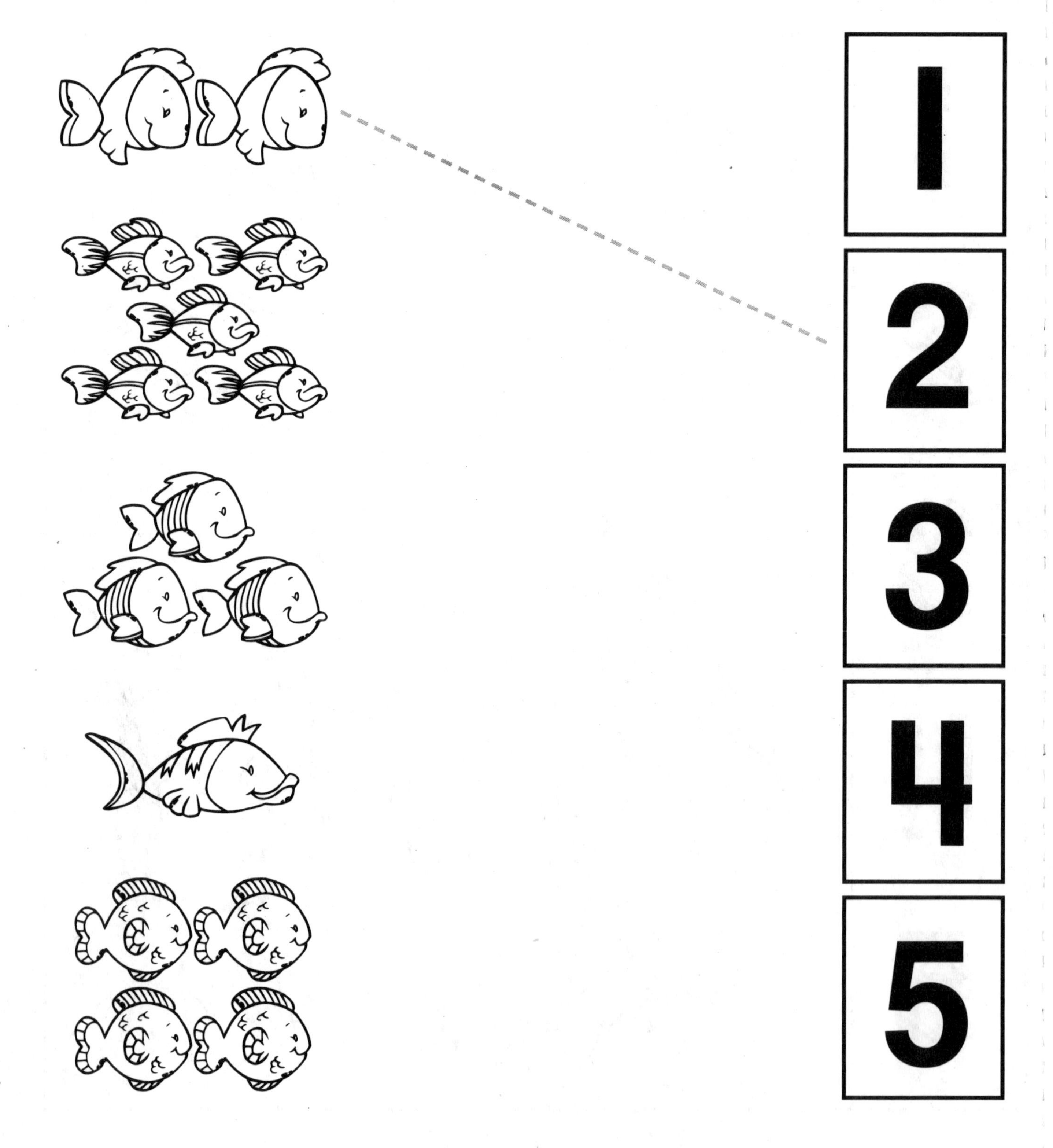

Counting to 5; matching numerals with the correct number of objects

Ask the child to count the number of sea creatures in each group. Then have him or her circle the number that shows how many there are.

Under the Sea

Circle the correct number.

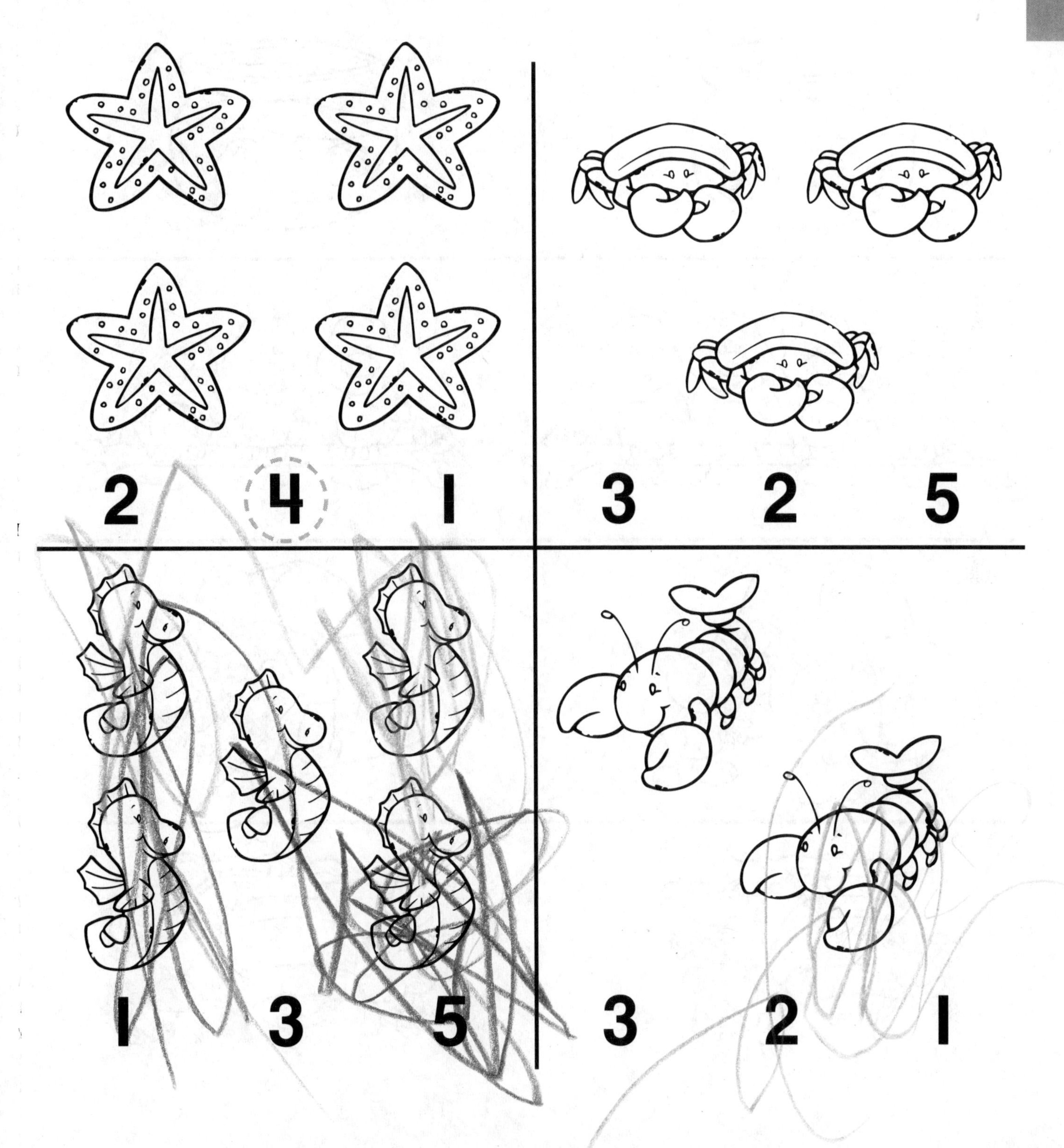

Ask the child to count the number of objects in each group. Then have him or her circle the group with more in each row.

More

Circle the group with more.

Ask the child to count the number of objects in each group. Then have him or her circle the group with less in each row.

Less

Circle the group with less.

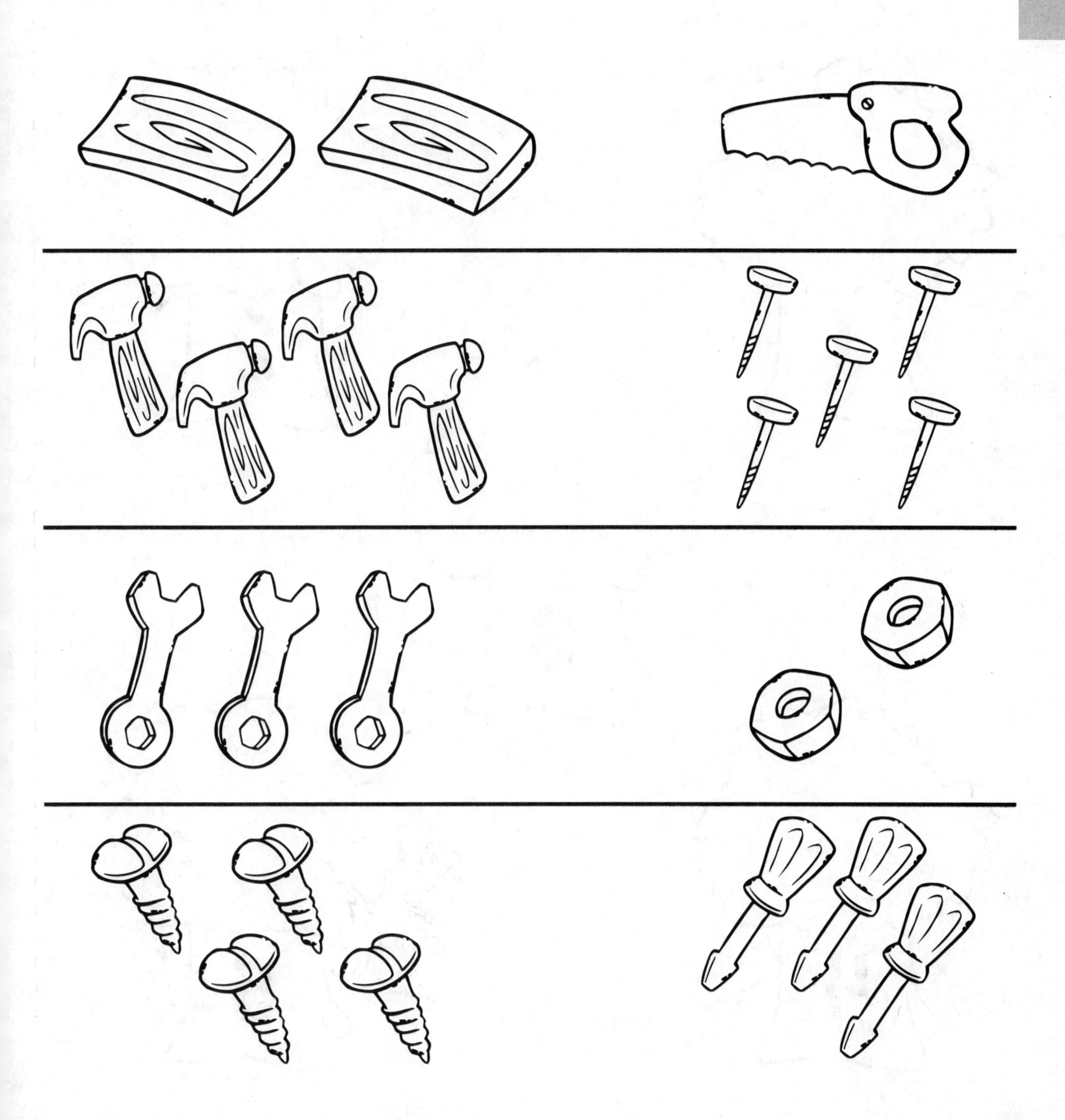

Ask the child to read the numeral on each tree trunk. Then have him or her draw that number of apples on the trees.

Apple Trees

Draw s on the .

Counting to 5; recognizing numerals; drawing to show numbers

Ask the child to count and color the picnic baskets, cats, clouds, ants, and trees in the picture. Then have him or her circle the number that he or she counted for each.

The Cats' Picnic

Count and color. Circle how many.

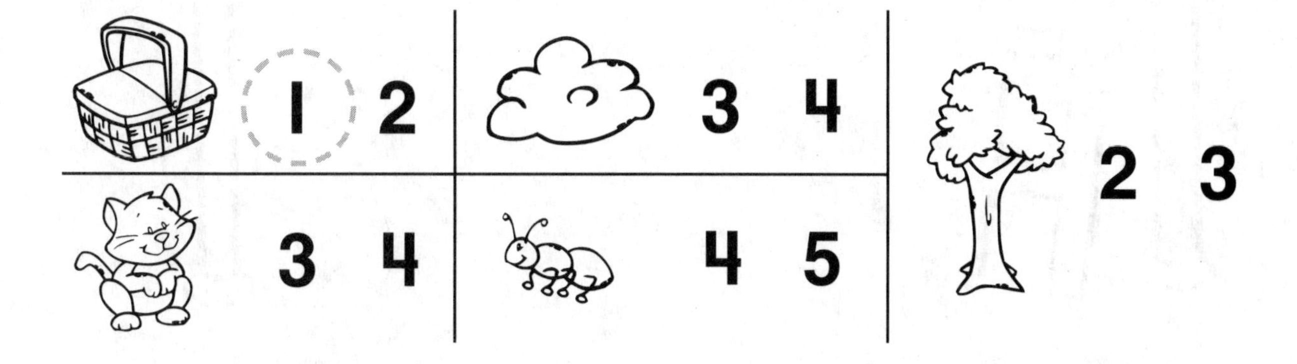

Ask the child to predict what the picture will show when completed. Then have him or her connect the dots in numerical order and color the picture.

High Wire Dot-to-Dot

Connect the dots from **1** to **5**.

Understanding numerical order; developing fine motor control

Ask the child to predict what the picture will show when completed. Then have him or her connect the dots in numerical order and color the picture.

Raccoon Dot-to-Dot

Connect the dots from **1** to **5**.

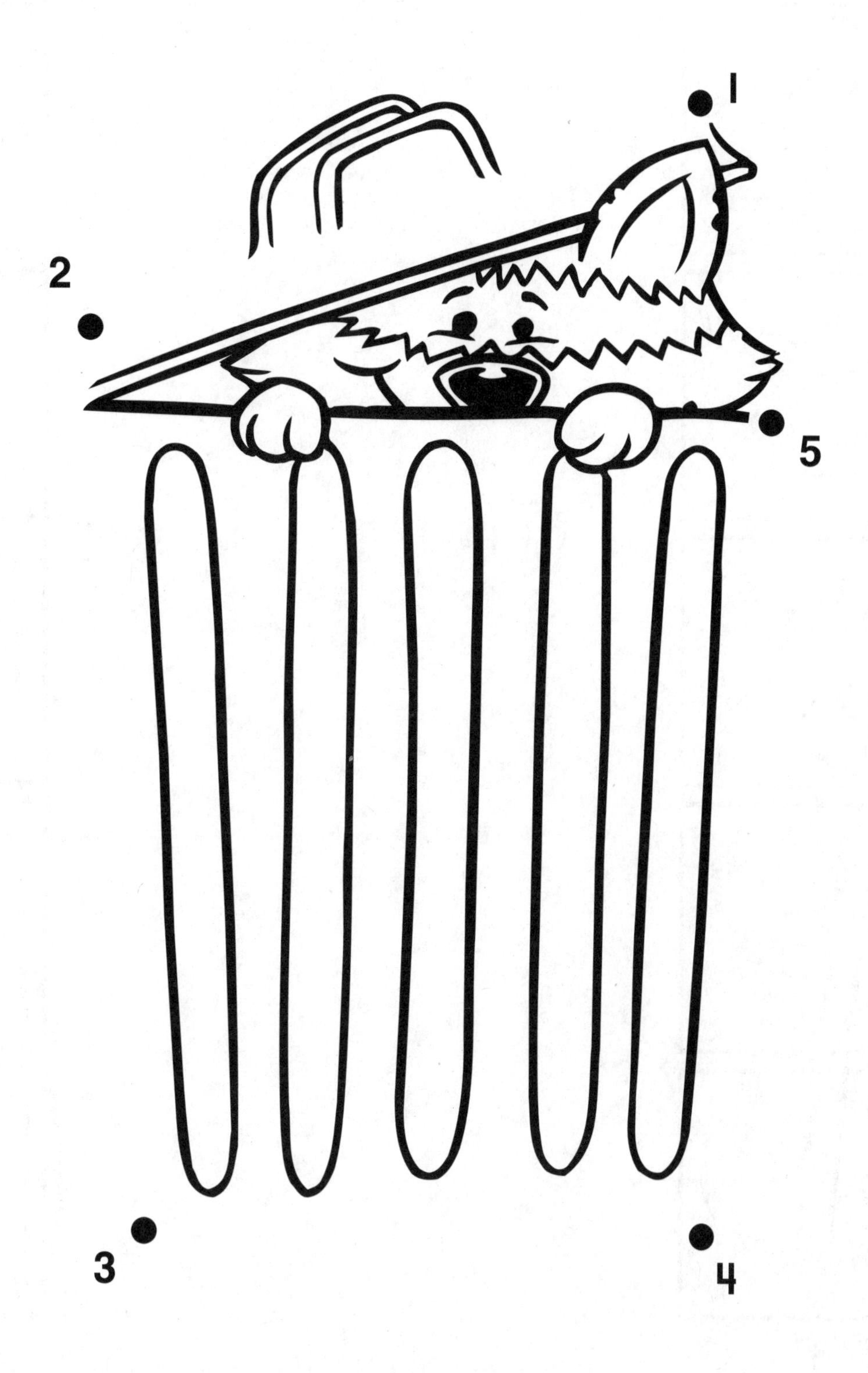

Understanding numerical order; developing fine motor control

Ask the child to count the items in each box. Then have him or her draw a line to the number that shows how many there are.

Brrrr! It's Cold Out!

Match.

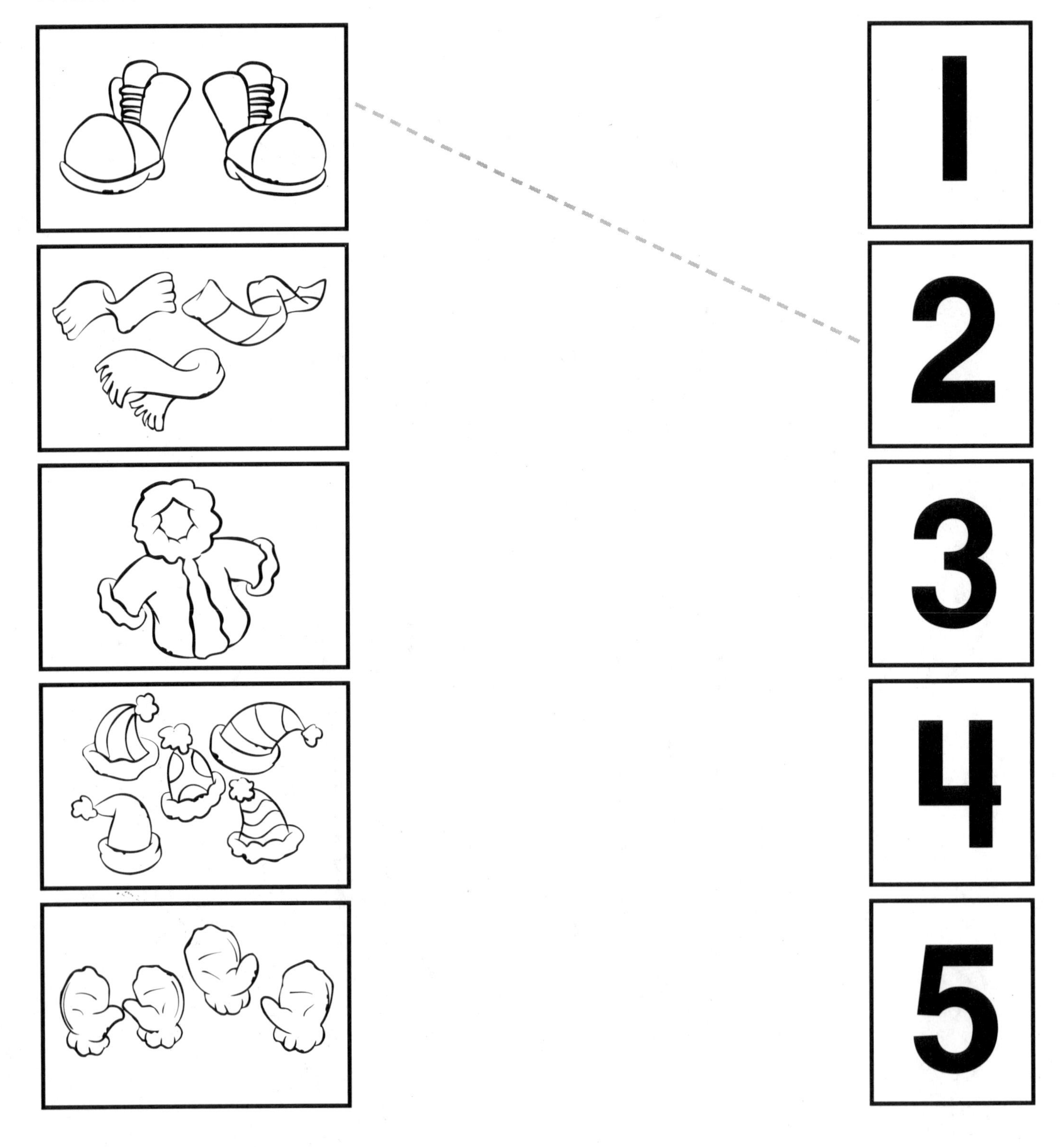

Counting to 5; matching numerals with the correct number of objects

Help the child identify the color of each crayon. Then point to and say the numeral on each dinosaur. Ask the child to use the code to color the dinosaurs.

Color by Number

Use the code to color the dinosaurs.

Ask the child to count the items in each row. Then have him or her trace the numerals.

Bake Shop

Trace the numerals.

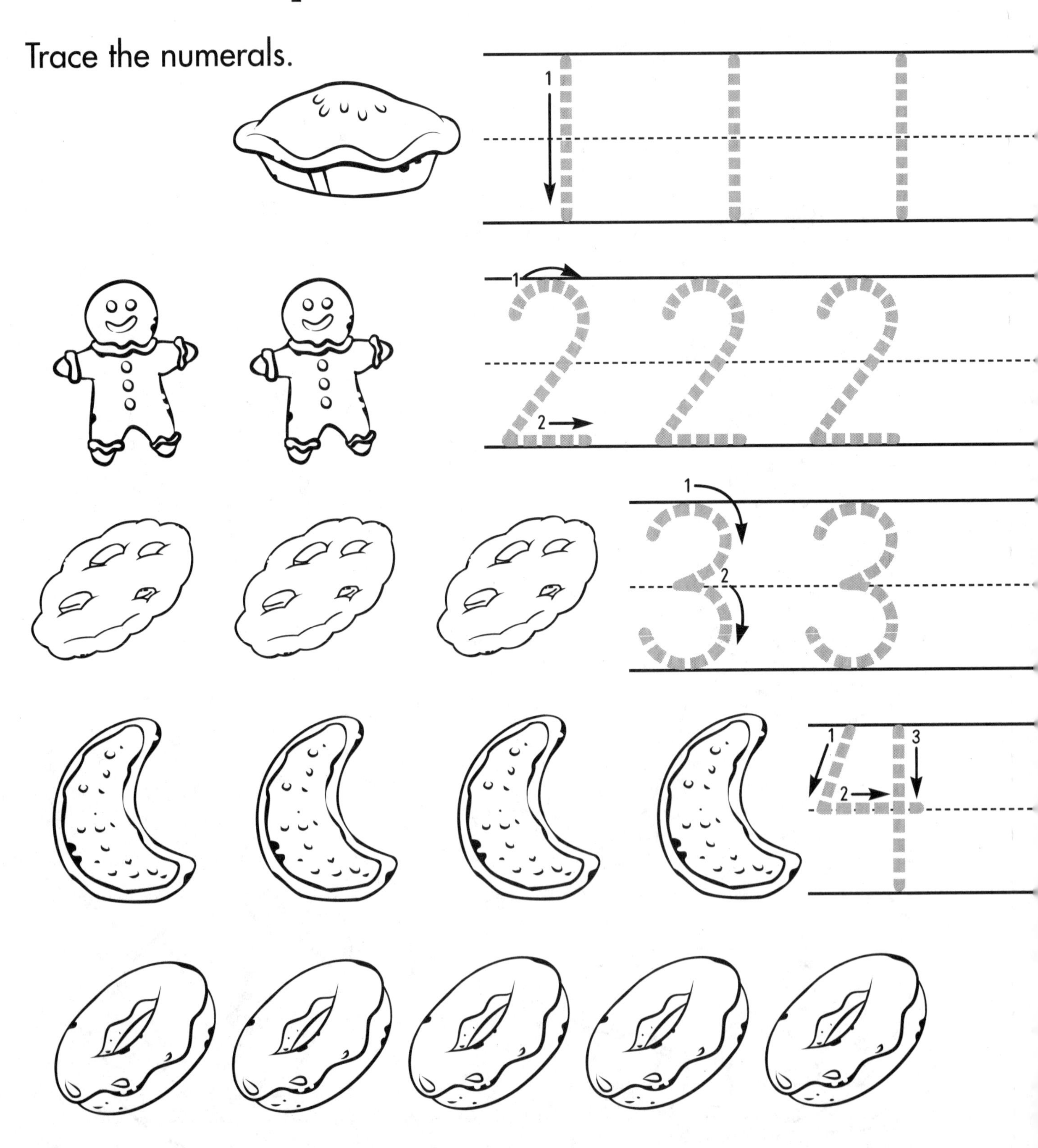

Understanding numbers; counting objects and tracing numerals

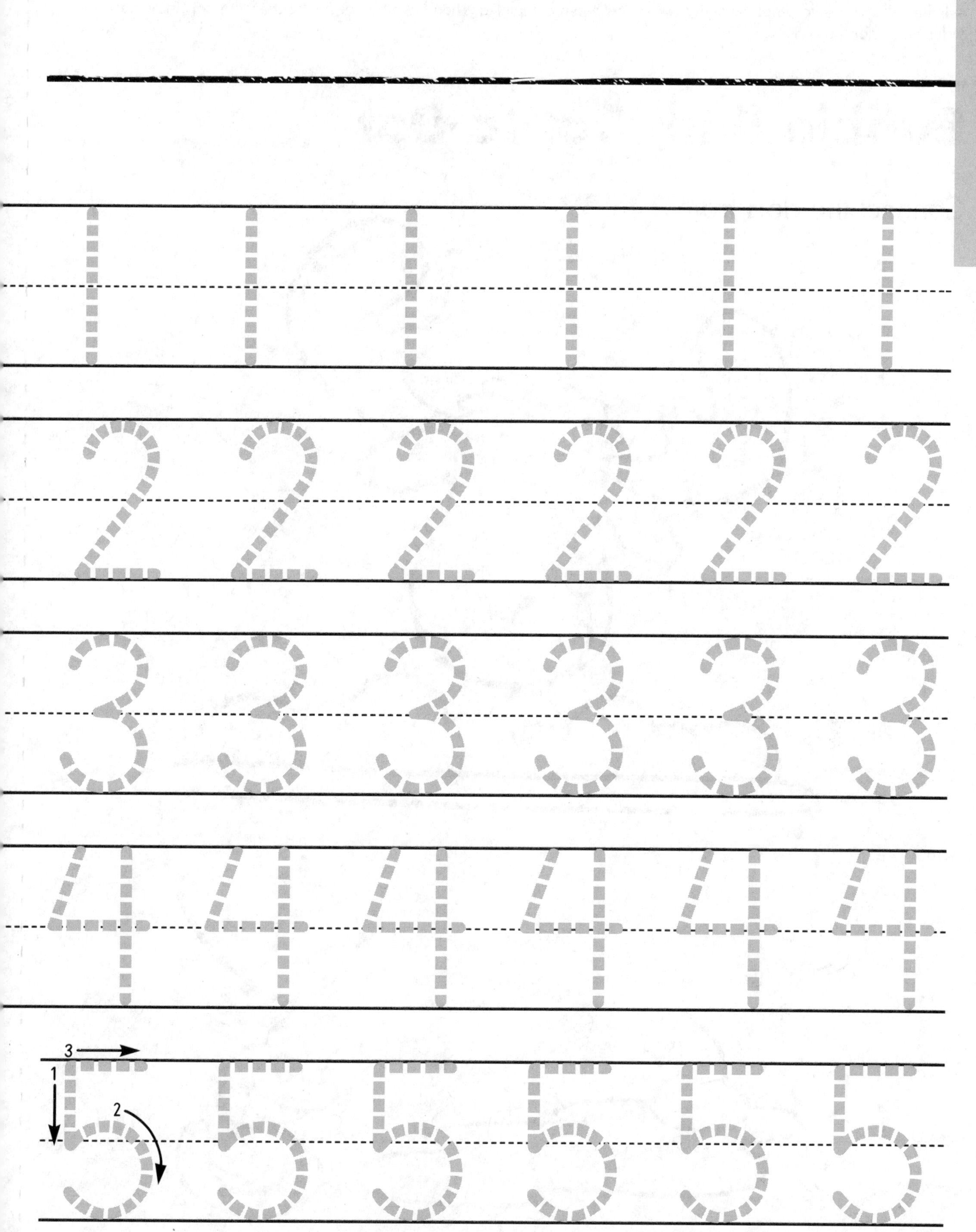
1
2
3

Ask the child to predict what the picture will show when completed. Then have him or her connect the dots in numerical order and color the picture.

Bubble Bath Dot-to-Dot

Connect the dots from **1** to **5**.

Understanding numerical order; developing fine motor control

Answer Key

As the child completes the pages in this section, review his or her answers. When you take the time to correct the work and explain mistakes, you're showing your child that you feel learning is important.

page 2

Point to and say the numeral. Ask the child to count and color the bird at the top of the page. Then ask him or her to count and circle one bird at the bottom.

Counting 1

Count and color **1**.

Count and circle **1**.

2 Understanding numbers: identifying a set of one

page 3

Ask the child to count and color one item in each group.

Numbers I

Showing 1

Count and color **1** in each group.

Understanding numbers: identifying a set of one 3

page 4

Point to and say the numeral. Ask the child to count and color the gingerbread houses at the top of the page. Then ask him or her to count and circle two gingerbread men at the bottom.

Counting 2

Count and color **2**.

Count and circle **2**.

4 Understanding numbers: identifying a set of two

page 5

Ask the child to count and color two items in each group.

Numbers I

Showing 2

Count and color **2** in each group.

Understanding numbers: identifying a set of two 5

page 6

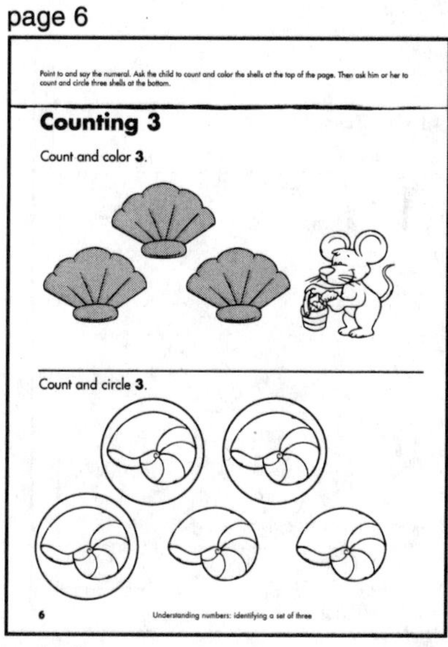

Point to and say the numeral. Ask the child to count and color the shells at the top of the page. Then ask him or her to count and circle three shells at the bottom.

Counting 3

Count and color **3**.

Count and circle **3**.

6 Understanding numbers: identifying a set of three

page 7

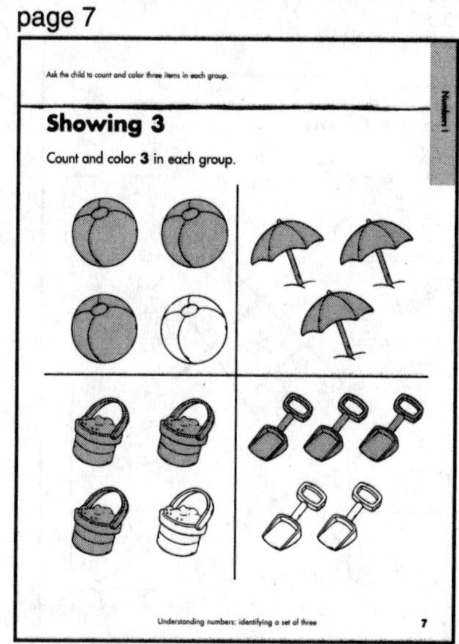

Ask the child to count and color three items in each group.

Numbers I

Showing 3

Count and color **3** in each group.

Understanding numbers: identifying a set of three 7

page 8

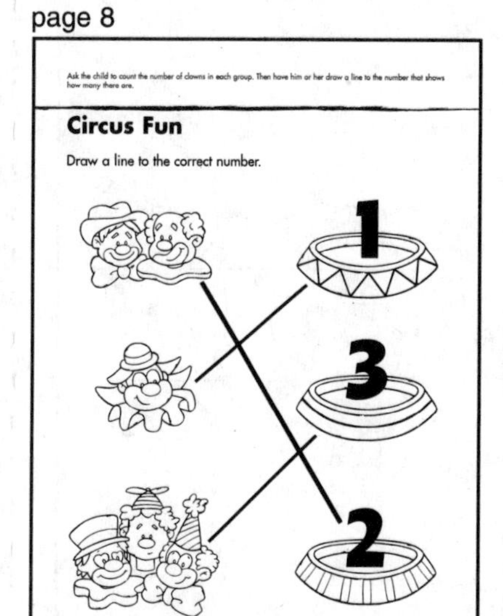

Ask the child to count the number of clowns in each group. Then have him or her draw a line to the number that shows how many there are.

Circus Fun

Draw a line to the correct number.

1

3

2

8 Understanding numbers: matching groups of objects and numerals 1-3

page 9

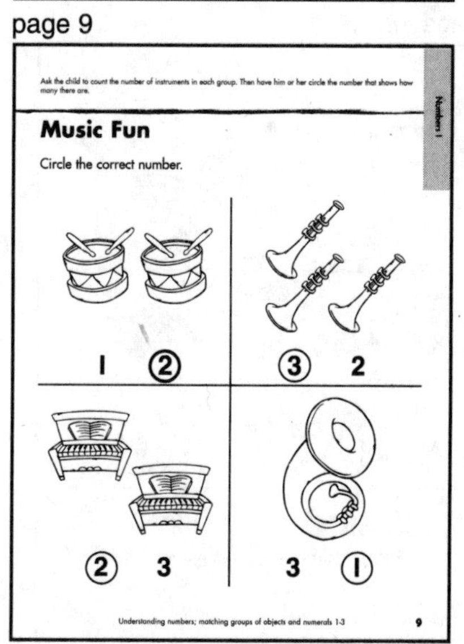

Ask the child to count the number of instruments in each group. Then have him or her circle the number that shows how many there are.

Numbers I

Music Fun

Circle the correct number.

1 ② ③ 2

② 3 3 ①

Understanding numbers: matching groups of objects and numerals 1-3 9

page 10

Point to and say the numeral. Ask the child to count and color the bears at the top of the page. Then ask him or her to count and circle four dolls at the bottom.

Counting 4

Count and color **4**.

Count and circle **4**.

10 Understanding numbers: identifying a set of four

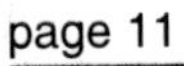
page 11

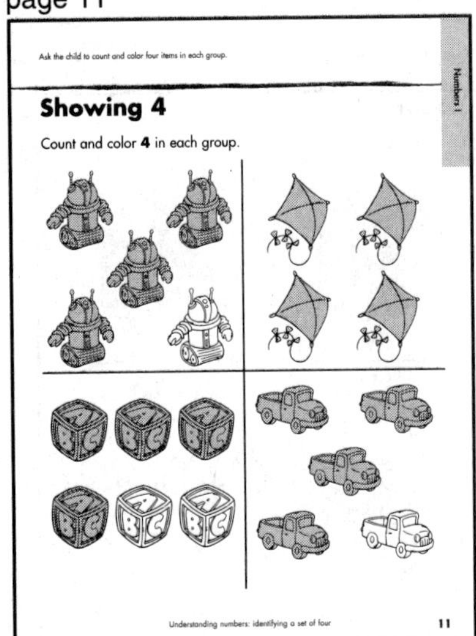
Ask the child to count and color four items in each group.

Numbers 1

Showing 4

Count and color **4** in each group.

Understanding numbers: identifying a set of four 11

page 12

Point to and say the numeral. Ask the child to count and color the easels at the top of the page. Then ask him or her to count and circle five paint trays at the bottom.

Counting 5

Count and color **5**.

Count and circle **5**.

12 Understanding numbers: identifying a set of five

page 13

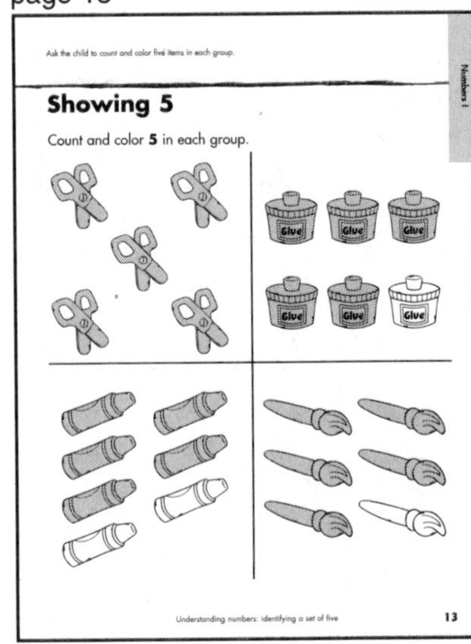
Ask the child to count and color five items in each group.

Numbers 1

Showing 5

Count and color **5** in each group.

Understanding numbers: identifying a set of five 13

page 14

Ask the child to count the number of animals in each box. Then have him or her draw a line between the groups with the same number.

On the Farm

Match.

14 Understanding numbers; matching sets of 1-5

page 15

Ask the child to read the numeral at the beginning of each row. Then have him or her color that number of animals in the row.

Numbers 1

At the Zoo

Color the correct number.

1

2

3

4

5

Counting to 5; matching numerals with the correct number of objects 15

page 16

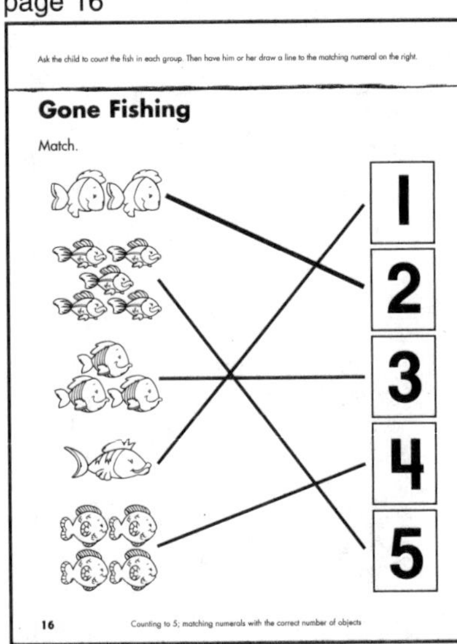
Ask the child to count the fish in each group. Then have him or her draw a line to the matching numeral on the right.

Gone Fishing

Match.

1

2

3

4

5

16 Counting to 5; matching numerals with the correct number of objects

page 17

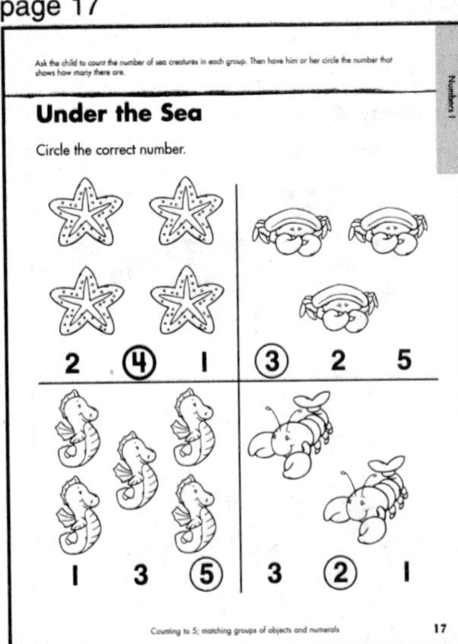
Ask the child to count the number of sea creatures in each group. Then have him or her circle the number that shows how many there are.

Numbers 1

Under the Sea

Circle the correct number.

2 (4) 1 | (3) 2 5

1 3 (5) | 3 (2) 1

Counting to 5; matching groups of objects and numerals 17

page 18

Ask the child to count the number of objects in each group. Then have him or her circle the group with more in each row.

More

Circle the group with more.

18 Understanding more and less

page 19

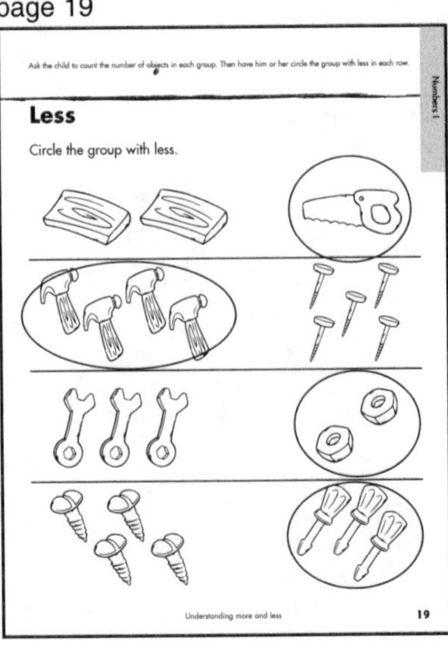
Ask the child to count the number of objects in each group. Then have him or her circle the group with less in each row.

Numbers 1

Less

Circle the group with less.

Understanding more and less 19

page 20

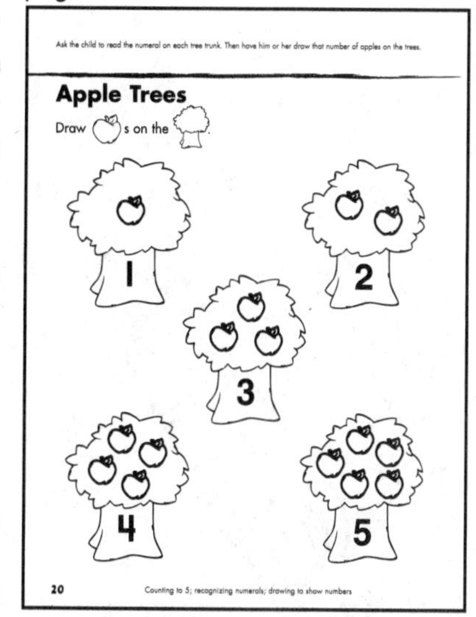

Ask the child to read the numeral on each tree trunk. Then have him or her draw that number of apples on the trees.

Apple Trees

Draw s on the .

1 2 3 4 5

20 Counting to 5; recognizing numerals; drawing to show numbers

page 21

Ask the child to count and color the picnic baskets, cats, clouds, ants, and trees in the picture. Then have him or her circle the number that he or she counted for each.

The Cats' Picnic

Count and color. Circle how many.

1 2 3 4 2 3
3 4 4 5

Counting to 5; recognizing numerals 21

page 22

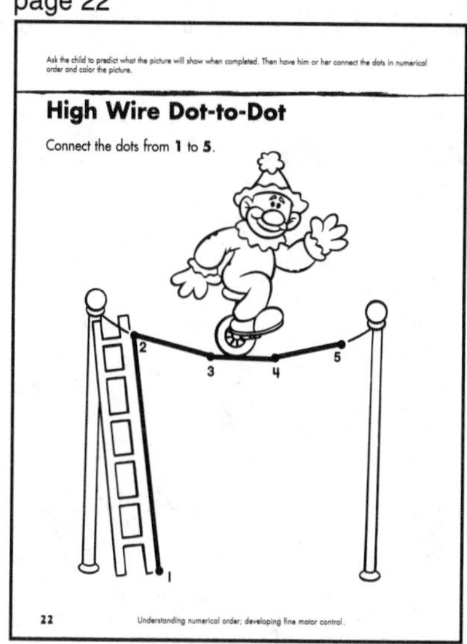

Ask the child to predict what the picture will show when completed. Then have him or her connect the dots in numerical order and color the picture.

High Wire Dot-to-Dot

Connect the dots from **1** to **5**.

22 Understanding numerical order; developing fine motor control.

page 23

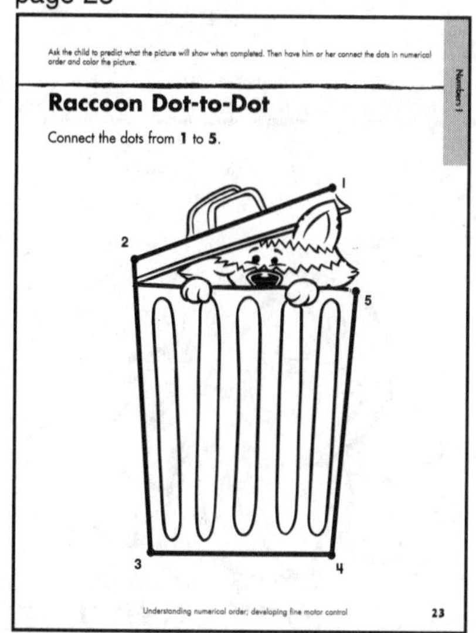

Ask the child to predict what the picture will show when completed. Then have him or her connect the dots in numerical order and color the picture.

Raccoon Dot-to-Dot

Connect the dots from **1** to **5**.

Understanding numerical order; developing fine motor control 23

page 24

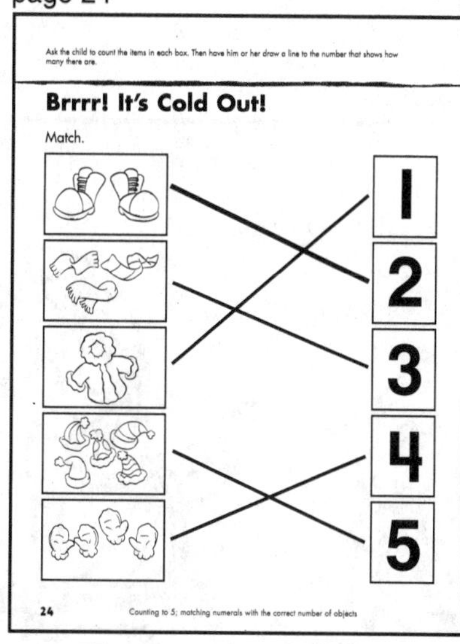

Ask the child to count the items in each box. Then have him or her draw a line to the number that shows how many there are.

Brrrr! It's Cold Out!

Match.

1 2 3 4 5

24 Counting to 5; matching numerals with the correct number of objects

page 25

Help the child identify the color of each crayon. Then point to and say the numeral on each dinosaur. Ask the child to use the code to color the dinosaurs.

Color by Number

Use the code to color the dinosaurs.

1 = yellow 2 = orange
3 = brown 4 = blue 5 = green

1 yellow
2 orange
3 brown
4 blue
5 green

Recognizing numerals; following directions 25

page 26

Ask the child to count the items in each row. Then have him or her trace the numerals.

Bake Shop

Trace the numerals.

1 1 1
2 2 2
3 3
4
5

26 Understanding numbers; counting objects and tracing numerals

page 27

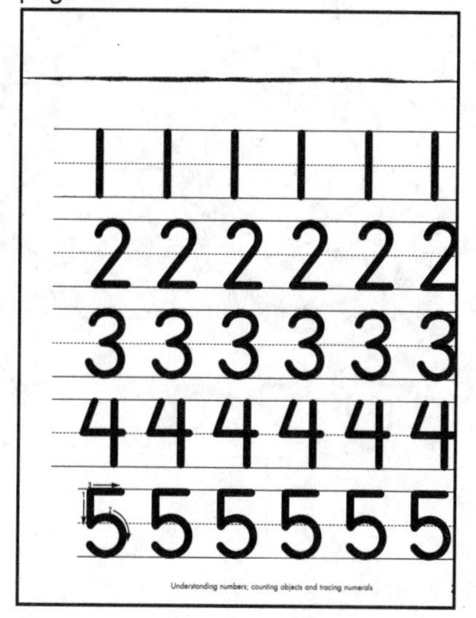

1 1 1 1 1 1
2 2 2 2 2 2
3 3 3 3 3 3
4 4 4 4 4 4
5 5 5 5 5 5

Understanding numbers; counting objects and tracing numerals

page 28

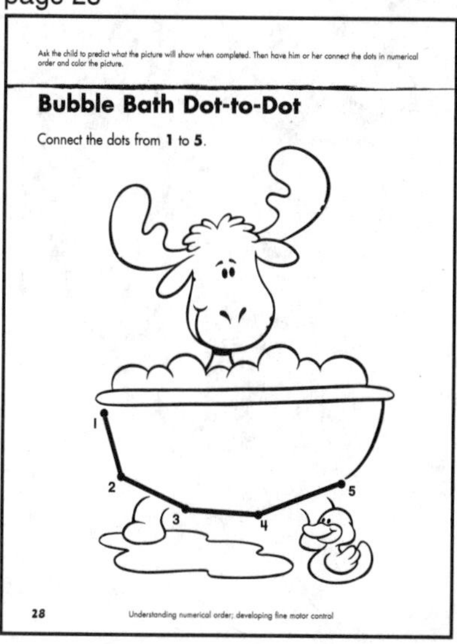

Ask the child to predict what the picture will show when completed. Then have him or her connect the dots in numerical order and color the picture.

Bubble Bath Dot-to-Dot

Connect the dots from **1** to **5**.

28 Understanding numerical order; developing fine motor control

Point to and say the numeral. Ask the child to count and color the rockets at the top of the page. Then ask him or her to count and circle six astronauts at the bottom.

Counting 6

Count and color **6**.

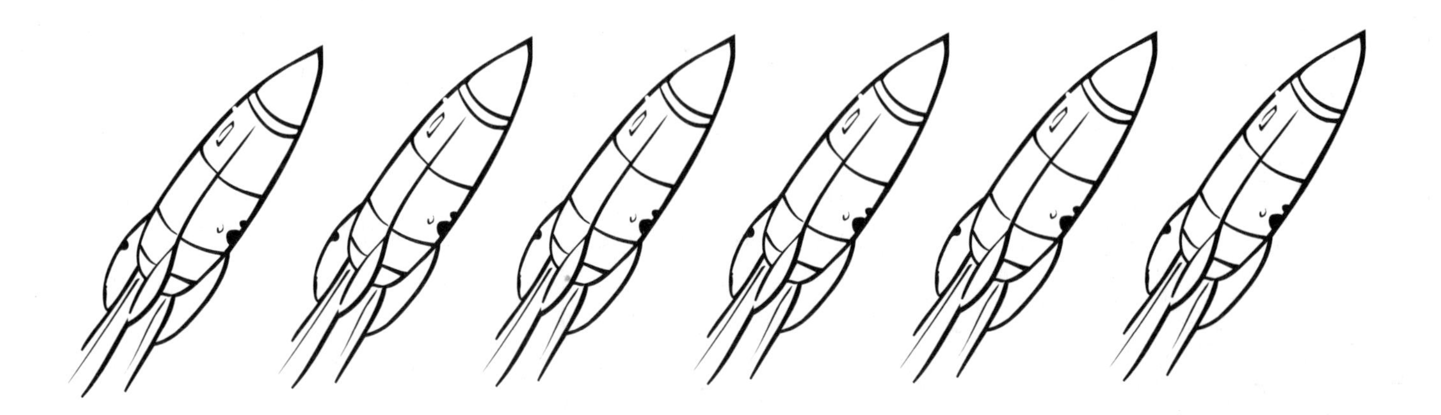

Count and circle **6**.

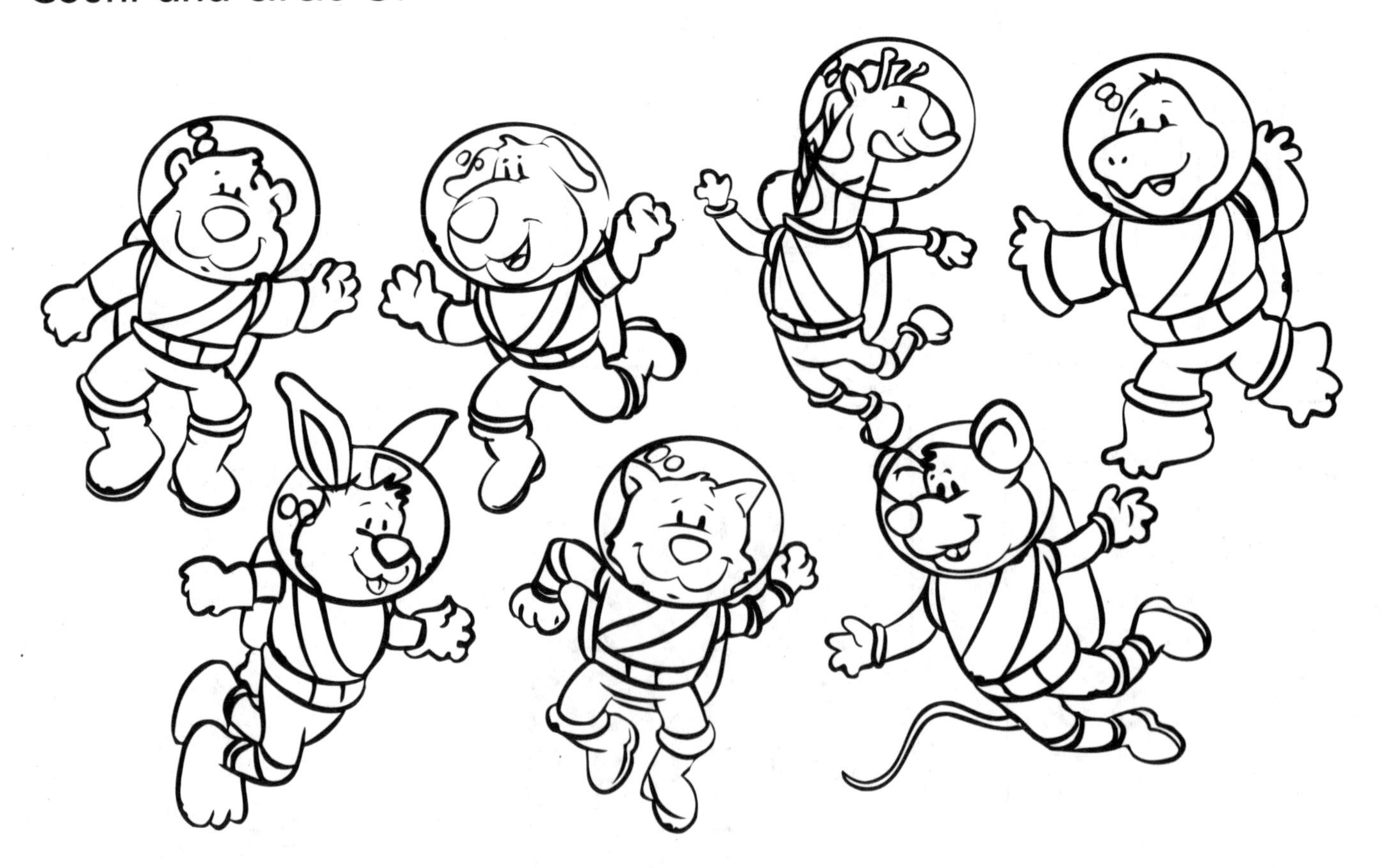

Ask the child to count and color six pictures in each group.

Showing 6

Count and color **6** in each group.

Numbers II

Point to and say the numeral. Ask the child to count and color the tubes at the top of the page. Then ask him or her to count and circle seven umbrellas at the bottom.

Counting 7

Count and color **7**.

Count and circle **7**.

Ask the child to count and color seven items in each group.

Showing 7

Count and color **7** in each group.

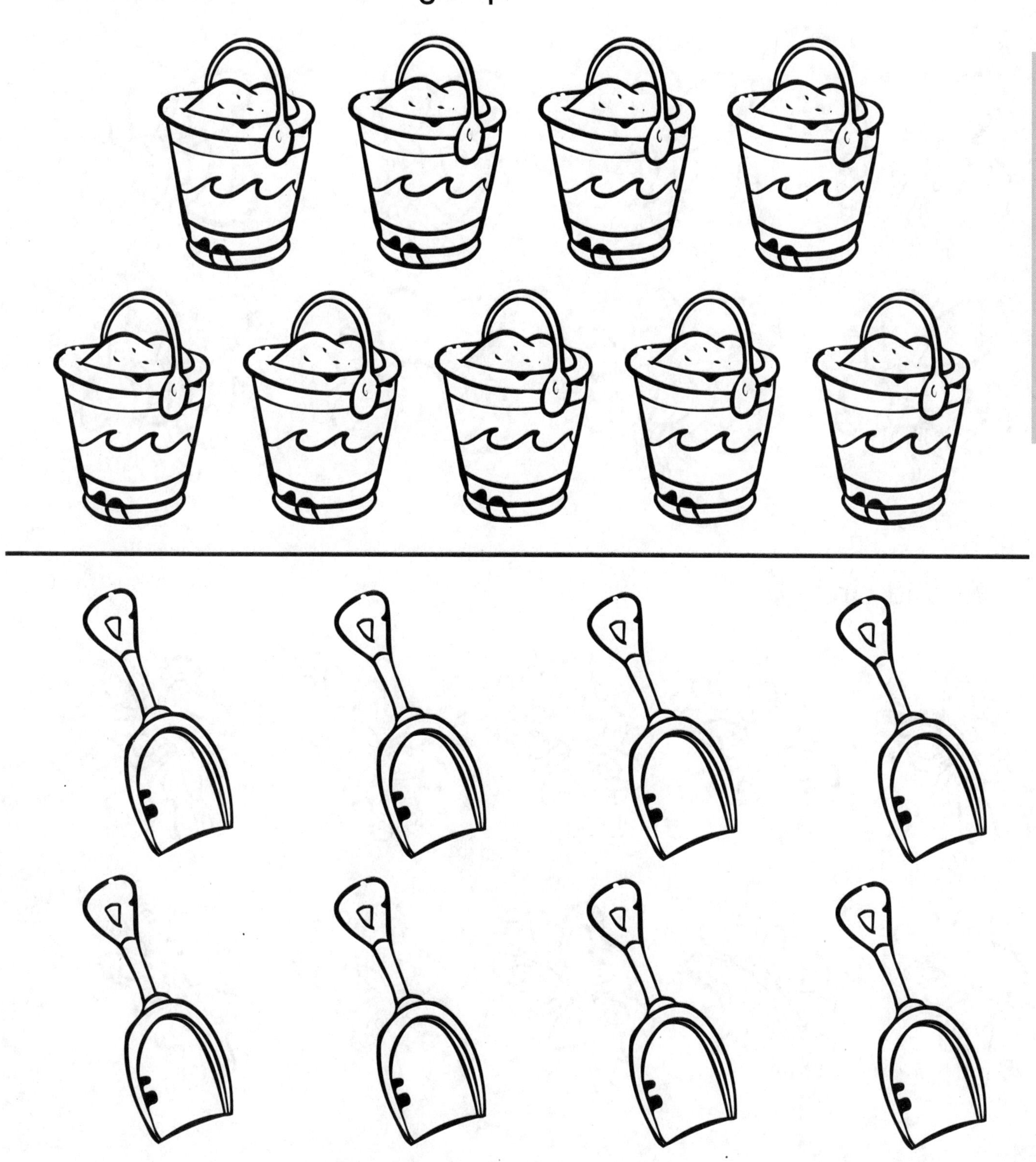

Point to and say the numeral. Ask the child to count and color the bees at the top of the page. Then ask him or her to count and circle eight butterflies at the bottom.

Counting 8

Count and color **8**.

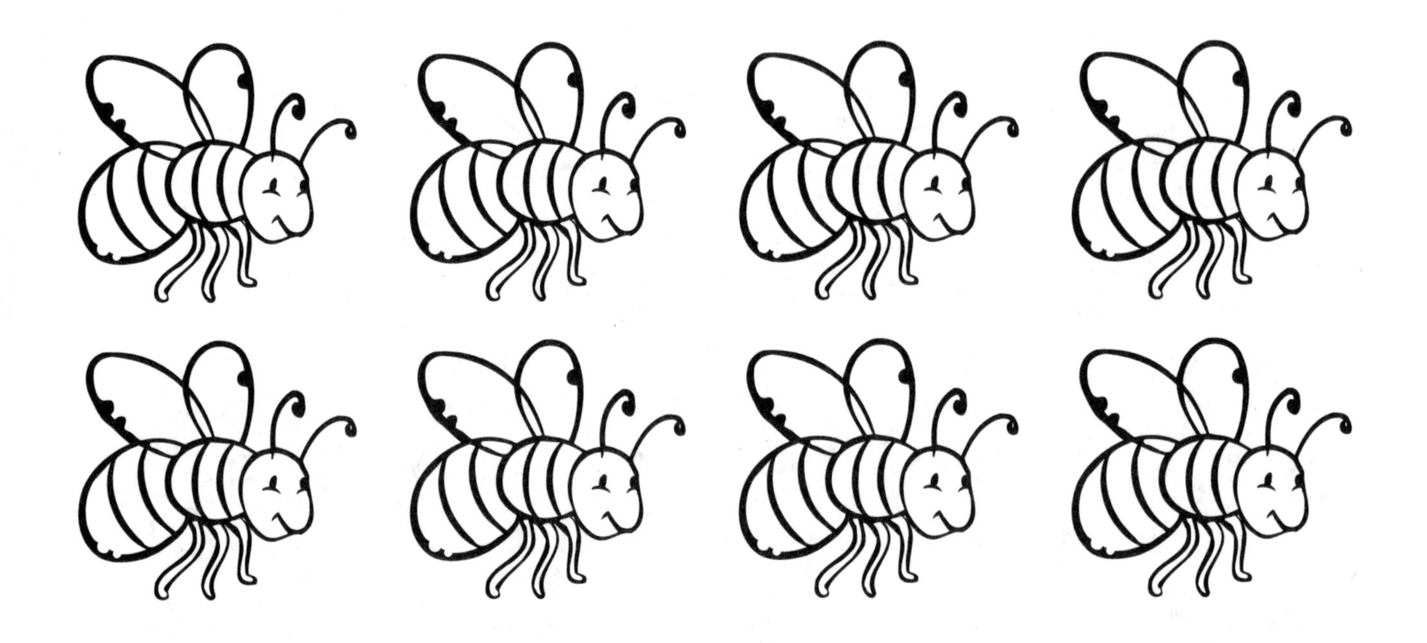

Count and circle **8**.

Ask the child to count and color eight bugs in each group.

Showing 8

Count and color **8** in each group.

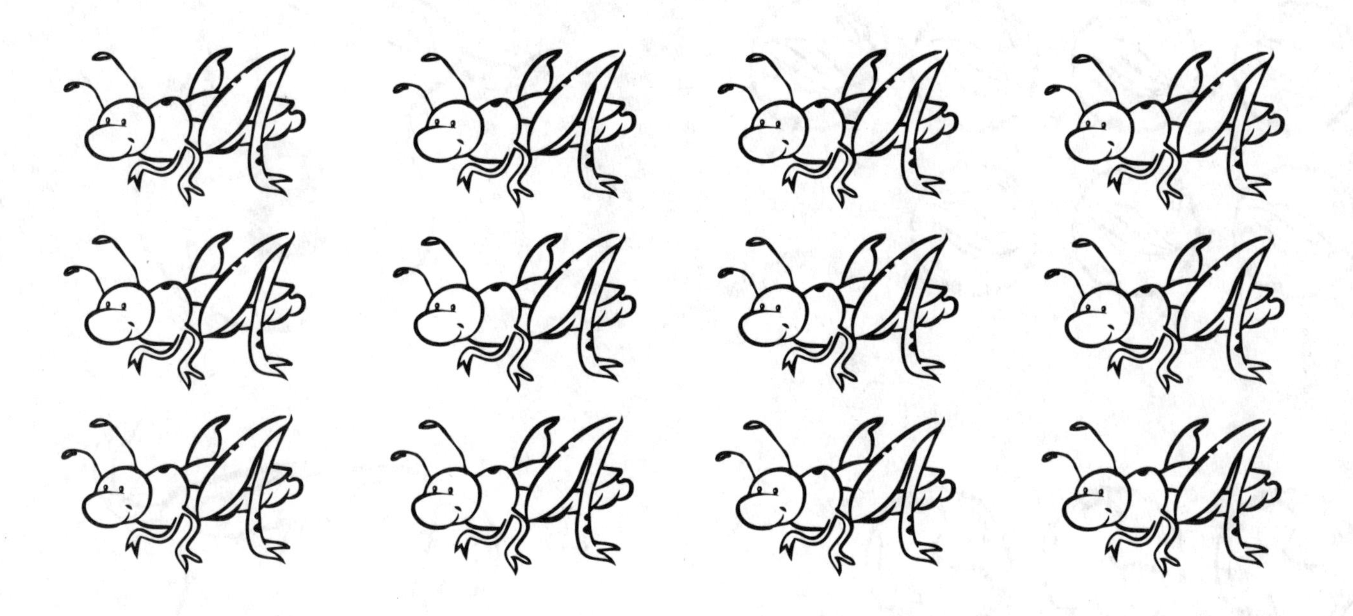

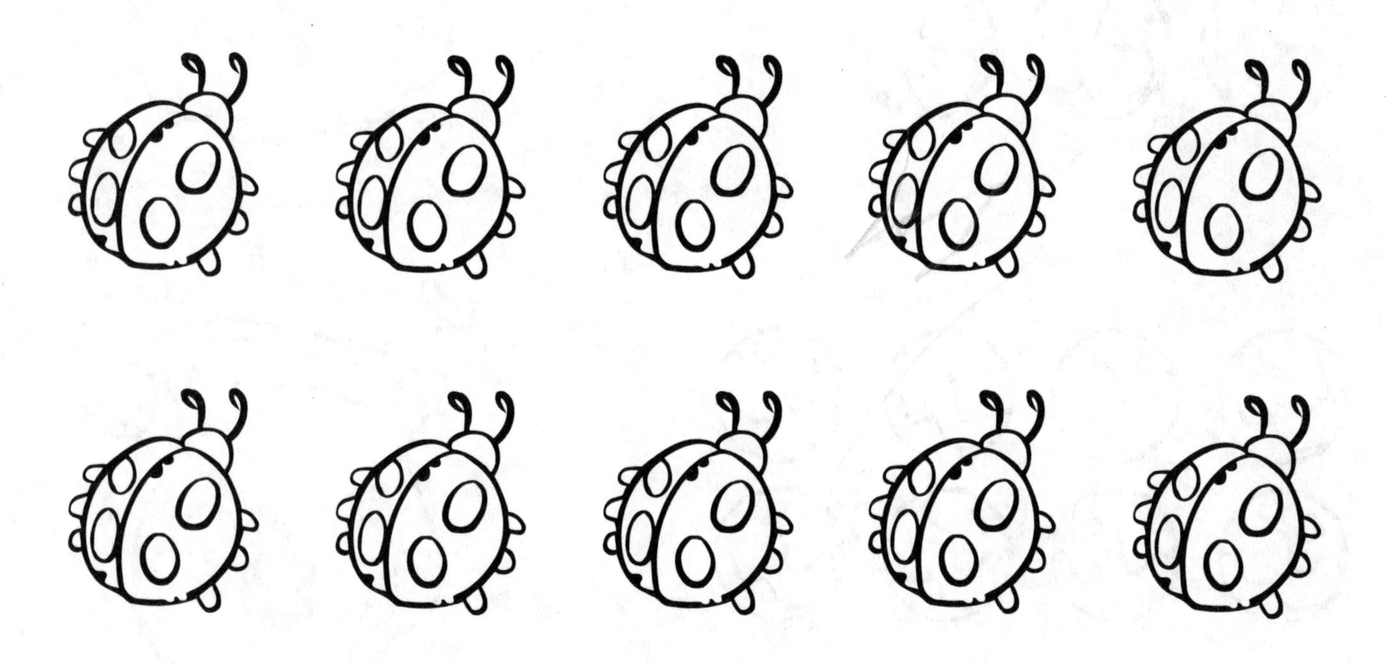

Ask the child to count the marbles in each group. Then have him or her draw a line to the number that shows how many there are.

Let's Play Marbles

Draw a line to the correct number.

Understanding numbers; matching groups of objects and numerals 6-8

Ask the child to count the number of items in each group. Then have him or her circle the number that shows how many there are.

Music Fun

Circle the correct number.

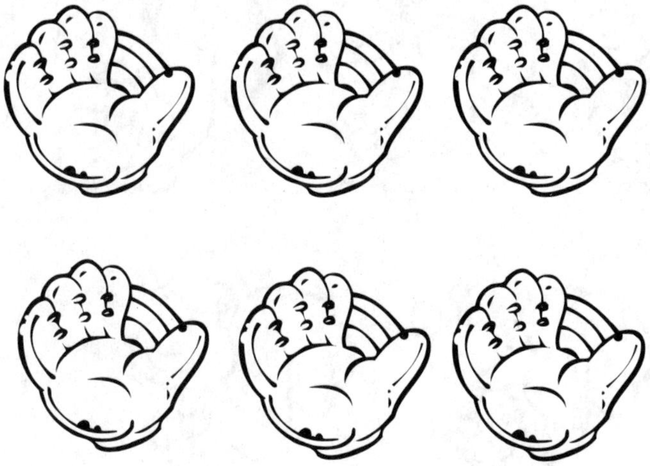

6 7

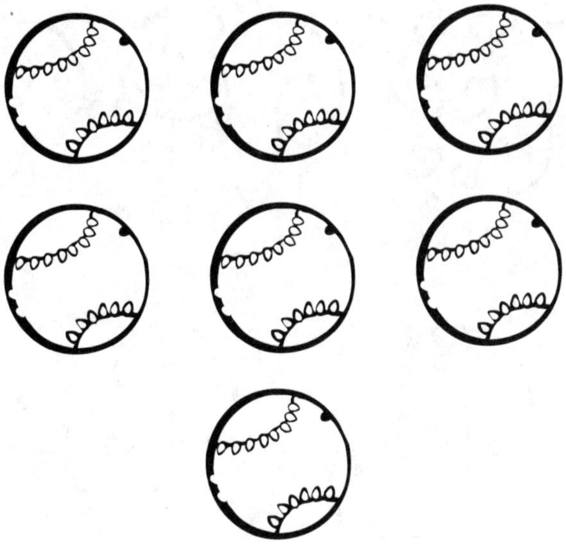

7 8

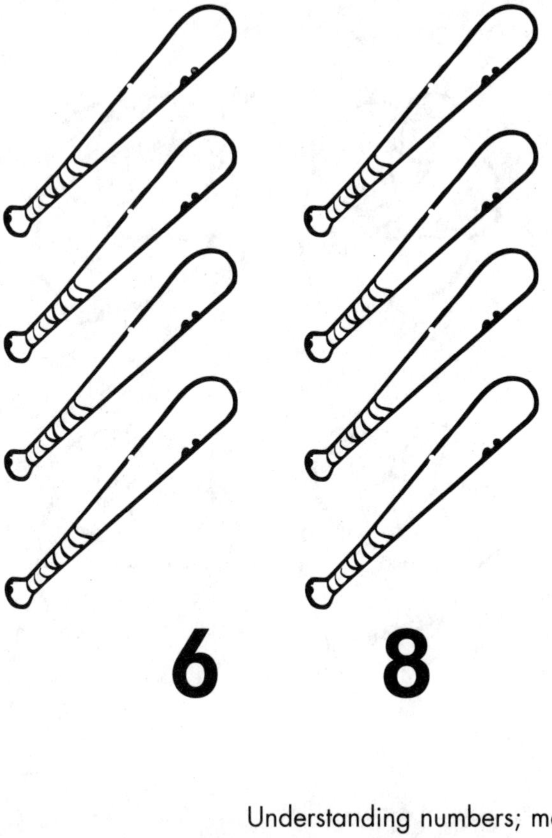

6 8

6 7

Point to and say the numeral. Ask the child to count and color the squirrels at the top of the page. Then ask him or her to count and circle nine acorns at the bottom.

Counting 9

Count and color **9**.

Count and circle **9**.

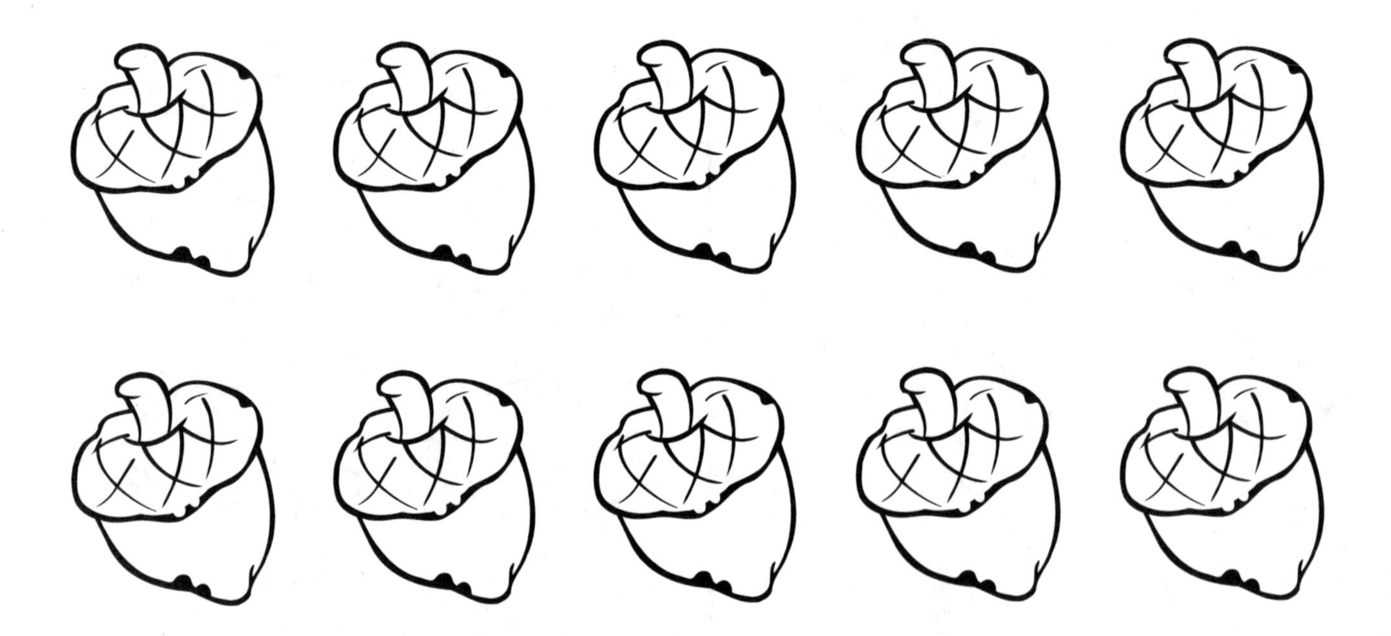

Ask the child to count and color nine items in each group.

Showing 9

Count and color **9** in each group.

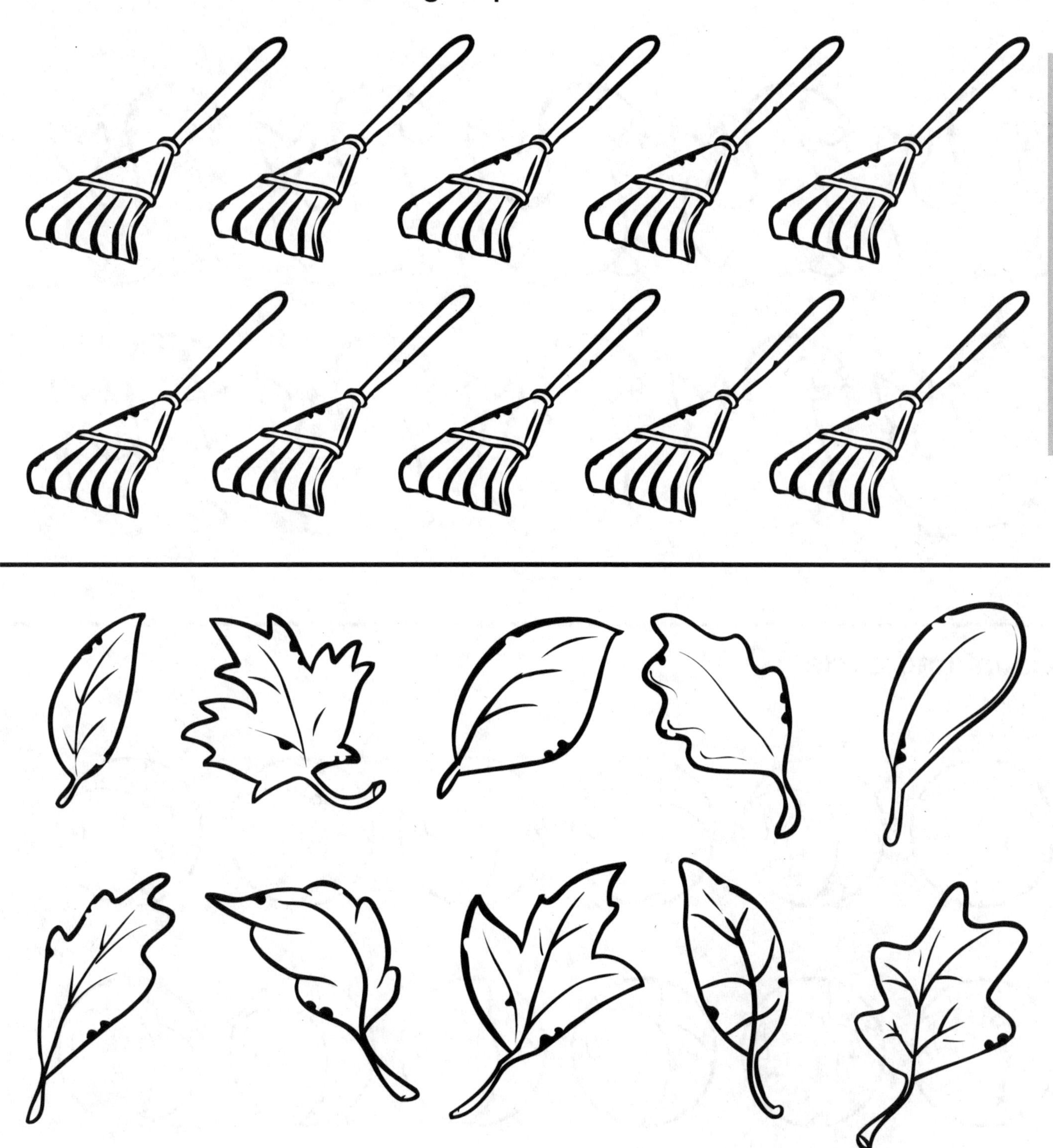

Point to and say the numeral. Ask the child to count and color the seals at the top of the page. Then ask him or her to count and circle ten balls at the bottom.

Counting 10

Count and color **10**.

Count and circle **10**.

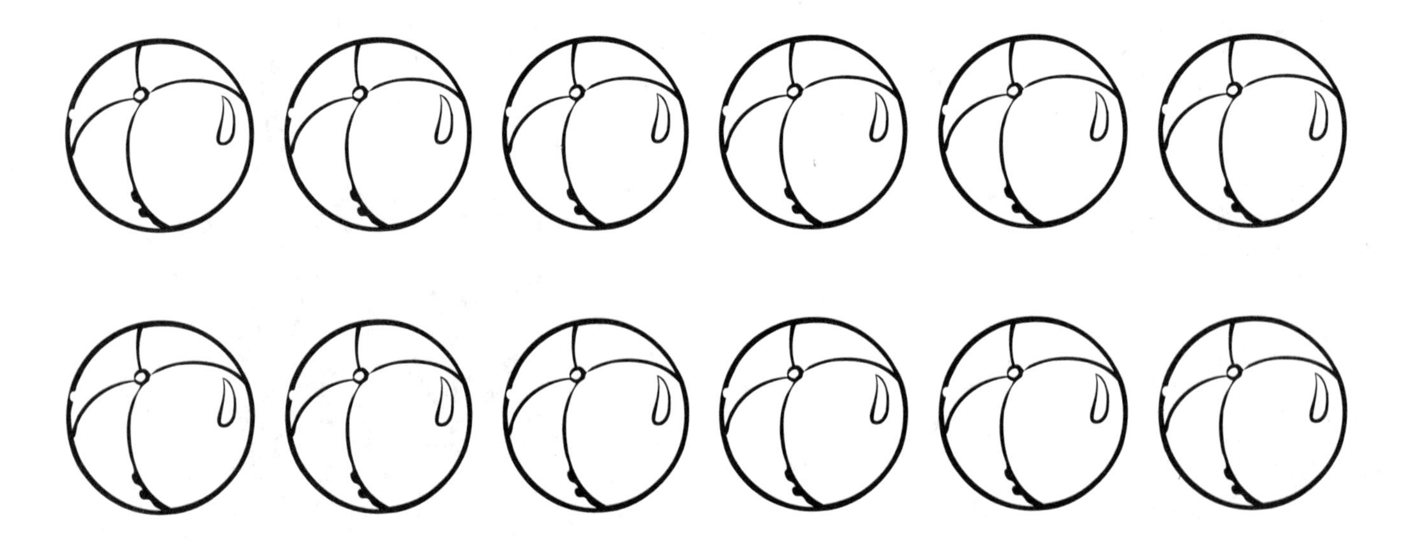

Ask the child to count and color ten pictures in each group.

Showing 10

Count and color **10** in each group.

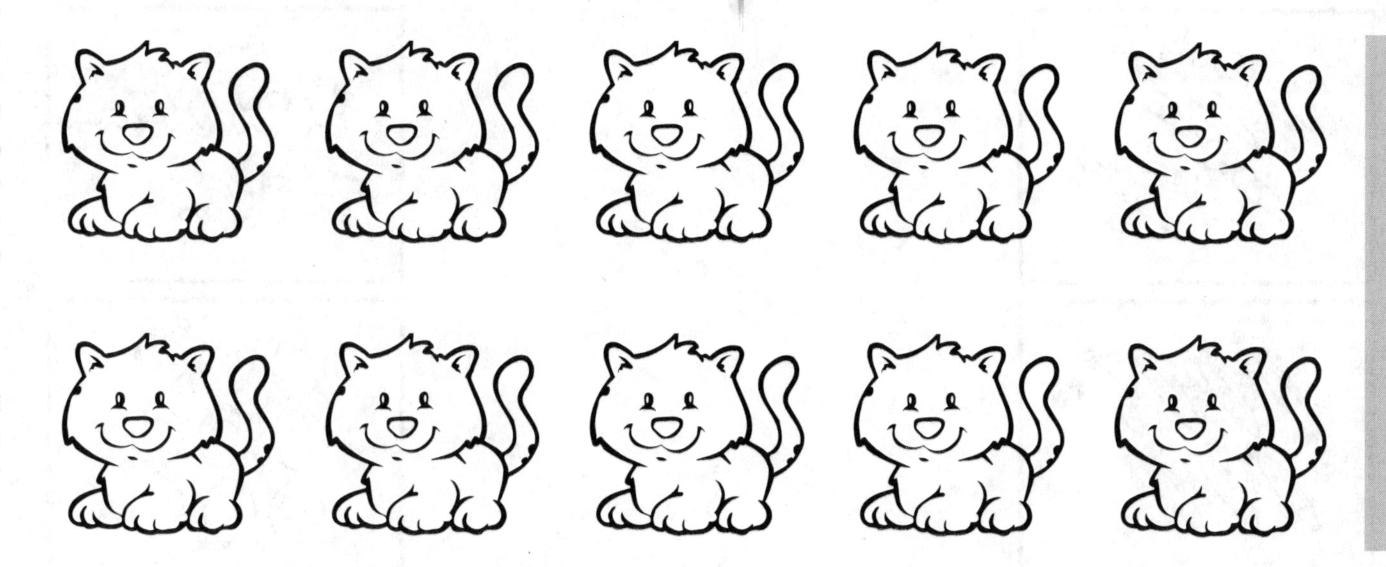

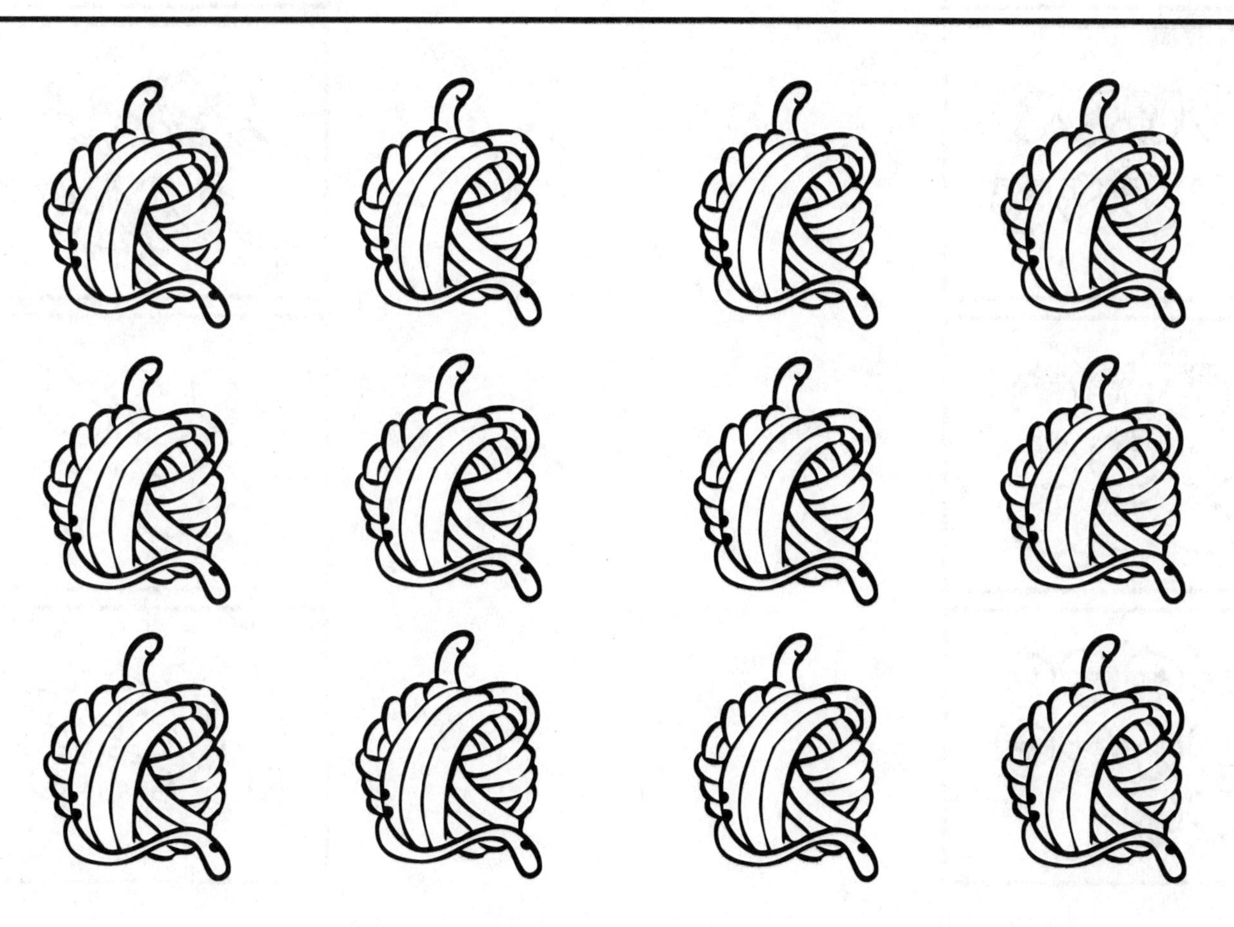

Numbers II

Ask the child to count the number of vegetables in each box. Then have him or her draw a line between the groups with the same number.

Vegetable Patch

Match.

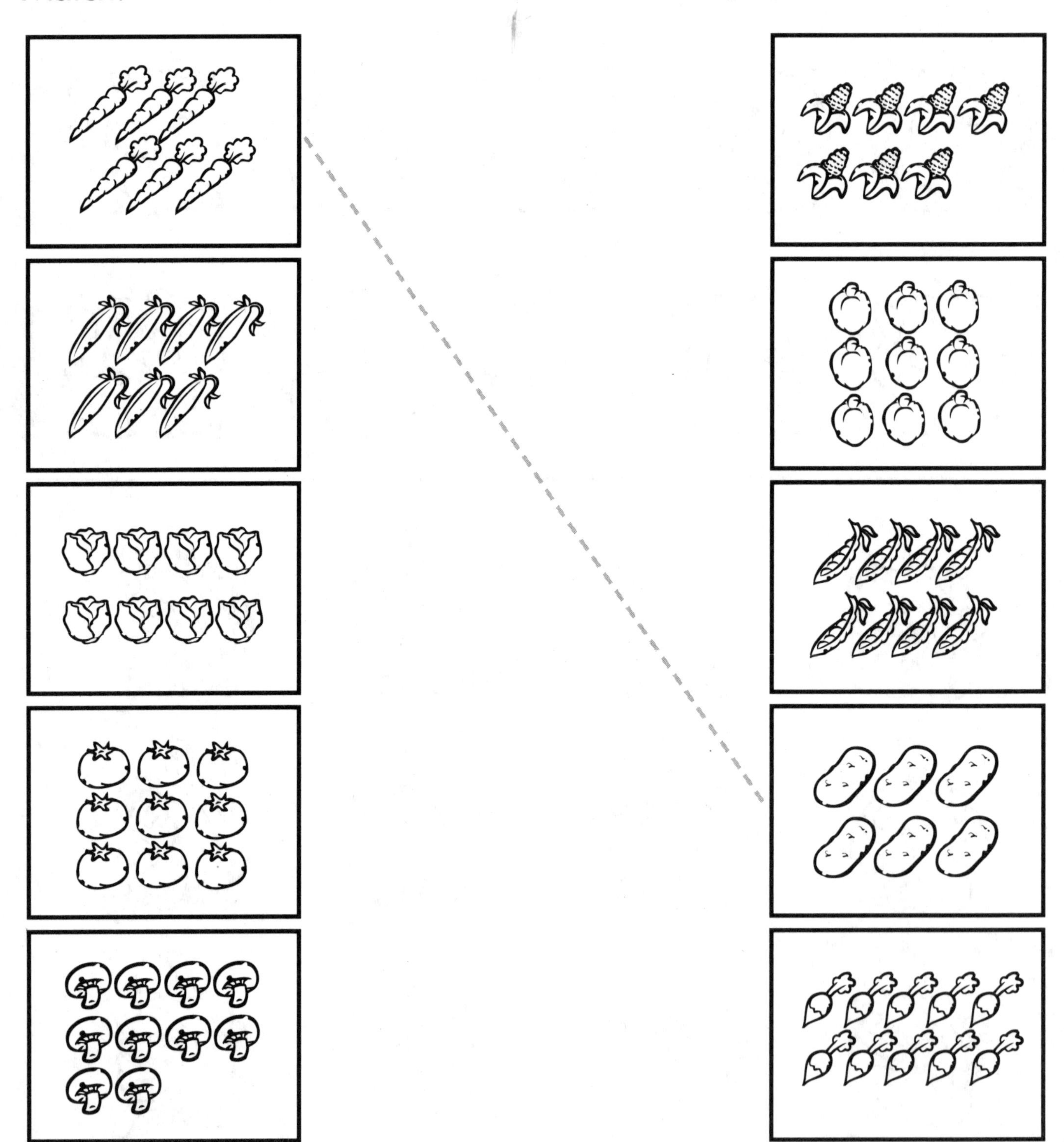

Understanding numbers; matching sets of 6-10

Ask the child to read the numeral at the beginning of each row. Then have him or her color that number of birds in the row.

Feathered Friends

Color the correct number.

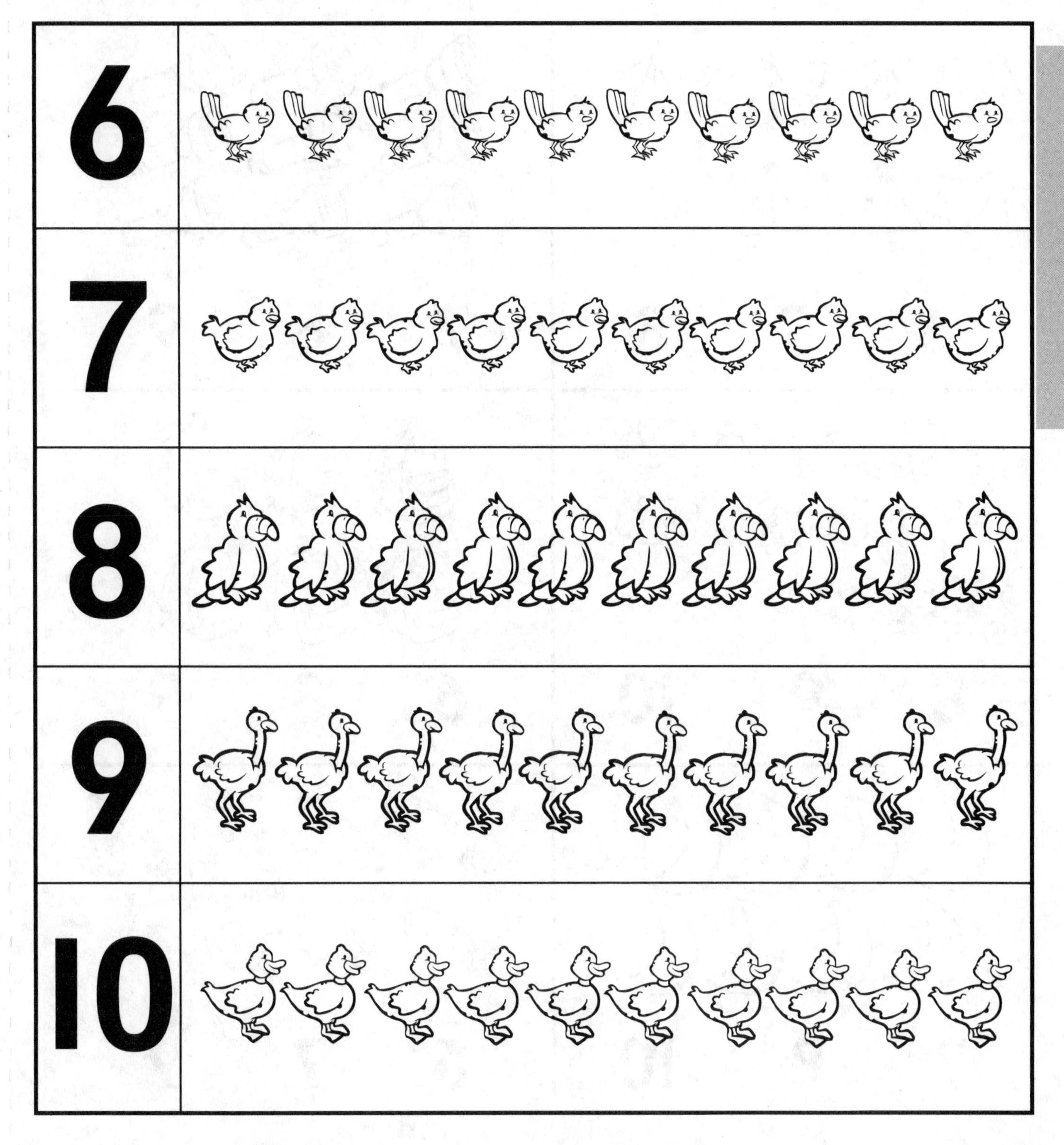

Ask the child to count the number of items in each group. Then have him or her circle the number that shows how many there are.

Camping Out

Circle the correct number.

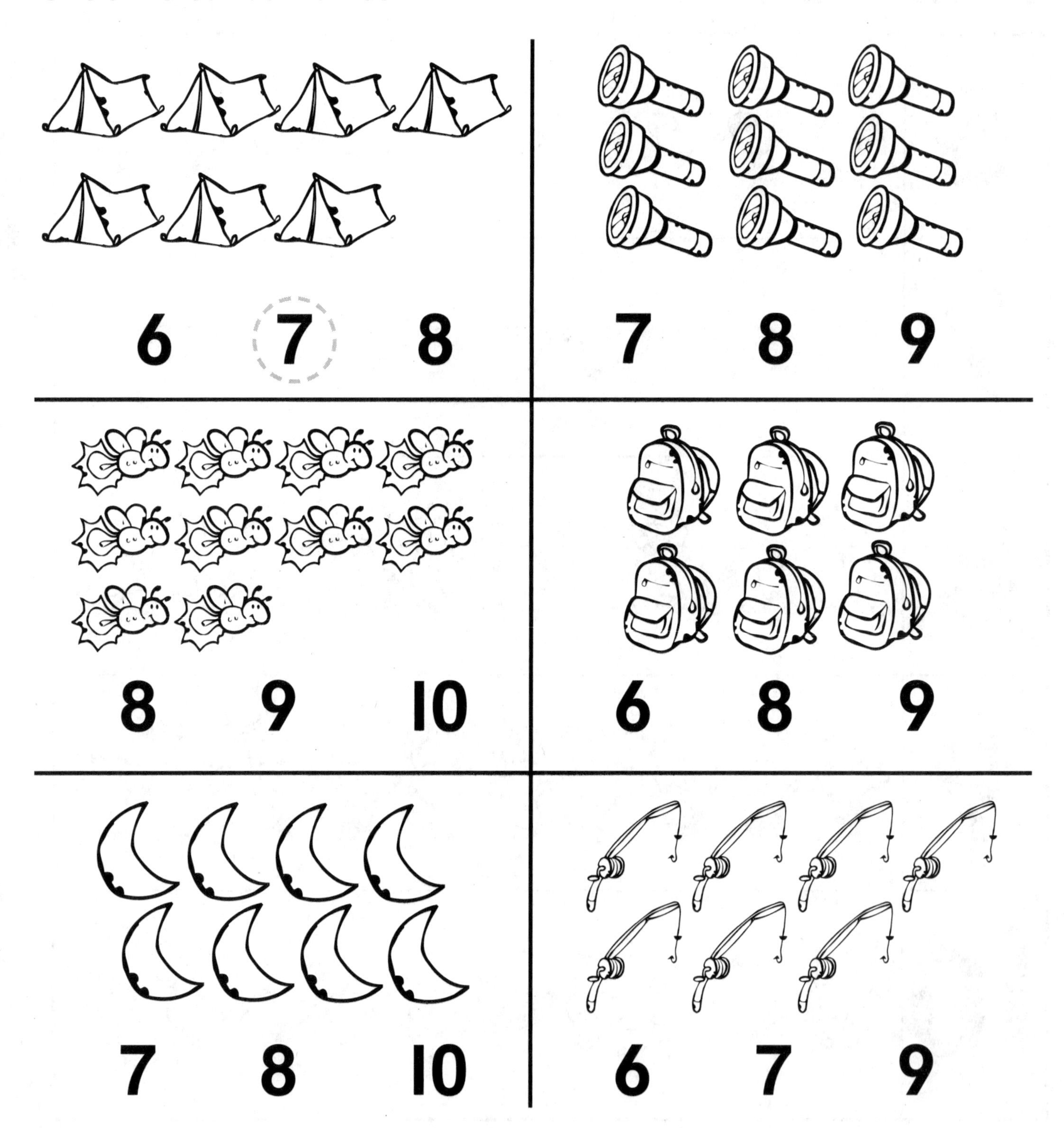

Ask the child to count the jellybeans in each group. Then have him or her draw a line to that number on the right.

Jellybean Jars

Match.

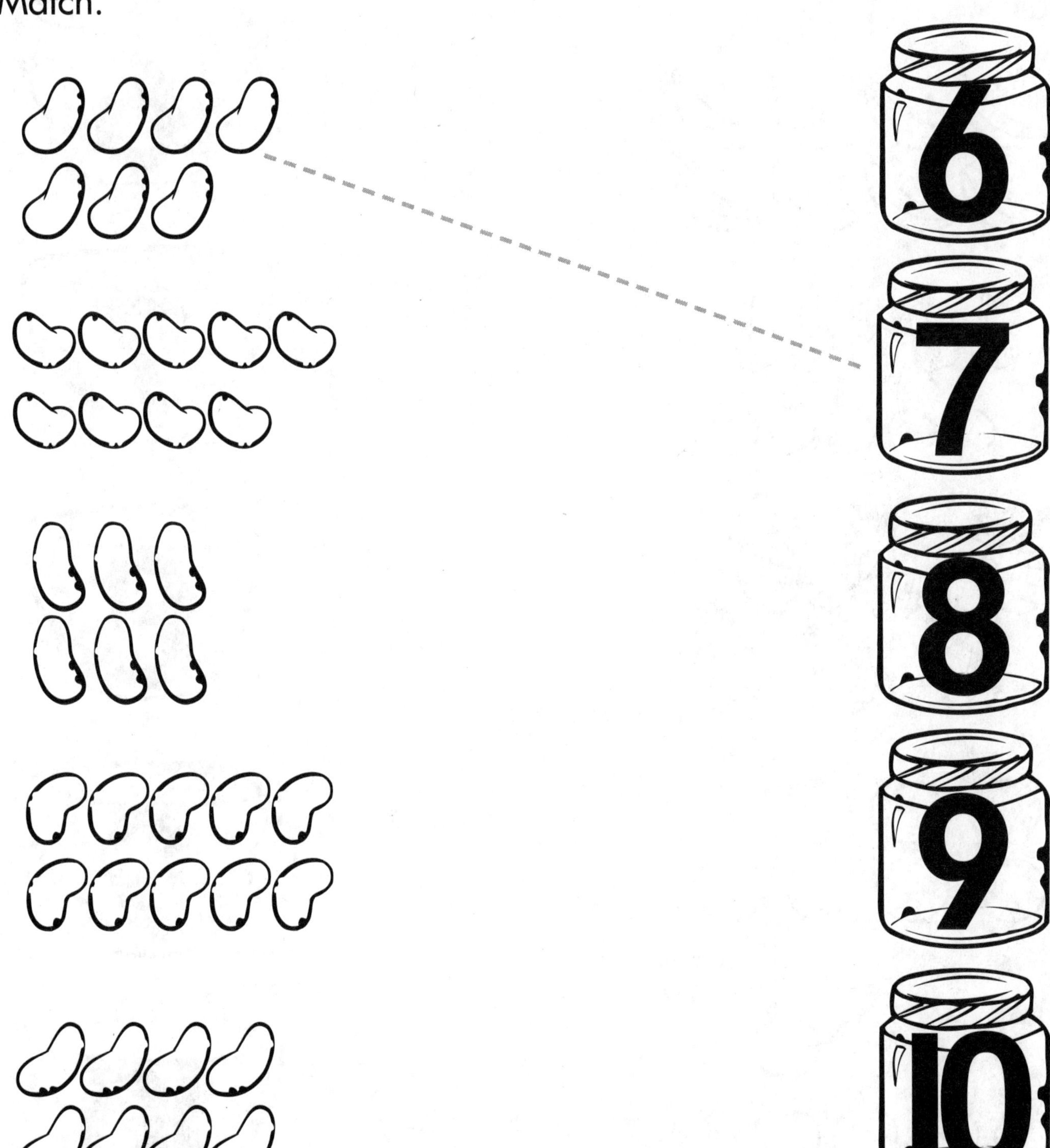

Ask the child to count the fruit in each group. Then have him or her draw a line to that number on the right.

Fruit Bowls

Match.

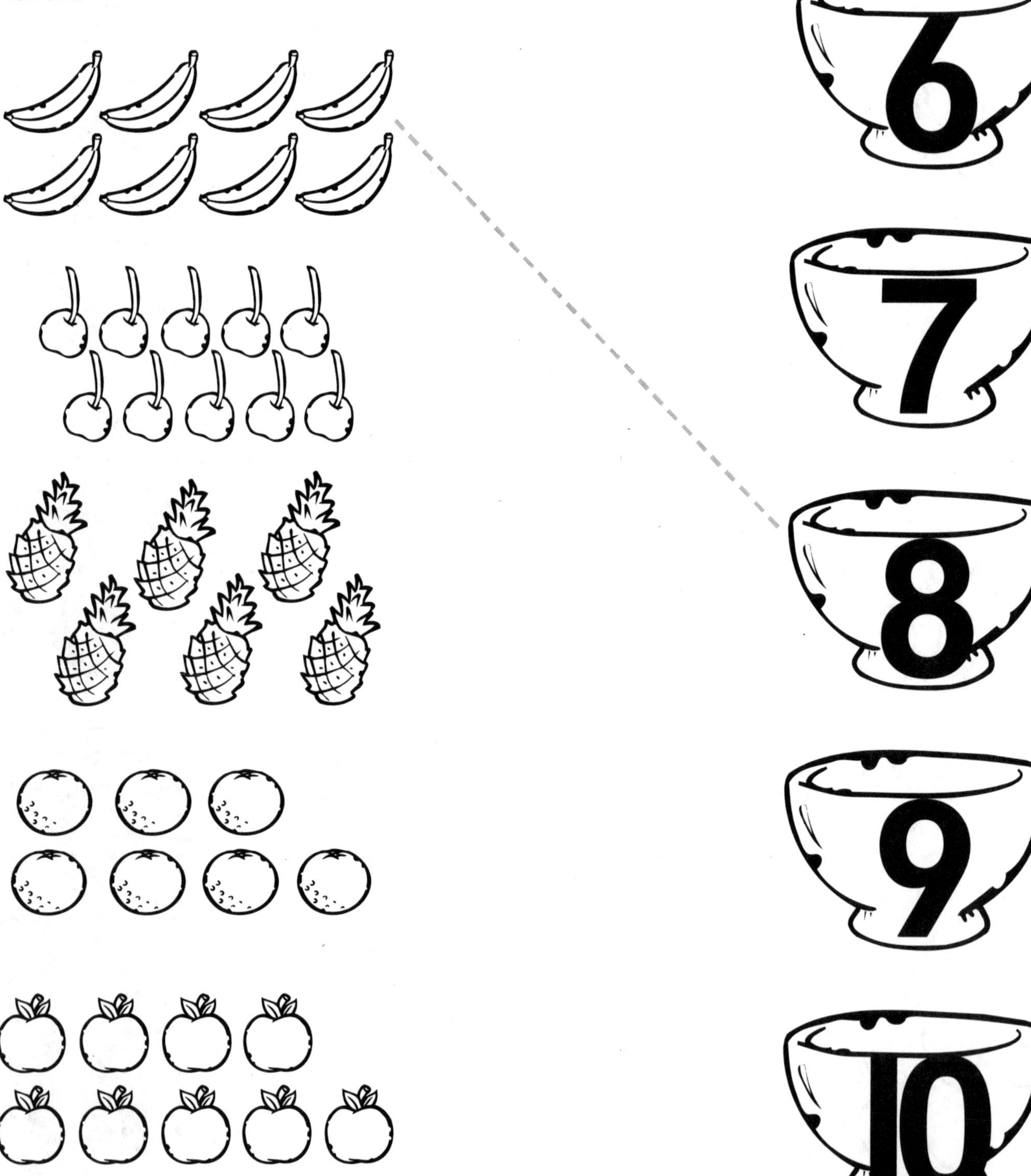

Counting 6 to 10; matching numerals with the correct number of objects

Ask the child to read the numeral next to each cookie. Then have him or her draw that number of chocolate chips on the cookies.

Chocolate Chip Cookies

Draw s on the .

6

7

8

9

10

Ask the child to count and color the scarecrows, pigs, pitchforks, cows, sheep, pieces of corn, trees, chickens, haystacks, and cornstalks in the picture on page 51. Then have him or her circle the number that he or she counted for each.

On the Farm

Count and color. Circle how many.

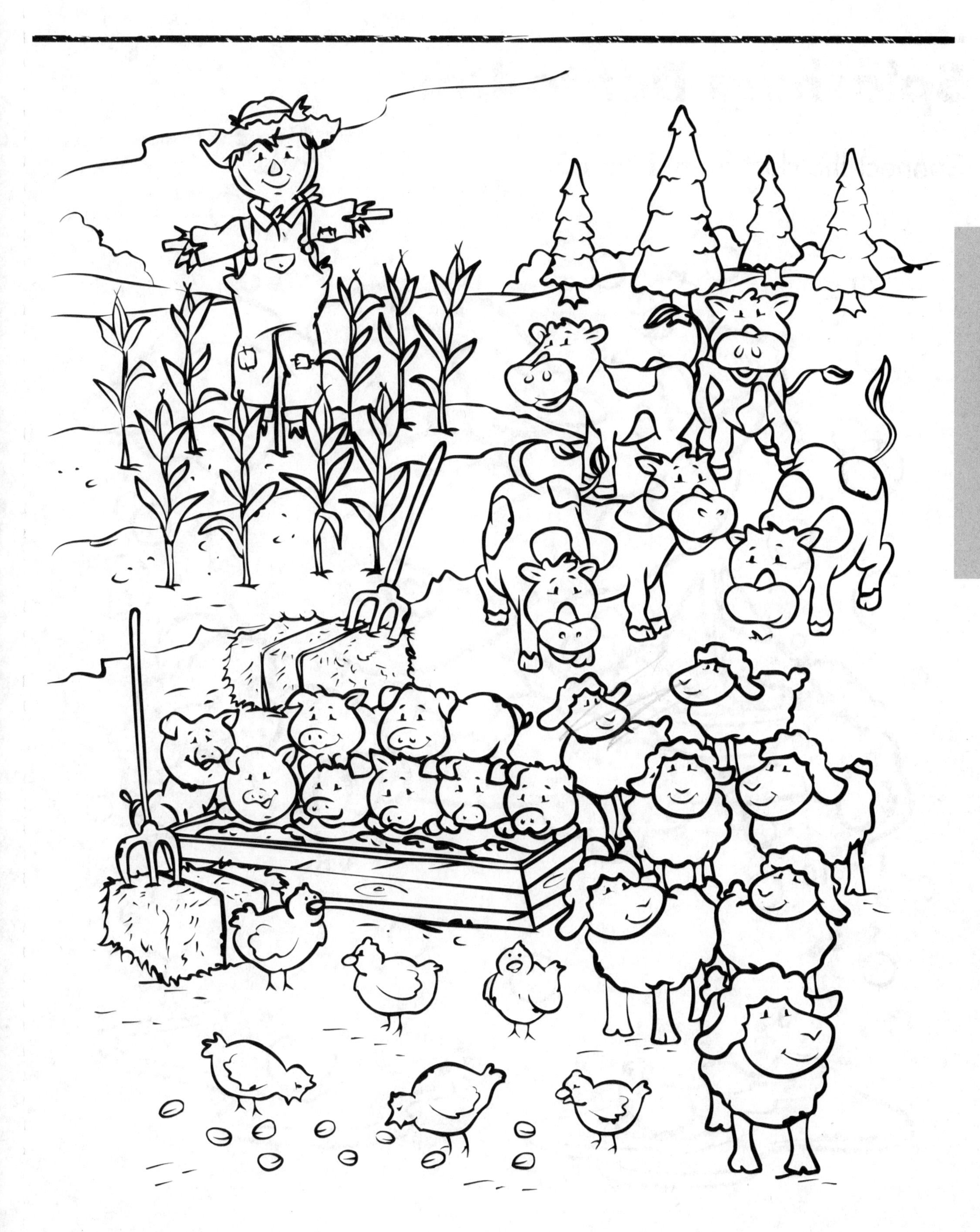

Ask the child to predict what the picture will show when completed. Then have him or her connect the dots in numerical order and color the picture.

Splashing Dot-to-Dot

Connect the dots from **1** to **10**.

 Understanding numerical order; developing fine motor control

Ask the child to read the numeral next to each crayon. Then help him or her identify the crayon color. Ask the child to use the code to color the picture.

Playing Dress Up

Use the code to color the picture.

Ask the child to predict what the picture will show when completed. Then have him or her connect the dots in numerical order and color the picture.

Splashing Dot-to-Dot

Connect the dots from **1** to **10**.

 Understanding numerical order; developing fine motor control

Ask the child to read the numeral next to each crayon. Then help him or her identify the crayon color. Ask the child to use the code to color the picture.

Go Fly a Kite

Use the code to color the picture.

Have the child trace the numerals at the top of the page. Then ask him or her to count the items in each row and write the number that shows how many there are.

Toy Count

Trace the numerals.

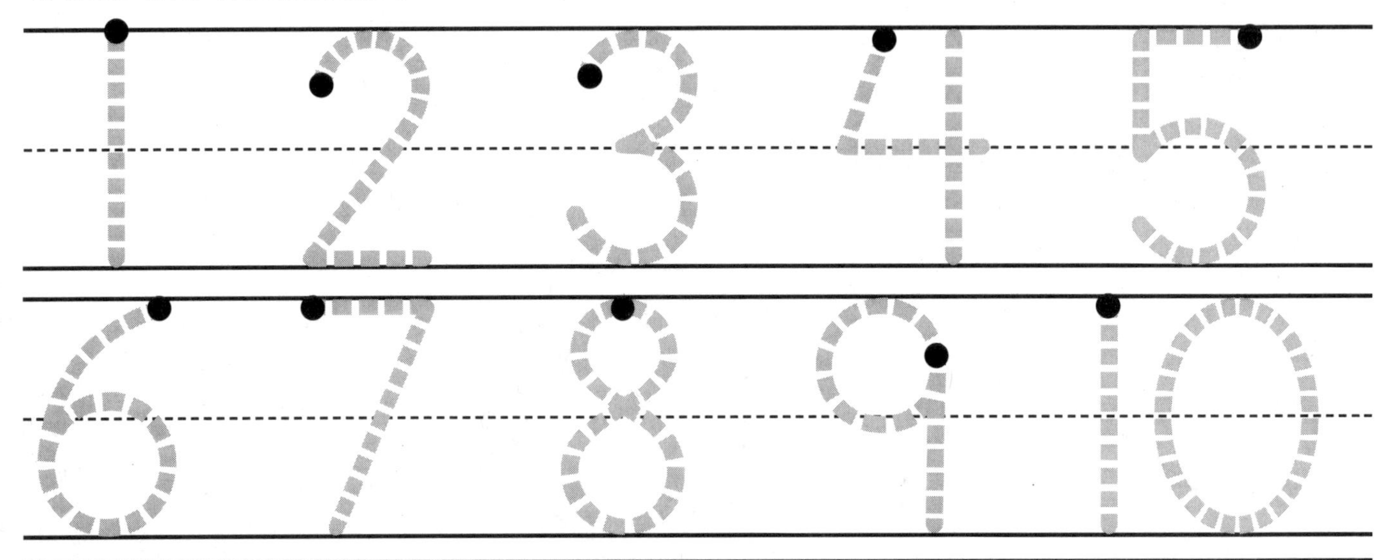

Count the toys and write the number.

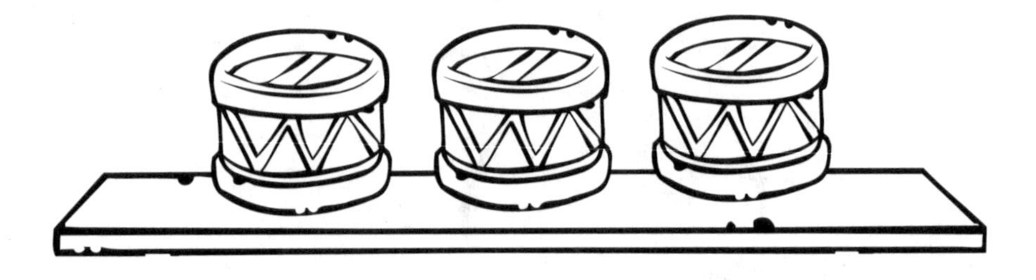

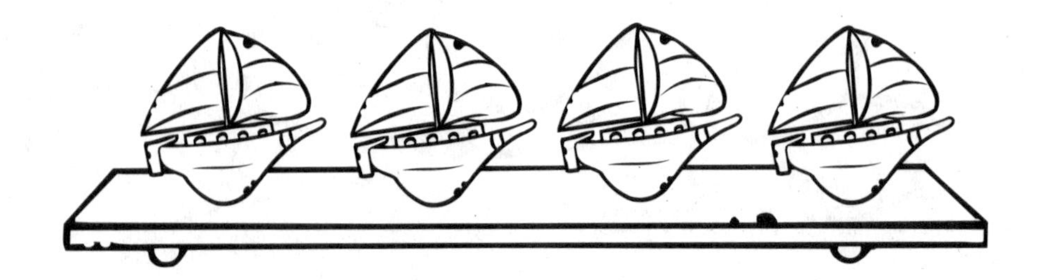

Point to the animals at the top of the page. Ask the child to count them in order from one to ten. Then have him or her write the missing numbers in the activity below.

What's Missing?

Write the missing numbers.

1   3   7   9

6   8   4   6

3   5   8   10

Answer Key

As the child completes the pages in this section, review his or her answers. When you take the time to correct the work and explain mistakes, you're showing your child that you feel learning is important.

page 32

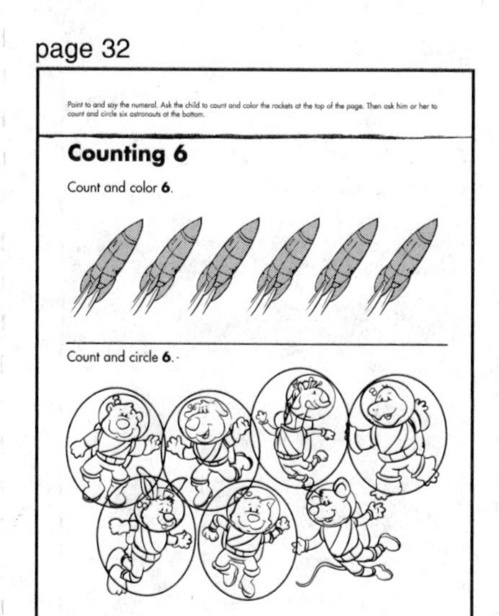

Point to and say the numeral. Ask the child to count and color the rockets at the top of the page. Then ask him or her to count and circle six astronauts at the bottom.

Counting 6

Count and color **6**.

Count and circle **6**.

32 Understanding numbers: identifying a set of six

page 33

Ask the child to count and color six pictures in each group.

Showing 6

Count and color **6** in each group.

Understanding numbers: identifying a set of six 33

page 34

Point to and say the numeral. Ask the child to count and color the tubes at the top of the page. Then ask him or her to count and circle seven umbrellas at the bottom.

Counting 7

Count and color **7**.

Count and circle **7**.

34 Understanding numbers: identifying a set of seven

page 35

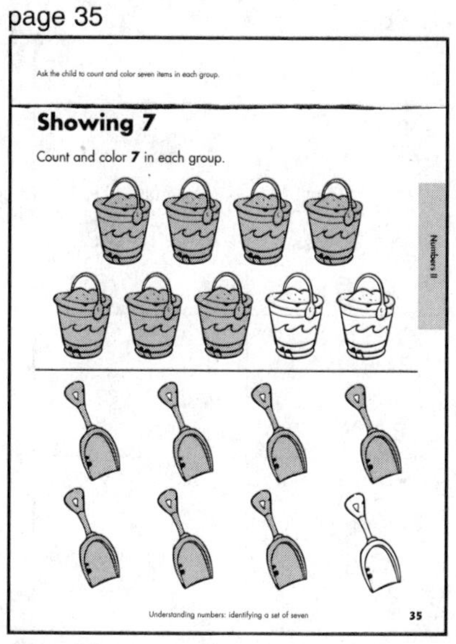

Ask the child to count and color seven items in each group.

Showing 7

Count and color **7** in each group.

Understanding numbers: identifying a set of seven 35

page 36

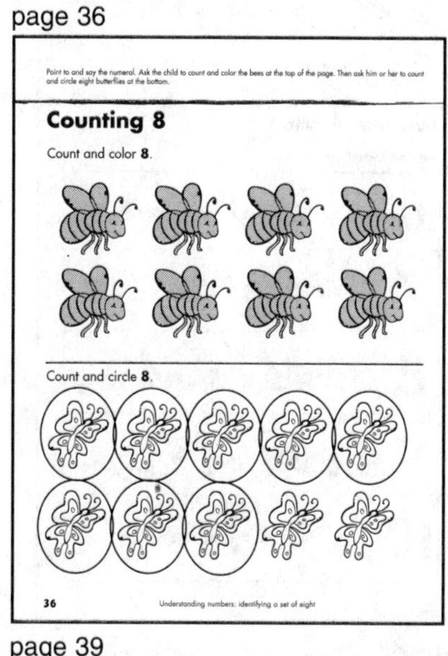

Point to and say the numeral. Ask the child to count and color the bees at the top of the page. Then ask him or her to count and circle eight butterflies at the bottom.

Counting 8

Count and color **8**.

Count and circle **8**.

36 Understanding numbers: identifying a set of eight

page 37

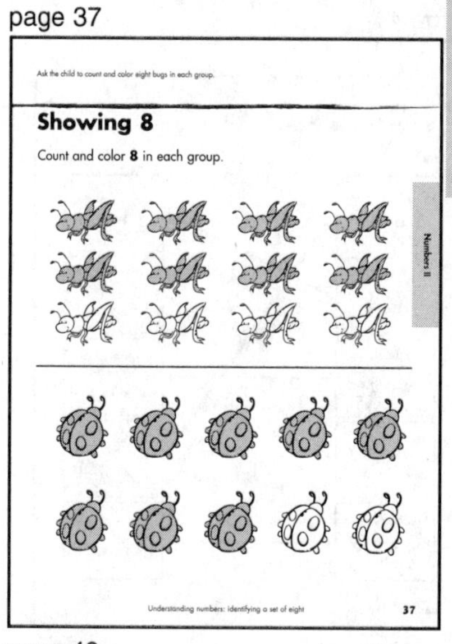

Ask the child to count and color eight bugs in each group.

Showing 8

Count and color **8** in each group.

Understanding numbers: identifying a set of eight 37

page 38

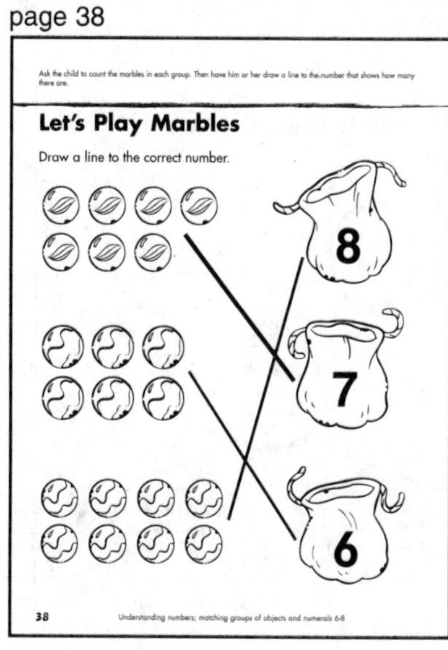

Ask the child to count the marbles in each group. Then have him or her draw a line to the number that shows how many there are.

Let's Play Marbles

Draw a line to the correct number.

8

7

6

38 Understanding numbers: matching groups of objects and numerals 6-8

page 39

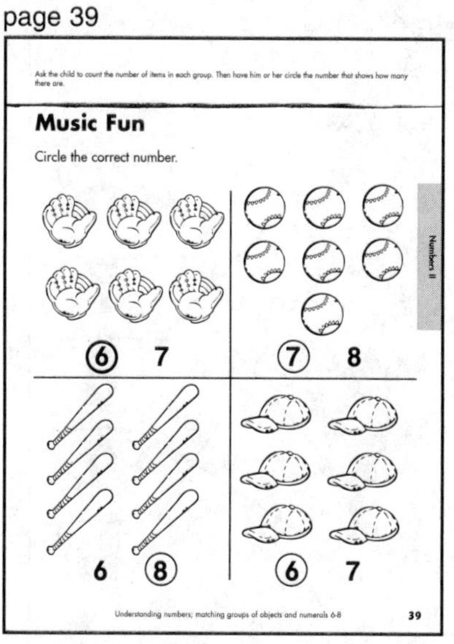

Ask the child to count the number of items in each group. Then have him or her circle the number that shows how many there are.

Music Fun

Circle the correct number.

(6) 7 (7) 8

6 (8) (6) 7

Understanding numbers: matching groups of objects and numerals 6-8 39

page 40

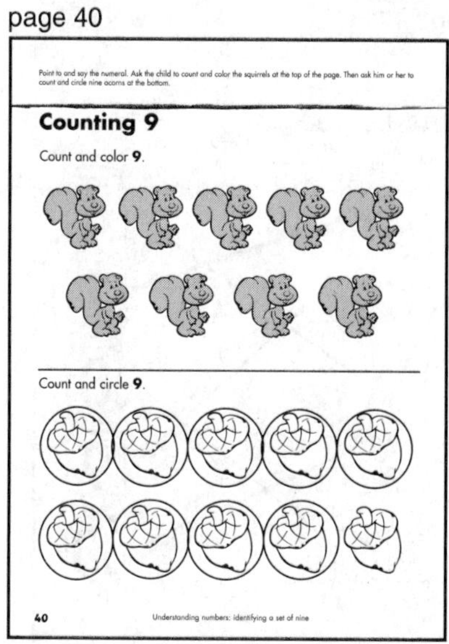

Point to and say the numeral. Ask the child to count and color the squirrels at the top of the page. Then ask him or her to count and circle nine acorns at the bottom.

Counting 9

Count and color **9**.

Count and circle **9**.

40 Understanding numbers: identifying a set of nine

page 41

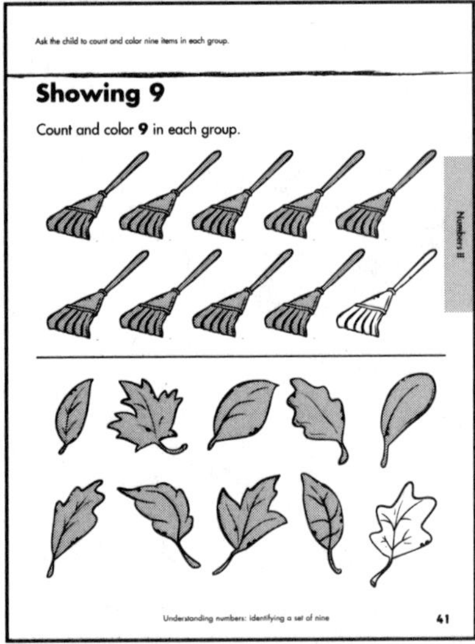
Showing 9

Count and color **9** in each group.

Understanding numbers: identifying a set of nine

41

page 42

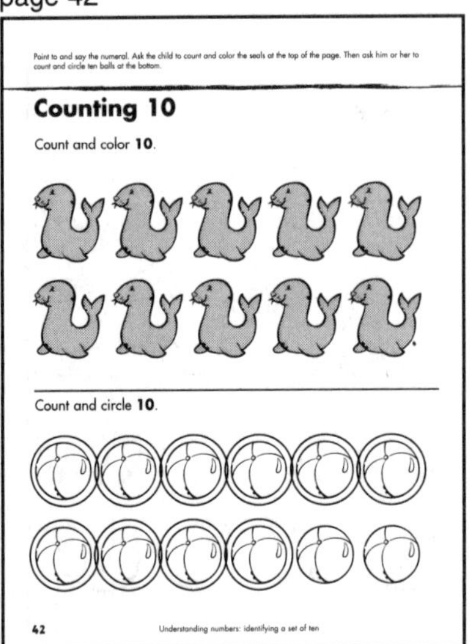
Counting 10

Count and color **10**.

Count and circle **10**.

42

Understanding numbers: identifying a set of ten

page 43

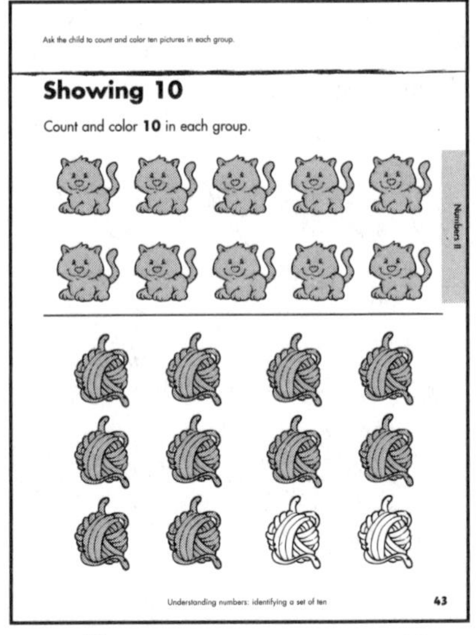
Showing 10

Count and color **10** in each group.

Understanding numbers: identifying a set of ten

43

page 44

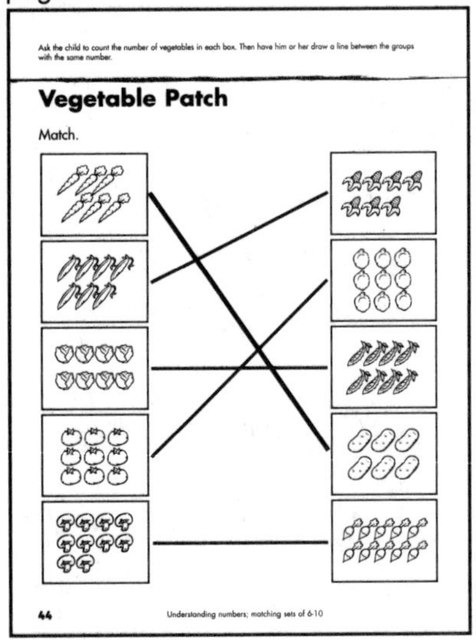
Vegetable Patch

Match.

44

Understanding numbers: matching sets of 6-10

page 45

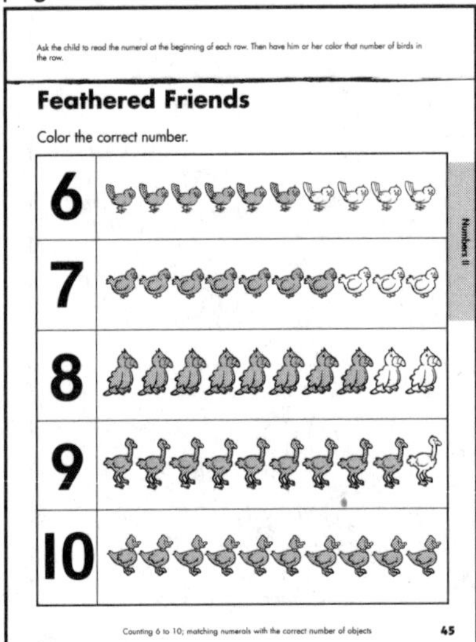
Feathered Friends

Color the correct number.

6

7

8

9

10

Counting 6 to 10; matching numerals with the correct number of objects

45

page 46

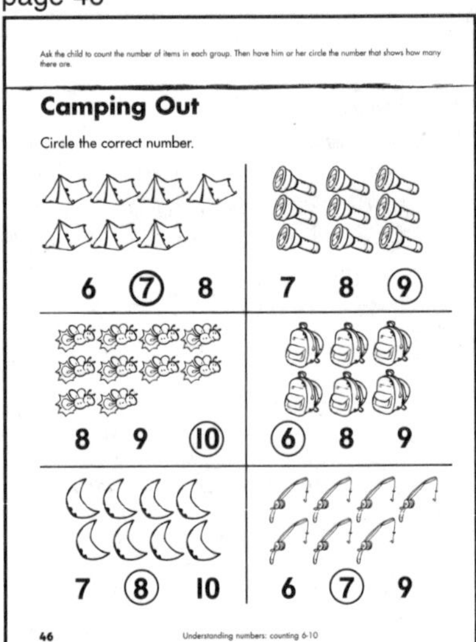
Camping Out

Circle the correct number.

6 (7) 8

7 8 (9)

8 9 (10)

(6) 8 9

7 (8) 10

6 (7) 9

46

Understanding numbers: counting 6-10

page 47

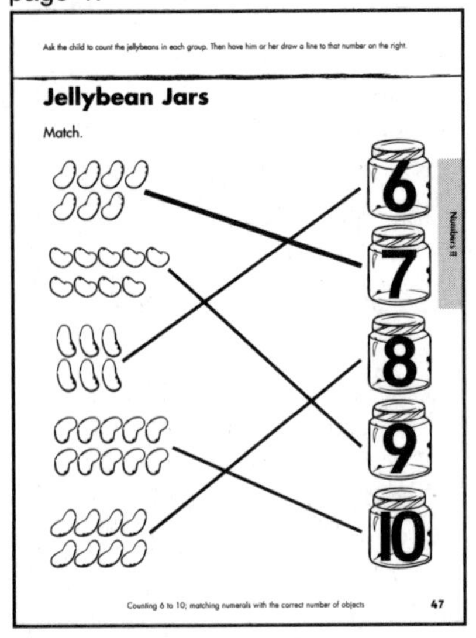
Jellybean Jars

Match.

6

7

8

9

10

Counting 6 to 10; matching numerals with the correct number of objects

47

page 48

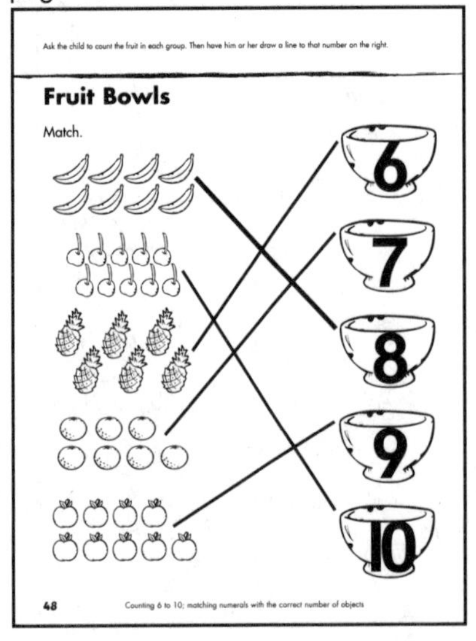
Fruit Bowls

Match.

6

7

8

9

10

48

Counting 6 to 10; matching numerals with the correct number of objects

page 49

Chocolate Chip Cookies

Draw s on the .

6

7

8

9

10

Counting to 10; recognizing numerals; drawing to show numbers

49

page 50

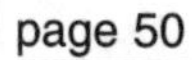

On the Farm

Count and color. Circle how many.

Counting to 10; recognizing numerals

page 52

Splashing Dot-to-Dot

Connect the dots from **1** to **10**.

Understanding numerical order; developing fine motor control

page 53

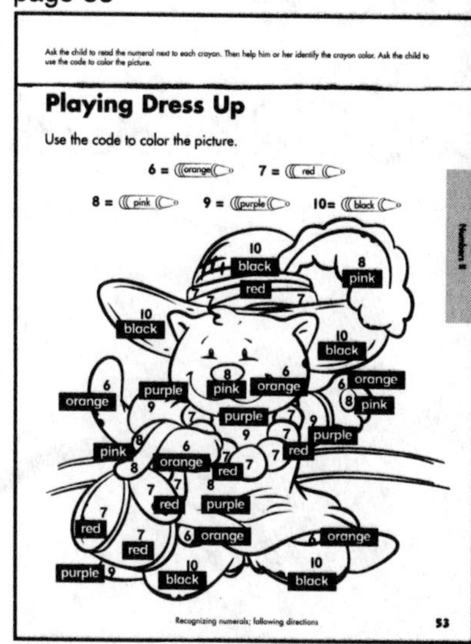

Playing Dress Up

Use the code to color the picture.

6 = orange 7 = red 8 = pink 9 = purple 10 = black

Recognizing numerals; following directions

page 54

Splashing Dot-to-Dot

Connect the dots from **1** to **10**.

Understanding numerical order; developing fine motor control

page 55

Go Fly a Kite

Use the code to color the picture.

6 = yellow 7 = blue 8 = red 9 = green 10 = brown

Recognizing numerals; following directions

page 56

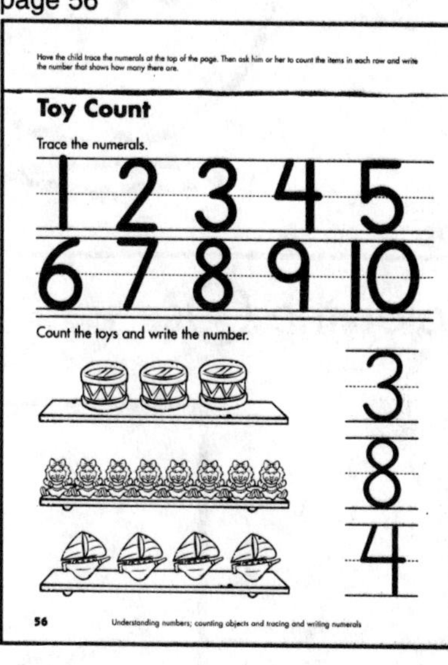

Toy Count

Trace the numerals.

1 2 3 4 5 6 7 8 9 10

Count the toys and write the number.

3 8 4

Understanding numbers; counting objects and tracing and writing numerals

page 57

6 2 9 5 10

Understanding numbers; counting objects and tracing and writing numerals

page 58

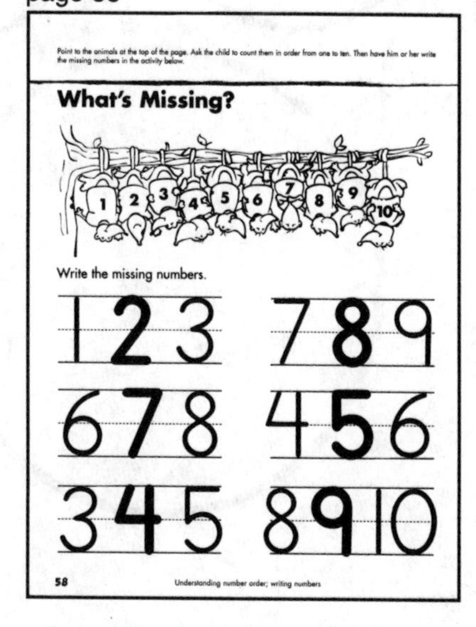

What's Missing?

Write the missing numbers.

1 2 3 7 8 9

6 7 8 4 5 6

3 4 5 8 9 10

Understanding number order; writing numbers

Point to the circle in the picture at the top of the page. Say the shape and trace it with your finger. Have the child color the circle. Then ask the child to color all the circles at the bottom.

Circle

Look closely. Color the ○.

Color the ○s.

Ask the child to find and color all the circles in the picture.

Circle Search

Look closely. Color the ◯s.

Point to the square in the picture at the top of the page. Say the shape and trace it with your finger. Have the child color the square. Then ask the child to color all the squares at the bottom.

Square

Look closely. Color the □.

Color the □s.

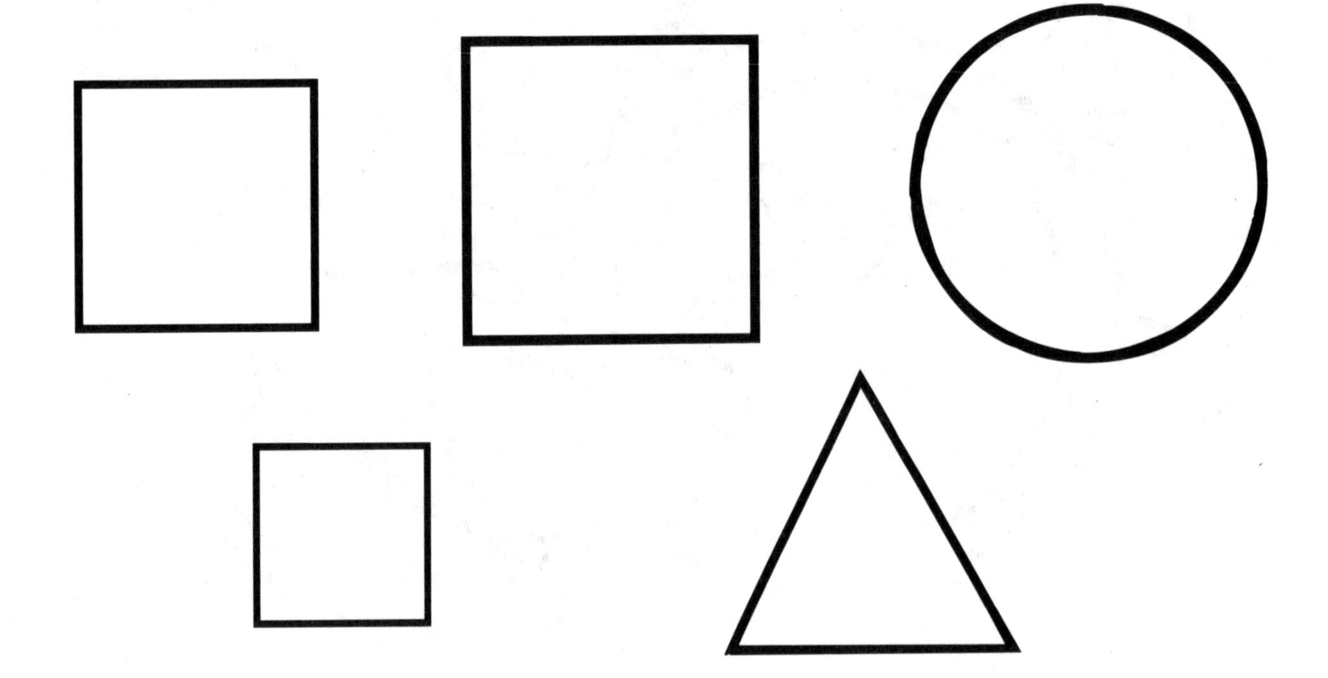

Ask the child to find and color all the squares in the picture.

Square Search

Look closely. Color the □s.

Have the child trace the circles on the caterpillar with his or her finger. Then have him or her trace the circles with a crayon and color the caterpillar.

Trace Circles

Trace the ○s. Color the caterpillar.

Have the child trace the squares on the fire truck with his or her finger. Then have him or her trace the squares with a crayon and color the fire truck.

Trace Squares

Trace the □s. Color the fire truck.

Shapes & Sizes

Point to the triangle in the picture at the top of the page. Say the shape and trace it with your finger. Have the child color the triangle. Then ask the child to color all the triangles at the bottom.

Triangle

Look closely. Color the △.

Color the △s.

Ask the child to find and color all the triangles in the picture.

Triangle Search

Look closely. Color the △s.

Point to the rectangle in the picture at the top of the page. Say the shape and trace it with your finger. Have the child color the rectangle. Then ask the child to color all the rectangles at the bottom.

Rectangle

Look closely. Color the □.

Color the □s.

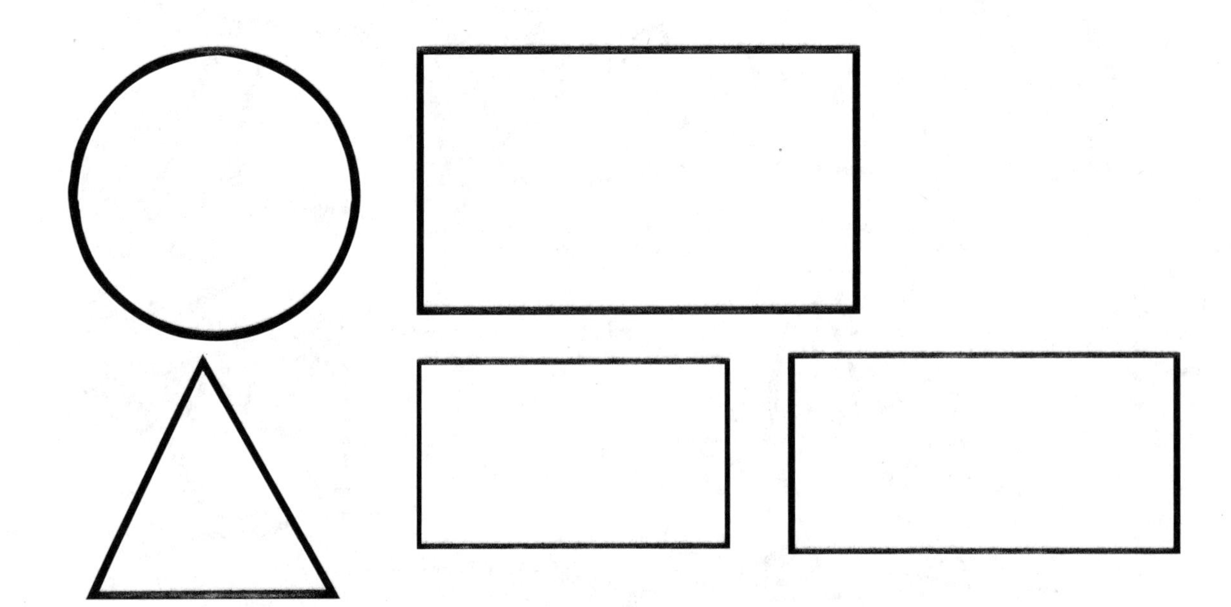

Understanding shapes; recognizing shape names

Ask the child to find and color all the rectangles in the picture.

Rectangle Search

Look closely. Color the ▭s.

Have the child trace the triangle-shaped slices of pizza with his or her finger. Then have him or her trace the triangles with a crayon and color the pizza. Ask the child to color the blank slice like his or her favorite kind of pizza.

Trace Triangles

Trace the △s. Color the pizza.

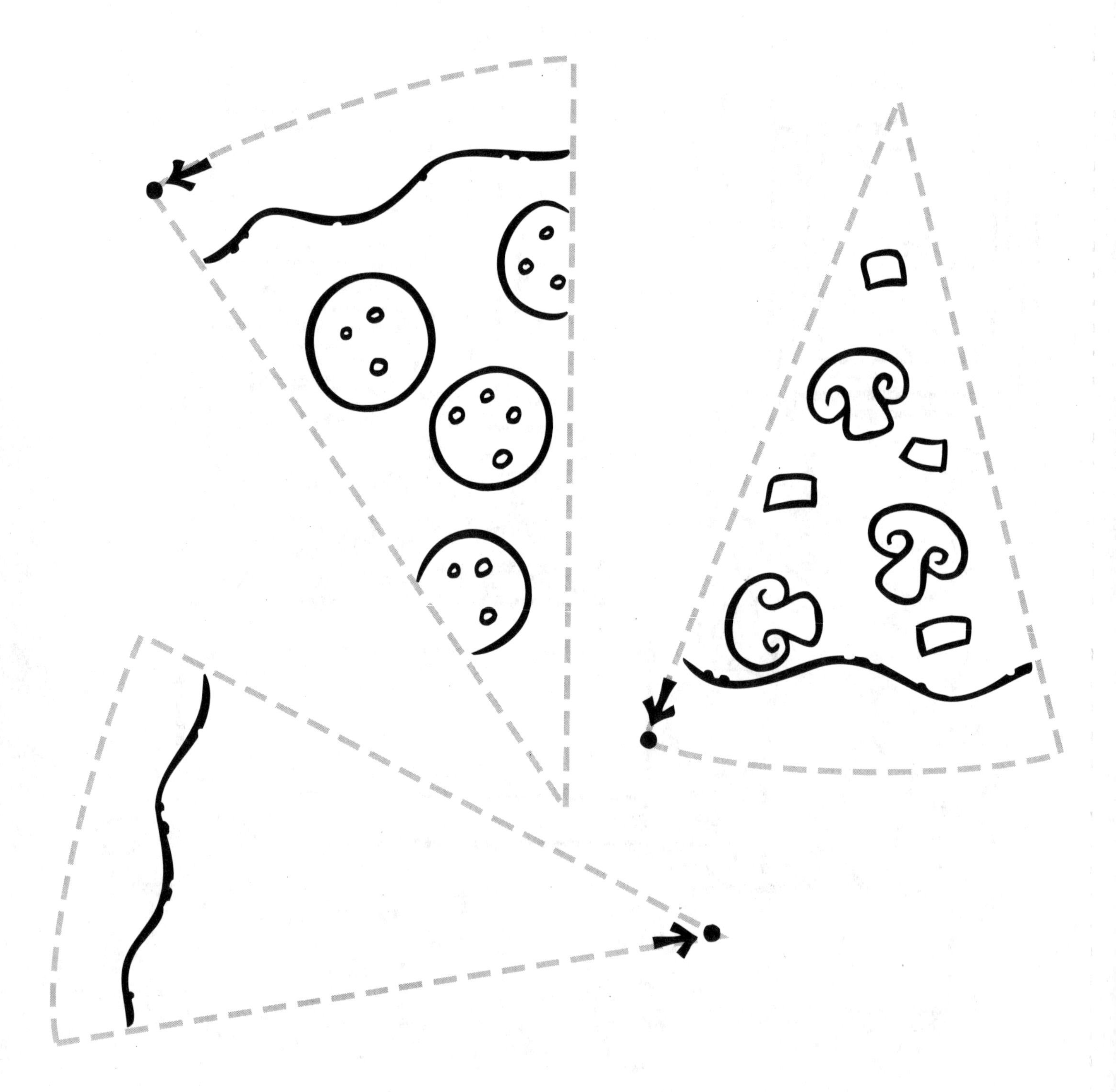

Have the child trace the rectangles on the flag with his or her finger. Then have him or her trace the rectangles with a crayon and color the flag.

Trace Rectangles

Trace the ▭s. Color the flag.

Ask the child to color the shapes in each row that are the same. Then have him or her name the shapes.

Shapes in a Row

Color the shapes that are the same.

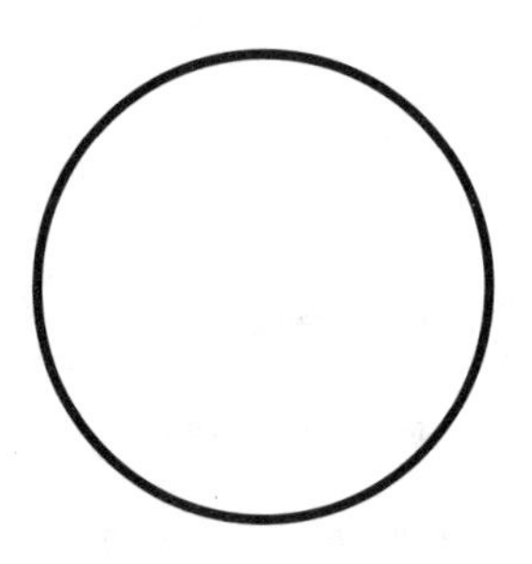 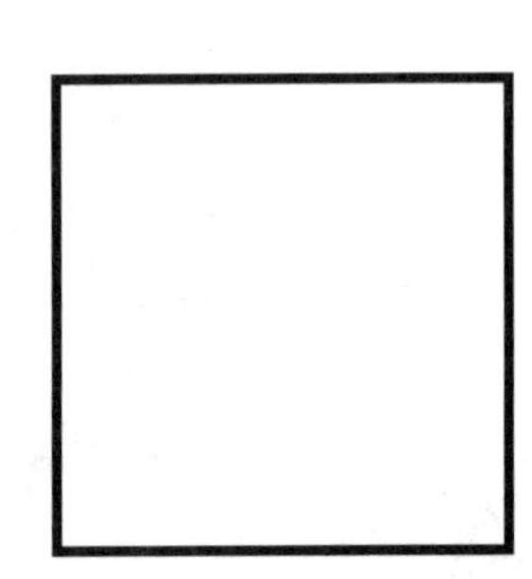 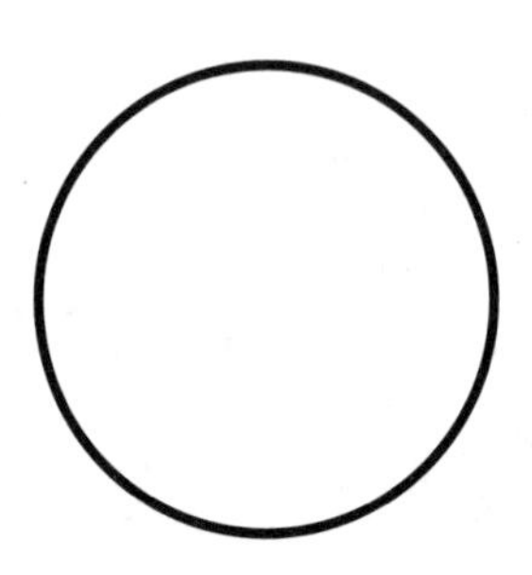

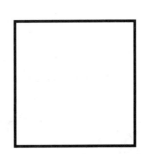  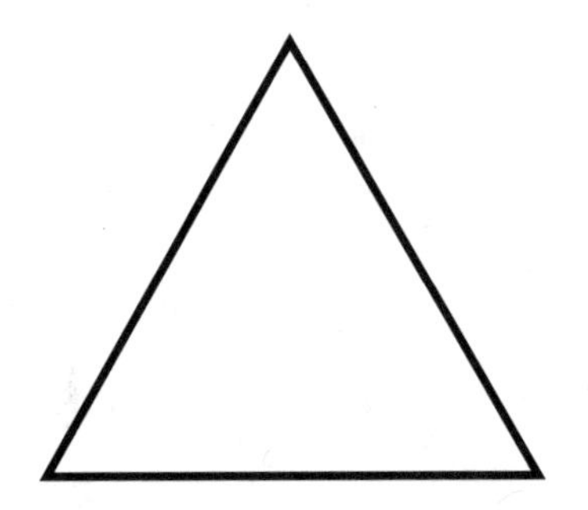

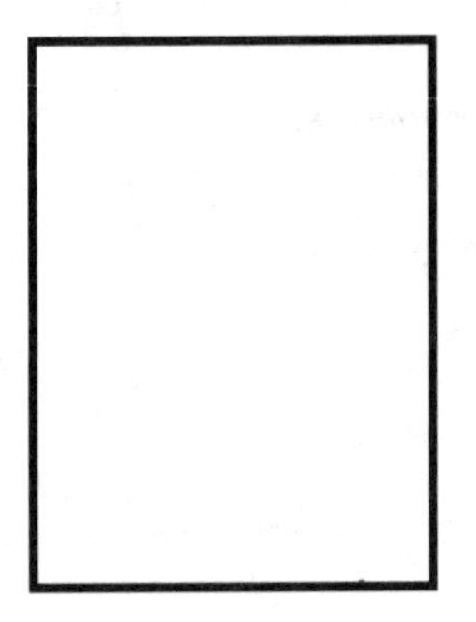 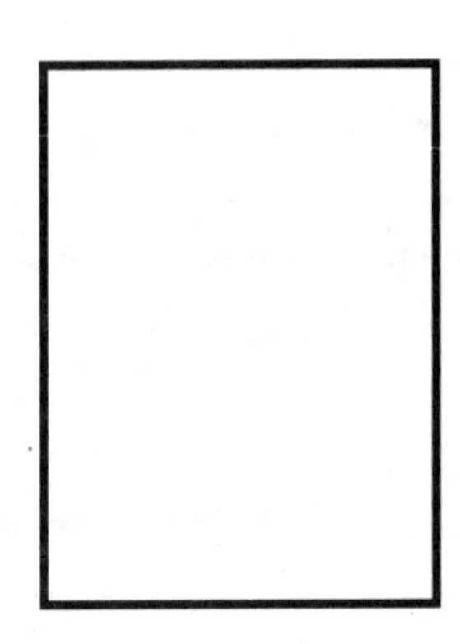 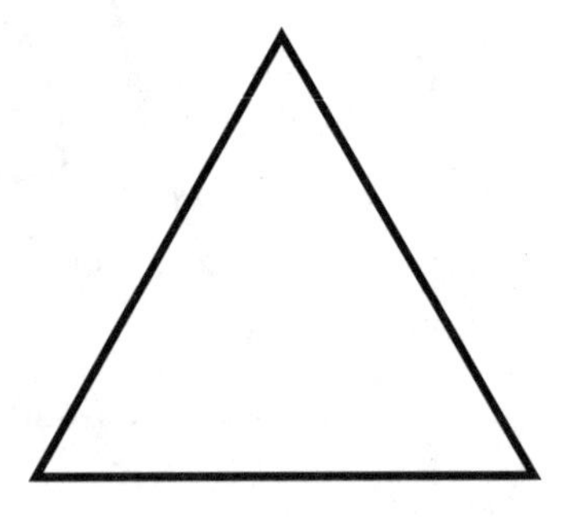

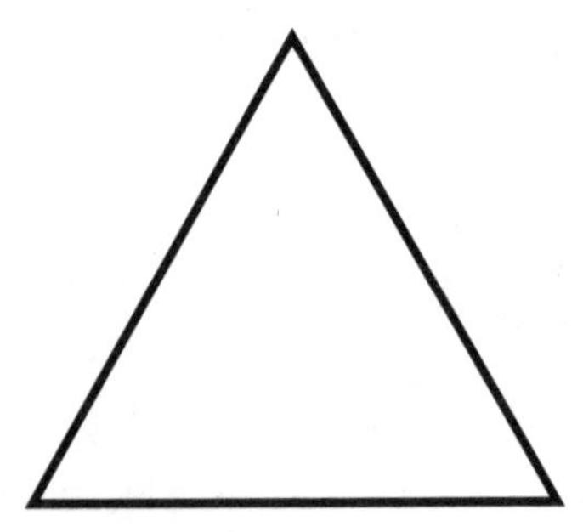 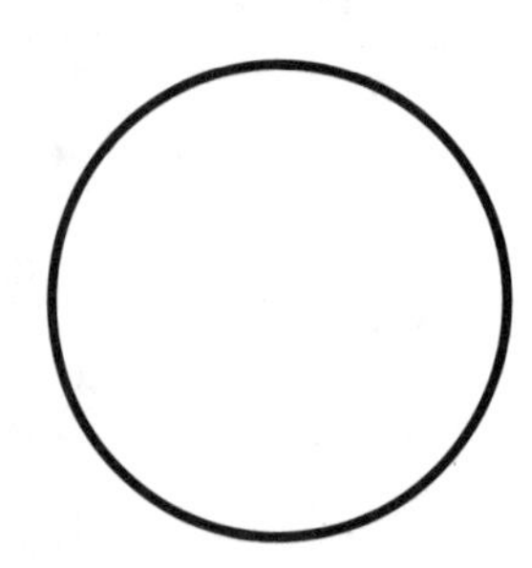 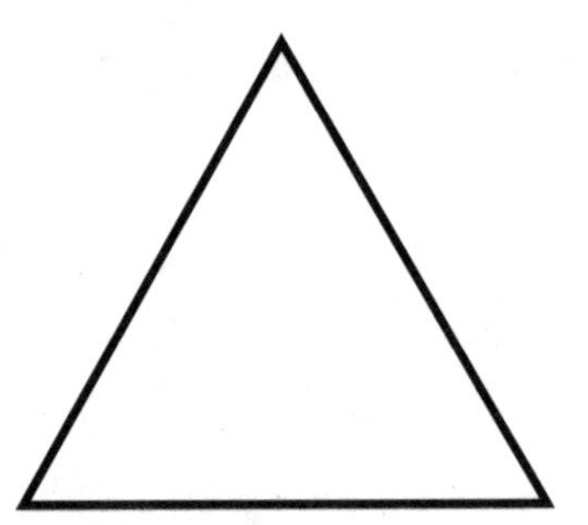

Point to and name each shape. Have the child draw a line between the shapes that are the same.

Shape Match

Match.

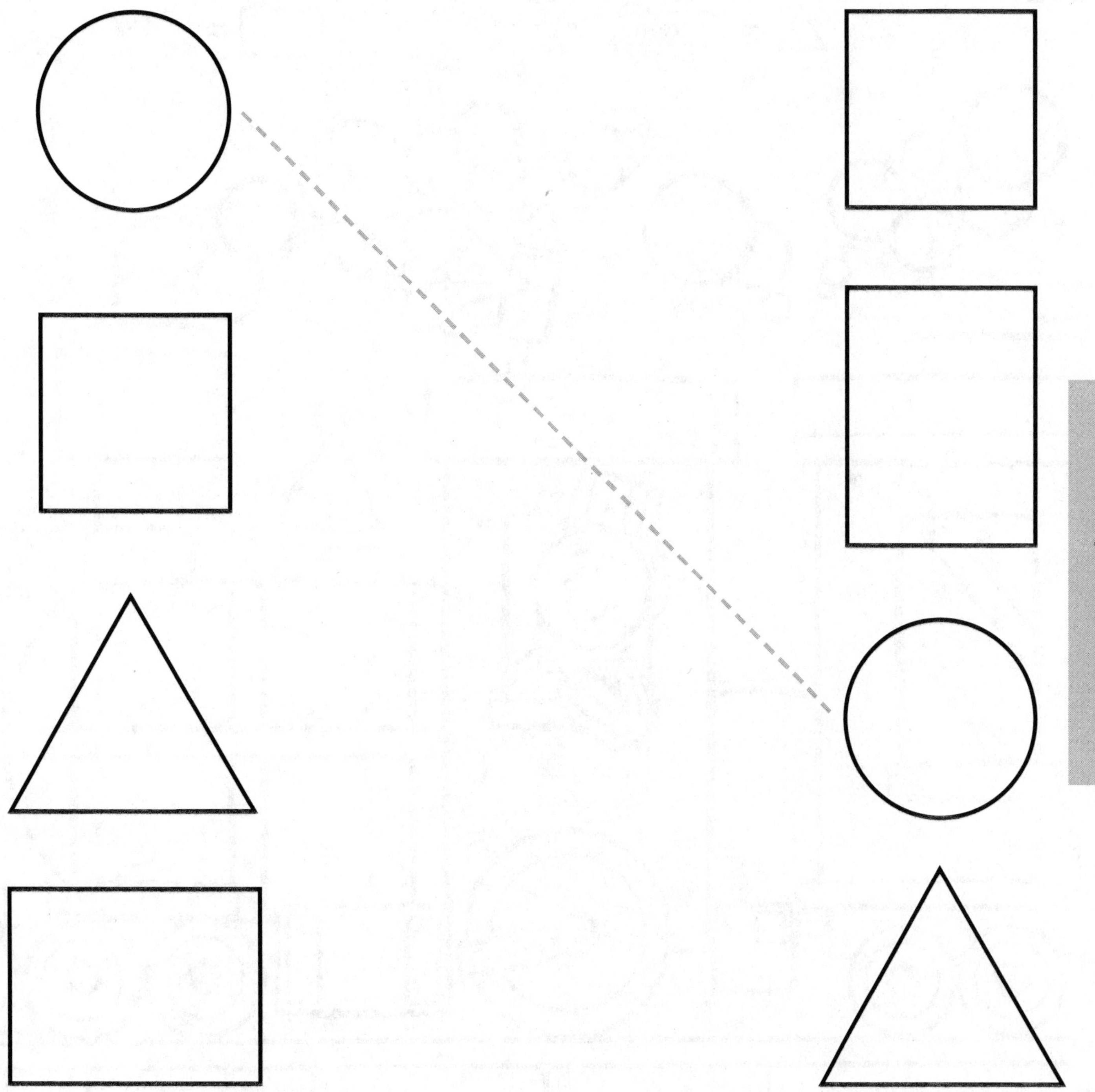

Help the child identify each shape in the code and the color of each crayon. Then have him or her color the shapes in the picture using the code.

All Aboard!

Use the code to color the picture.

Shapes & Sizes

Point to and name each shape. Then have the child draw a line between the shapes that are the same.

Snack Time

Match.

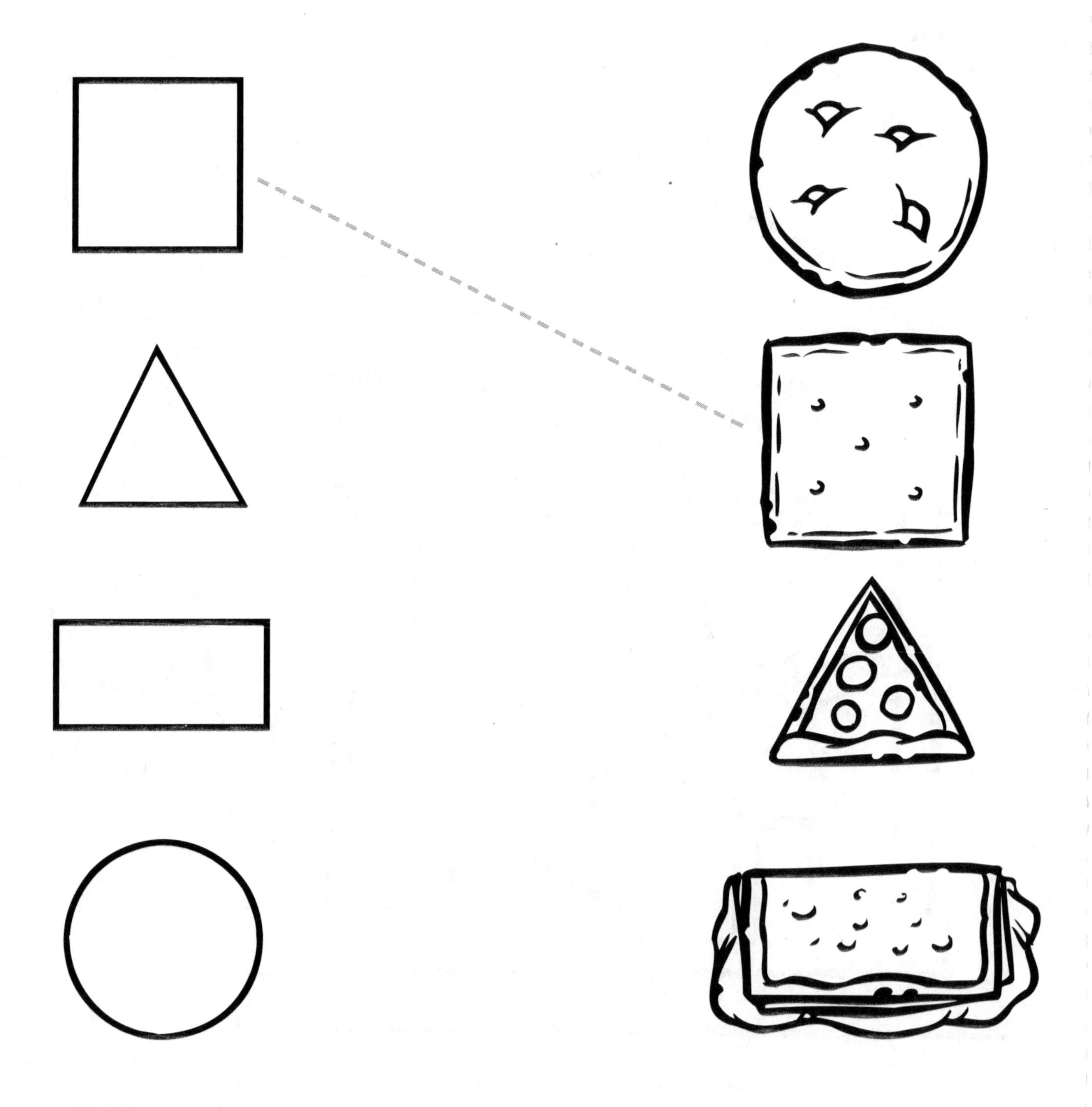

Ask the child to find and color the circles, squares, triangles, and rectangles hidden in the picture.

In the Kitchen

Look closely. Color the ◯s, □s, △s, and ▭s.

Shapes & Sizes

Ask the child to identify the different shapes on the page. Then have him or her color all the squares to make a path from the dog to the doghouse.

A-maze-ing

Color the □s.

Ask the child to identify the different shapes on the page. Then have him or her color all the triangles to make a path from the bird to the nest.

Home Sweet Home

Color the △s.

Shapes & Sizes

Ask the child to look closely at the fruit and trace the shape of each picture with his or her finger. Then have him or her draw a line between the shapes that are the same.

Fruit Bowl

Match.

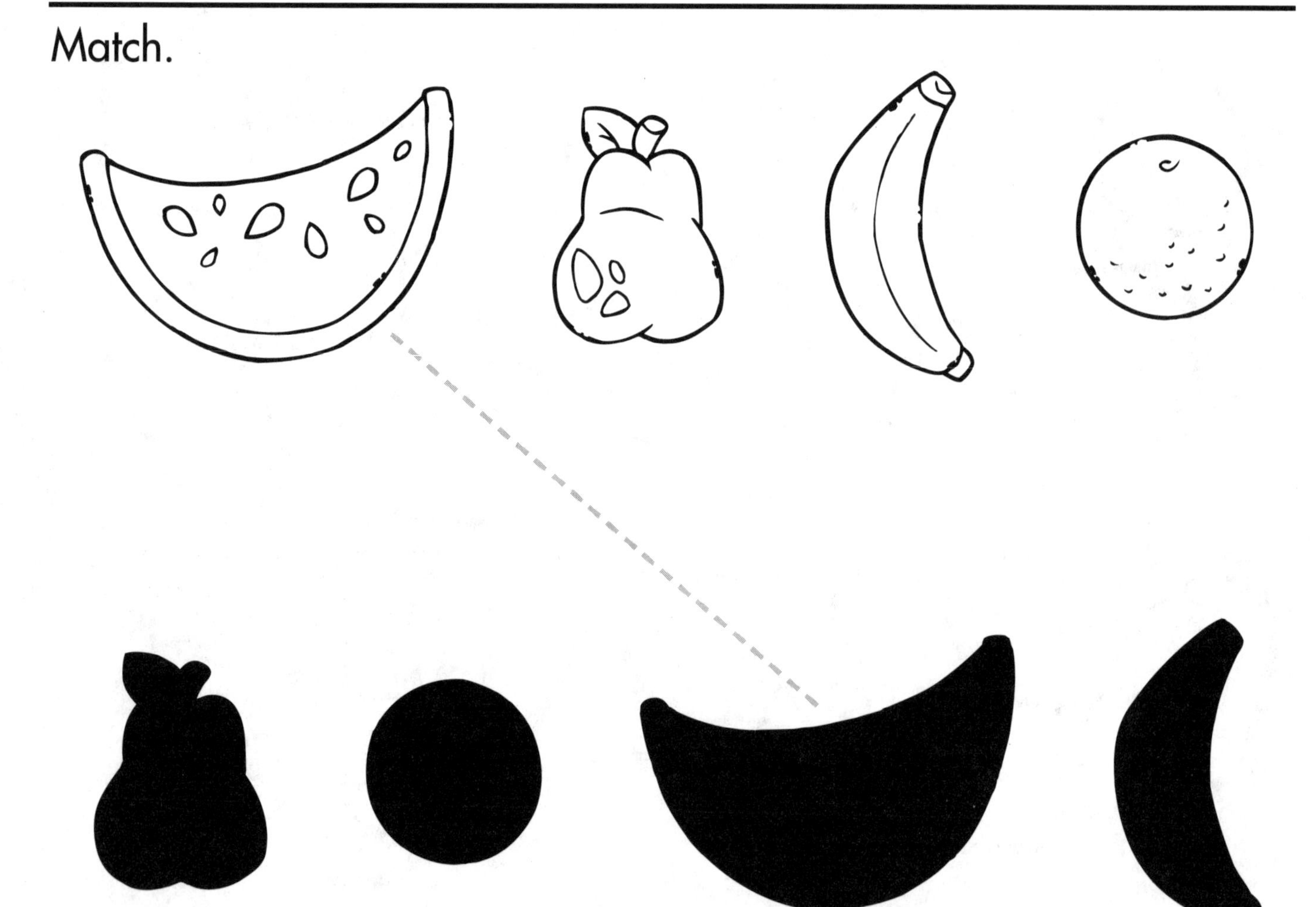

Ask the child to look closely at the presents and trace the shape of each picture with his or her finger. Then have him or her draw a line between the shapes that are the same.

A Present for You

Match.

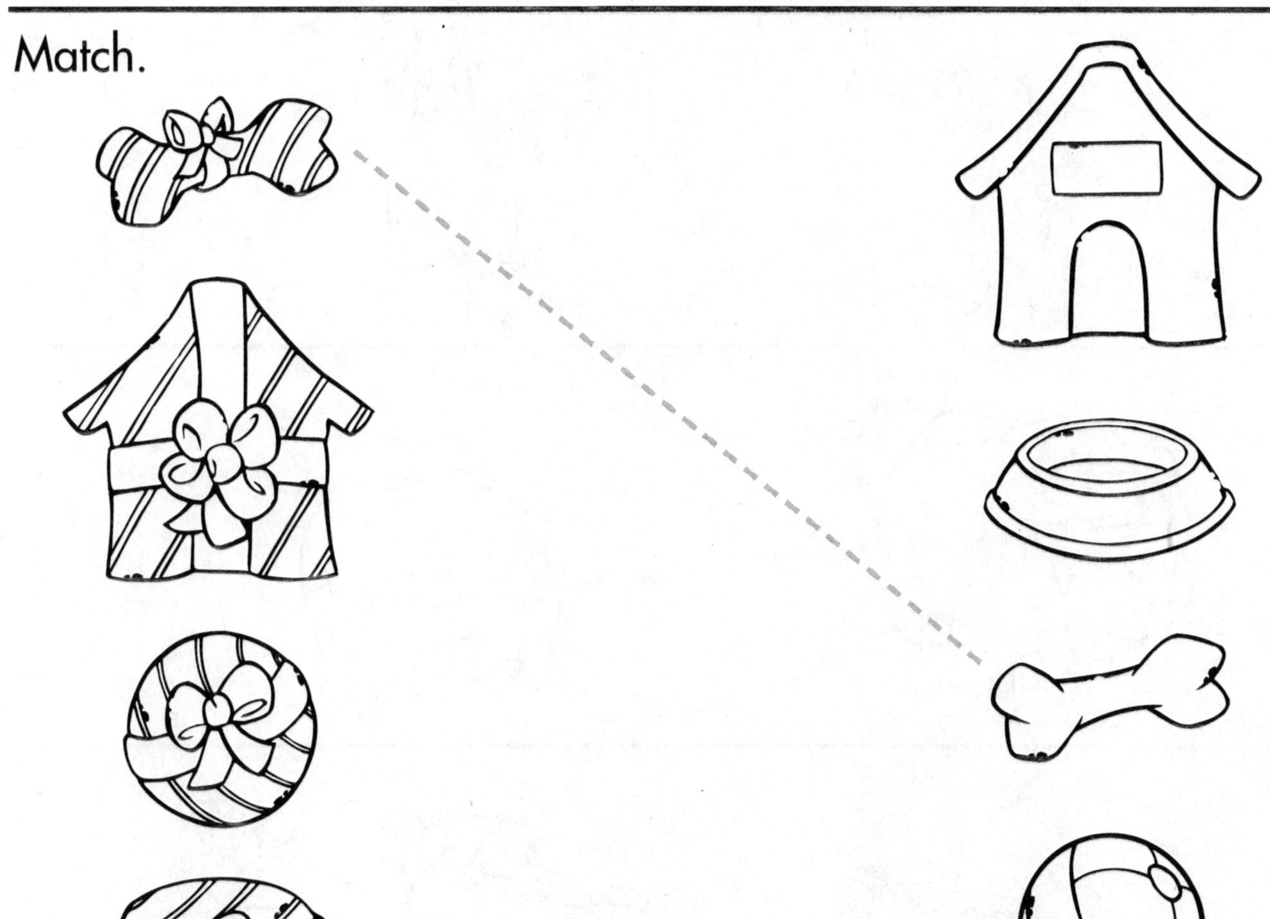

Shapes & Sizes

Point to the big lion and then to the little lion. Ask the child to color the big animal and circle the little animal in each row.

Big and Little

Color the big animal. Circle the little animal.

Point to the long ribbon and then to the short ribbon. Ask the child to color the long object in each group red and the short object in each group blue.

Long and Short

Color the long ones red. Color the short ones blue.

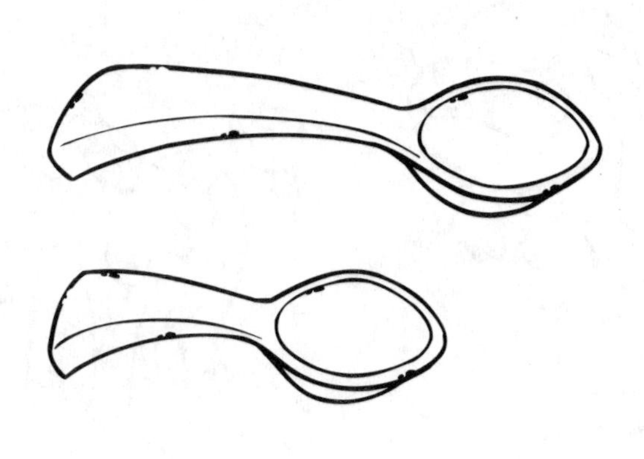

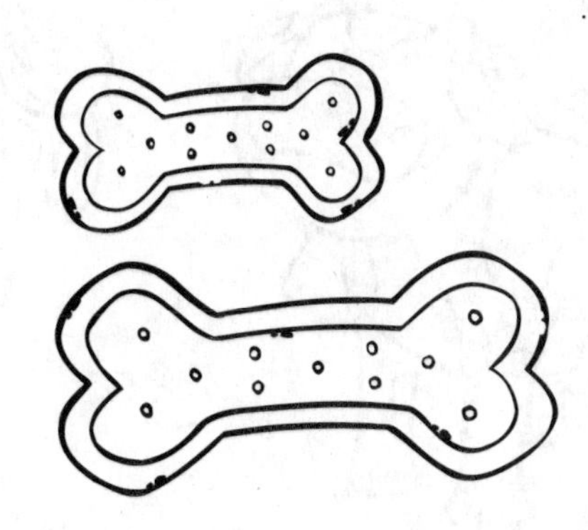

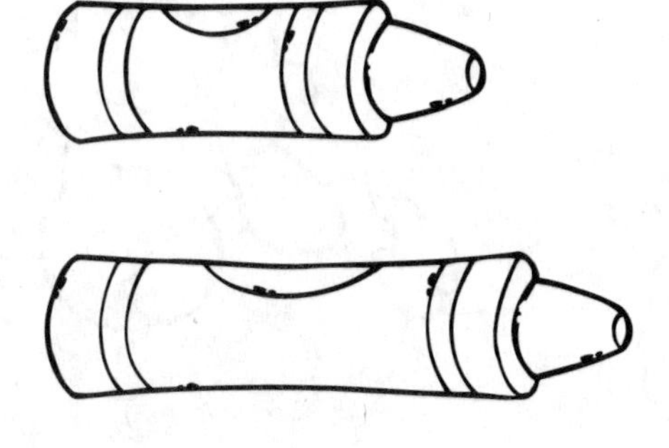

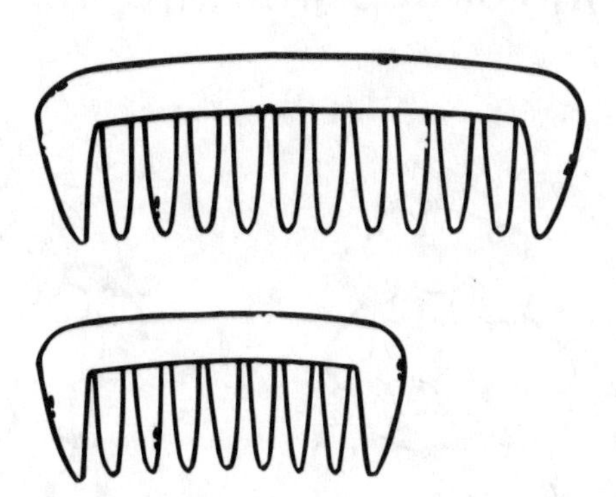

Shapes & Sizes

Point to the two turkeys and explain that they are the same size. Then ask the child to circle the cows and sheep that are the same size.

Same Size

Circle the cows that are the same size.

Circle the sheep that are the same size.

Point to the littlest boat and then to the biggest boat. Ask the child to color the biggest vehicle and circle the littlest vehicle in each row.

Littlest and Biggest

Color the biggest. Circle the littlest.

Point to the longest caterpillar and then to the shortest caterpillar. Ask the child to color the longest animal in each group yellow and the shortest animal in each group green.

Longest and Shortest

Color the longest ones yellow. Color the shortest ones green.

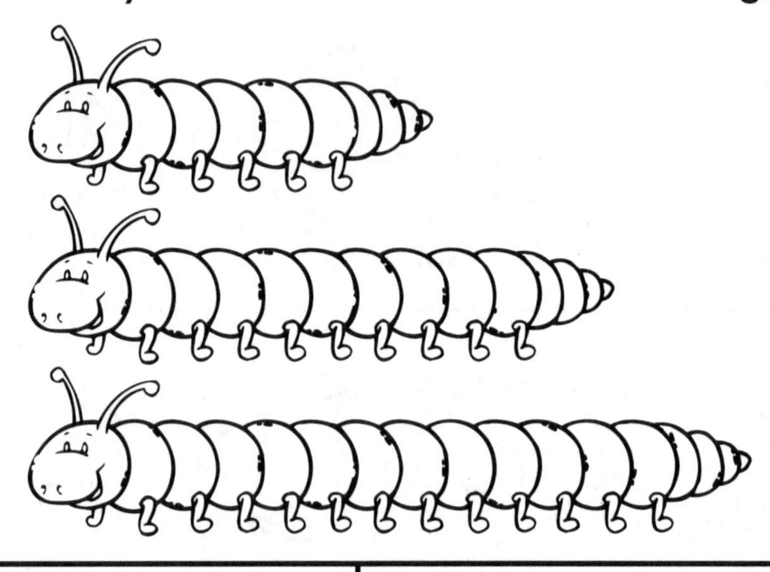

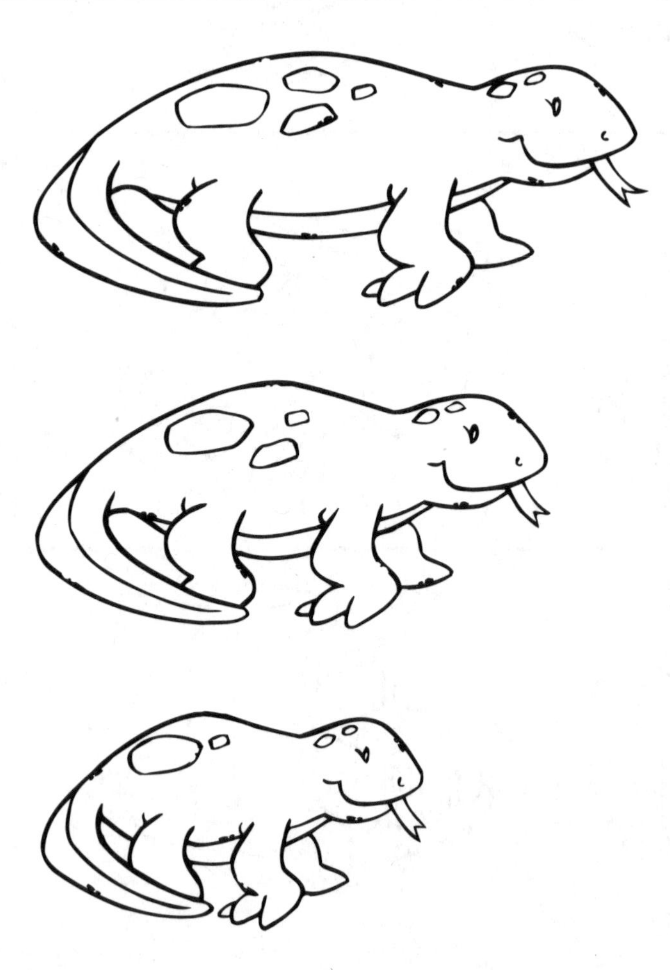

Answer Key

As the child completes the pages in this section, review his or her answers. When you take the time to correct the work and explain mistakes, you're showing your child that you feel learning is important.

page 62

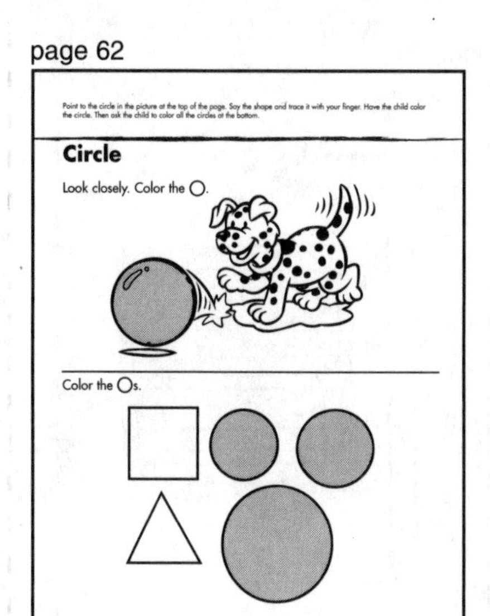

page 63

page 64

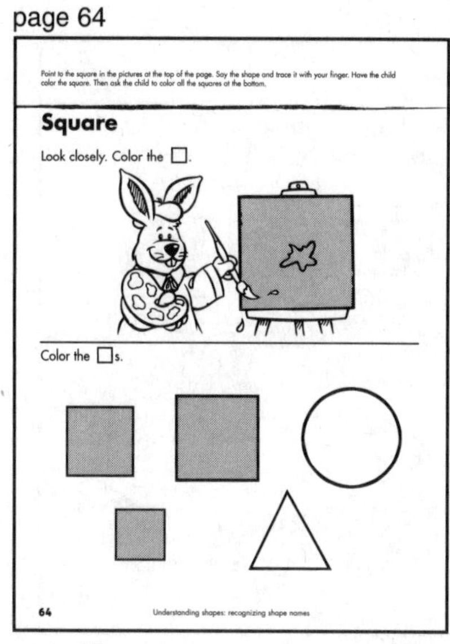

page 65

page 66

page 67

page 68

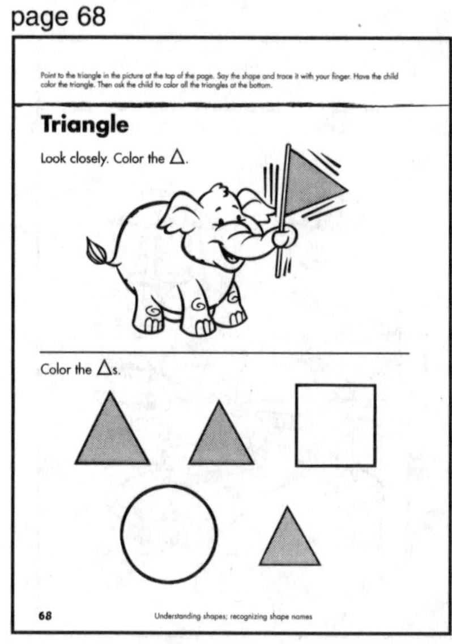

page 69

page 70

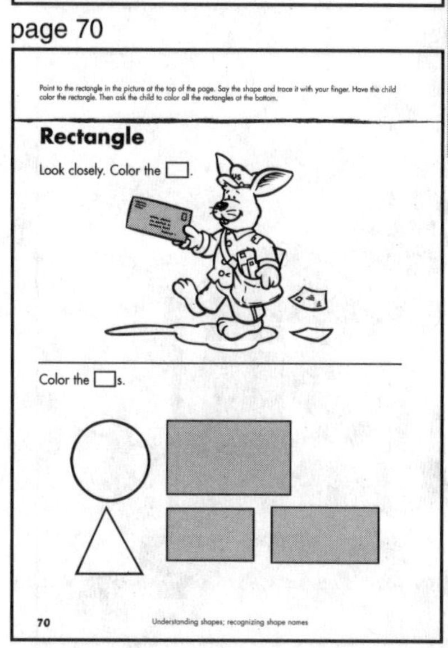

Shapes & Sizes

page 71

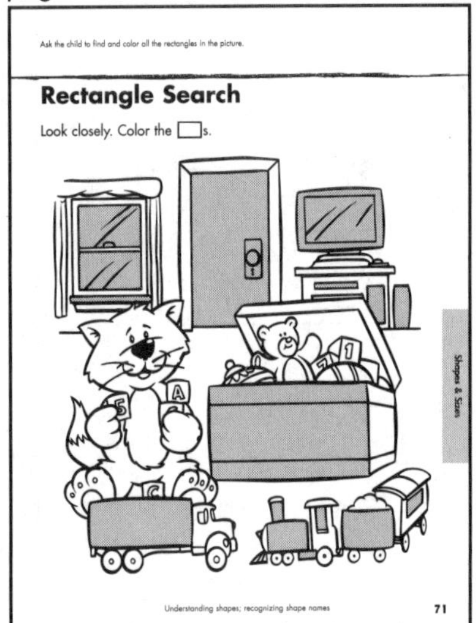
Ask the child to find and color all the rectangles in the picture.
Rectangle Search
Look closely. Color the ▭s.
Shapes & Sizes
Understanding shapes; recognizing shape names
71

page 72

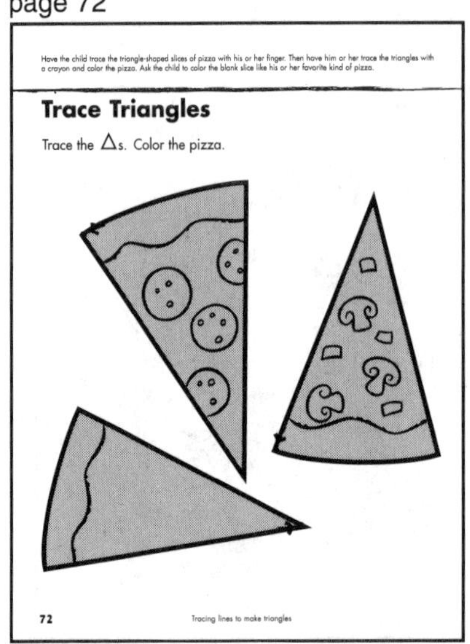
Trace Triangles
Trace the △s. Color the pizza.
72
Tracing lines to make triangles

page 73

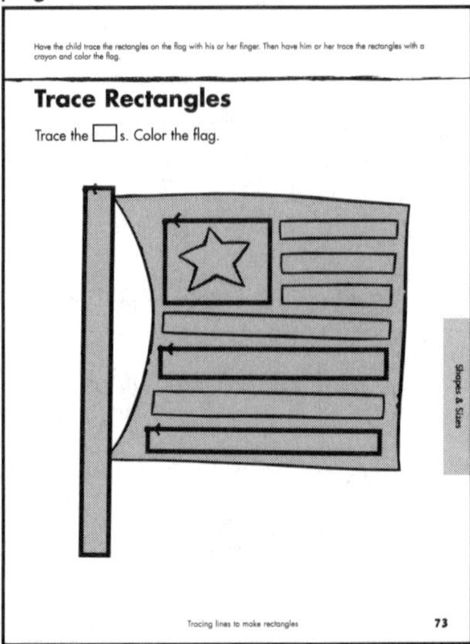
Trace Rectangles
Trace the ▭s. Color the flag.
Shapes & Sizes
Tracing lines to make rectangles
73

page 74

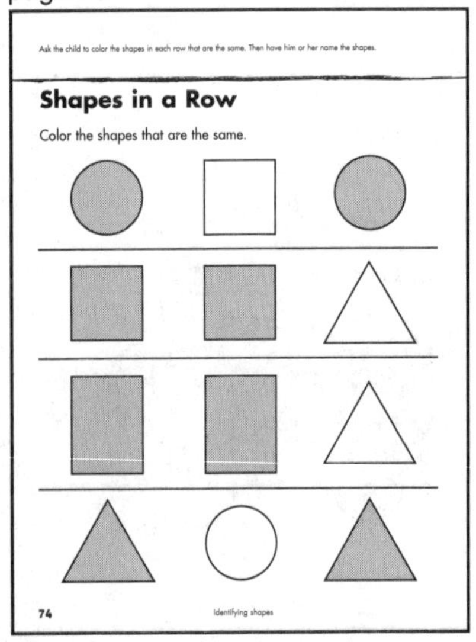
Shapes in a Row
Color the shapes that are the same.
74
Identifying shapes

page 75

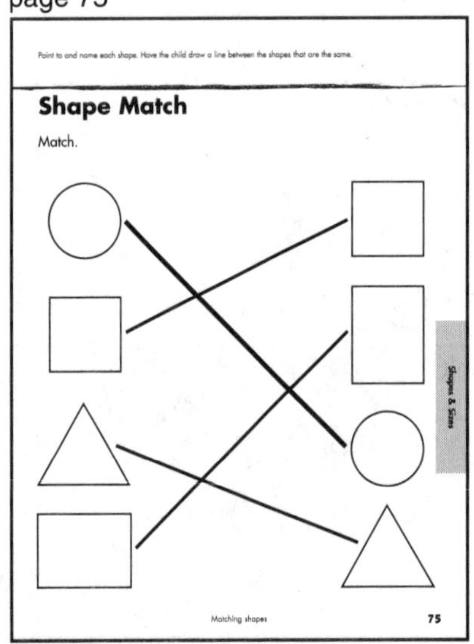
Shape Match
Match.
Shapes & Sizes
Matching shapes
75

page 76

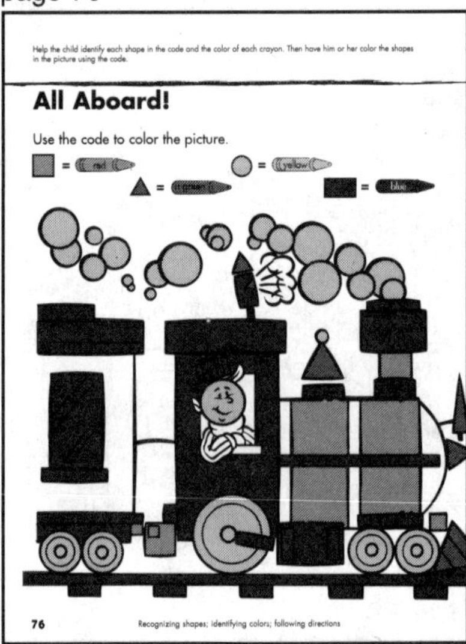
All Aboard!
Use the code to color the picture.
red
yellow
green
blue
76
Recognizing shapes; identifying colors; following directions

page 77

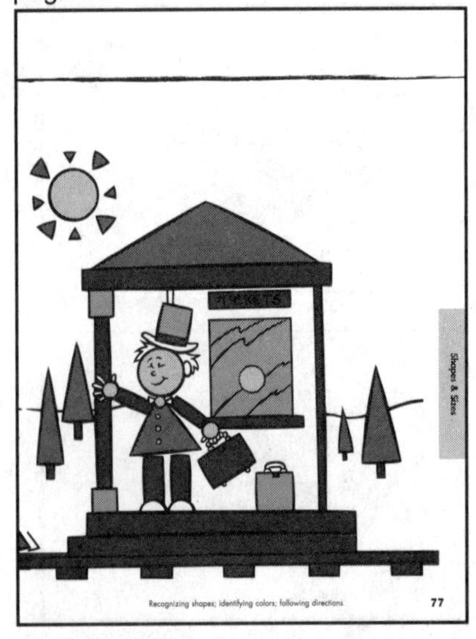
TICKETS
Shapes & Sizes
Recognizing shapes; identifying colors; following directions
77

page 78

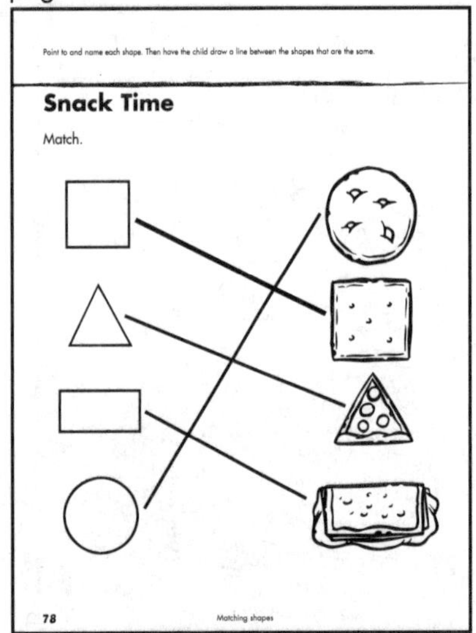
Point to and name each shape. Then have the child draw a line between the shapes that are the same.
Snack Time
Match.
78
Matching shapes

page 79

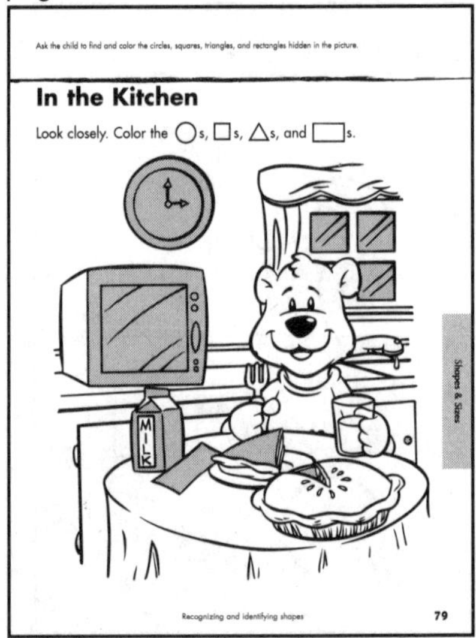
Ask the child to find and color the circles, squares, triangles, and rectangles hidden in the picture.
In the Kitchen
Look closely. Color the ○s, □s, △s, and ▭s.
MILK
Shapes & Sizes
Recognizing and identifying shapes
79

page 80

Ask the child to identify the different shapes on the page. Then have him or her color all the squares to make a path from the dog to the doghouse.

A-maze-ing

Color the □s.

80 Identifying shapes

page 81

Ask the child to identify the different shapes on the page. Then have him or her color all the triangles to make a path from the bird to the nest.

Home Sweet Home

Color the △s.

Shapes & Sizes

Identifying shapes 81

page 82

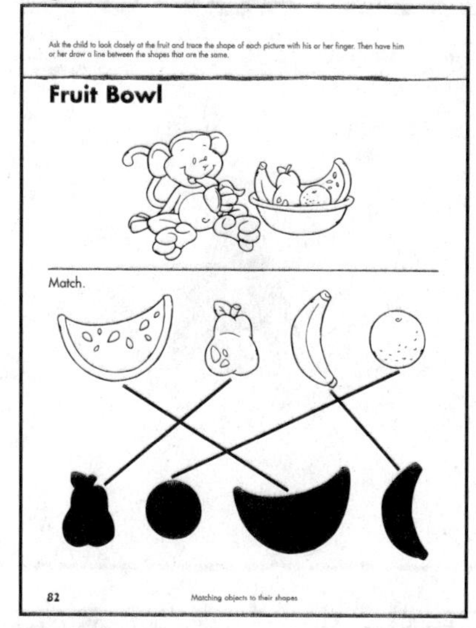

Ask the child to look closely at the fruit and trace the shape of each picture with his or her finger. Then have him or her draw a line between the shapes that are the same.

Fruit Bowl

Match.

82 Matching objects to their shapes

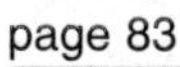

page 83

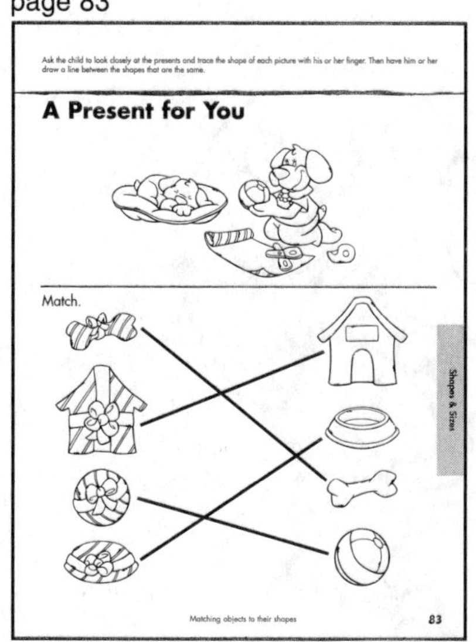

Ask the child to look closely at the presents and trace the shape of each picture with his or her finger. Then have him or her draw a line between the shapes that are the same.

A Present for You

Match.

Shapes & Sizes

Matching objects to their shapes 83

page 84

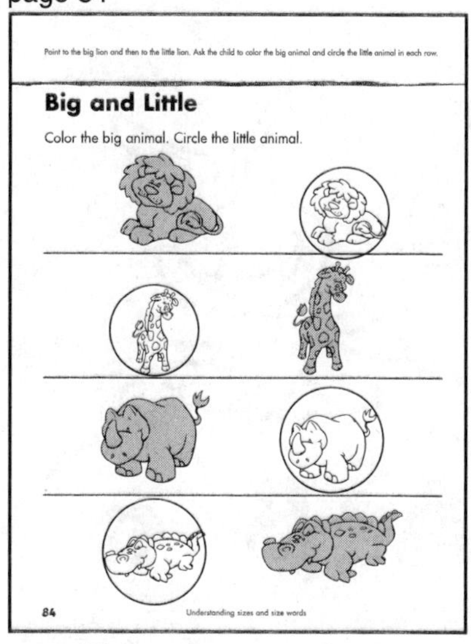

Point to the big lion and then to the little lion. Ask the child to color the big animal and circle the little animal in each row.

Big and Little

Color the big animal. Circle the little animal.

84 Understanding sizes and size words

page 85

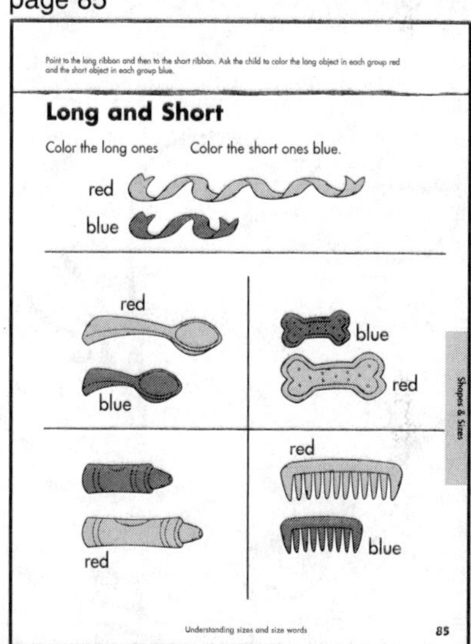

Point to the long ribbon and then to the short ribbon. Ask the child to color the long object in each group red and the short object in each group blue.

Long and Short

Color the long ones Color the short ones blue.

Shapes & Sizes

Understanding sizes and size words 85

page 86

Point to the two turkeys and explain that they are the same size. Then ask the child to circle the cows and sheep that are the same size.

Same Size

Circle the cows that are the same size.

Circle the sheep that are the same size.

86 Understanding sizes and size words

page 87

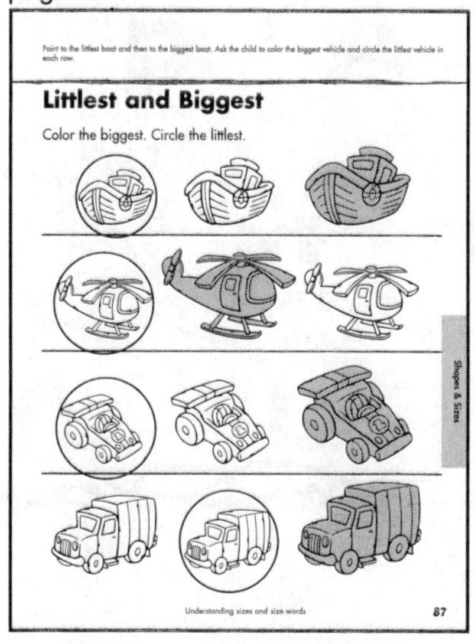

Point to the littlest boat and then to the biggest boat. Ask the child to color the biggest vehicle and circle the littlest vehicle in each row.

Littlest and Biggest

Color the biggest. Circle the littlest.

Shapes & Sizes

Understanding sizes and size words 87

page 88

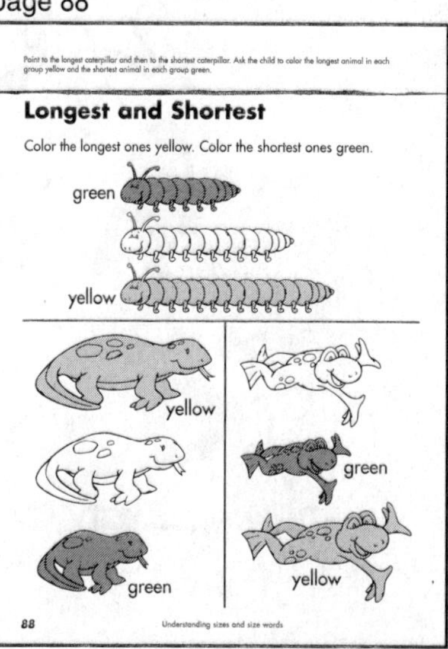

Point to the longest caterpillar and then to the shortest caterpillar. Ask the child to color the longest animal in each group yellow and the shortest animal in each group green.

Longest and Shortest

Color the longest ones yellow. Color the shortest ones green.

88 Understanding sizes and size words

Point to and say the capital and lowercase letters **A** and **a** at the top of the page. Ask the child to find and circle all the letters **A** and **a** on the anthill.

The Letters A and a

Circle the letters **A** and **a**.

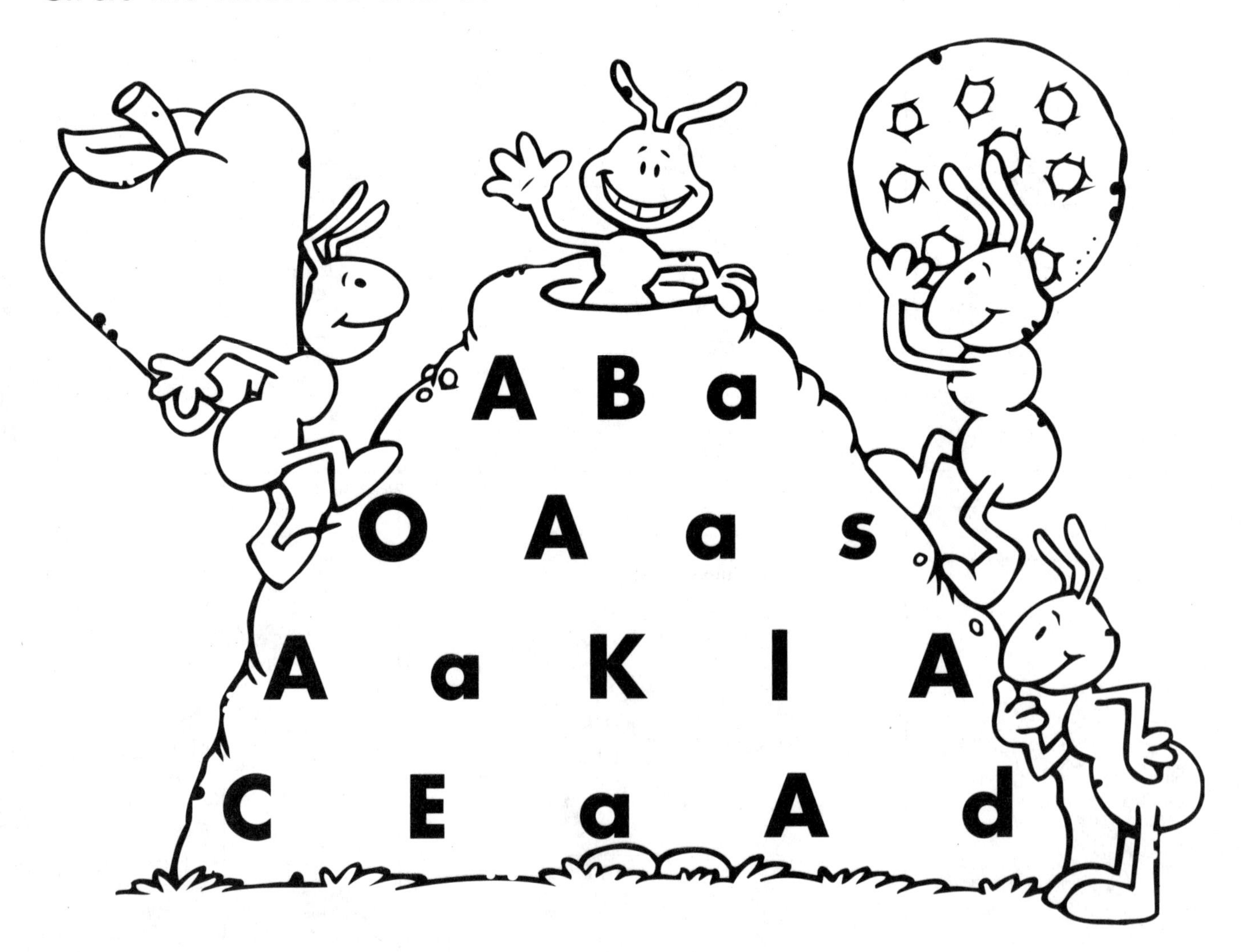

Name the pictures at the top of the page that begin with the letter **Aa**. Have the child follow the arrows to trace the letters with his or her finger. Then have him or her color the letters. Ask the child to trace and write the letters at the bottom.

Writing Aa

Color the letters.

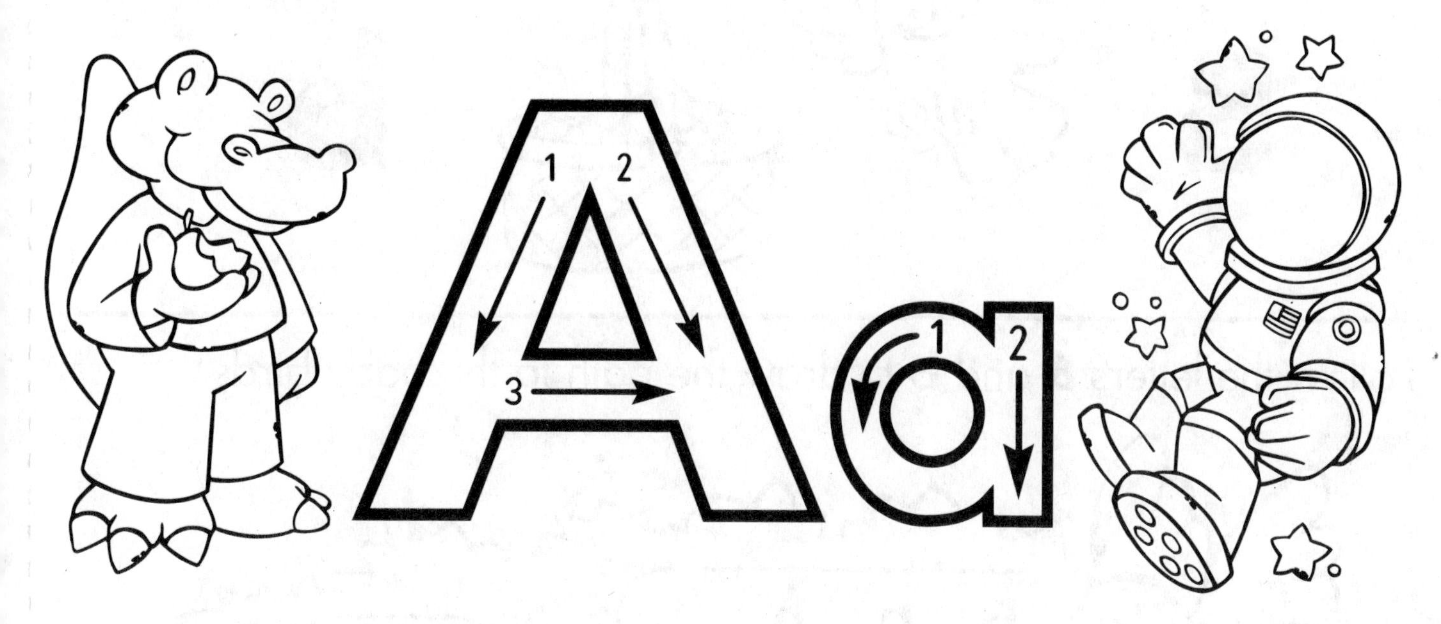

Trace and write the letters.

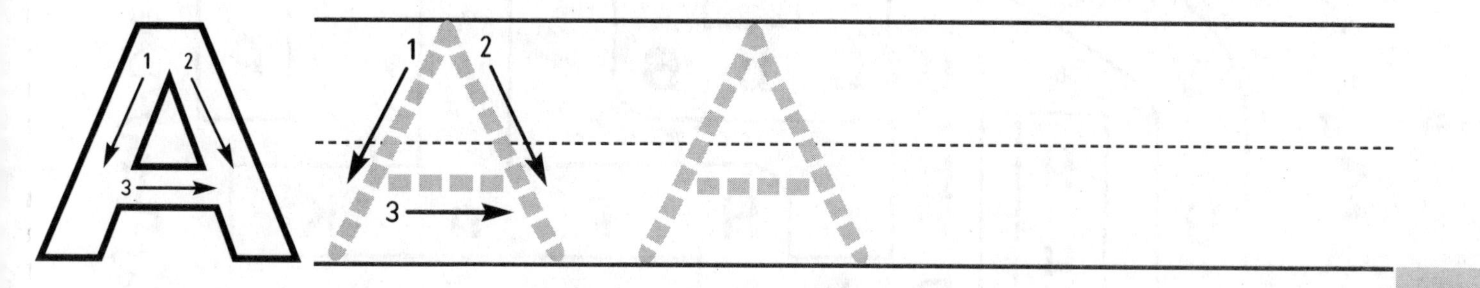

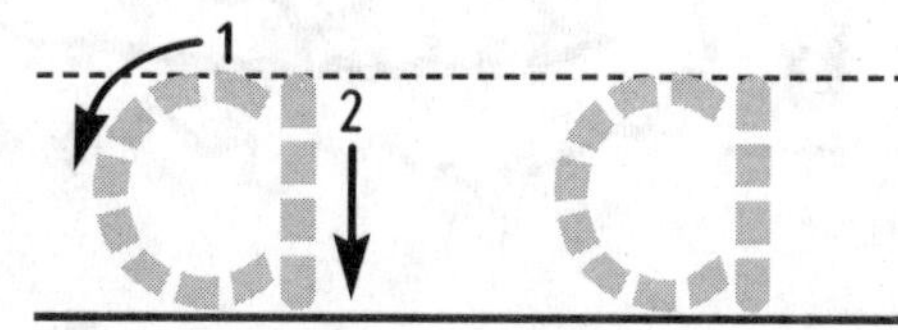

Point to and say the capital and lowercase letters **B** and **b** at the top of the page. Ask the child to draw a line from the mother bird to her babies by following the letters **B** and **b**.

The Letters B and b

Follow the letters **B** and **b** to draw the path to the baby birds.

Name the pictures at the top of the page that begin with the letter **Bb**. Have the child follow the arrows to trace the letters with his or her finger. Then have him or her color the letters. Ask the child to trace and write the letters at the bottom.

Writing Bb

Color the letters.

Trace and write the letters.

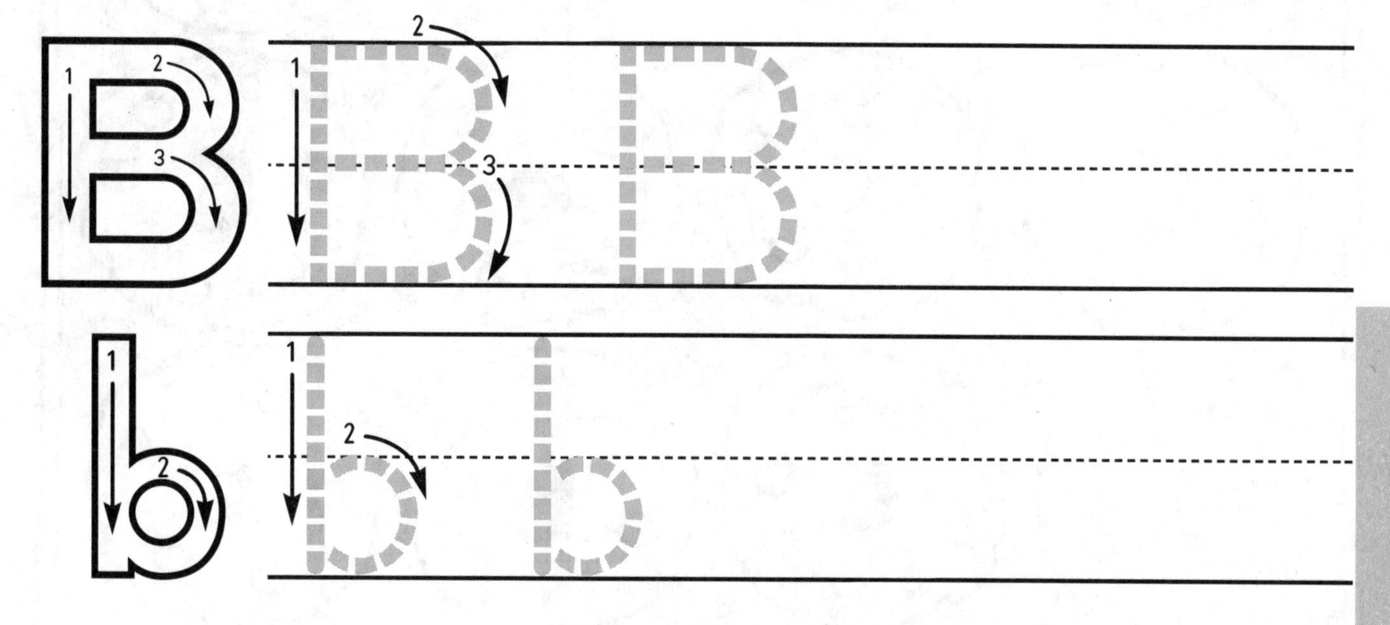

Point to and say the capital and lowercase letters **C** and **c** at the top of the page. Ask the child to find and color the cookies with the letters **C** or **c**.

The Letters C and c

Color the (cookie)s with **C** or **c**.

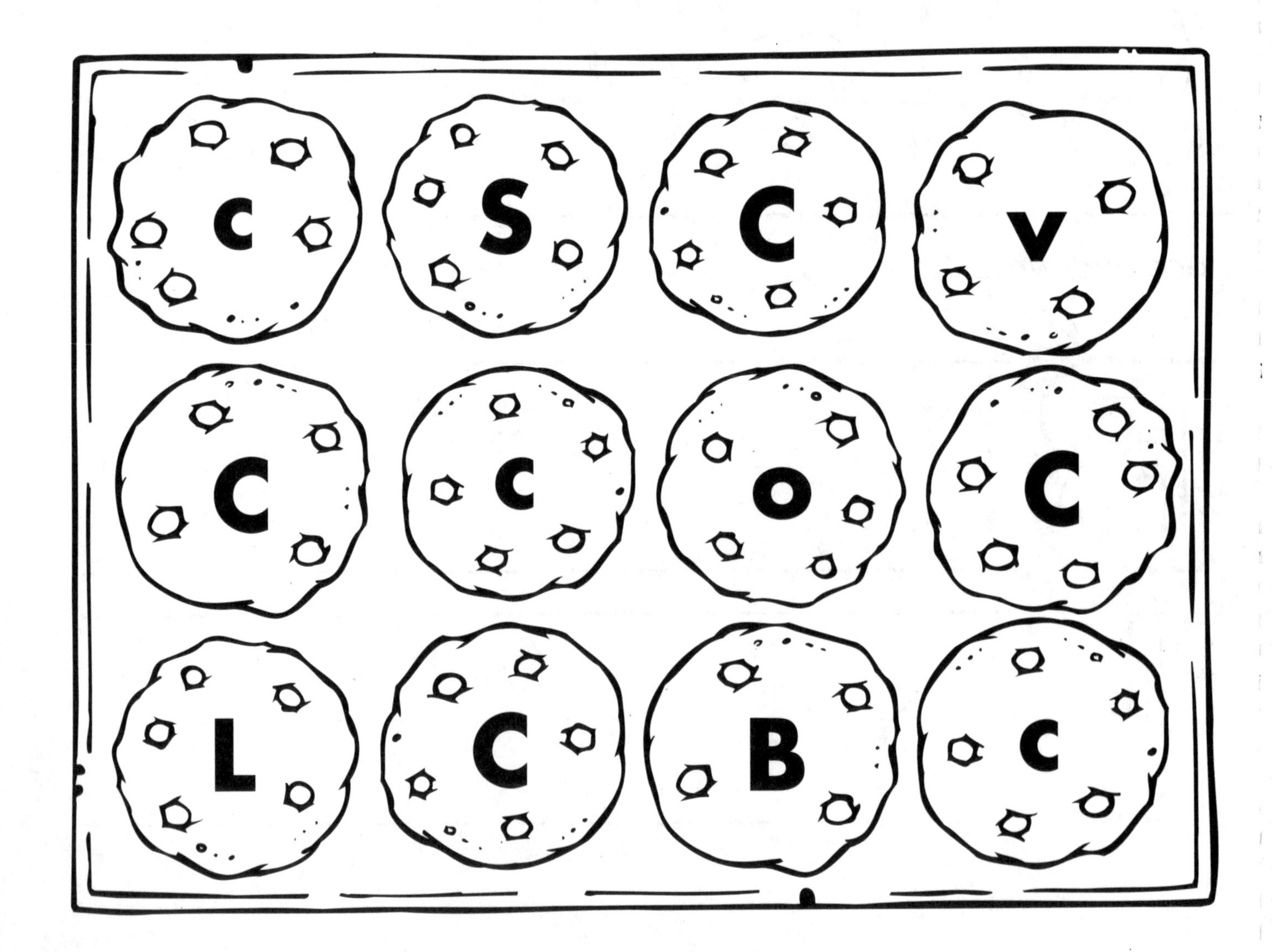

Name the pictures at the top of the page that begin with the letter **Cc**. Have the child follow the arrows to trace the letters with his or her finger. Then have him or her color the letters. Ask the child to trace and write the letters at the bottom.

Writing Cc

Color the letters.

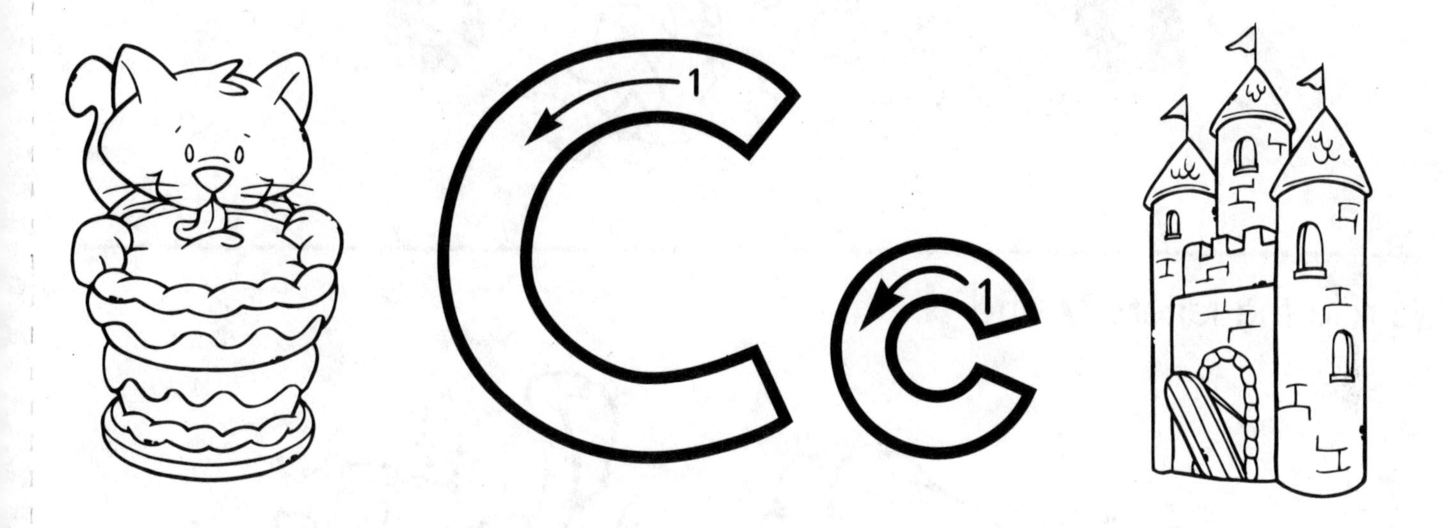

Trace and write the letters.

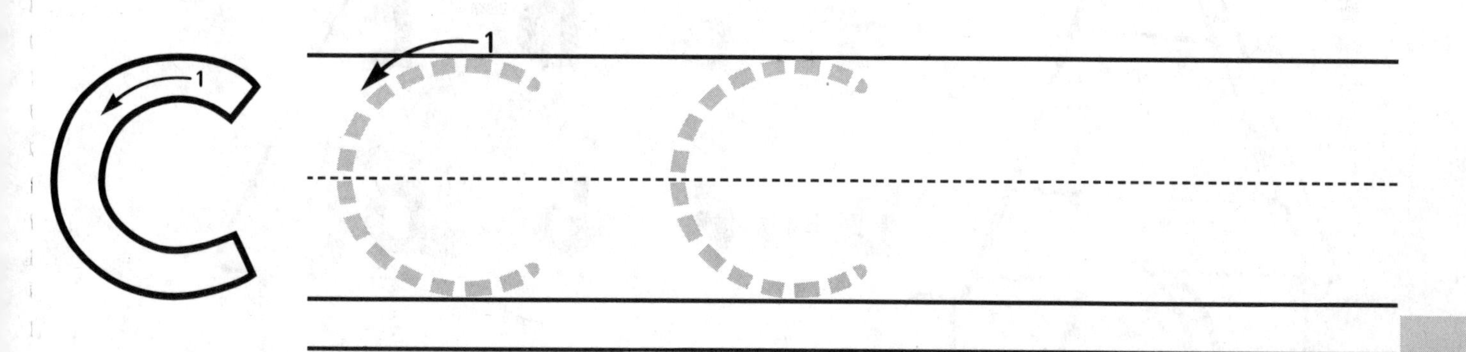

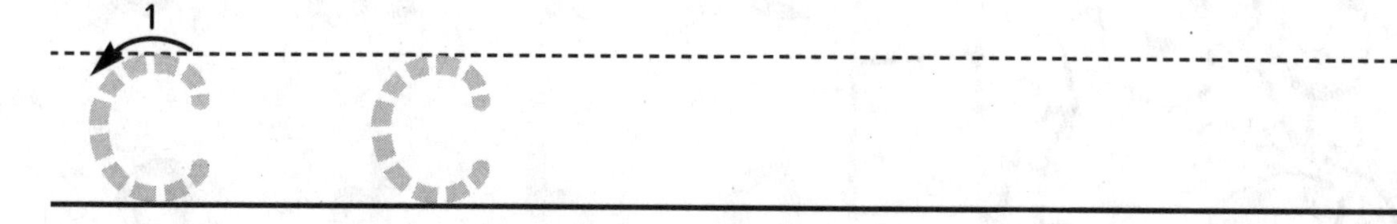

Point to and say the capital and lowercase letters **D** and **d** at the top of the page. Ask the child to find and circle all the letters **D** and **d** on the doghouse.

The Letters D and d

Circle the letters **D** and **d**.

Name the pictures at the top of the page that begin with the letter **Dd**. Have the child follow the arrows to trace the letters with his or her finger. Then have him or her color the letters. Ask the child to trace and write the letters at the bottom.

Writing Dd

Color the letters.

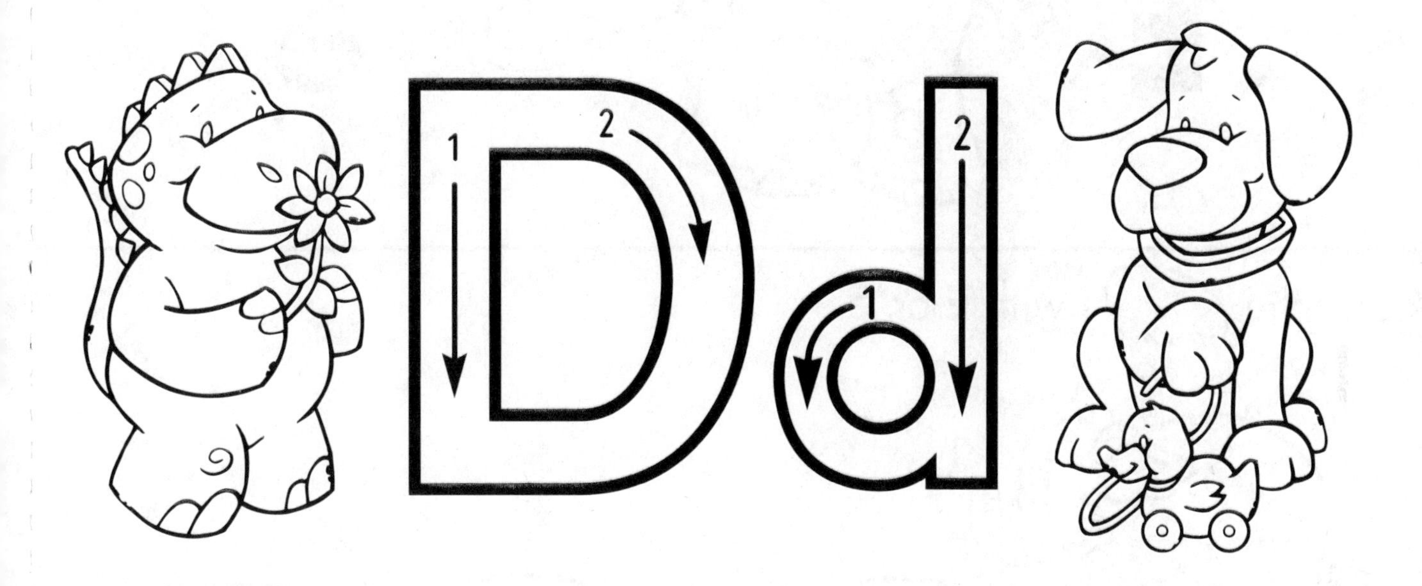

Trace and write the letters.

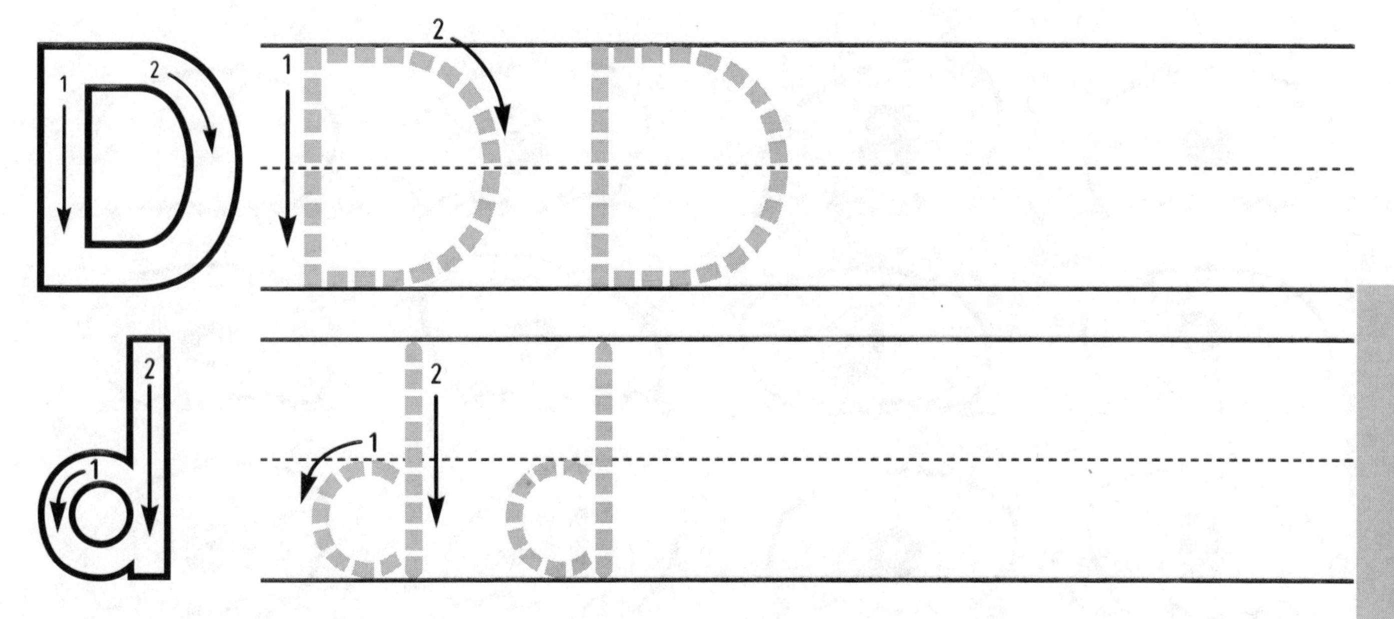

Letters I

Point to and say the capital and lowercase letters **E** and **e** at the top of the page. Ask the child to find and color the eggs with the letters **E** or **e**.

The Letters E and e

Color the (egg)s with **E** or **e**.

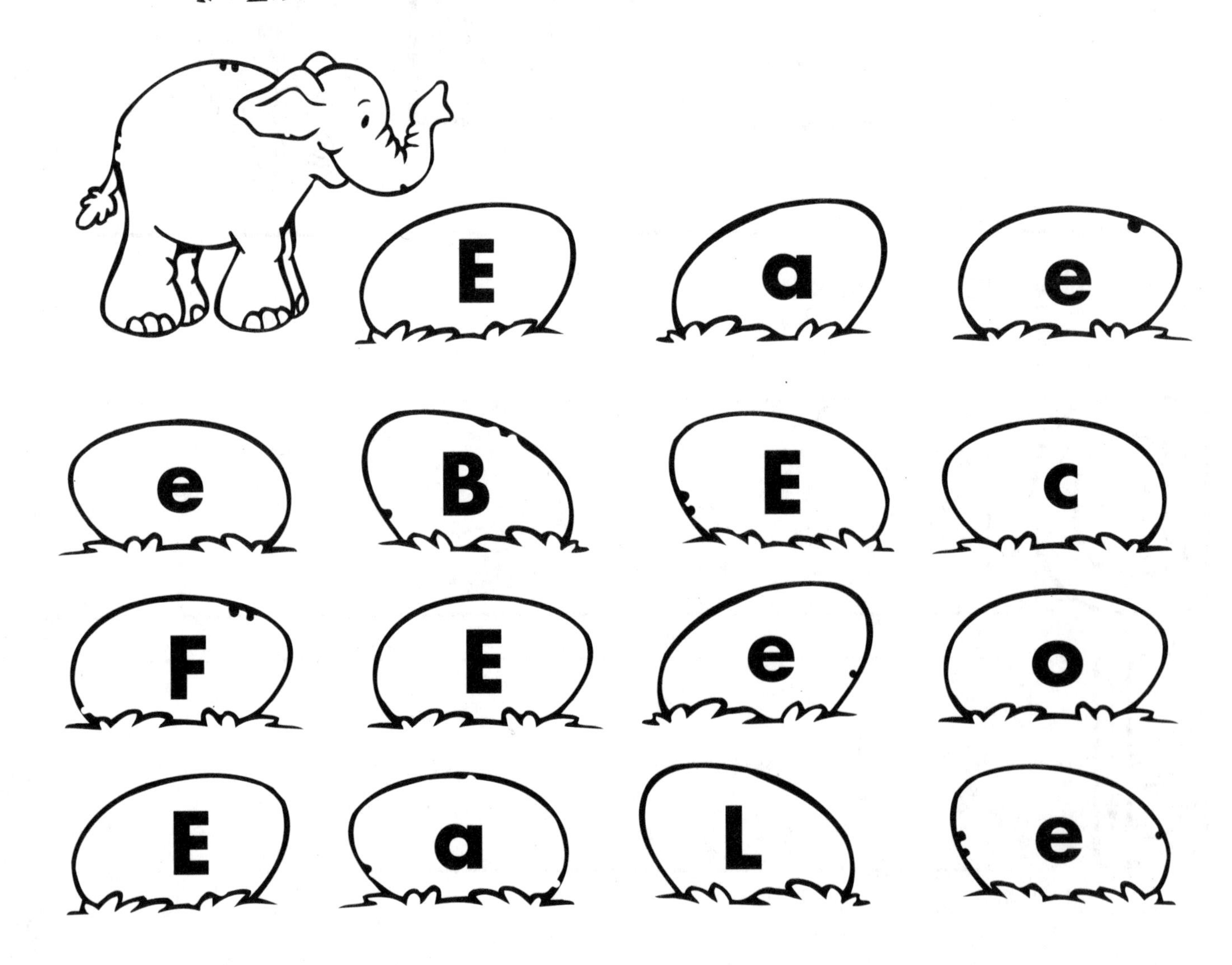

Name the pictures at the top of the page that begin with the letter **Ee**. Have the child follow the arrows to trace the letters with his or her finger. Then have him or her color the letters. Ask the child to trace and write the letters at the bottom.

Writing Ee

Color the letters.

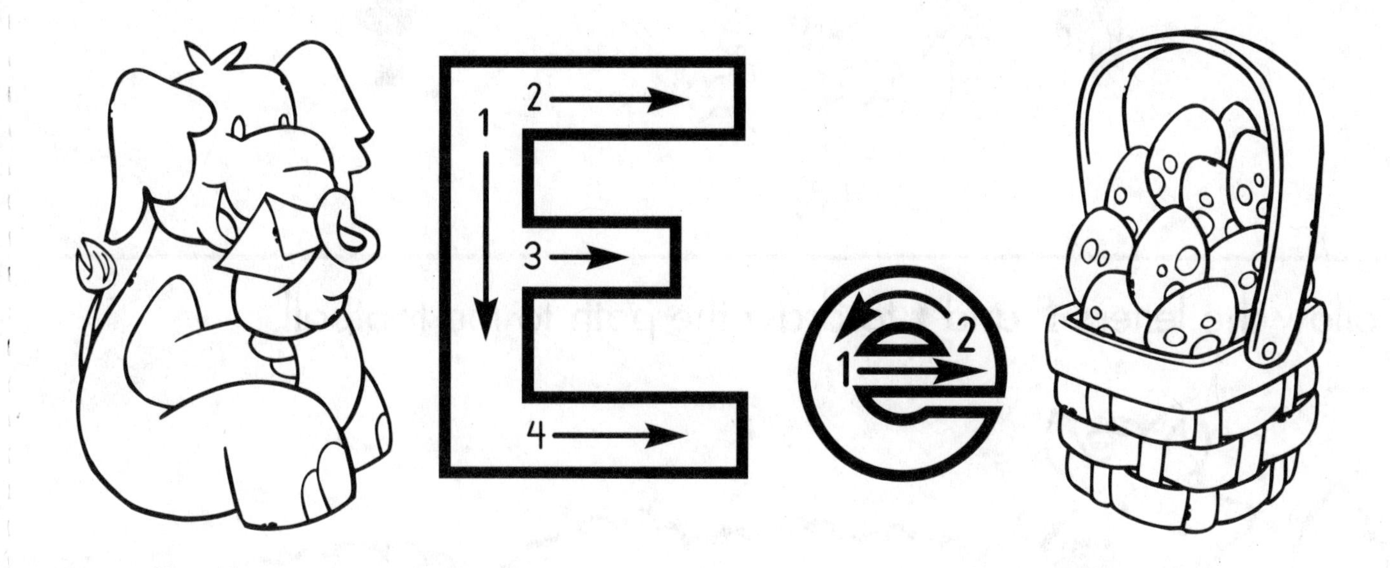

Trace and write the letters.

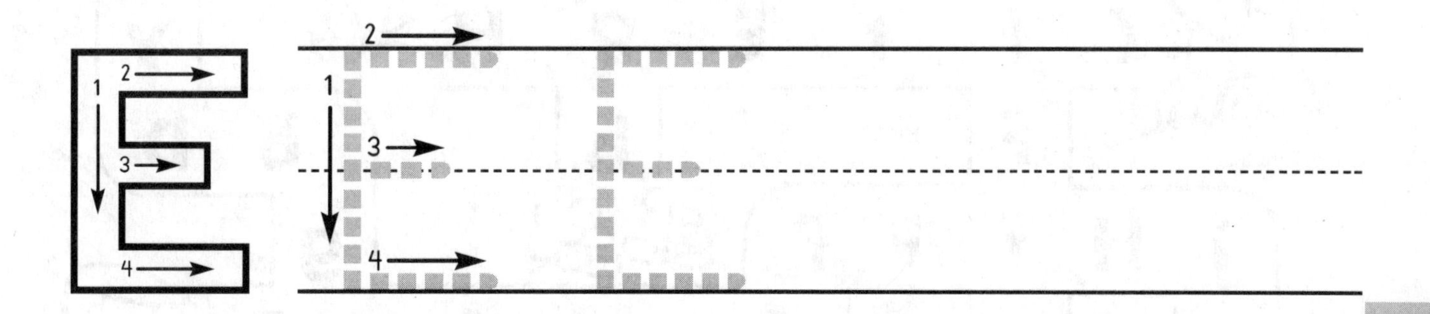

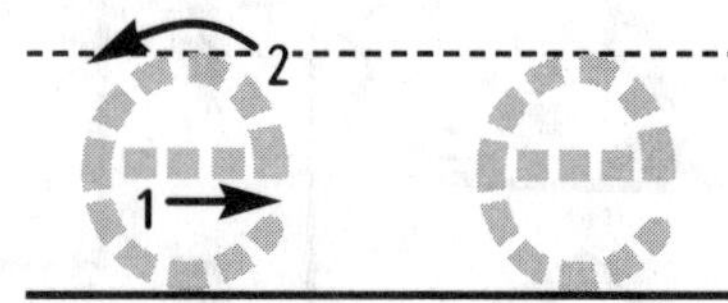

Letters I

Point to and say the capital and lowercase letters **F** and **f** at the top of the page. Ask the child to draw a line from the fox to the football by following the letters **F** and **f**.

The Letters F and f

Follow the letters **F** and **f** to draw the path to the football.

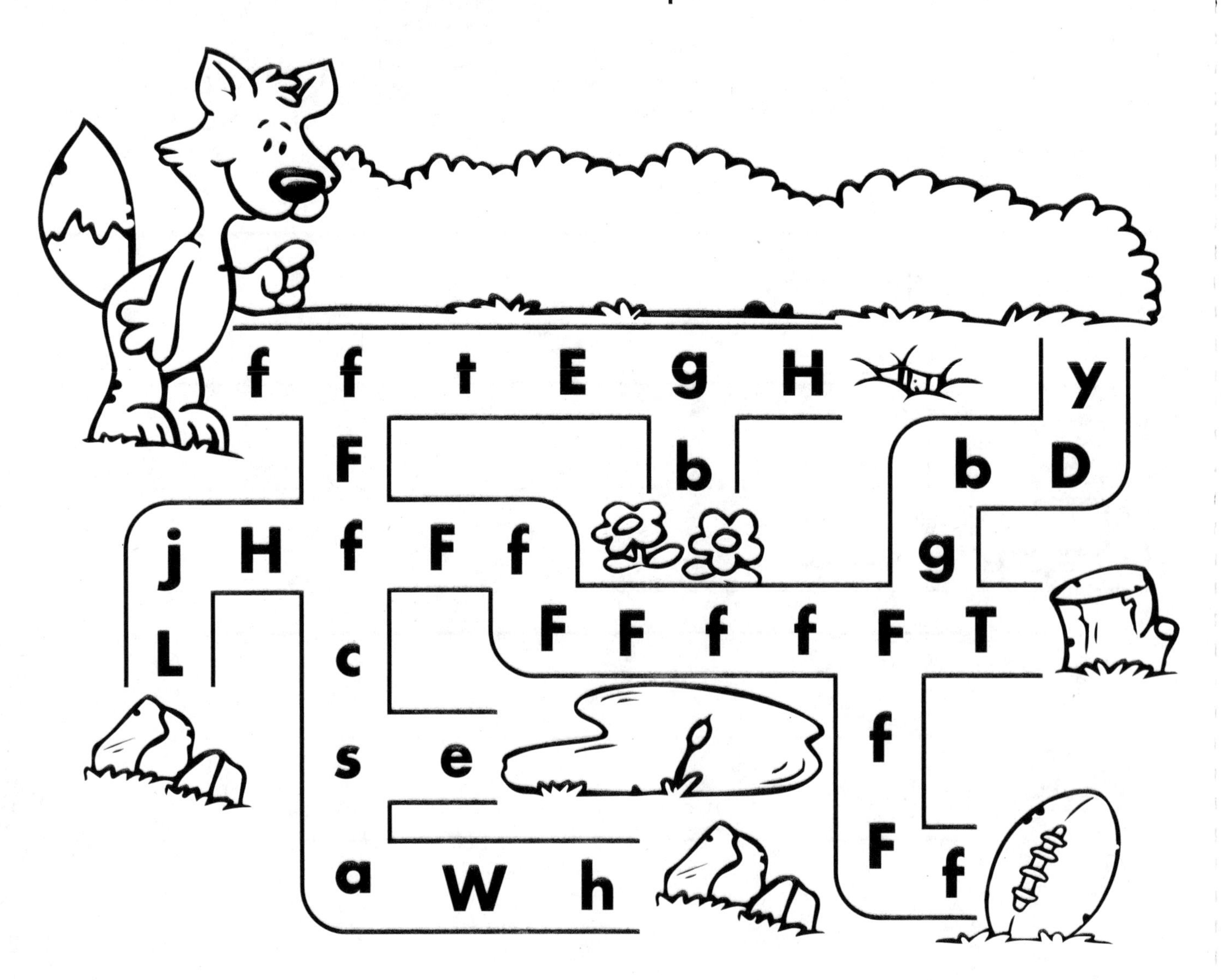

Name the pictures at the top of the page that begin with the letter **Ff**. Have the child follow the arrows to trace the letters with his or her finger. Then have him or her color the letters. Ask the child to trace and write the letters at the bottom.

Writing Ff

Color the letters.

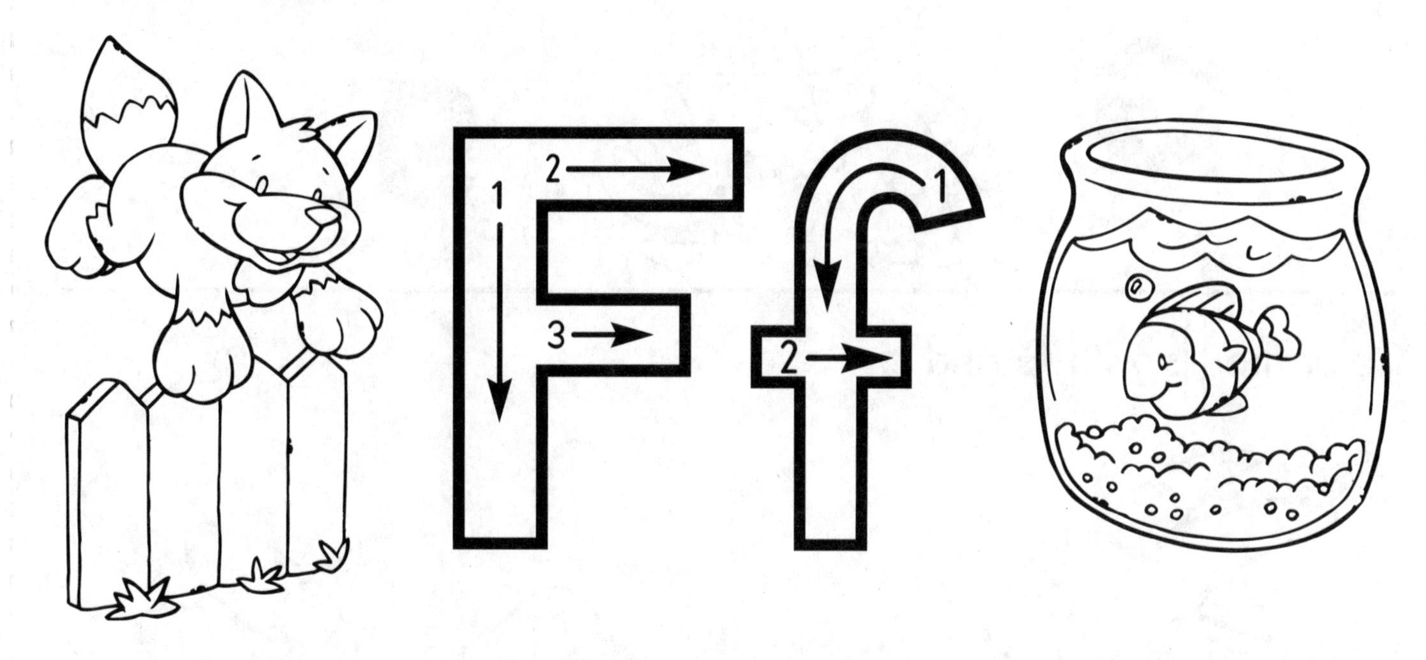

Trace and write the letters.

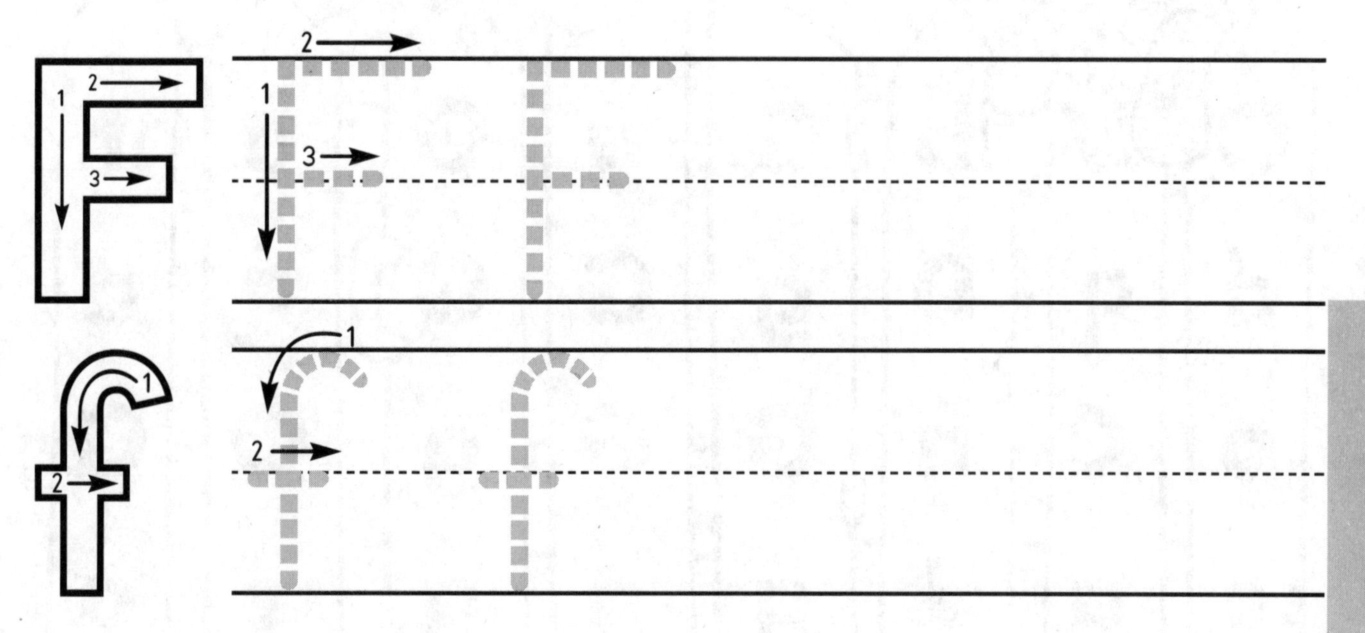

Letters I

Point to and say the capital and lowercase letters **G** and **g** at the top of the page. Ask the child to find and color the fence posts with the letters **G** and **g**.

The Letters G and g

Color the s with **G** and **g**.

Name the pictures at the top of the page that begin with the letter **Gg**. Have the child follow the arrows to trace the letters with his or her finger. Then have him or her color the letters. Ask the child to trace and write the letters at the bottom.

Writing Gg

Trace and write the letters.

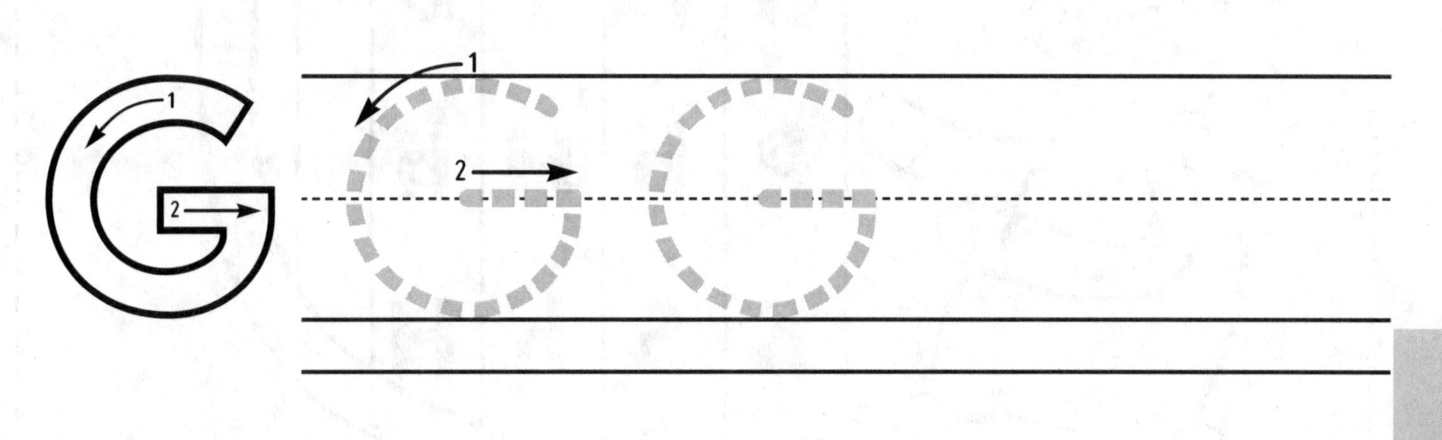

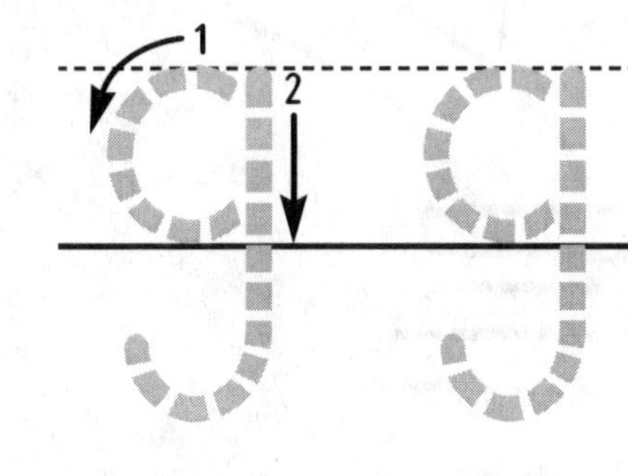

Letters I

Point to and say the capital and lowercase letters **H** and **h** at the top of the page. Ask the child to find and circle all the letters **H** and **h** on the harp.

The Letters H and h

Circle the letters **H** and **h**.

Name the pictures at the top of the page that begin with the letter **Hh**. Have the child follow the arrows to trace the letters with his or her finger. Then have him or her color the letters. Ask the child to trace and write the letters at the bottom.

Writing Hh

Color the letters.

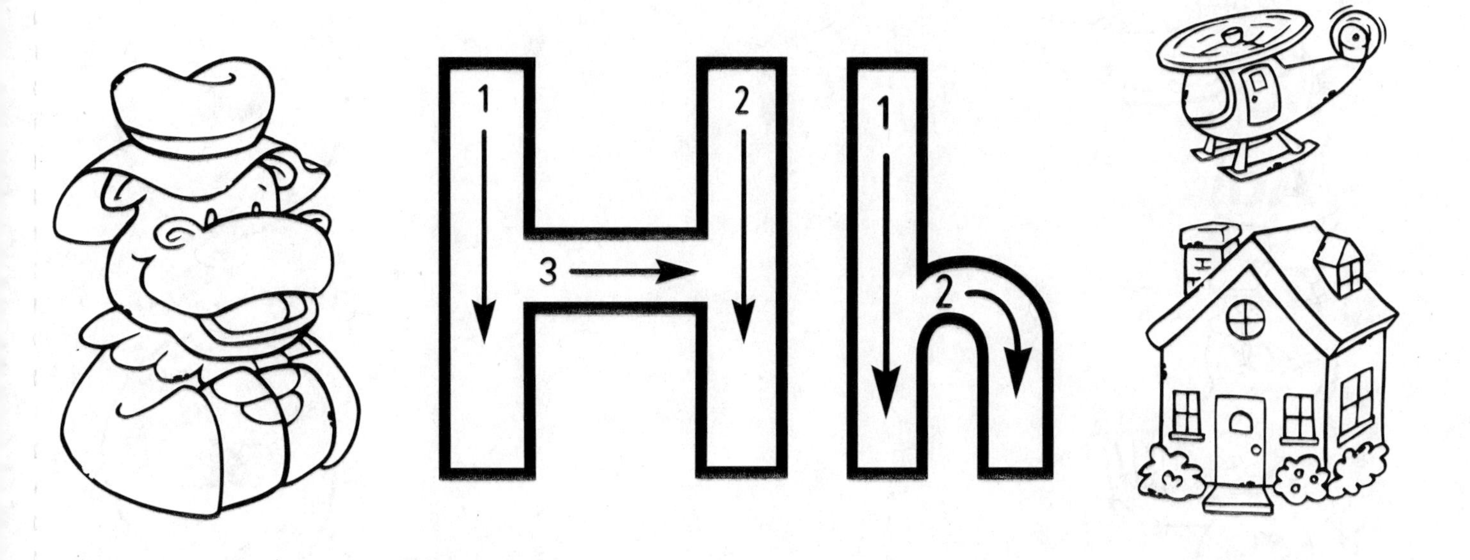

Trace and write the letters.

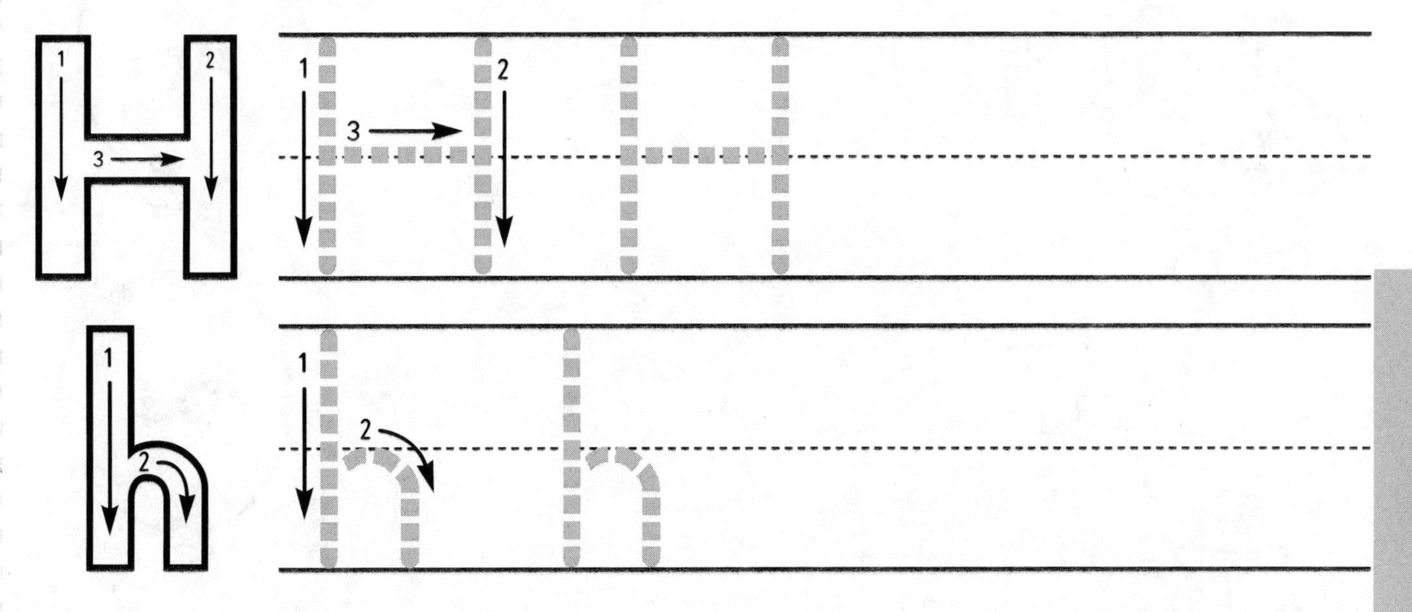

Letters I

Help the child say the letters on the animals' shirts. Then have him or her draw a line from each animal to the balloon with the matching letters and color the pictures.

It's a Party!

Match. Color the pictures.

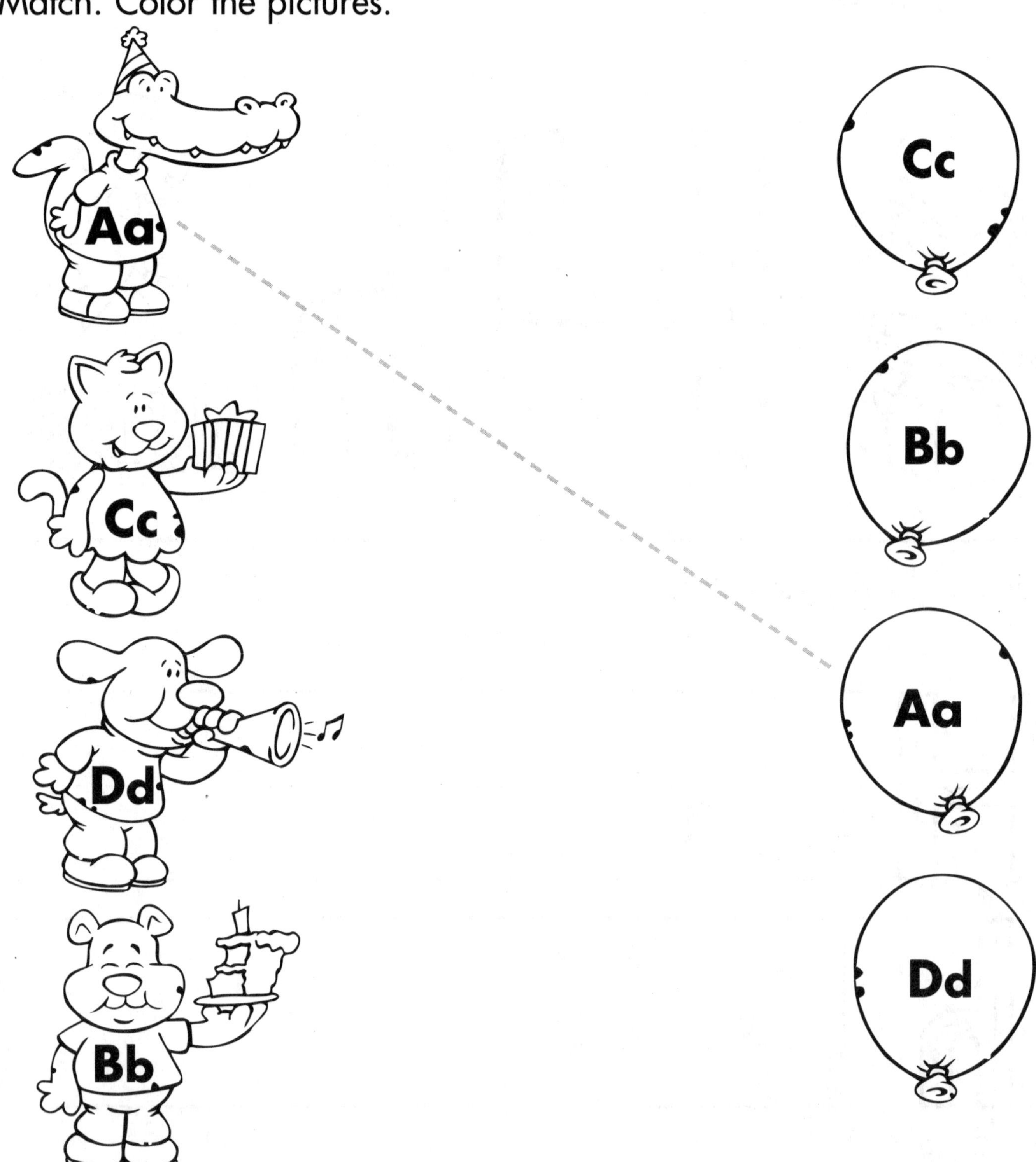

Help the child say the letters on the animals' bags. Then have him or her draw a line from each animal to the mailbox with the matching letters and color the pictures.

Heading Home

Match. Color the pictures.

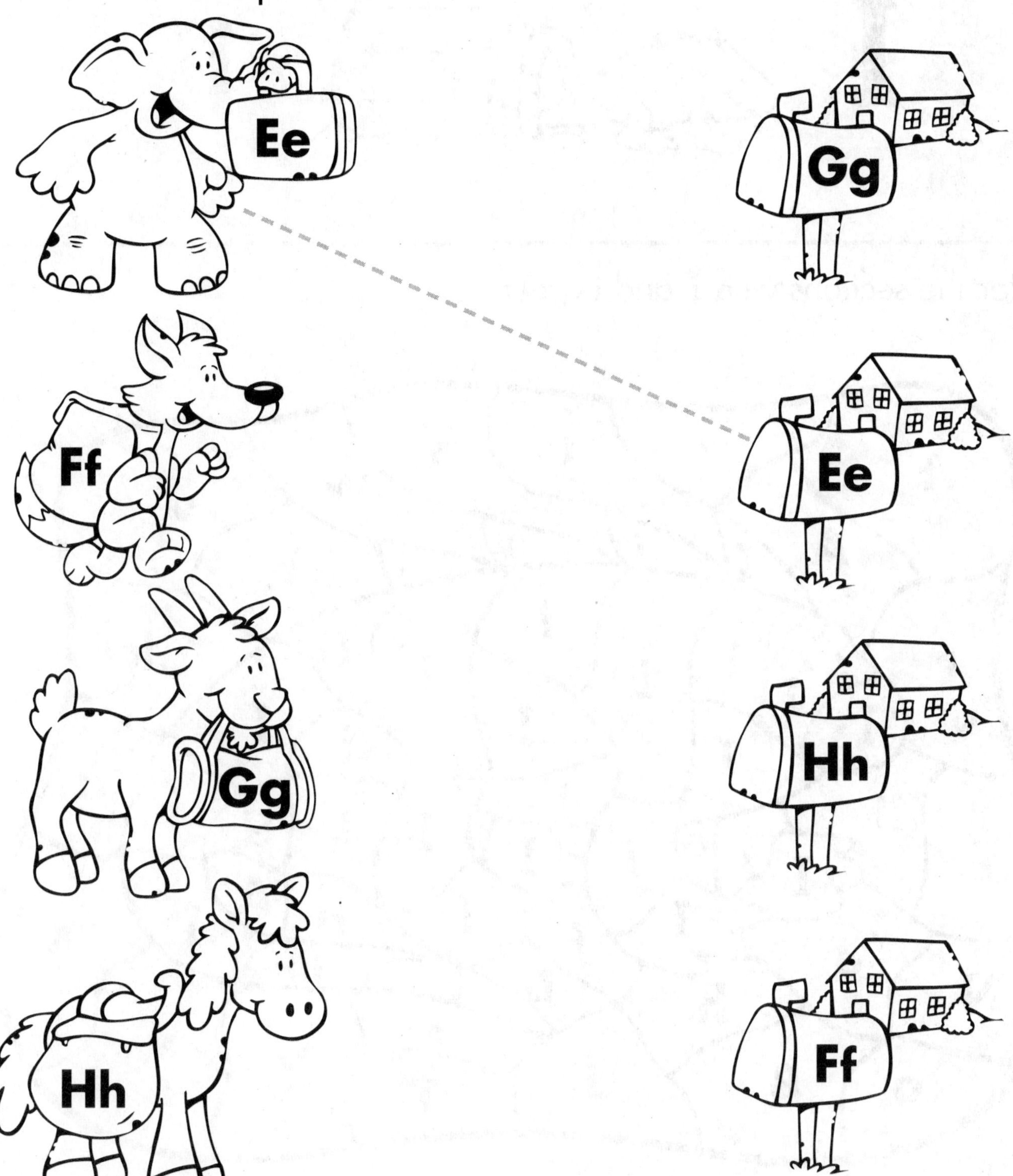

Letters I

Point to and say the capital and lowercase letters **I** and **i** at the top of the page. Ask the child to find and color all the letters **I** and **i** green to reveal the hidden picture.

The Letters I and i

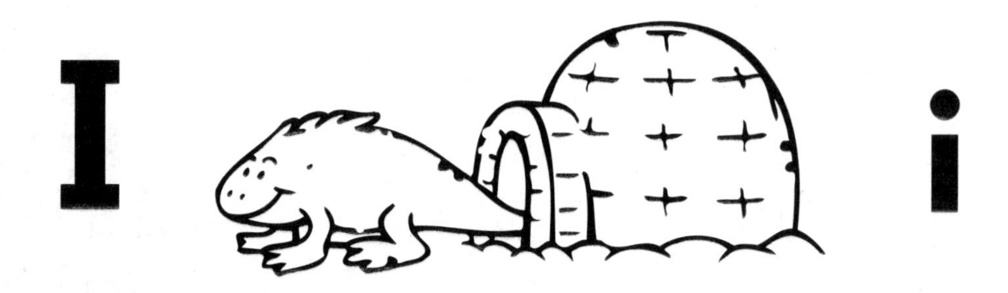

Color the sections with **I** and **i** green.

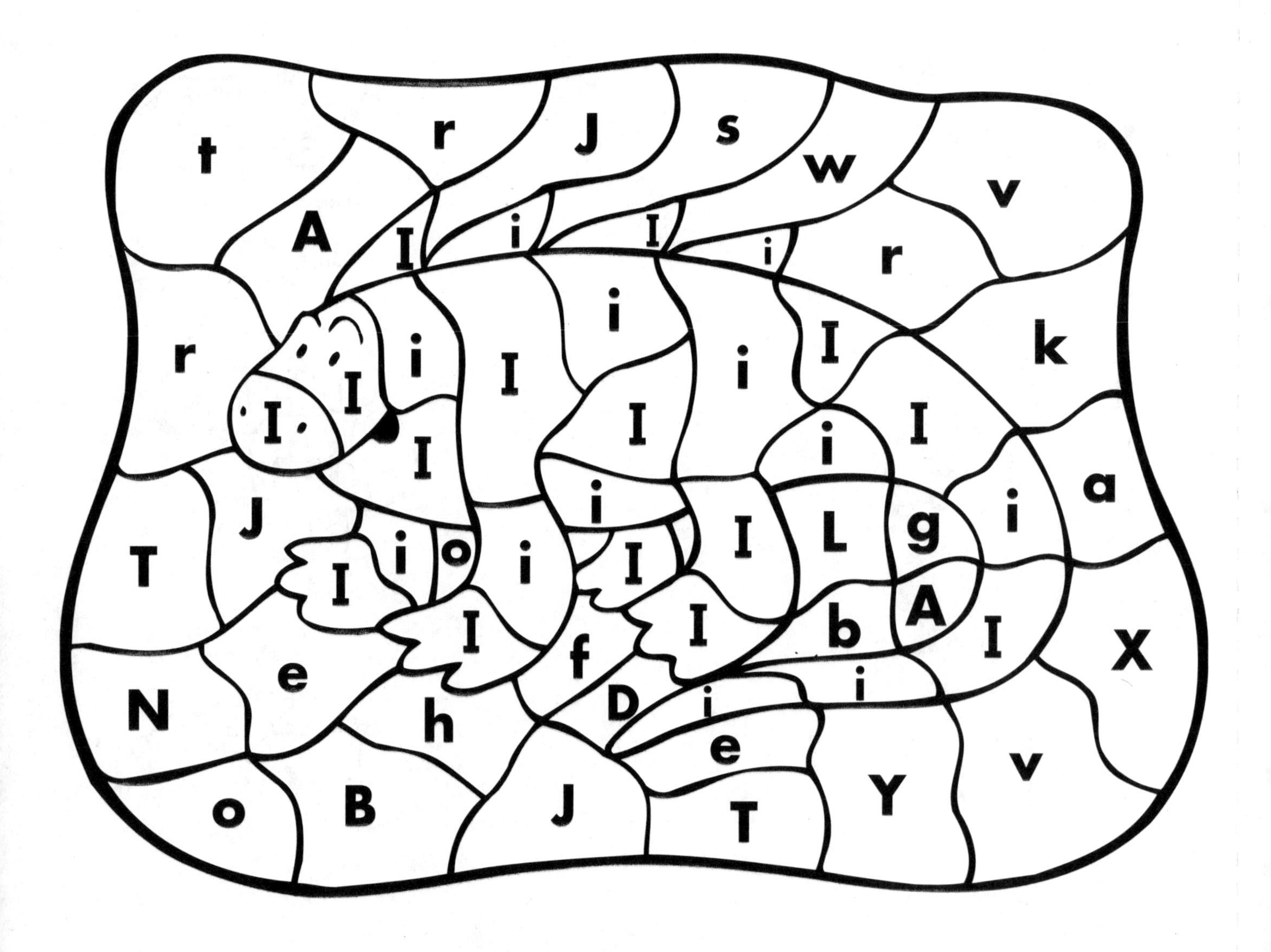

Name the pictures at the top of the page that begin with the letter **Ii**. Have the child follow the arrows to trace the letters with his or her finger. Then have him or her color the letters. Ask the child to trace and write the letters at the bottom.

Writing Ii

Color the letters.

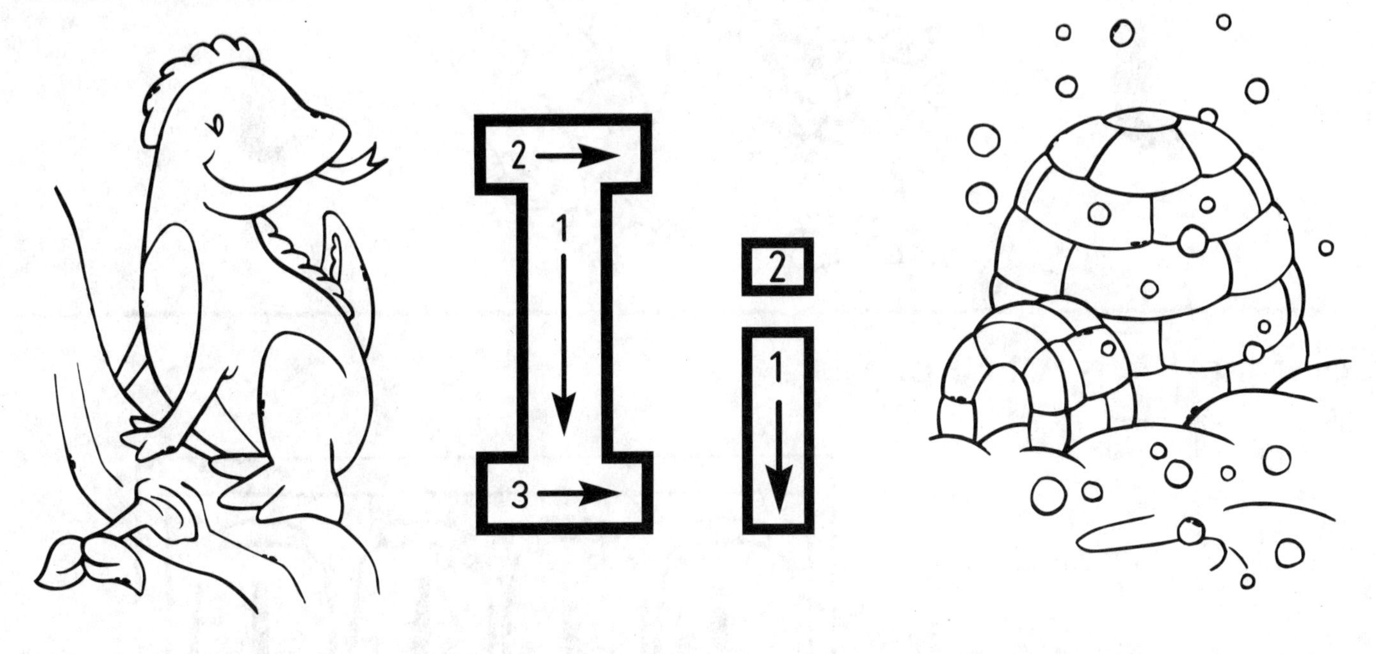

Trace and write the letters.

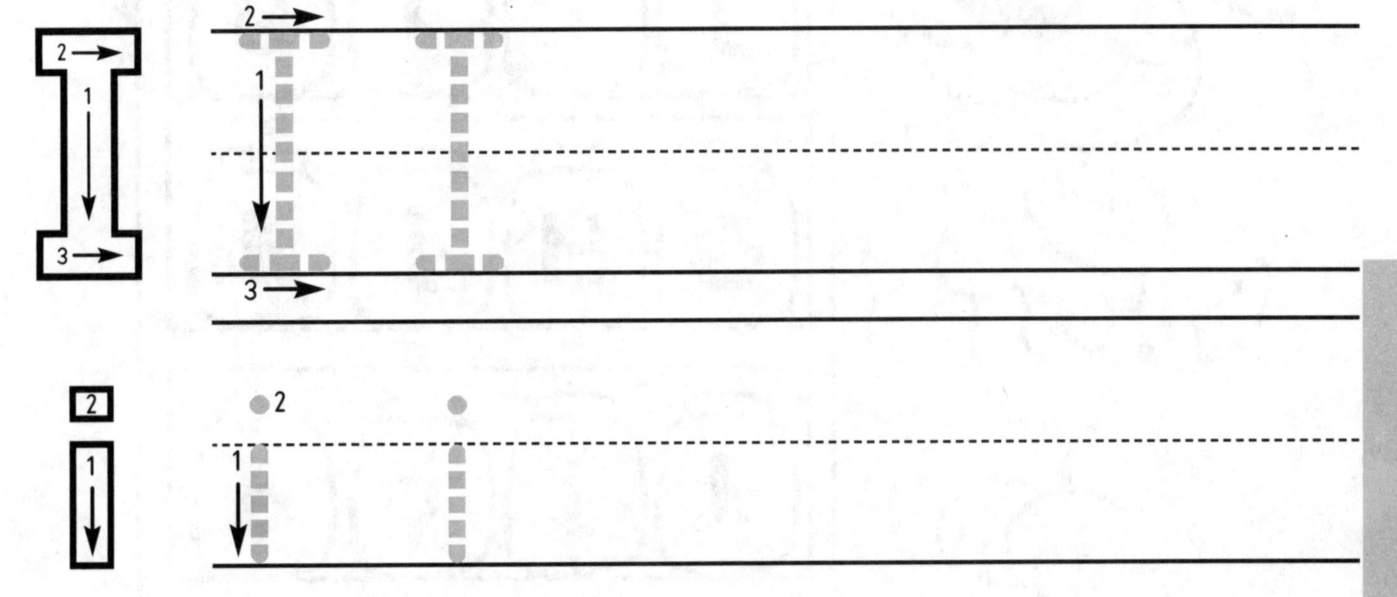

Letters I

Point to and say the capital and lowercase letters **J** and **j** at the top of the page. Ask the child to find and color the jars with the letters **J** or **j**.

The Letters J and j

j

Color the s with **J** or **j**.

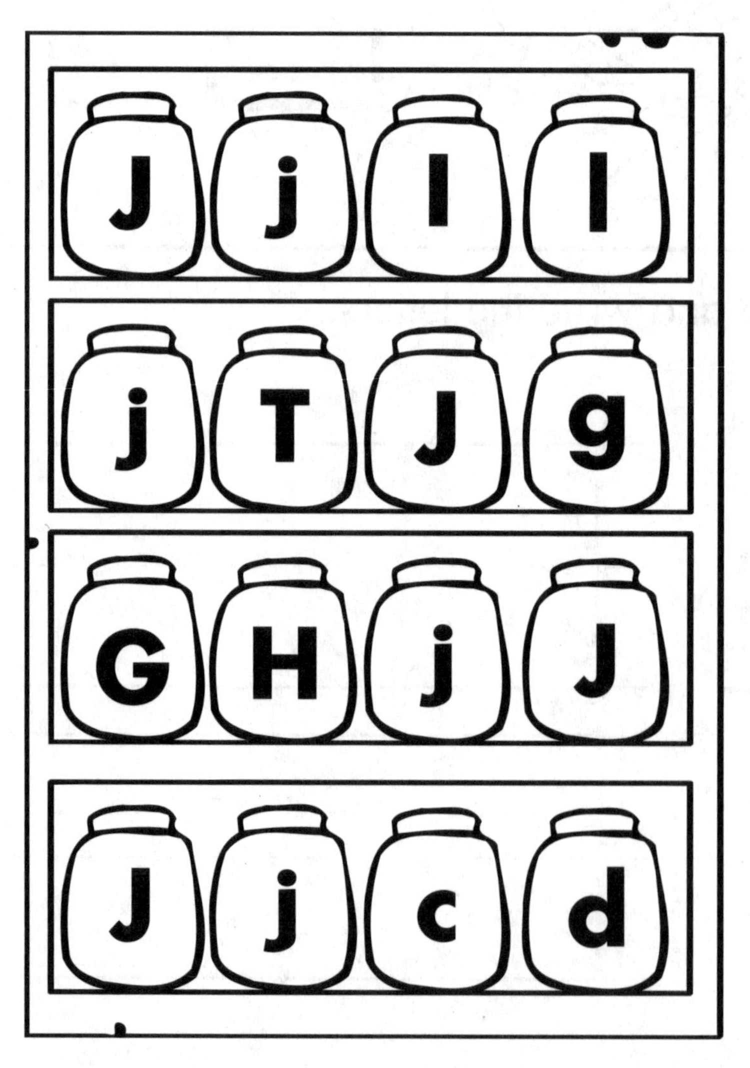

Name the pictures at the top of the page that begin with the letter **Jj**. Have the child follow the arrows to trace the letters with his or her finger. Then have him or her color the letters. Ask the child to trace and write the letters at the bottom.

Writing Jj

Color the letters.

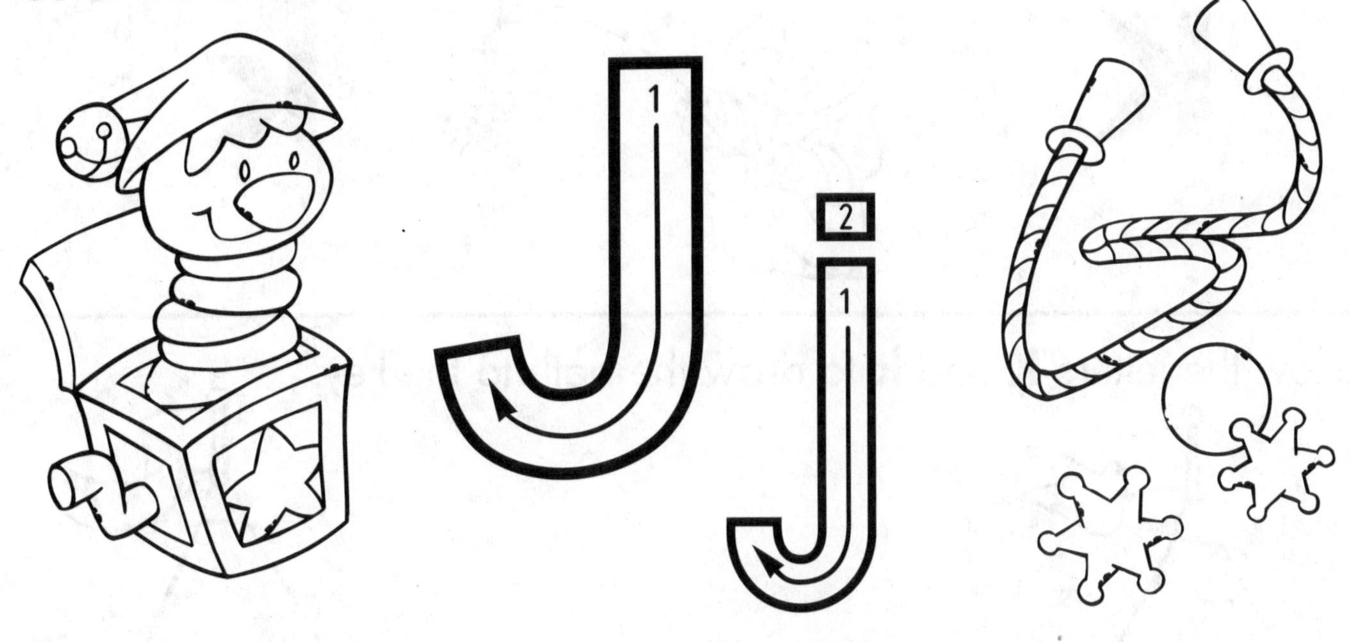

Trace and write the letters.

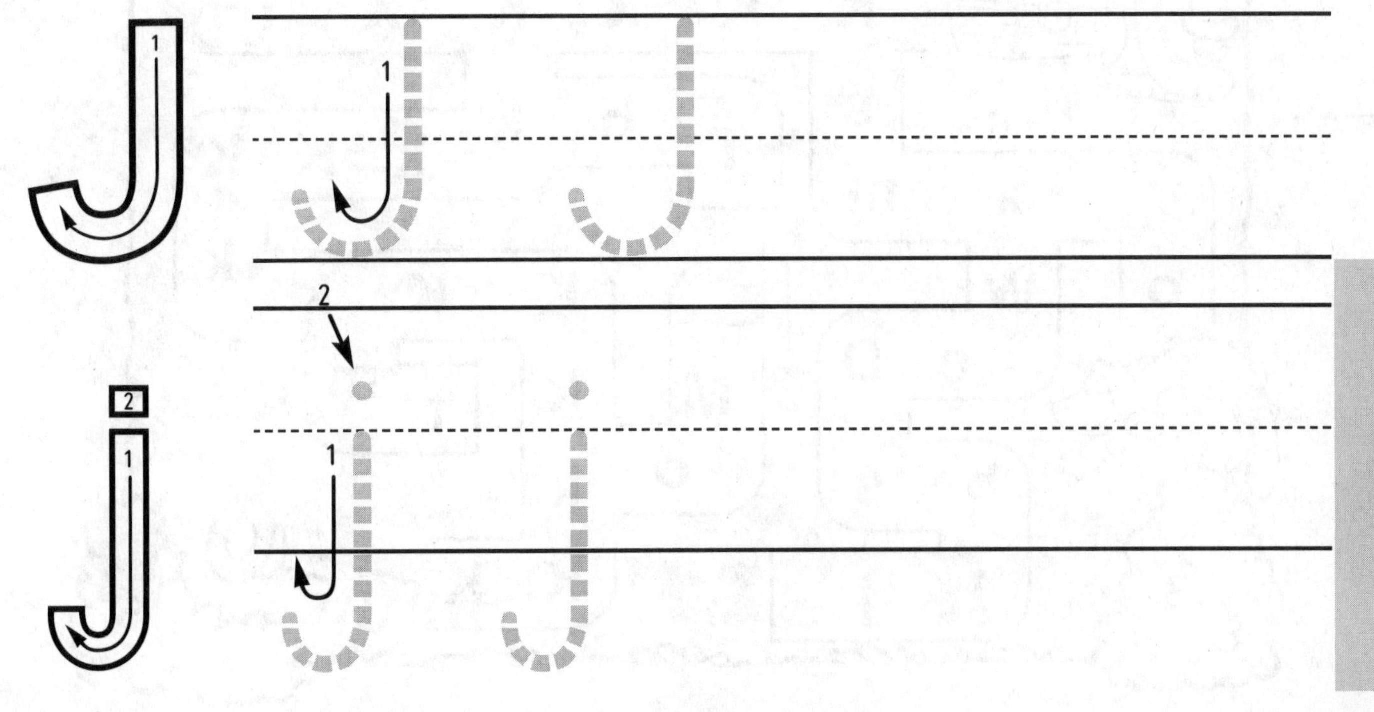

Letters I

Point to and say the capital and lowercase letters **K** and **k** at the top of the page. Ask the child to draw a line from the king to the key by following the letters **K** and **k**.

The Letters K and k

K

k

Follow the letters **K** and **k** to draw the path to the key.

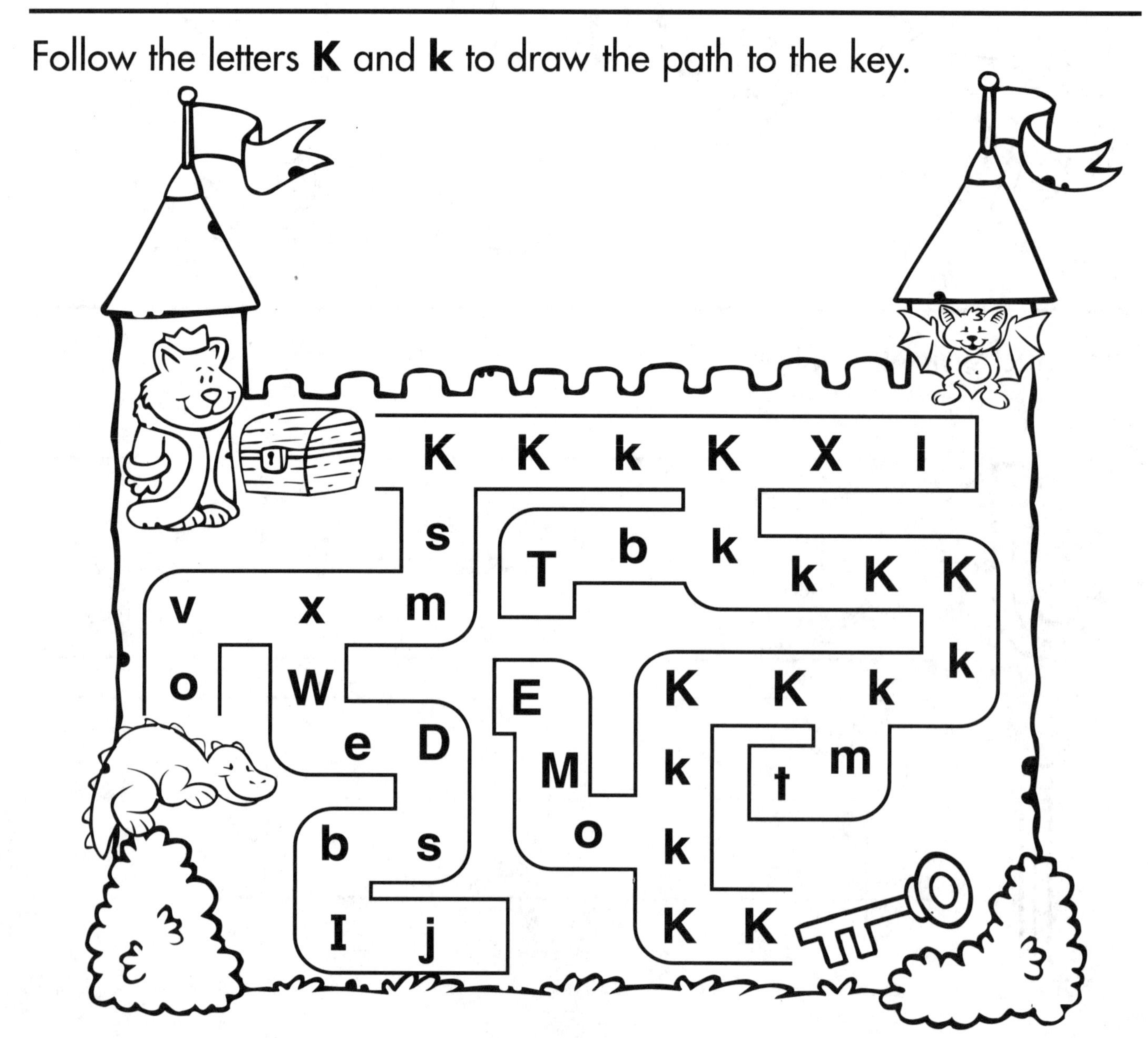

Name the pictures at the top of the page that begin with the letter **Kk**. Have the child follow the arrows to trace the letters with his or her finger. Then have him or her color the letters. Ask the child to trace and write the letters at the bottom.

Writing Kk

Color the letters.

Trace and write the letters.

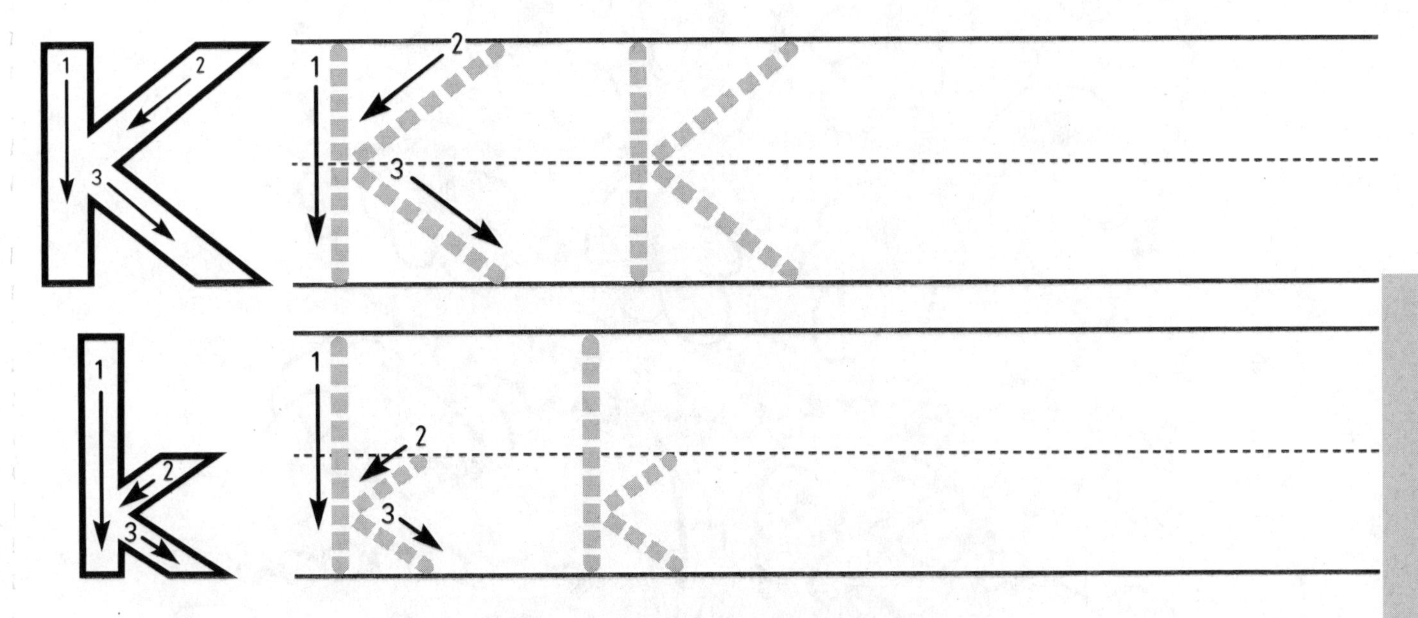

Point to and say the capital and lowercase letters **L** and **l** at the top of the page. Ask the child to find and color the leaves with the letters **L** or **l**.

The Letters L and l

Color the 🍂s with **L** or **l**.

Name the pictures at the top of the page that begin with the letter **Ll**. Have the child follow the arrows to trace the letters with his or her finger. Then have him or her color the letters. Ask the child to trace and write the letters at the bottom.

Writing Ll

Color the letters.

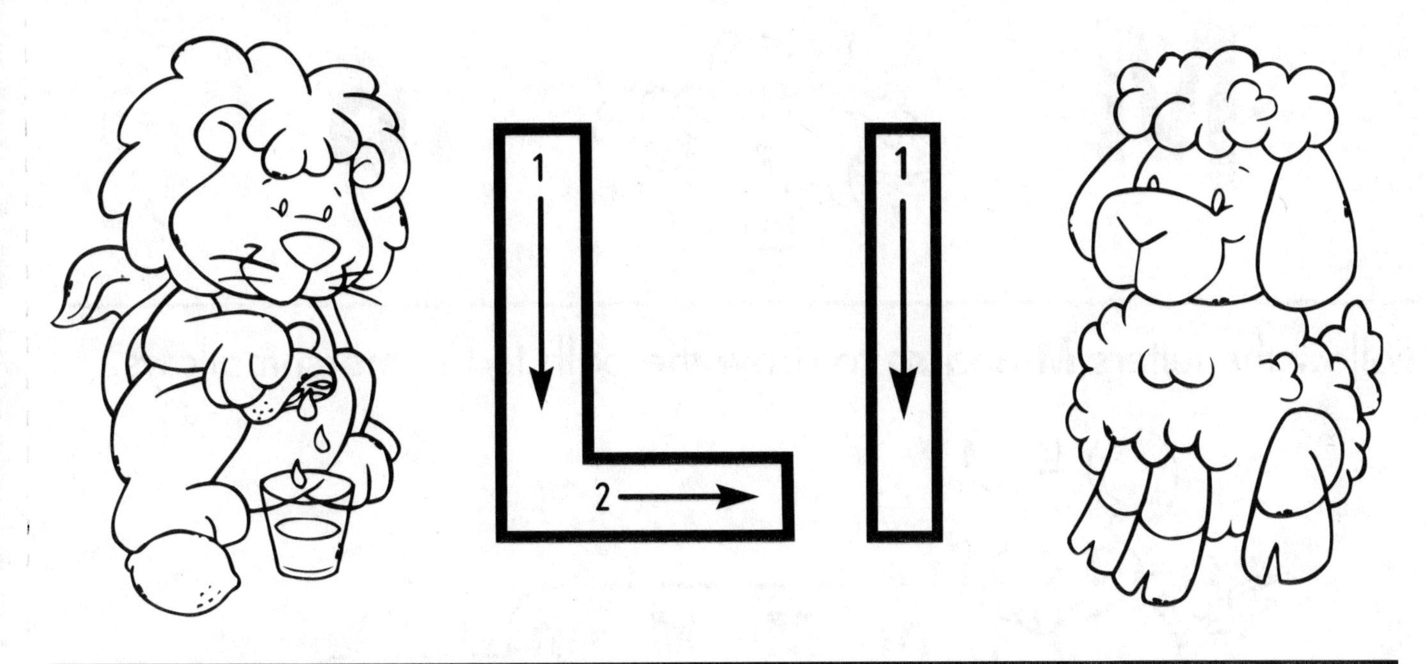

Trace and write the letters.

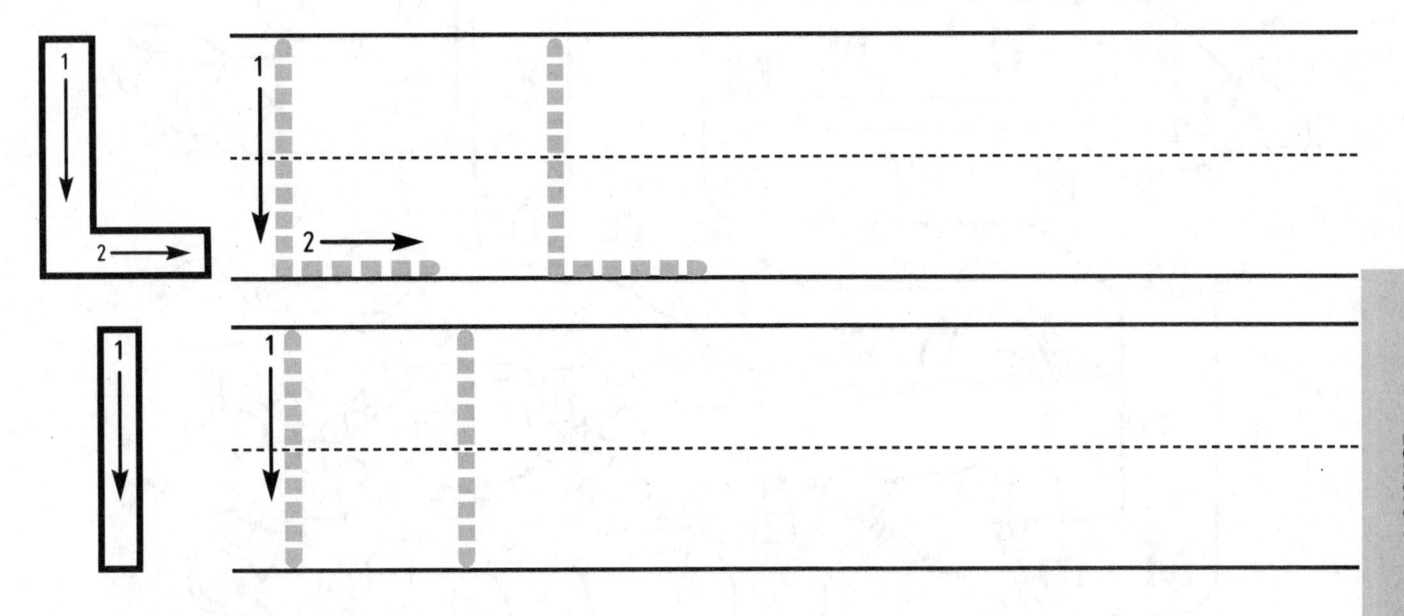

Letters l

Point to and say the capital and lowercase letters **M** and **m** at the top of the page. Ask the child to draw a line from the mouse to the marshmallows by following the letters **M** and **m**.

The Letters M and m

Follow the letters **M** and **m** to draw the path to the marshmallows.

Name the pictures at the top of the page that begin with the letter **Mm**. Have the child follow the arrows to trace the letters with his or her finger. Then have him or her color the letters. Ask the child to trace and write the letters at the bottom.

Writing Mm

Color the letters.

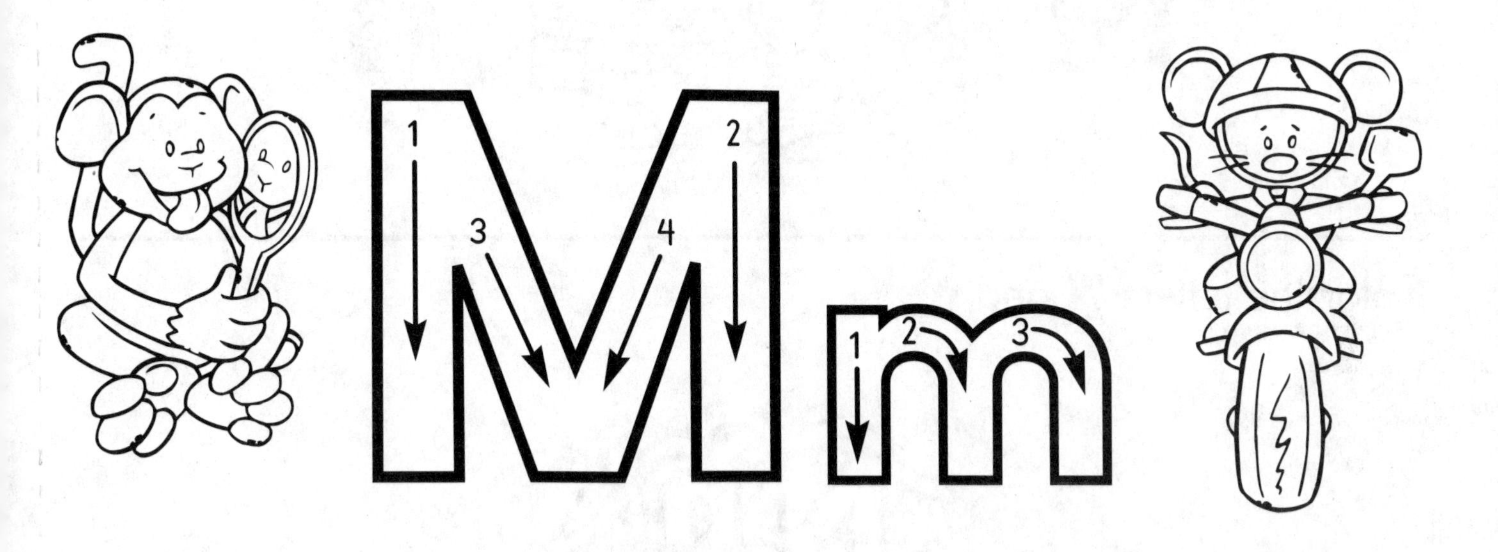

Trace and write the letters.

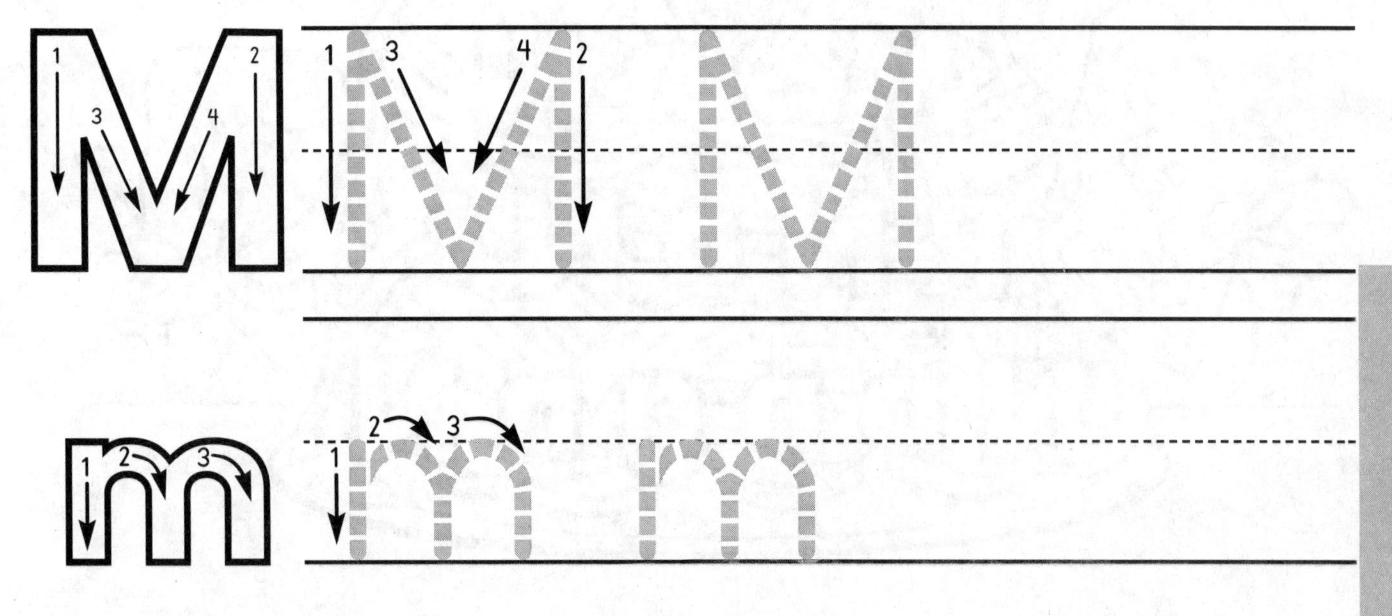

Letters I

Point to and say the capital and lowercase letters **N** and **n** at the top of the page. Ask the child to find and color all the letters **N** and **n** in the noodles.

The Letters N and n

Color the letters **N** and **n**.

Name the pictures at the top of the page that begin with the letter **Nn**. Have the child follow the arrows to trace the letters with his or her finger. Then have him or her color the letters. Ask the child to trace and write the letters at the bottom.

Writing Nn

Color the letters.

Trace and write the letters.

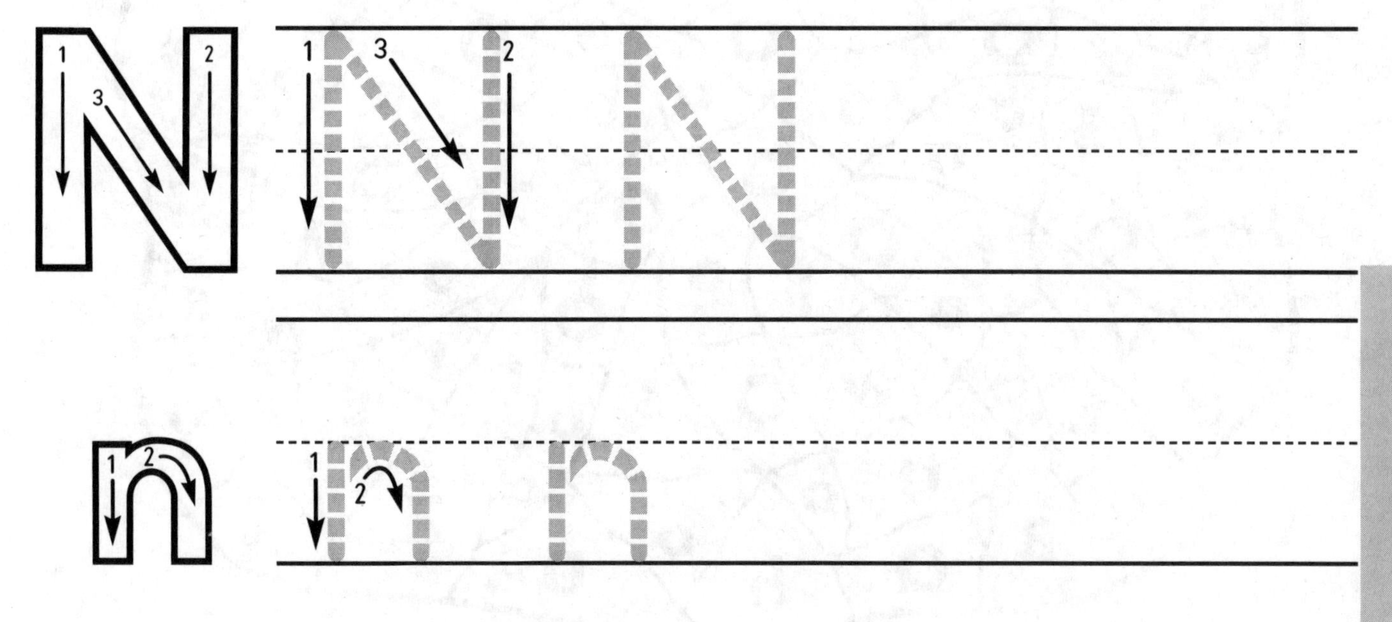

Letters I

Point to and say the capital and lowercase letters **O** and **o** at the top of the page. Ask the child to find and color all the sections with the letters **O** and **o** purple to reveal the hidden picture.

The Letters O and o

Color the sections with **O** and **o** purple.

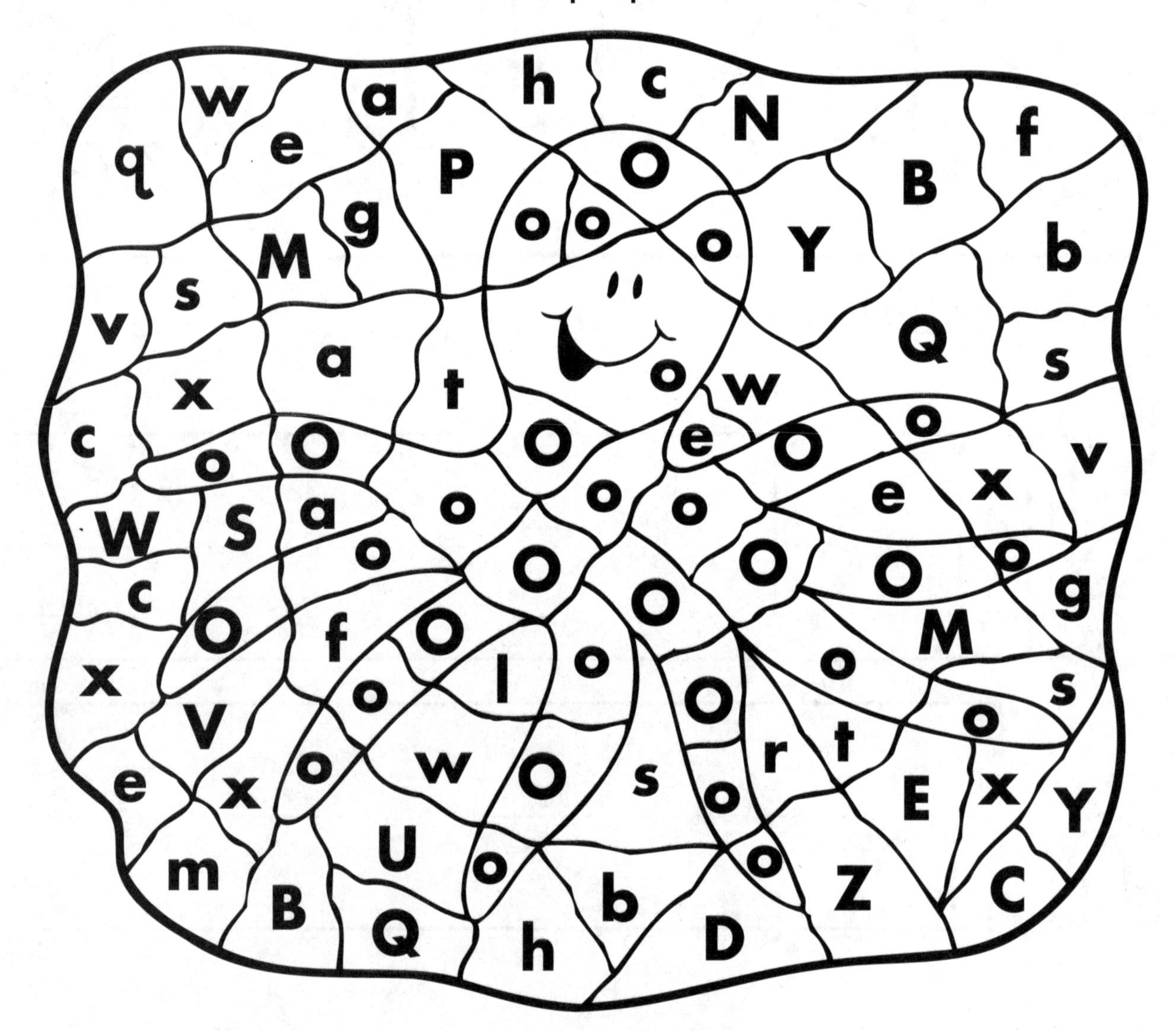

Name the pictures at the top of the page that begin with the letter **Oo**. Have the child follow the arrows to trace the letters with his or her finger. Then have him or her color the letters. Ask the child to trace and write the letters at the bottom.

Writing Oo

Color the letters.

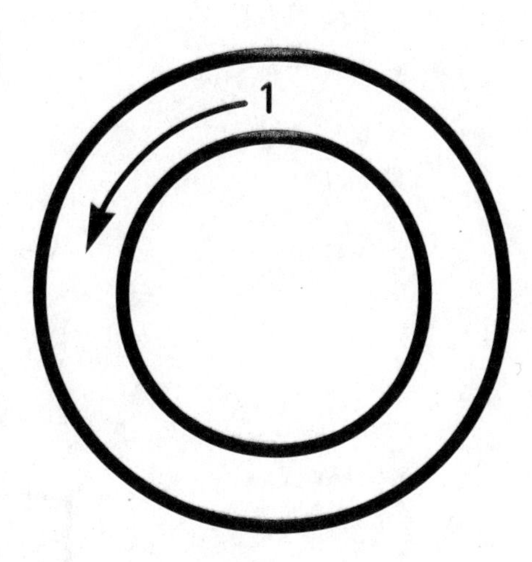

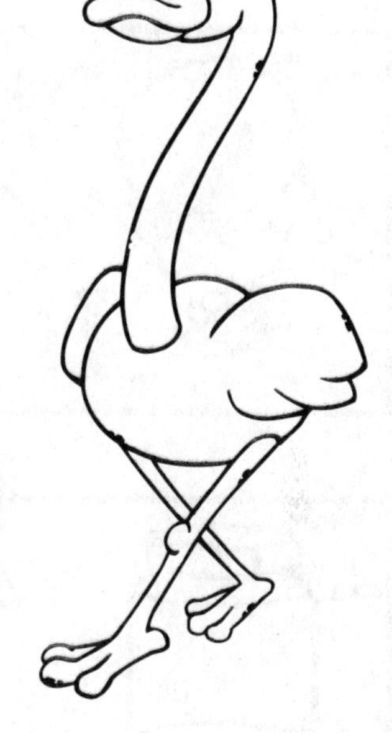

Trace and write the letters.

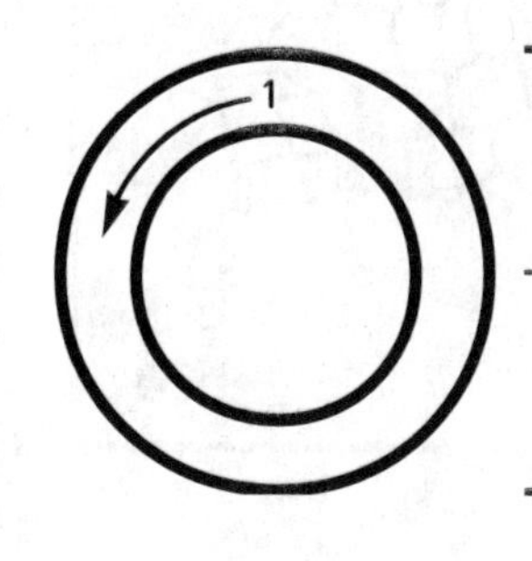

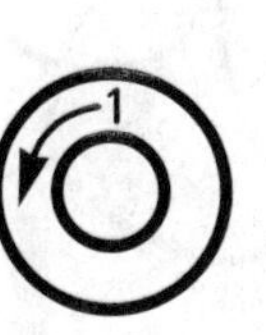

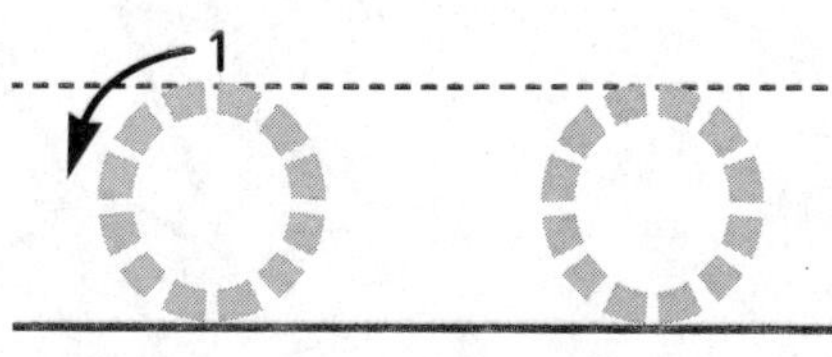

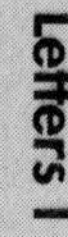

Help the child say the letters on the puzzle pieces. Then have him or her draw a line between the pieces with the same letters and color the pictures.

Puzzle Pieces

Match. Color the pictures.

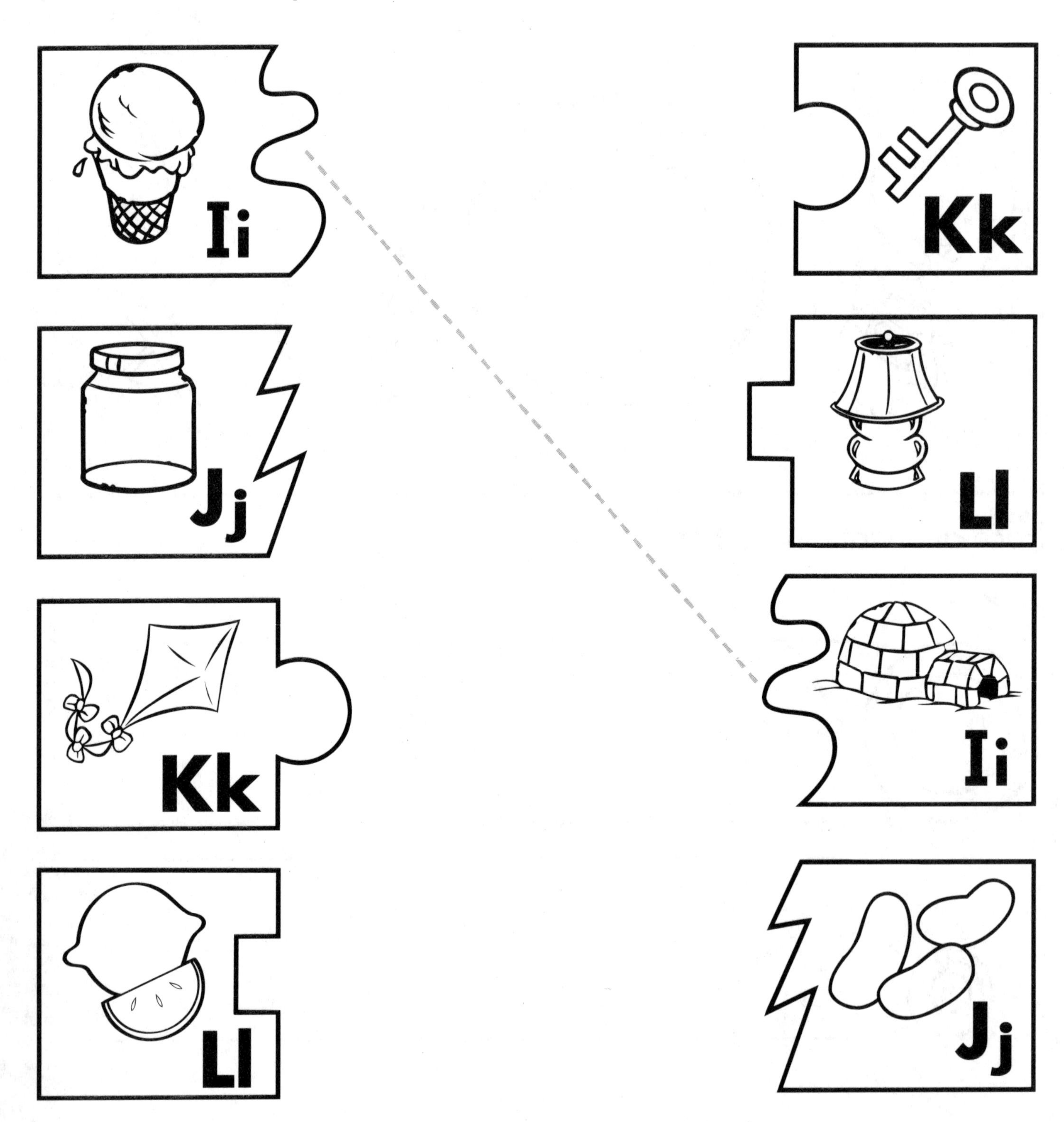

Answer Key

As the child completes the pages in this section, review his or her answers. When you take the time to correct the work and explain mistakes, you're showing your child that you feel learning is important.

page 92

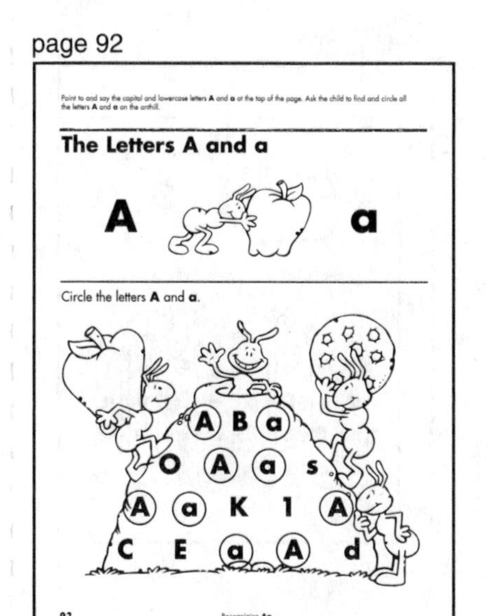

Point to and say the capital and lowercase letters **A** and **a** at the top of the page. Ask the child to find and circle all the letters **A** and **a** on the anthill.

The Letters A and a

Circle the letters **A** and **a**.

92 Recognizing **Aa**

page 93

Name the pictures at the top of the page that begin with the letter **Aa**. Have the child follow the arrows to trace the letters with his or her finger. Then have him or her color the letters. Ask the child to trace and write the letters at the bottom.

Writing Aa

Color the letters.

Trace and write the letters.

Recognizing, tracing, and writing **Aa** 93

page 94

Point to and say the capital and lowercase letters **B** and **b** at the top of the page. Ask the child to draw a line from the mother bird to her babies by following the letters **B** and **b**.

The Letters B and b

Follow the letters **B** and **b** to draw the path to the baby birds.

94 Recognizing **Bb**

page 95

Name the pictures at the top of the page that begin with the letter **Bb**. Have the child follow the arrows to trace the letters with his or her finger. Then have him or her color the letters. Ask the child to trace and write the letters at the bottom.

Writing Bb

Color the letters.

Trace and write the letters.

Recognizing, tracing, and writing **Bb** 95

page 96

Point to and say the capital and lowercase letters **C** and **c** at the top of the page. Ask the child to find and color the cookies with the letters **C** or **c**.

The Letters C and c

Color the cookies with **C** or **c**.

96 Recognizing **Cc**

page 97

Name the pictures at the top of the page that begin with the letter **Cc**. Have the child follow the arrows to trace the letters with his or her finger. Then have him or her color the letters. Ask the child to trace and write the letters at the bottom.

Writing Cc

Color the letters.

Trace and write the letters.

Recognizing, tracing, and writing **Cc** 97

page 98

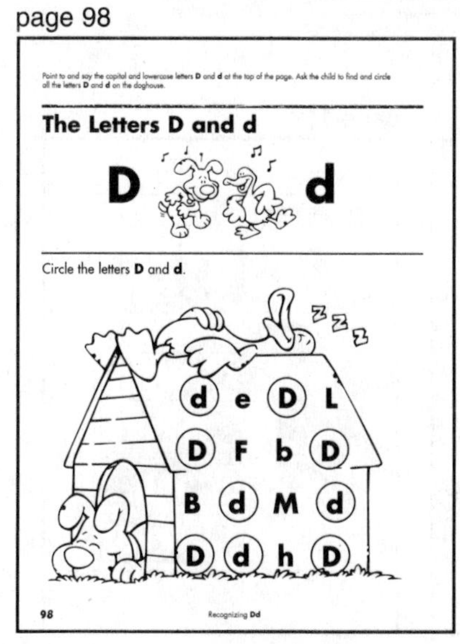

Point to and say the capital and lowercase letters **D** and **d** at the top of the page. Ask the child to find and circle all the letters **D** and **d** on the doghouse.

The Letters D and d

Circle the letters **D** and **d**.

98 Recognizing **Dd**

page 99

Name the pictures at the top of the page that begin with the letter **Dd**. Have the child follow the arrows to trace the letters with his or her finger. Then have him or her color the letters. Ask the child to trace and write the letters at the bottom.

Writing Dd

Color the letters.

Trace and write the letters.

Recognizing, tracing, and writing **Dd** 99

page 100

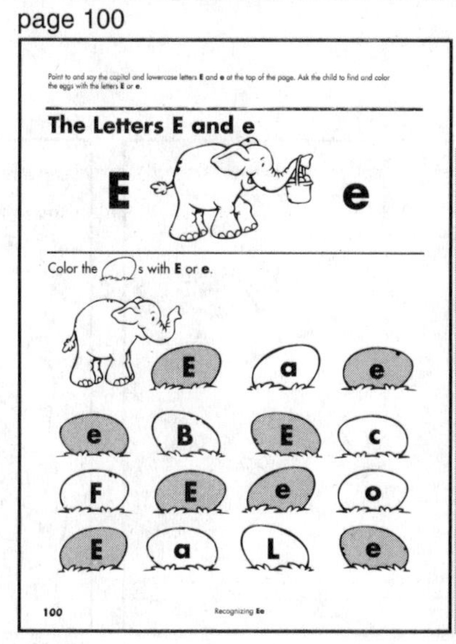

Point to and say the capital and lowercase letters **E** and **e** at the top of the page. Ask the child to find and color the eggs with the letters **E** or **e**.

The Letters E and e

Color the eggs with **E** or **e**.

100 Recognizing **Ee**

page 101

page 102

page 103

page 104

page 105

page 106

page 107

page 108

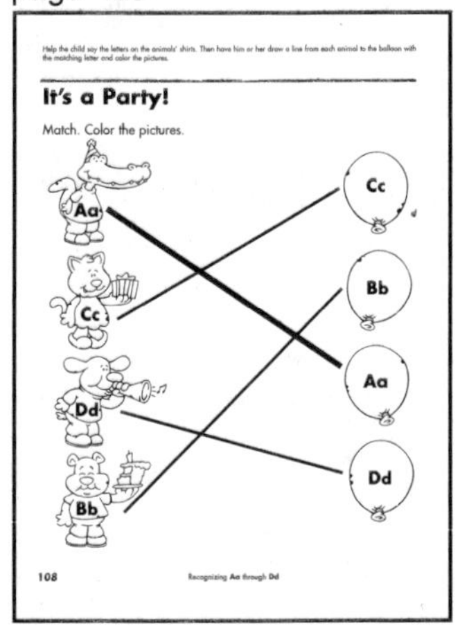

page 109

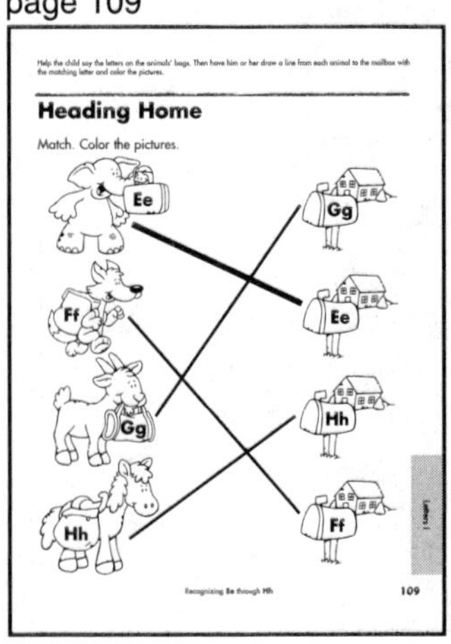

page 110

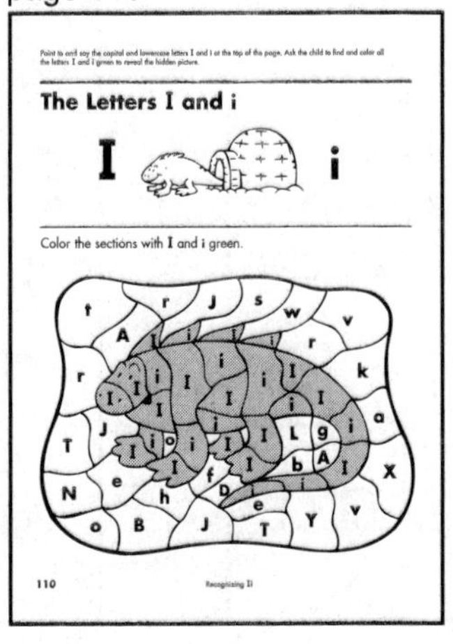

page 111

page 112

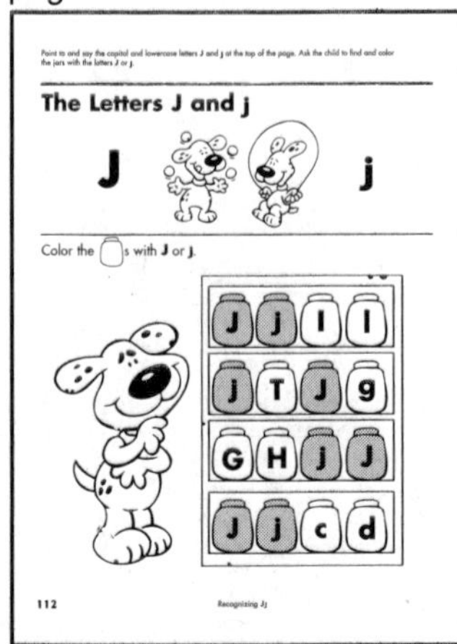

page 113

Writing Jj

Color the letters.

Trace and write the letters.

Recognizing, tracing, and writing Jj 113

page 114

The Letters K and k

K k

Follow the letters **K** and **k** to draw the path to the key.

114 Recognizing Kk

page 115

Writing Kk

Color the letters.

Trace and write the letters.

Recognizing, tracing, and writing Kk 115

page 116

The Letters L and l

L l

Color the leaves with L or l.

116 Recognizing Ll

page 117

Writing Ll

Color the letters.

Trace and write the letters.

Recognizing, tracing, and writing Ll 117

page 118

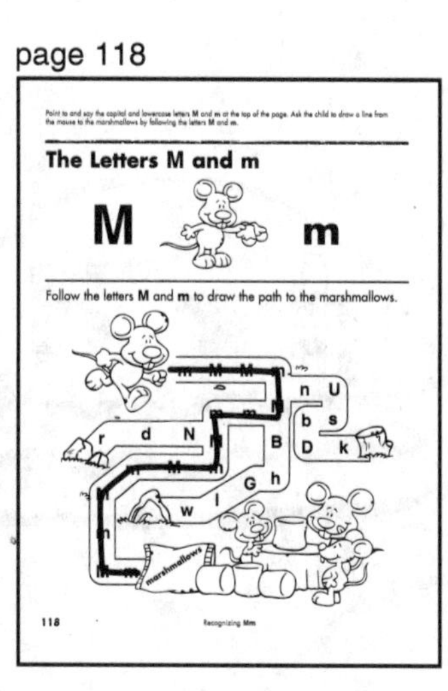
The Letters M and m

M m

Follow the letters **M** and **m** to draw the path to the marshmallows.

118 Recognizing Mm

page 119

Writing Mm

Color the letters.

Trace and write the letters.

Recognizing, tracing, and writing Mm 119

page 120

The Letters N and n

N n

Color the letters **N** and **n**.

120 Recognizing Nn

page 121

Writing Nn

Color the letters.

Trace and write the letters.

Recognizing, tracing, and writing Nn 121

page 122

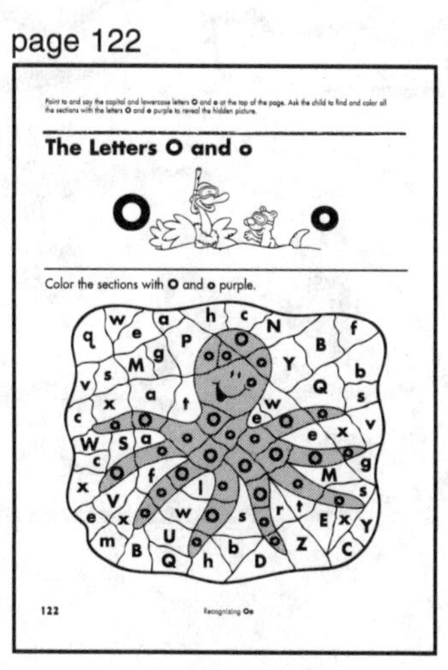
The Letters O and o

O o

Color the sections with **O** and **o** purple.

122 Recognizing Oo

page 123

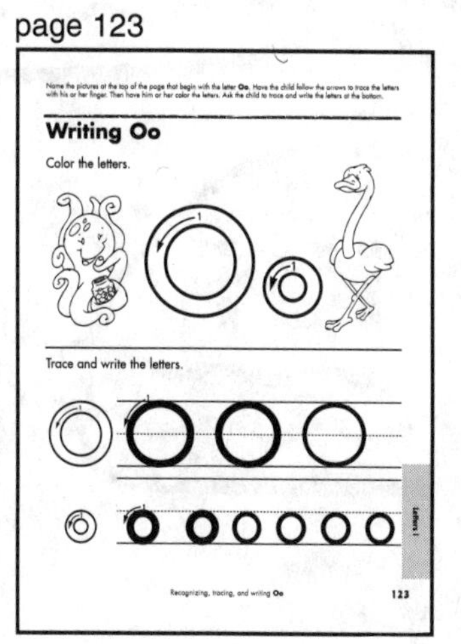
Writing Oo

Color the letters.

Trace and write the letters.

Recognizing, tracing, and writing Oo 123

page 124

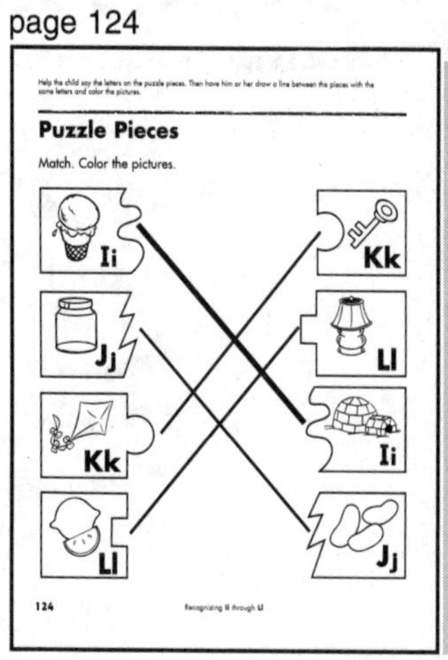
Puzzle Pieces

Match. Color the pictures.

124 Recognizing Ii through Ll

Letters I

Point to and say the capital and lowercase letters **P** and **p** at the top of the page. Ask the child to find and circle the letters **P** and **p** on each pie.

The Letters P and p

Circle the letters **P** and **p**.

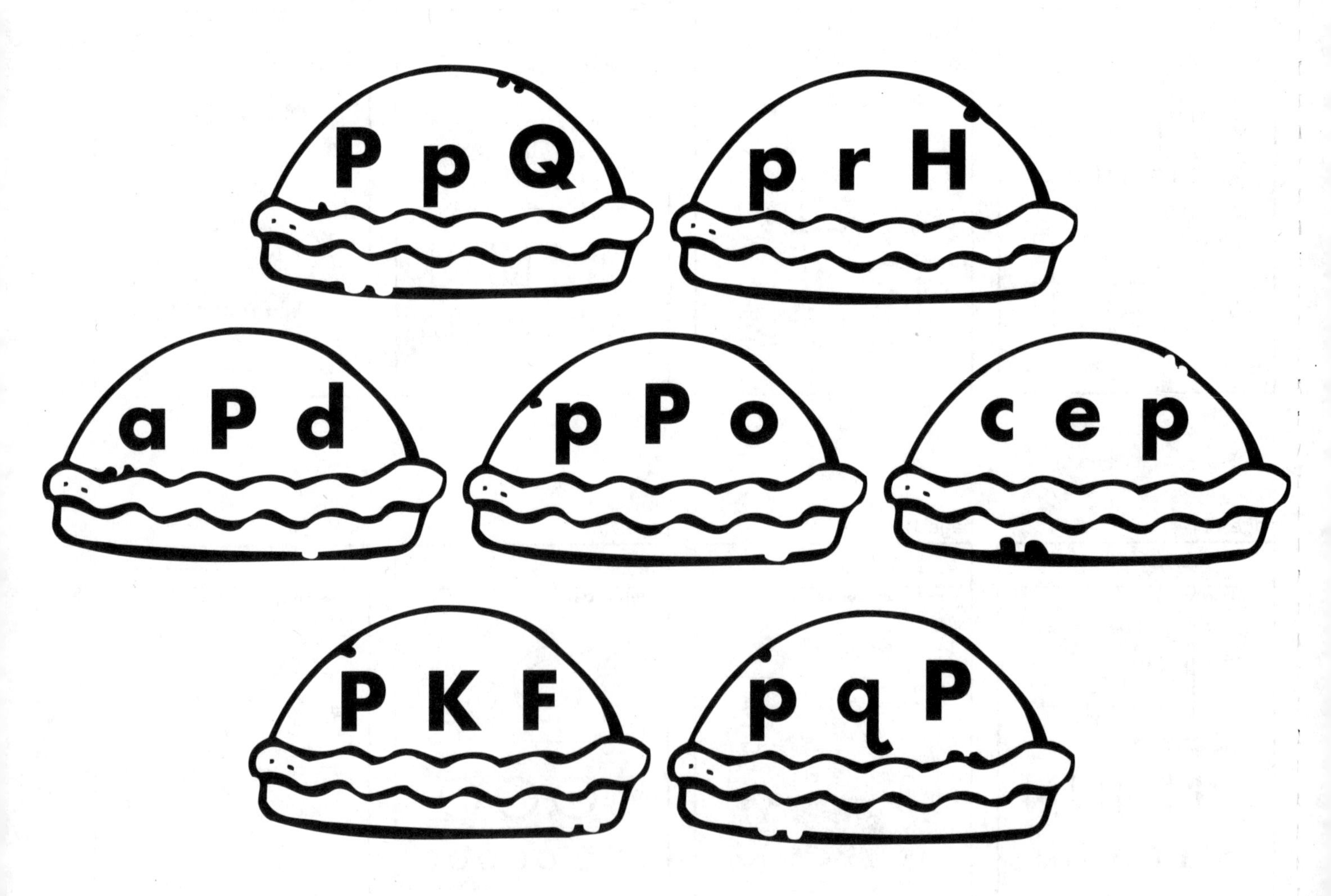

Name the pictures at the top of the page that begin with the letter **Pp**. Have the child follow the arrows to trace the letters with his or her finger. Then have him or her color the letters. Ask the child to trace and write the letters at the bottom.

Writing Pp

Color the letters.

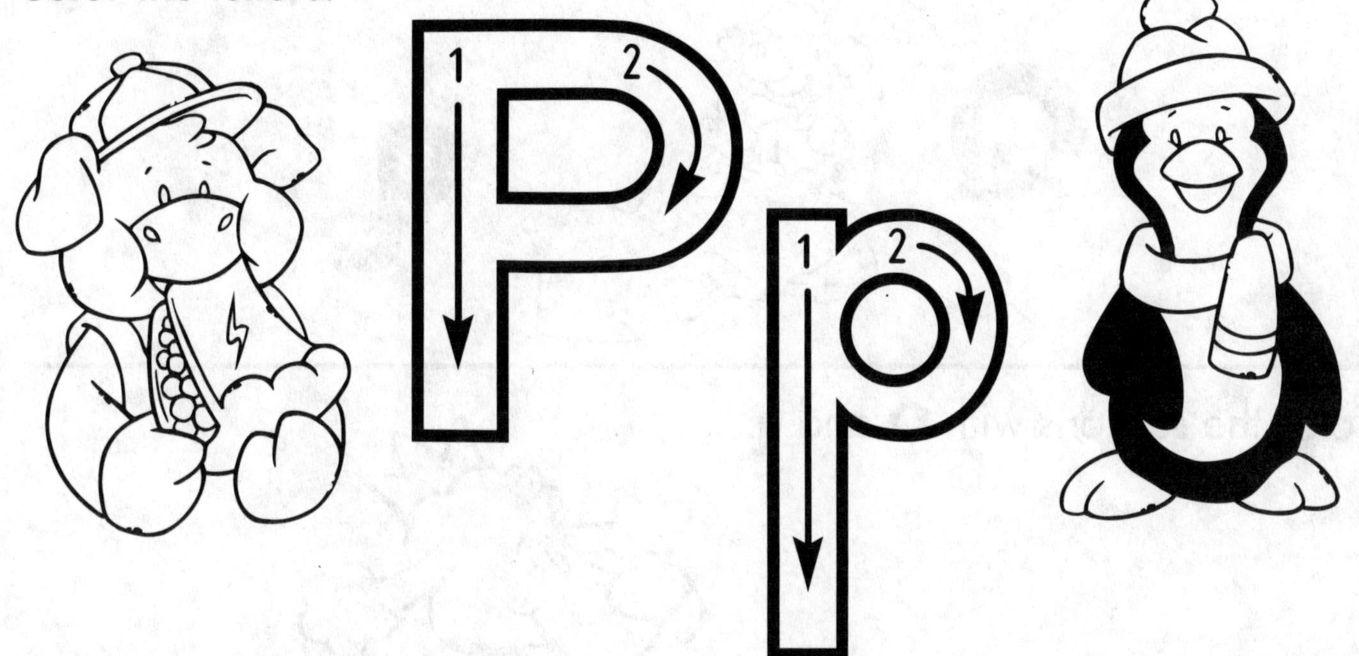

Trace and write the letters.

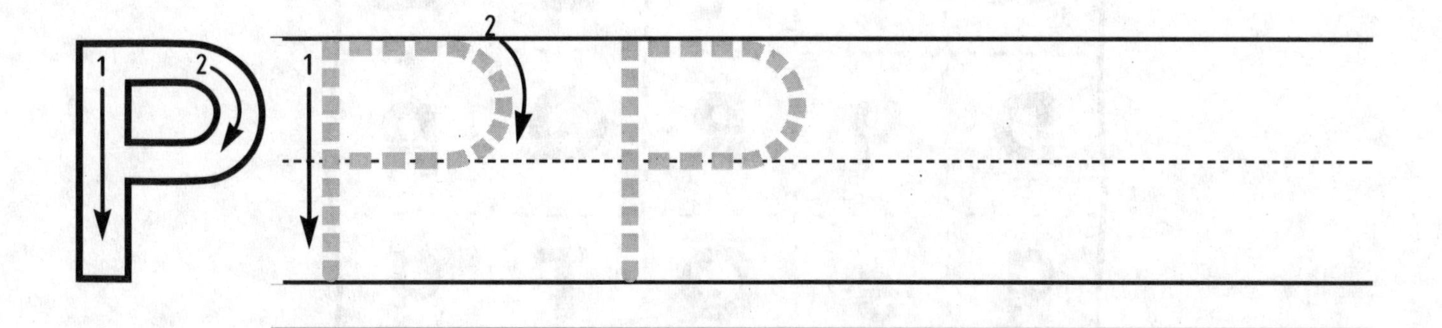

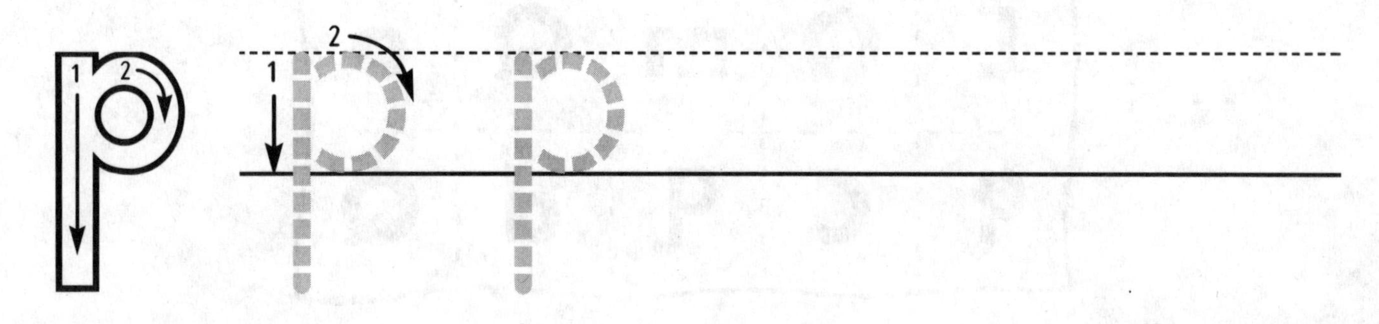

Letters II

Point to and say the capital and lowercase letters **Q** and **q** at the top of the page. Ask the child to find and color the areas on the quilt with the letters **Q** and **q**.

The Letters Q and q

Color the sections with **Q** and **q**.

Q	a	q	b	Q
D	q	R	Q	p
q	s	Q	T	q
L	Q	m	Q	o
q	c	q	d	Q

Name the pictures at the top of the page that begin with the letter **Qq**. Have the child follow the arrows to trace the letters with his or her finger. Then have him or her color the letters. Ask the child to trace and write the letters at the bottom.

Writing Qq

Color the letters.

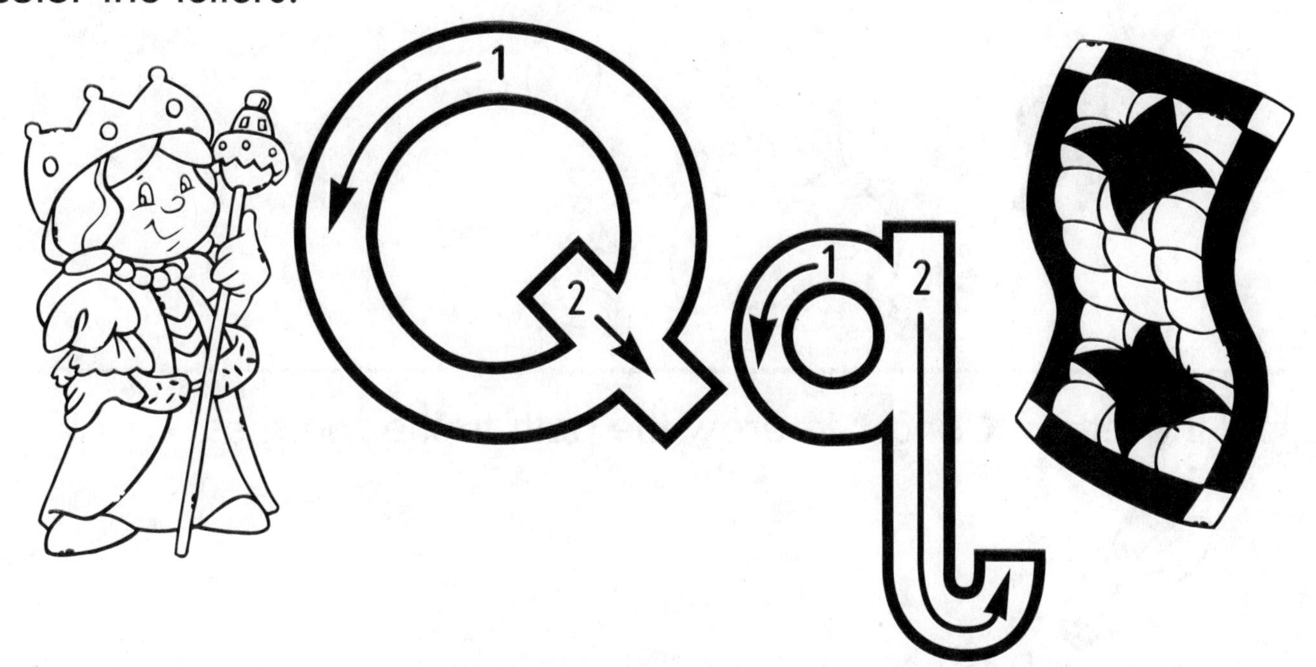

Trace and write the letters.

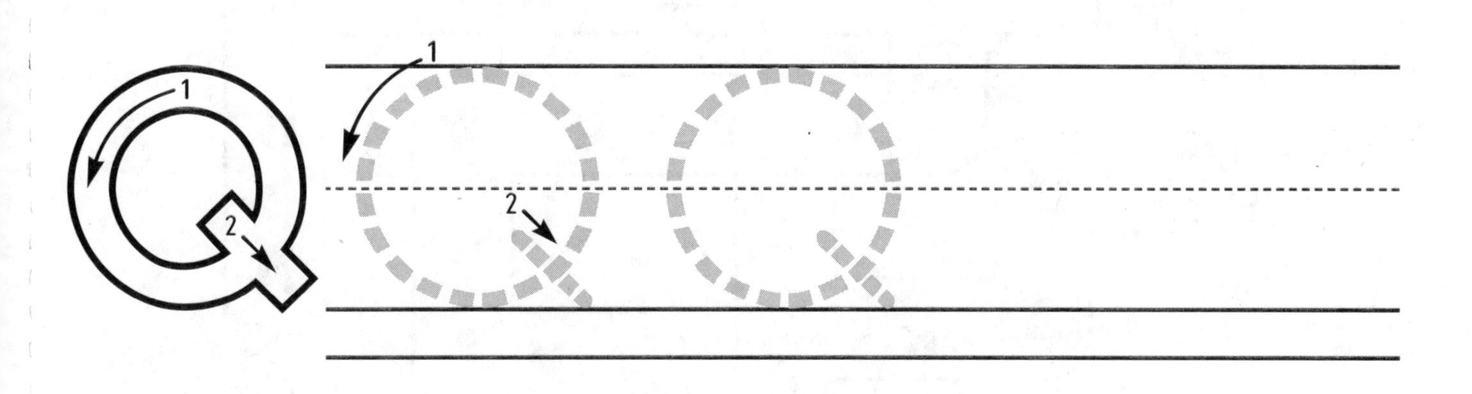

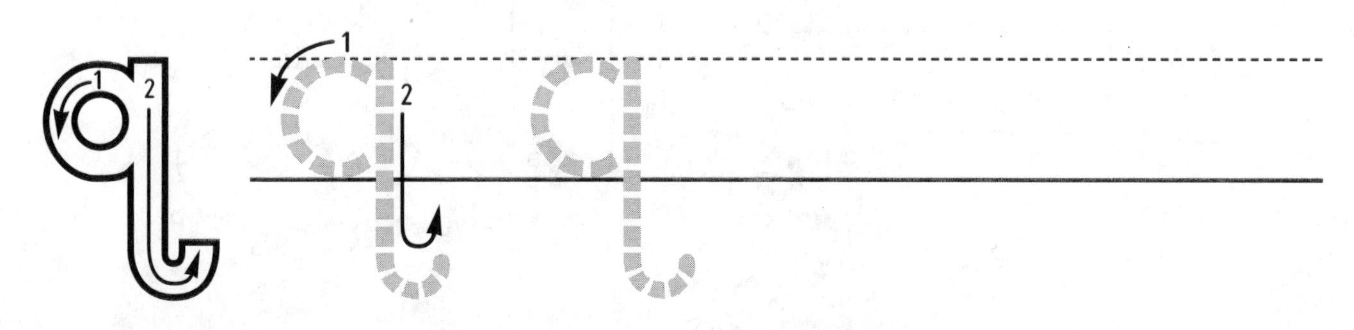

Letters II

Point to and say the capital and lowercase letters **R** and **r** at the top of the page. Ask the child to draw a line from the rabbit to the radishes by following the letters **R** and **r**.

The Letters R and r

Follow the letters **R** and **r** to draw the path to the radishes.

Name the pictures at the top of the page that begin with the letter **Rr**. Have the child follow the arrows to trace the letters with his or her finger. Then have him or her color the letters. Ask the child to trace and write the letters at the bottom.

Writing Rr

Color the letters.

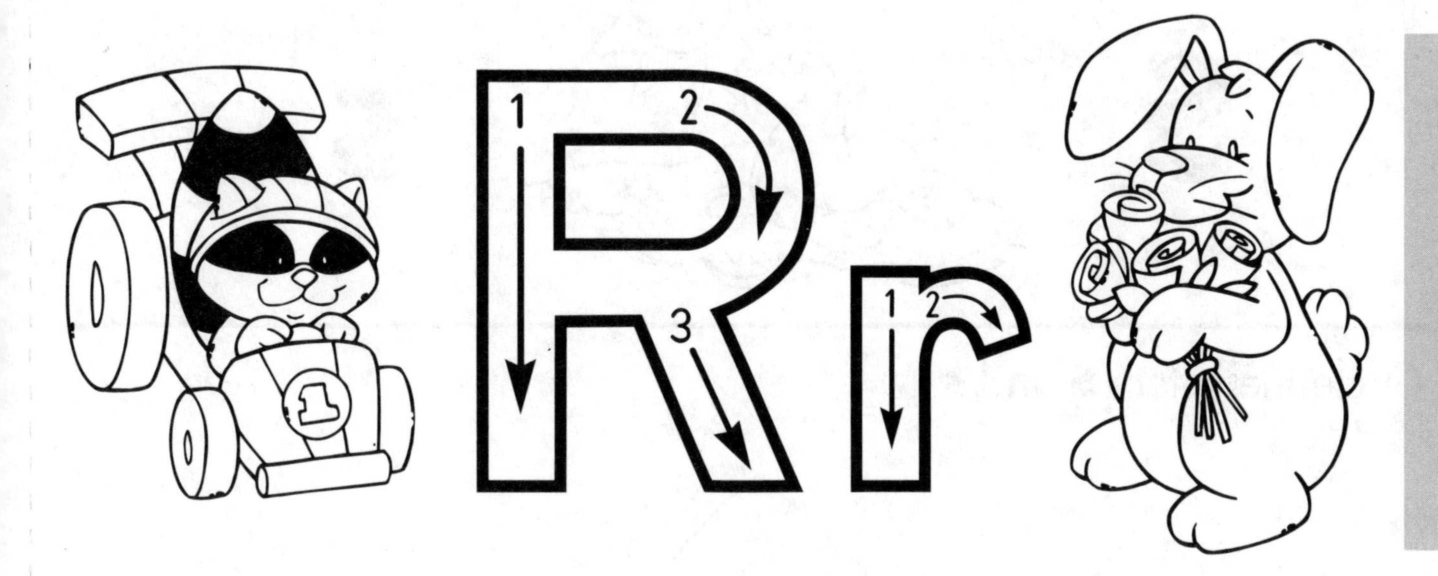

Letters II

Trace and write the letters.

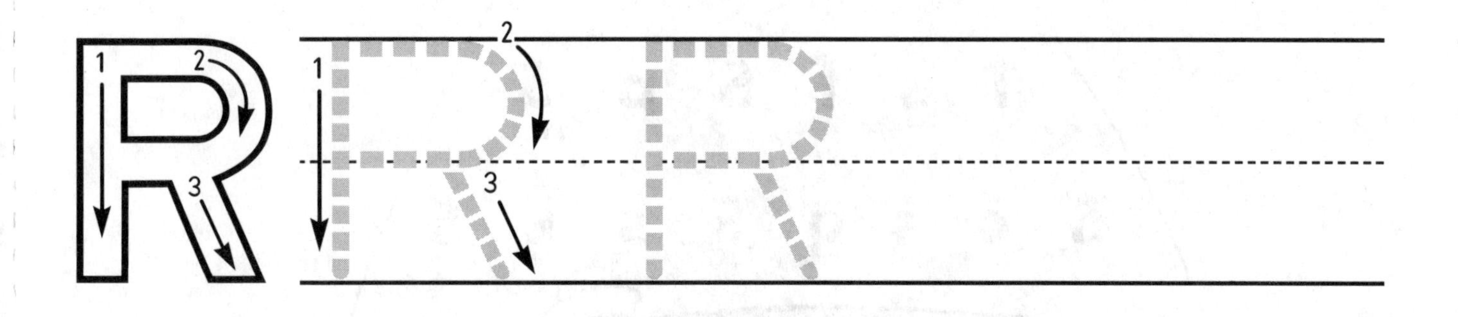

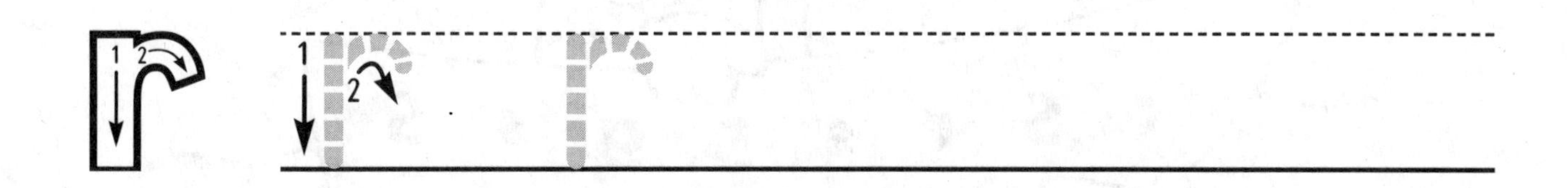

Point to and say the capital and lowercase letters **S** and **s** at the top of the page. Ask the child to find and circle all the letters **S** and **s** on the sailboat.

The Letters S and s

Circle the letters **S** and **s**.

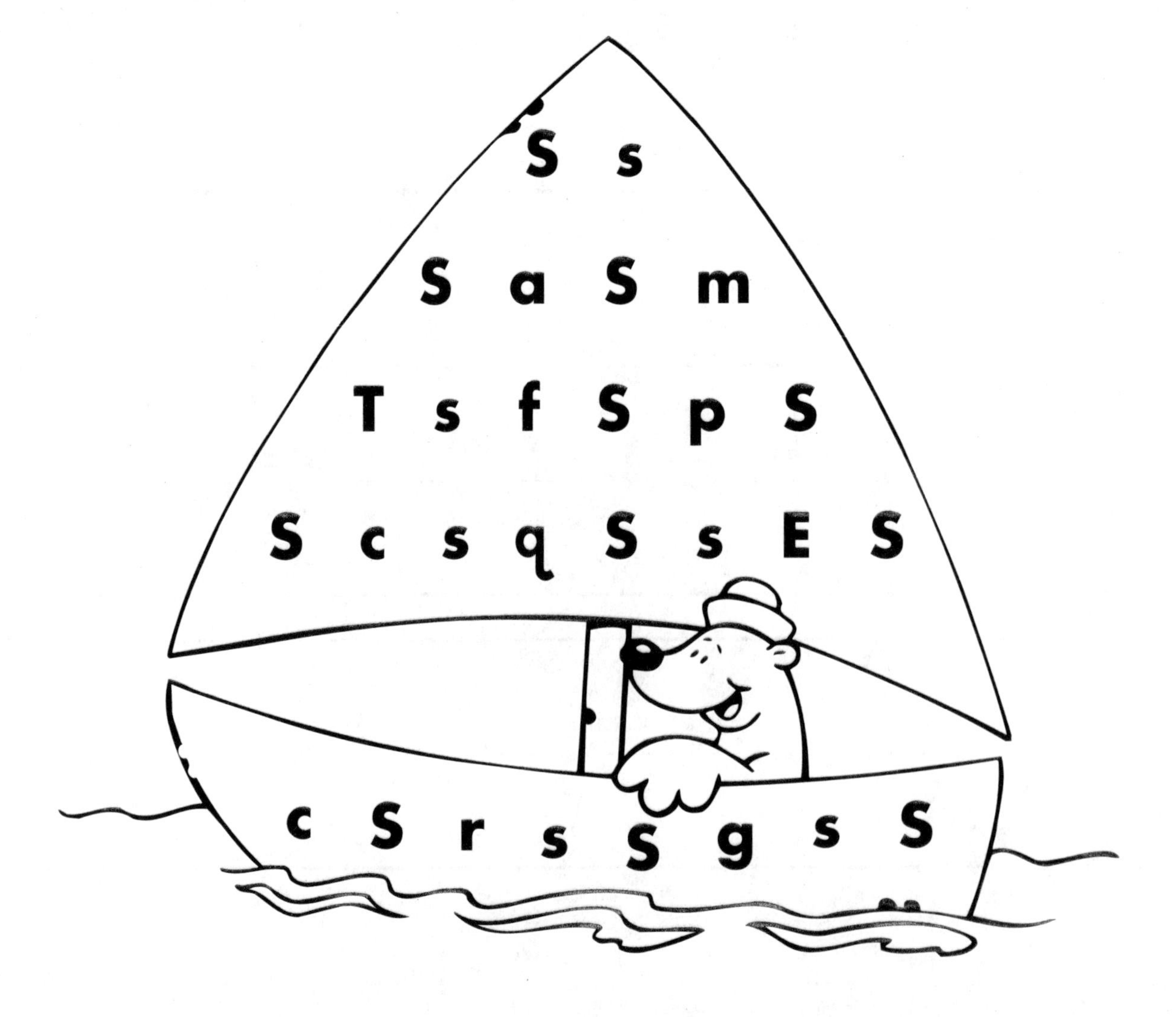

Name the pictures at the top of the page that begin with the letter **Ss**. Have the child follow the arrows to trace the letters with his or her finger. Then have him or her color the letters. Ask the child to trace and write the letters at the bottom.

Writing Ss

Color the letters.

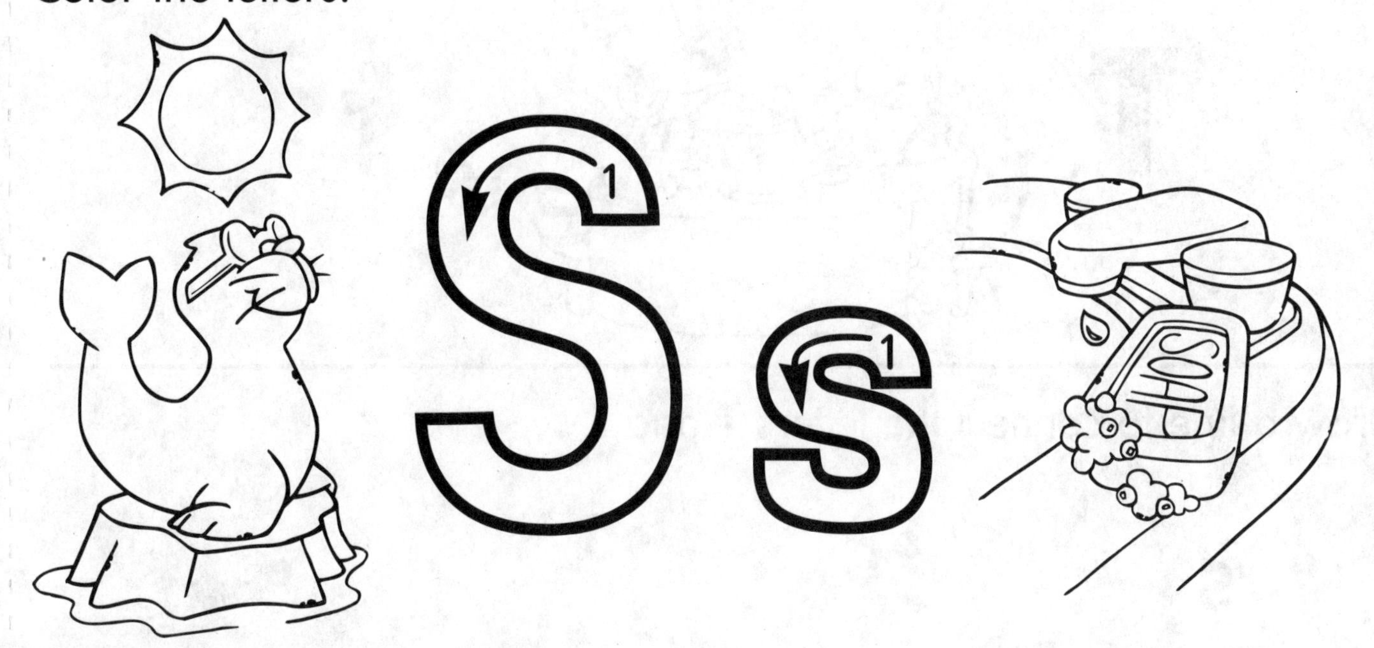

Letters II

Trace and write the letters.

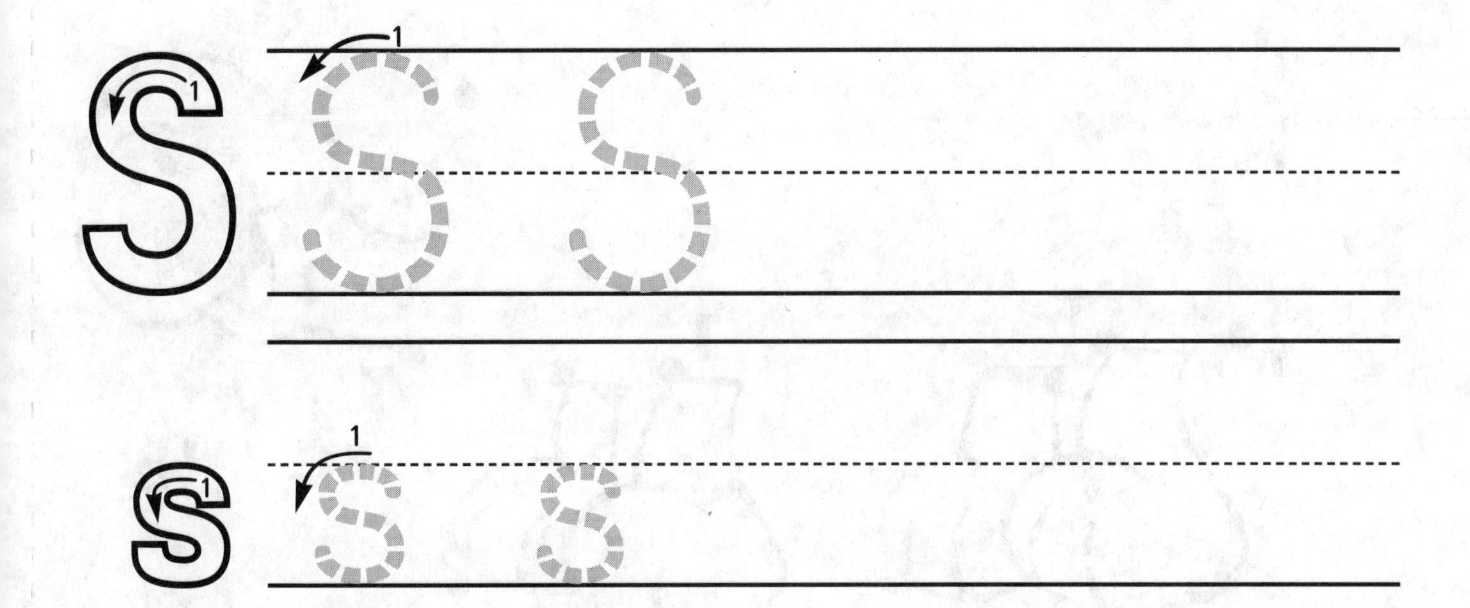

Point to and say the capital and lowercase letters **T** and **t** at the top of the page. Ask the child to draw a line connecting the letters **T** and **t** to finish the picture.

The Letters T and t

Draw a line to connect the letters **T** and **t**.

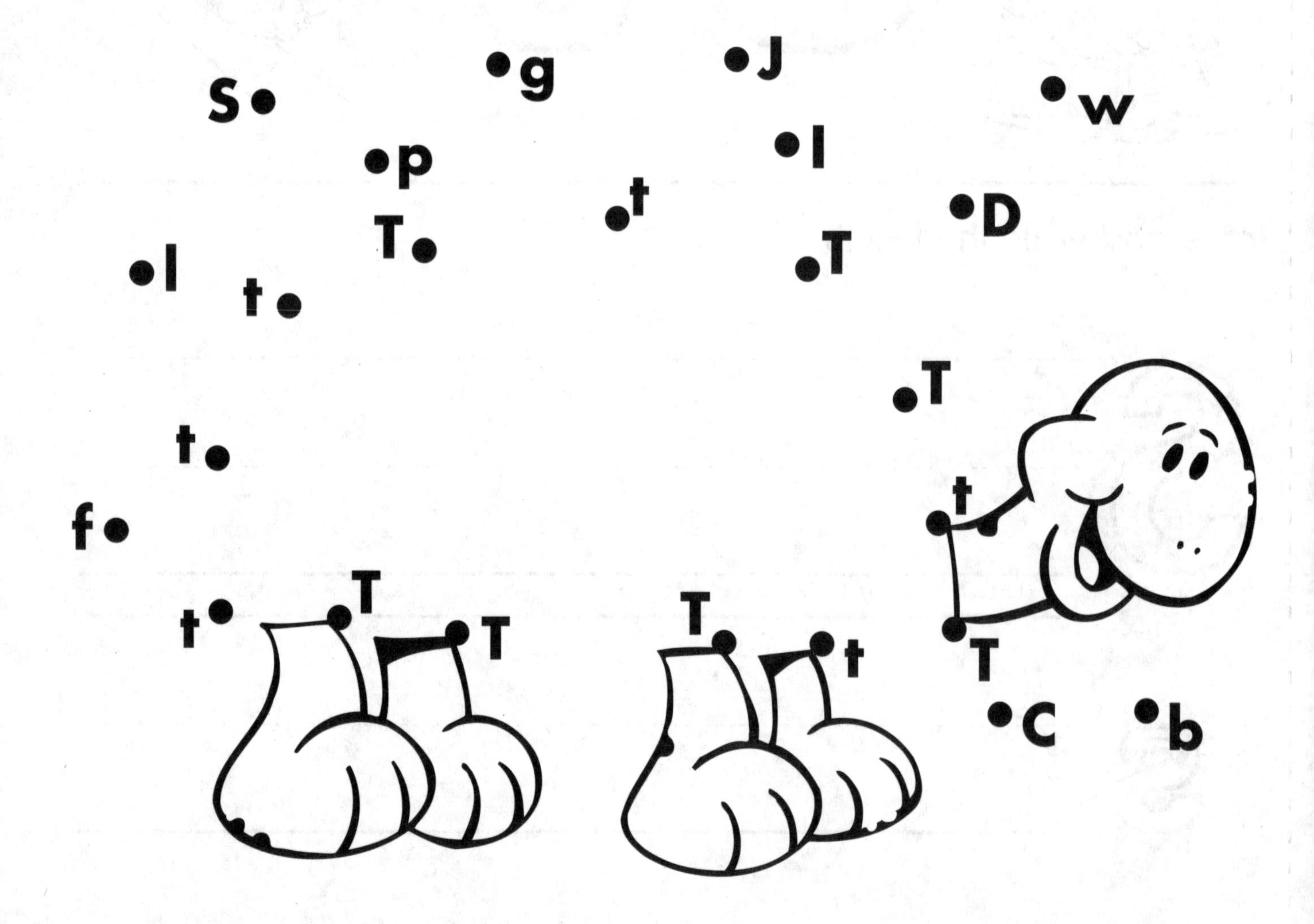

Name the pictures at the top of the page that begin with the letter **Tt**. Have the child follow the arrows to trace the letters with his or her finger. Then have him or her color the letters. Ask the child to trace and write the letters at the bottom.

Writing Tt

Color the letters.

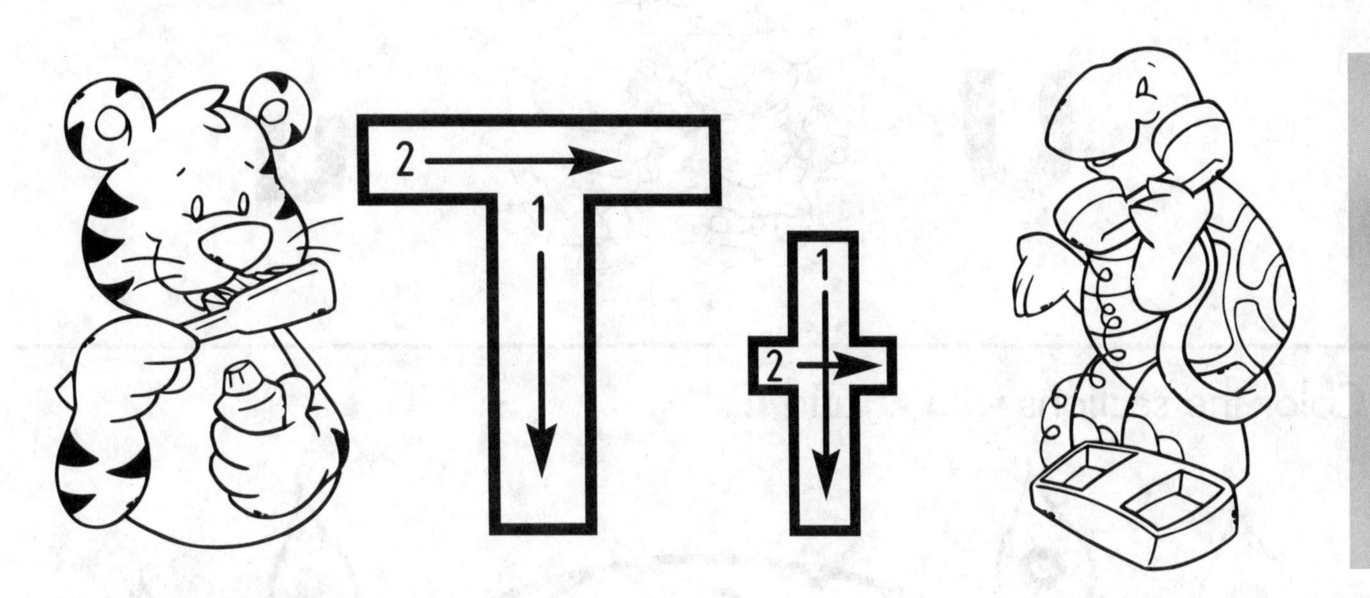

Letters II

Trace and write the letters.

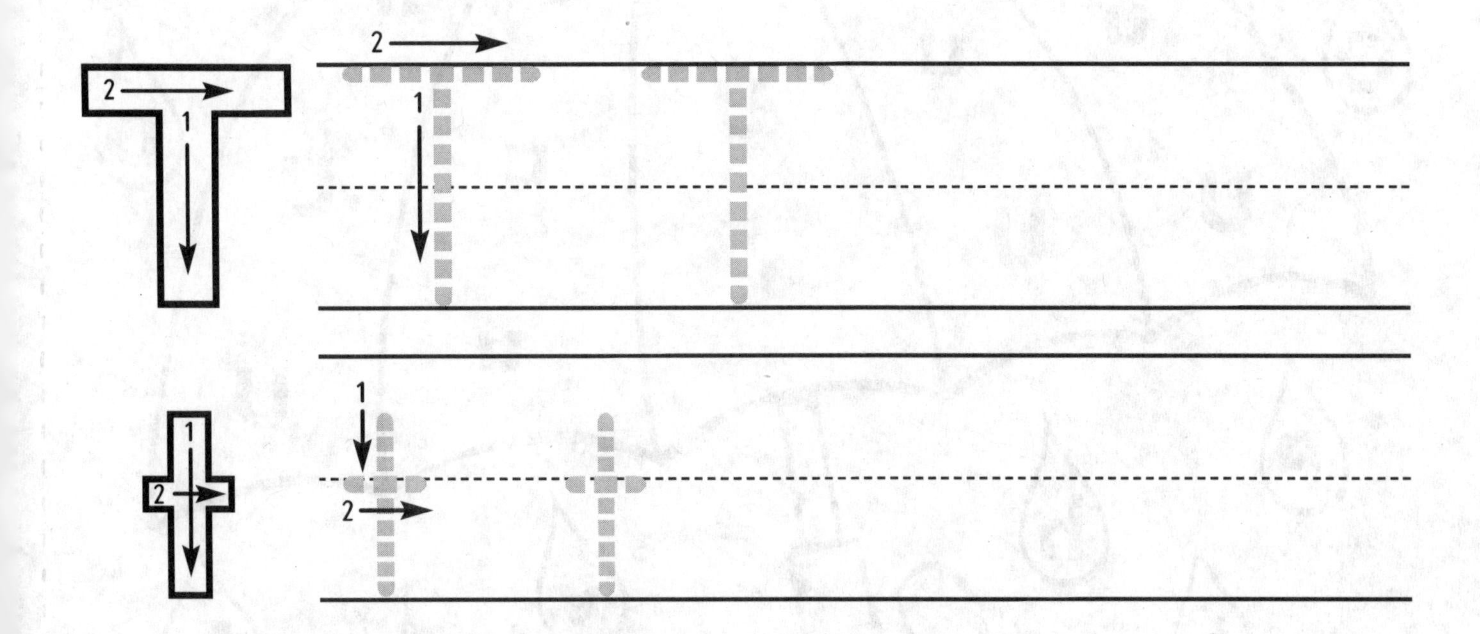

Point to and say the capital and lowercase letters **U** and **u** at the top of the page. Ask the child to find and color all the sections with the letters **U** and **u**.

The Letters U and u

Color the sections with **U** and **u**.

Name the pictures at the top of the page that begin with the letter **Uu**. Have the child follow the arrows to trace the letters with his or her finger. Then have him or her color the letters. Ask the child to trace and write the letters at the bottom.

Writing Uu

Color the letters.

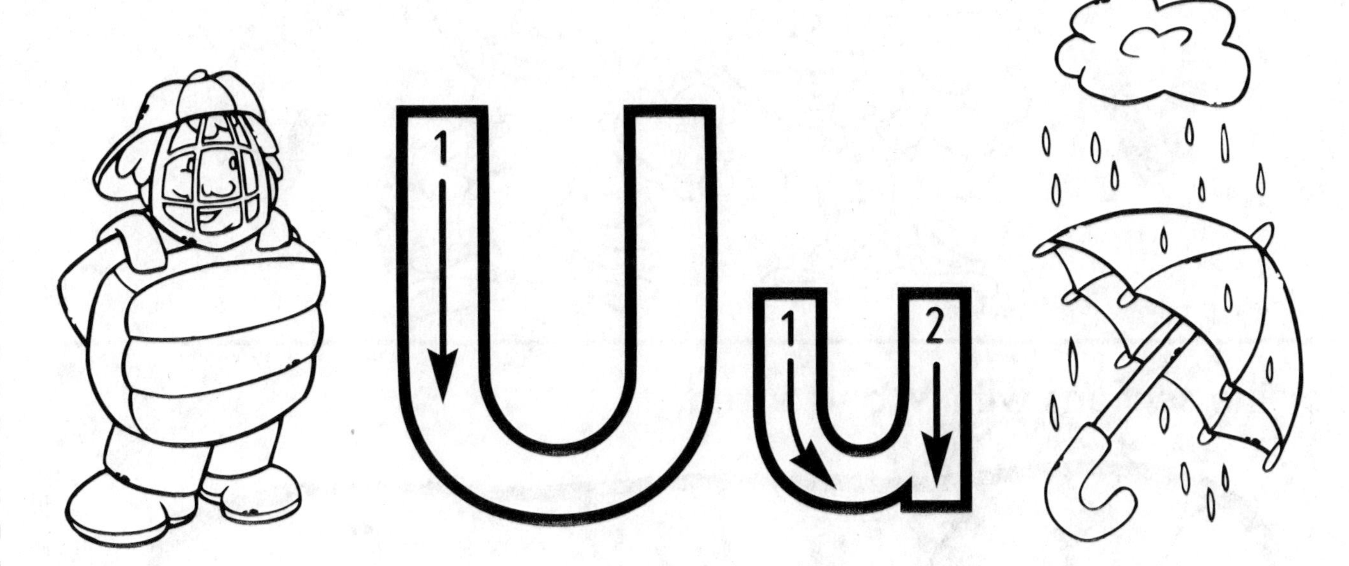

Trace and write the letters.

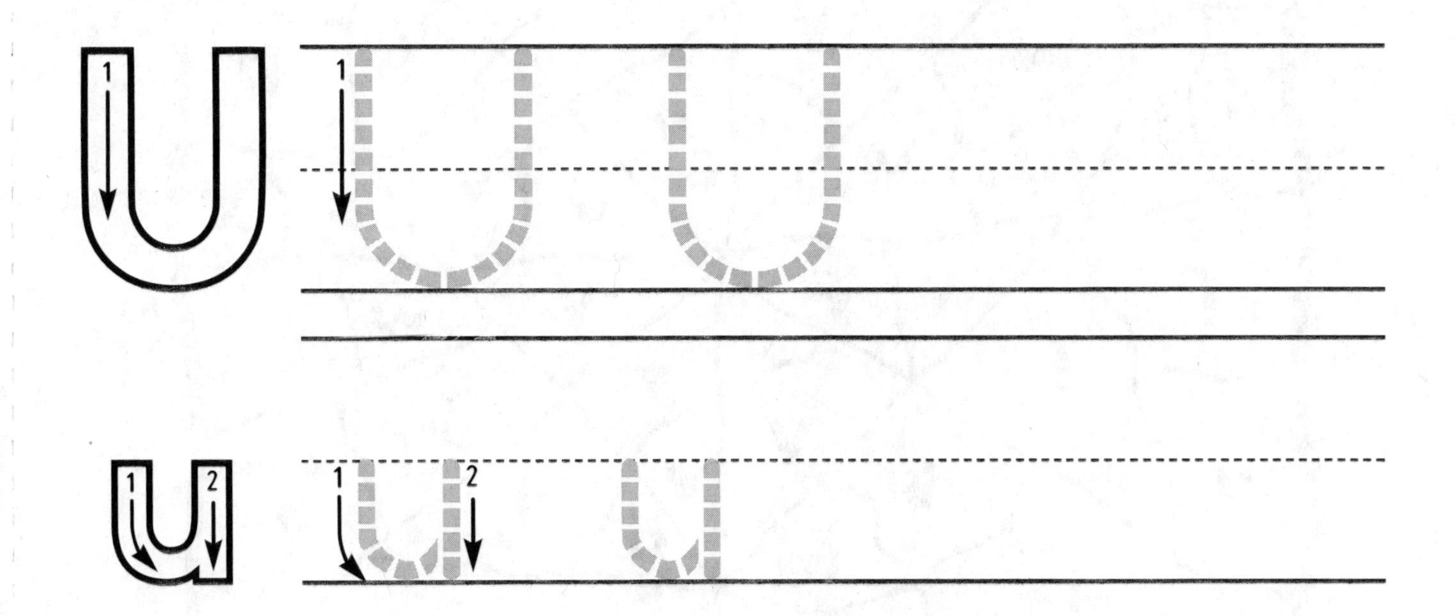

Point to and say the capital and lowercase letters **V** and **v** at the top of the page. Ask the child to find and color all the sections with the letters **V** and **v** red to reveal the hidden picture.

The Letters V and v

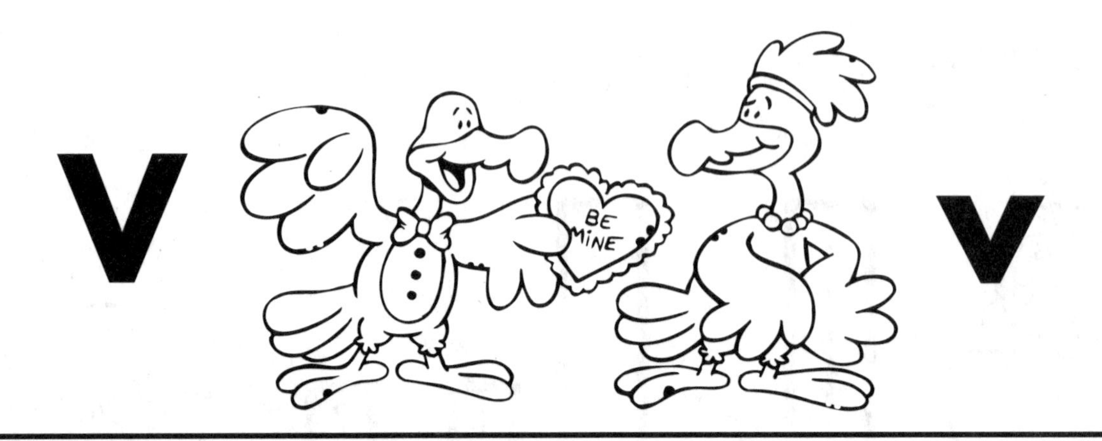

Color the sections with **V** and **v** red.

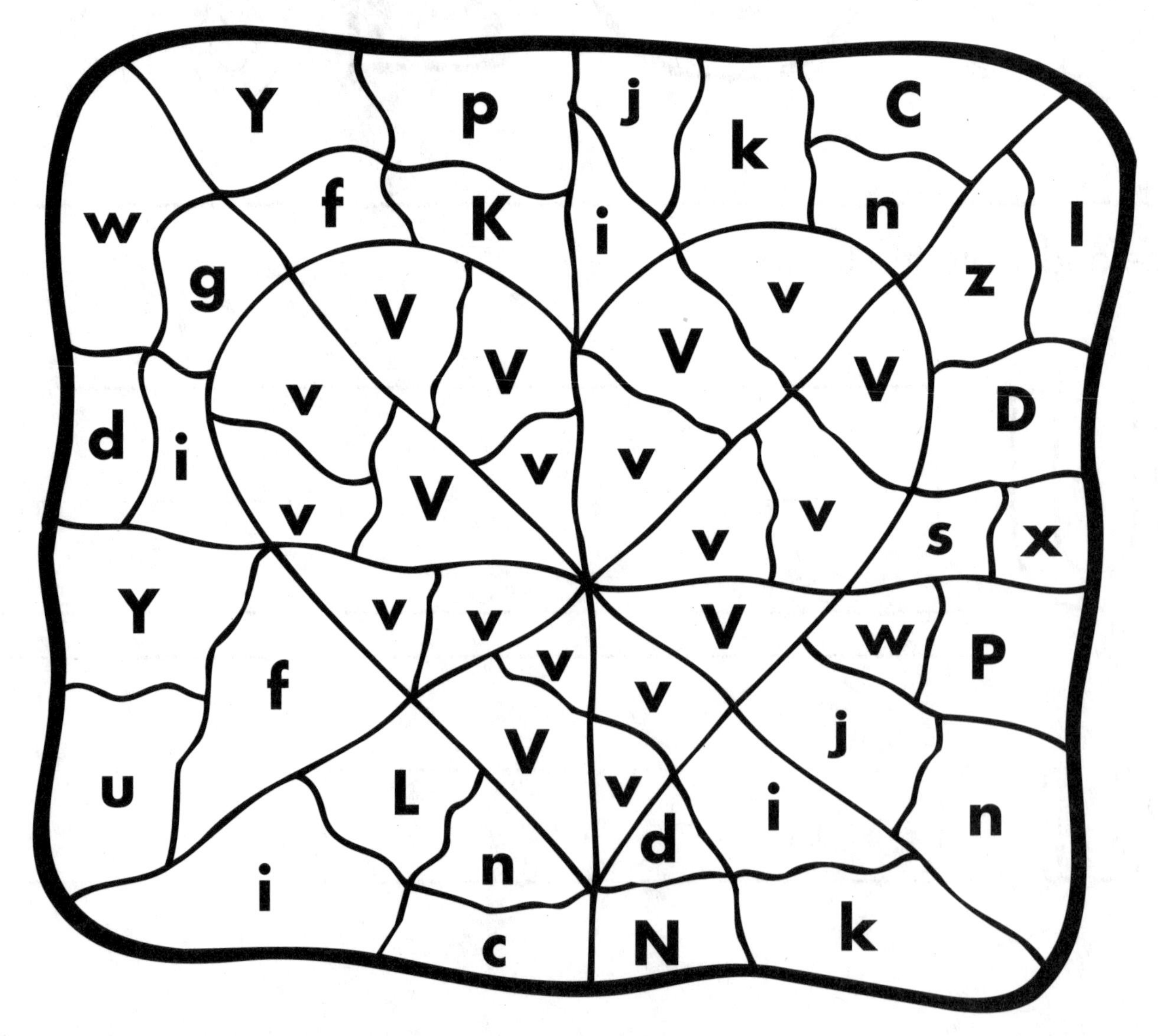

Name the pictures at the top of the page that begin with the letter **Vv**. Have the child follow the arrows to trace the letters with his or her finger. Then have him or her color the letters. Ask the child to trace and write the letters at the bottom.

Writing Vv

Color the letters.

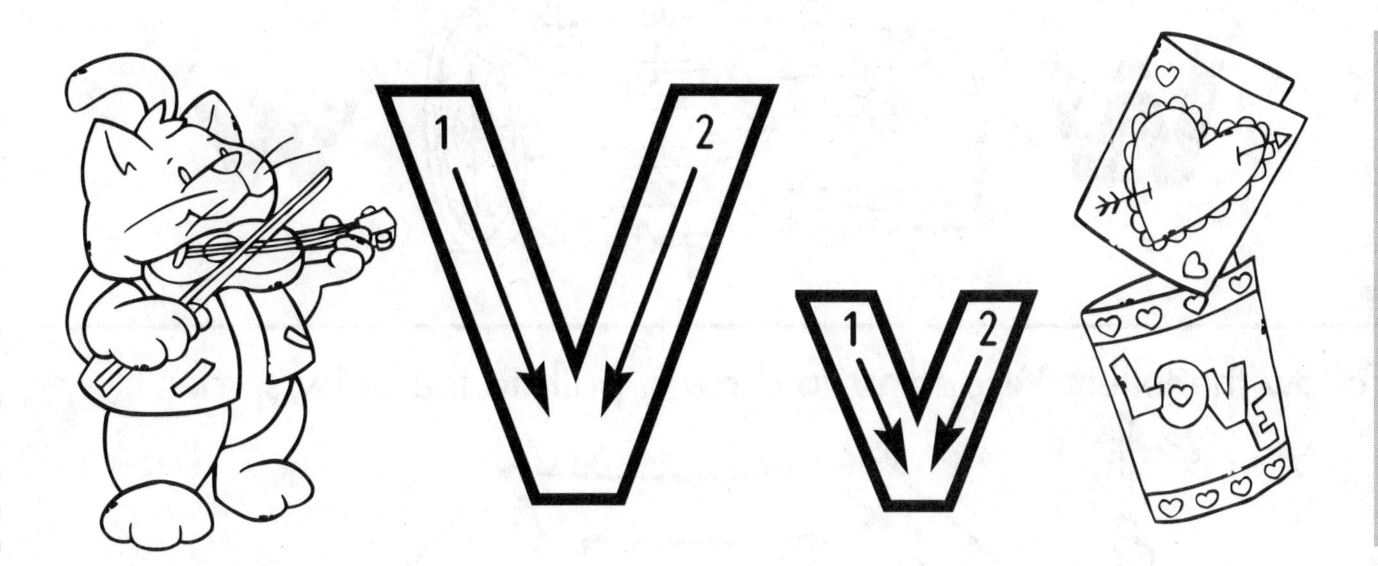

Trace and write the letters.

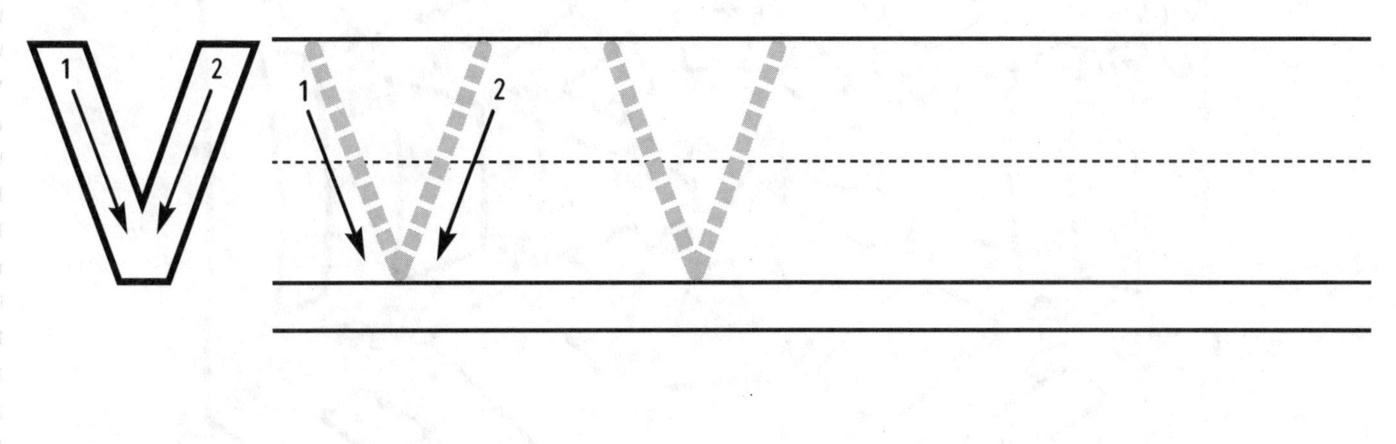

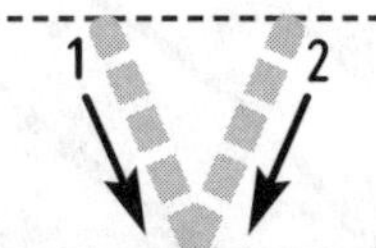

Point to and say the capital and lowercase letters **W** and **w** at the top of the page. Ask the child to draw a line through the web from the mother spider to the baby spider by following the letters **W** and **w**.

The Letters W and w

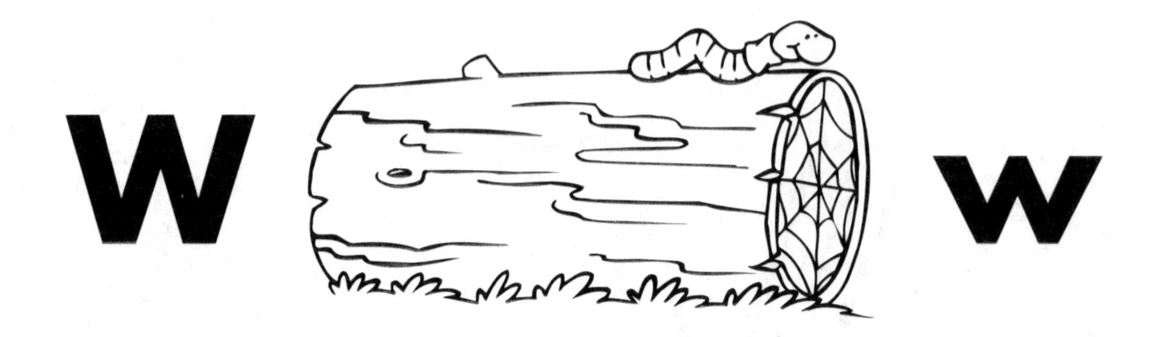

Follow the letters **W** and **w** to draw a path to the baby spider.

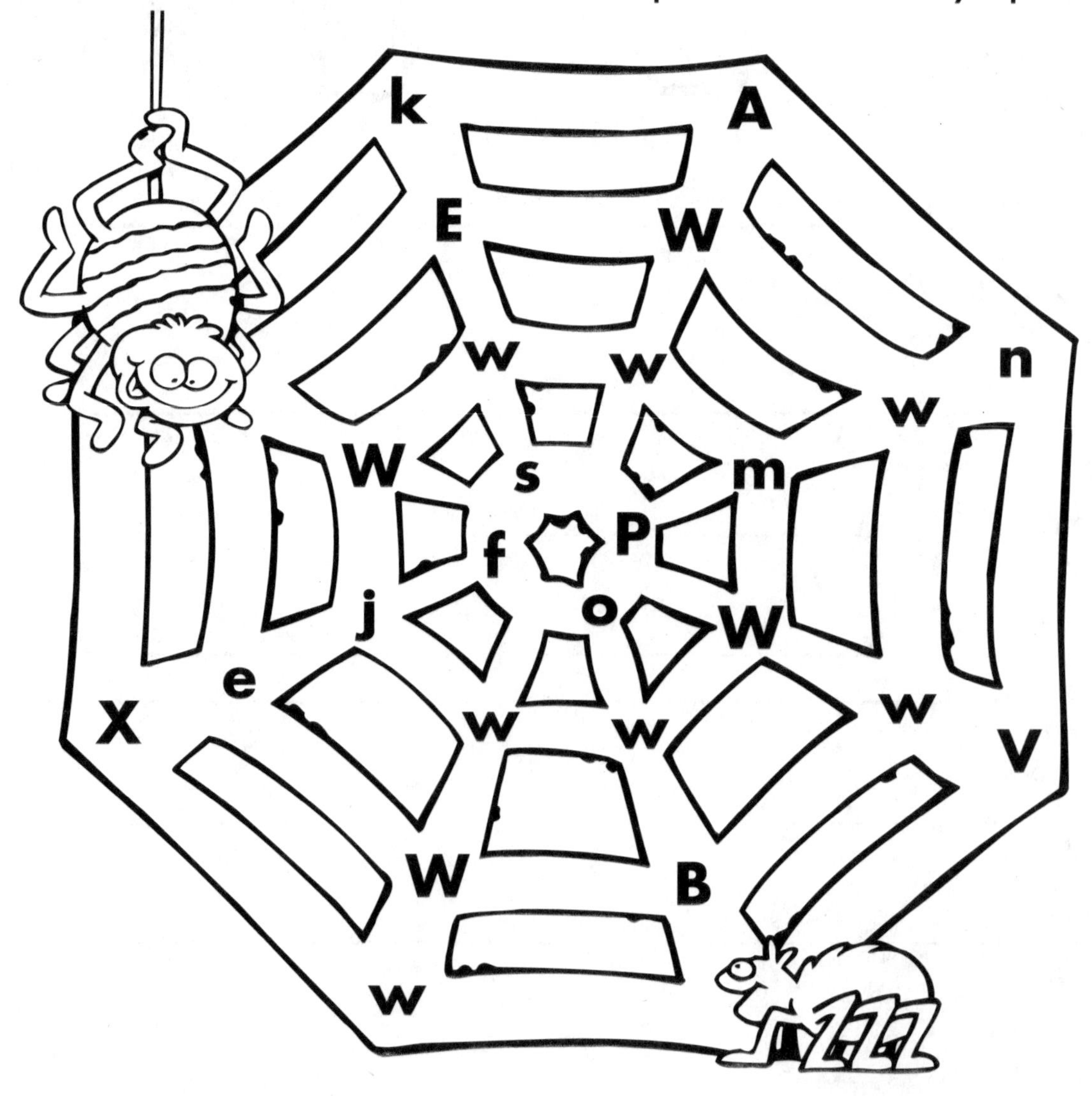

Name the pictures at the top of the page that begin with the letter **Ww**. Have the child follow the arrows to trace the letters with his or her finger. Then have him or her color the letters. Ask the child to trace and write the letters at the bottom.

Writing Ww

Color the letters.

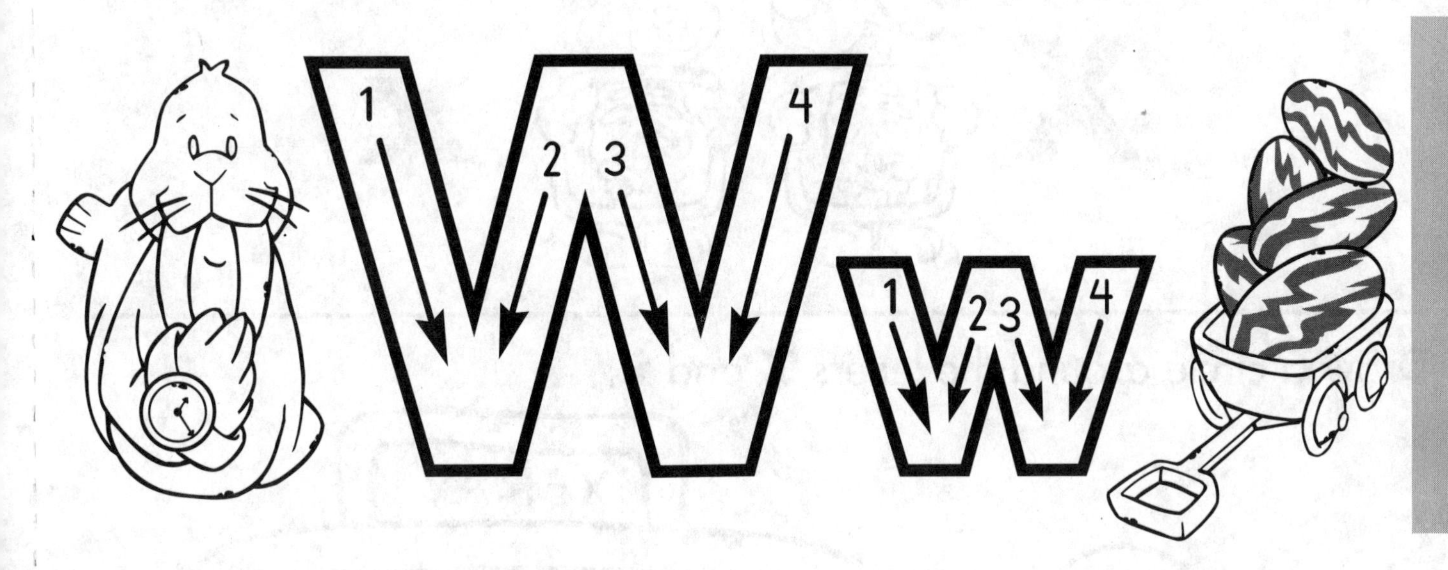

Trace and write the letters.

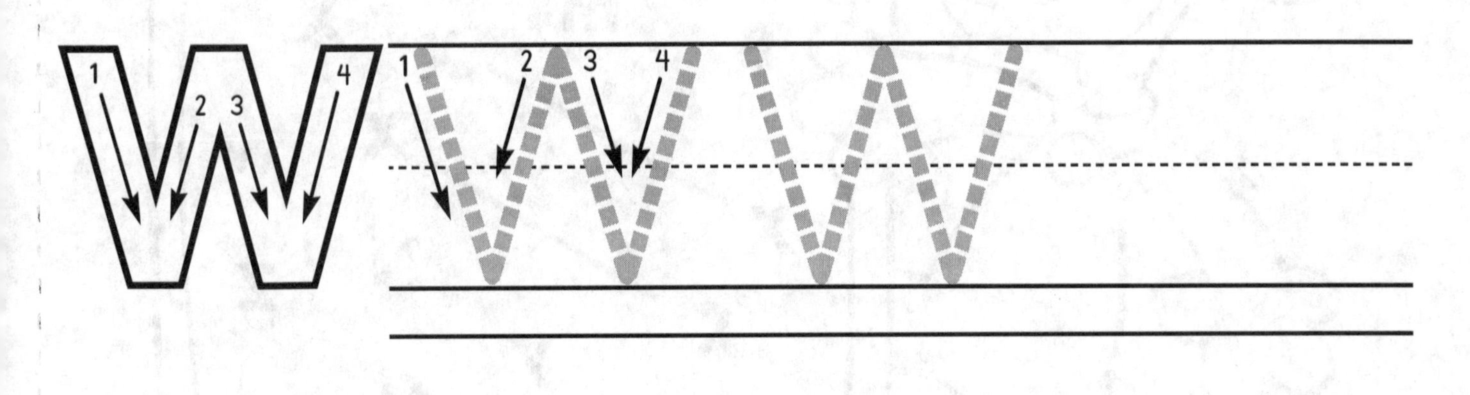

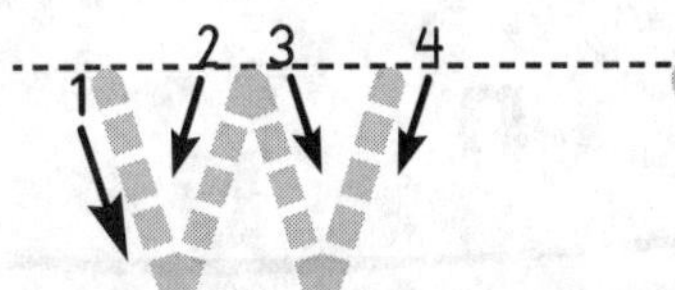

Point to and say the capital and lowercase letters **X** and **x** at the top of the page. Ask the child to draw a circle around each letter **X** and **x** to finish the picture.

The Letters X and x

Draw a circle around the letters **X** and **x**.

Name the pictures at the top of the page that begin with the letter **Xx**. Have the child follow the arrows to trace the letters with his or her finger. Then have him or her color the letters. Ask the child to trace and write the letters at the bottom.

Writing Xx

Color the letters.

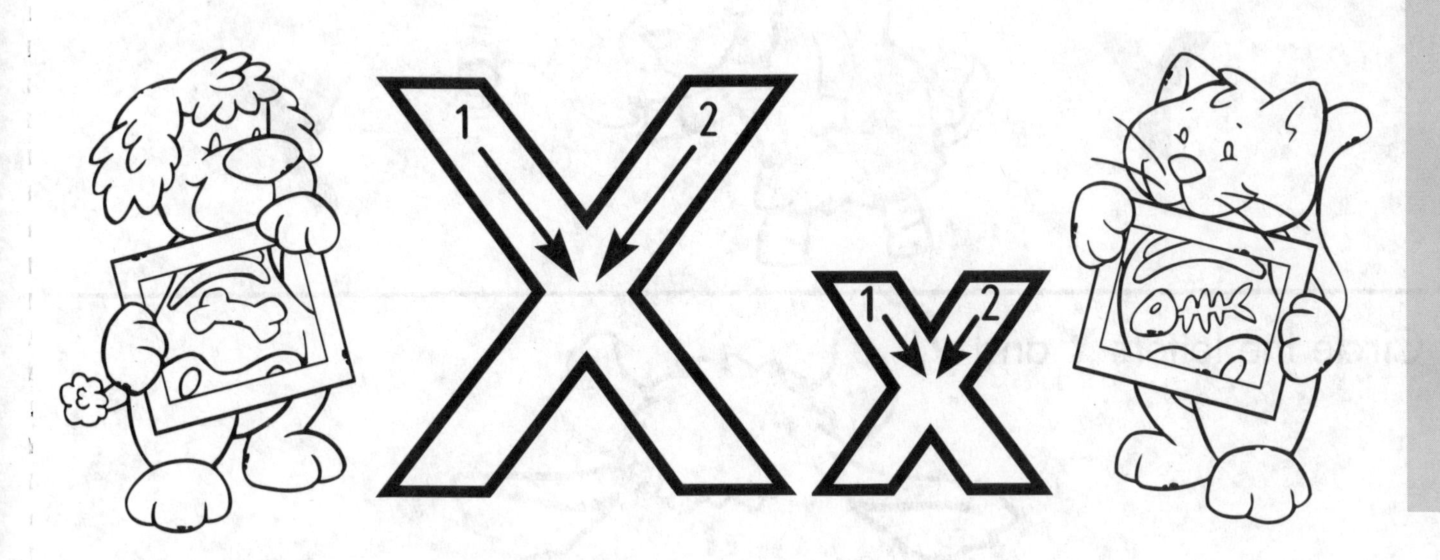

Trace and write the letters.

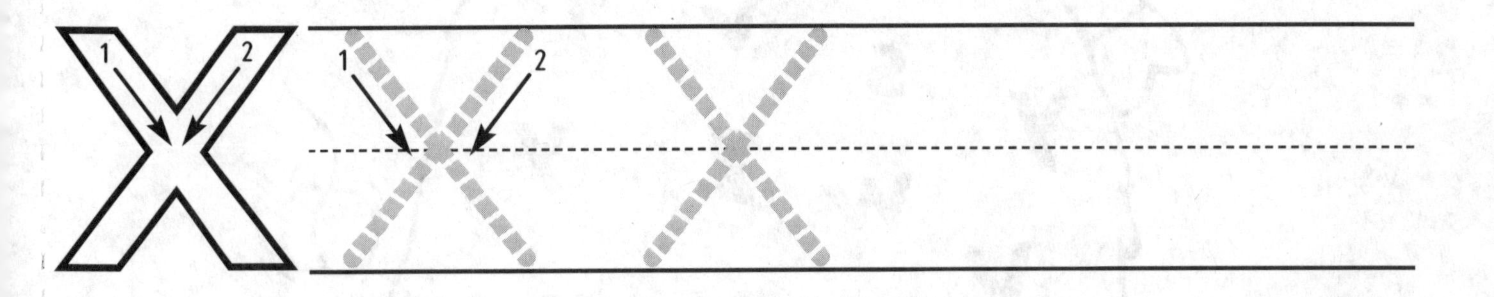

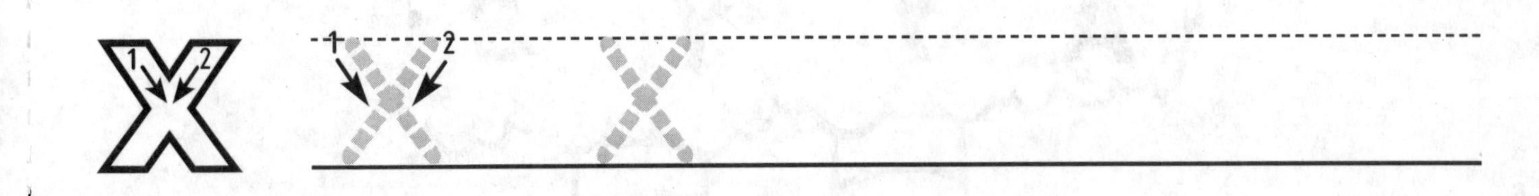

Letters II

Point to and say the capital and lowercase letters **Y** and **y** at the top of the page. Ask the child to find and circle all the letters **Y** and **y** on the yak.

The Letters Y and y

Circle the letters **Y** and **y**.

Name the pictures at the top of the page that begin with the letter **Yy**. Have the child follow the arrows to trace the letters with his or her finger. Then have him or her color the letters. Ask the child to trace and write the letters at the bottom.

Writing Yy

Color the letters.

Trace and write the letters.

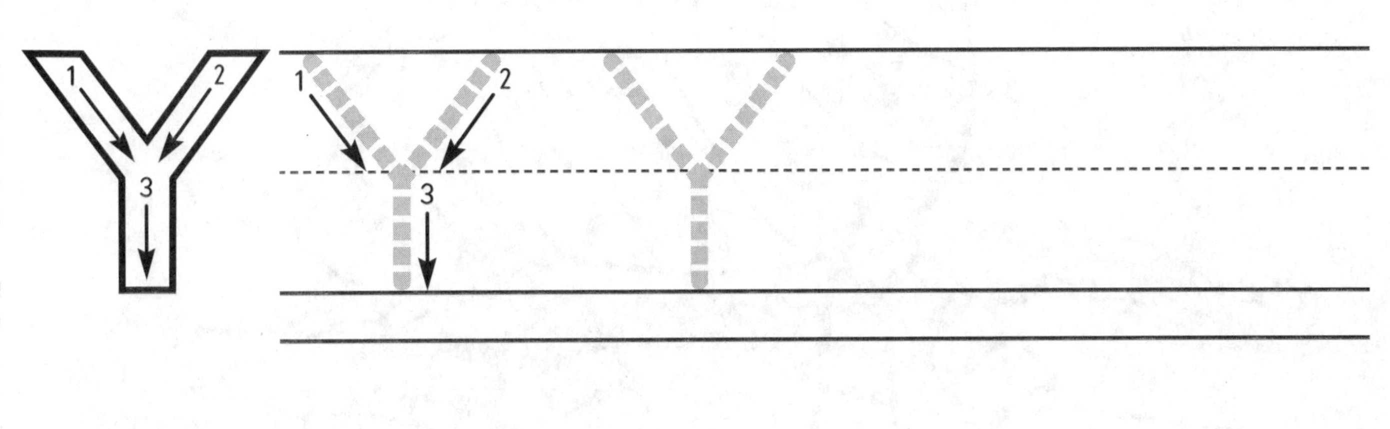

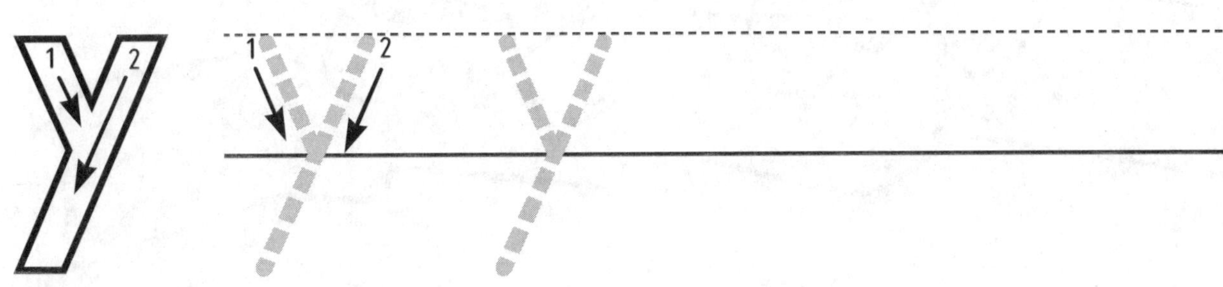

Point to and say the capital and lowercase letters **Z** and **z** at the top of the page. Ask the child to find and color the sections with the letters **Z** and **z** black.

The Letters Z and z

Z **z**

Color the sections with **Z** and **z** black.

Name the pictures at the top of the page that begin with the letter **Zz**. Have the child follow the arrows to trace the letters with his or her finger. Then have him or her color the letters. Ask the child to trace and write the letters at the bottom.

Writing Zz

Color the letters.

Letters II

Trace and write the letters.

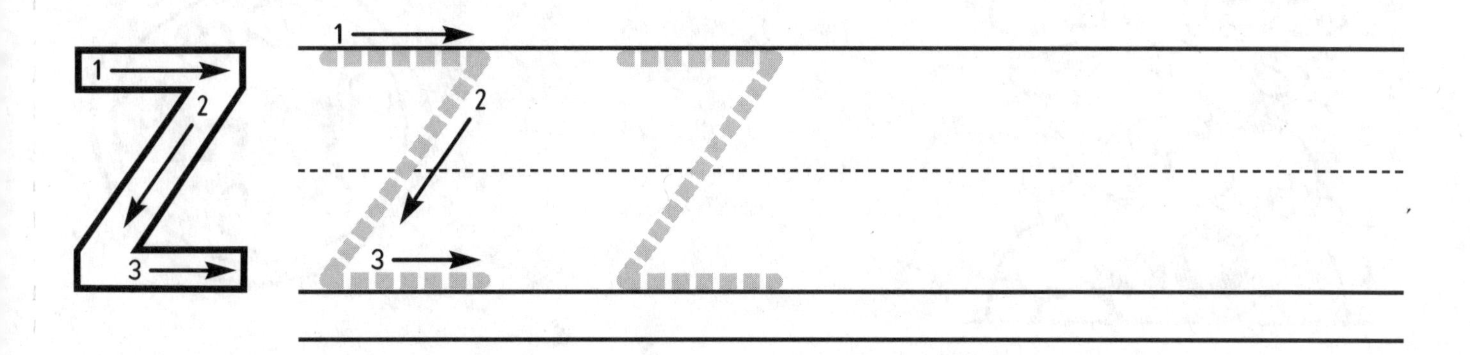

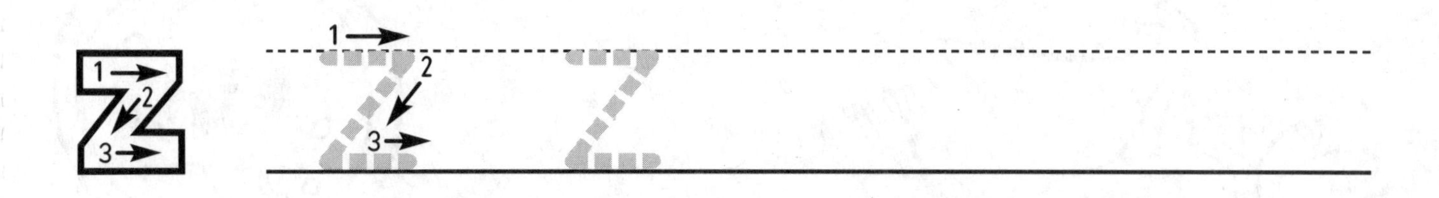

Help the child say the letters on the characters' napkins. Then have him or her draw a line to the pizza with the matching letters.

Pizza Time

Match.

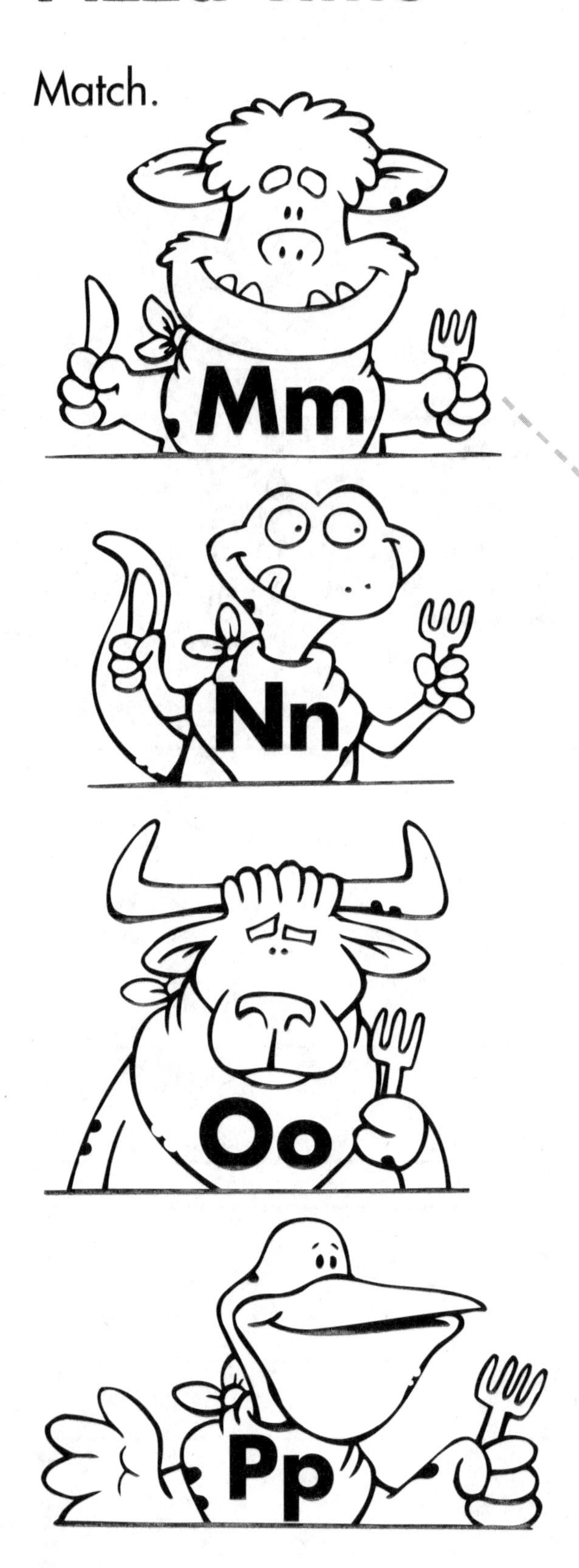

Help the child say the letters on the animals' easels. Then have him or her draw a line to the painting with the matching letters.

Fine Art

Match.

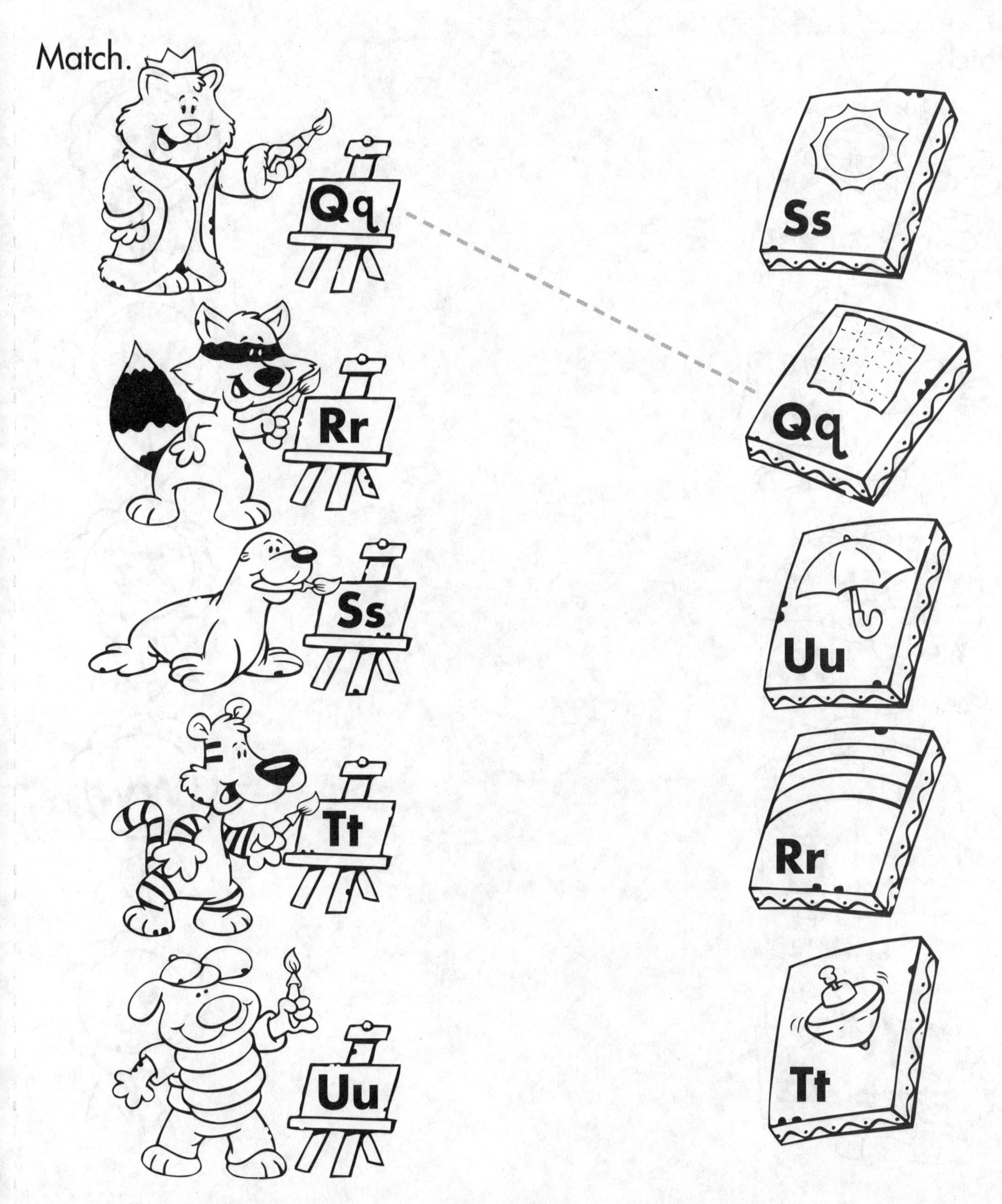

Help the child say the letters the animals are holding up. Then have him or her draw a line to the award with the matching letters.

Good Job!

Match.

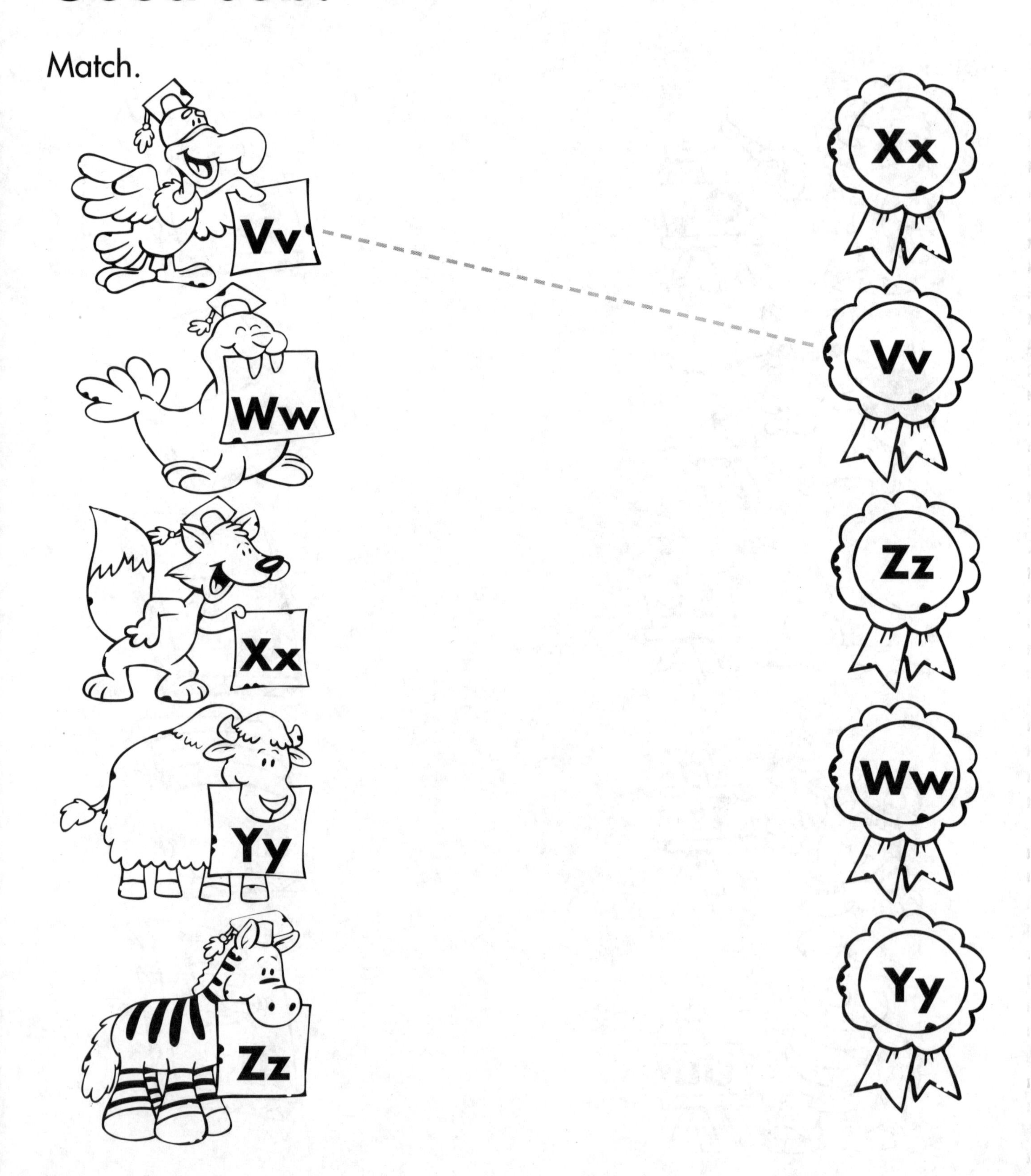

Help the child point to and say each letter. Then have him or her color the pictures and cut along the dashed lines to make alphabet cards. Shuffle the cards and place them on a table. Take turns picking cards from the deck, naming the letters, and tracing them with a finger.

Alphabet Cards

Color and cut out the cards.

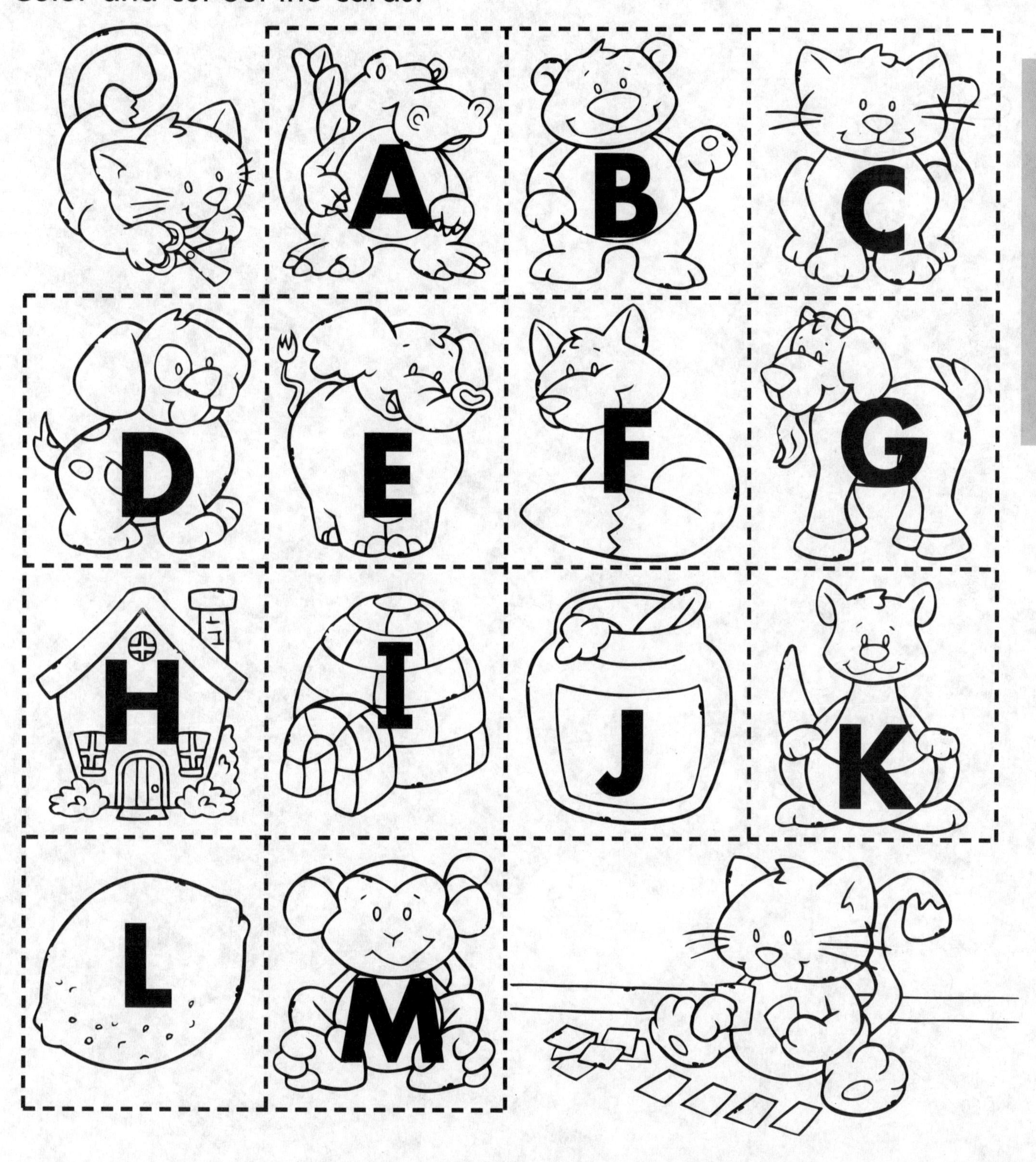

Help the child point to and say each letter. Then have him or her color the pictures and cut along the dashed lines to make alphabet cards. Shuffle the cards and place them on a table. Take turns picking cards from the deck, naming the letters, and tracing them with a finger.

Alphabet Cards

Color and cut out the cards.

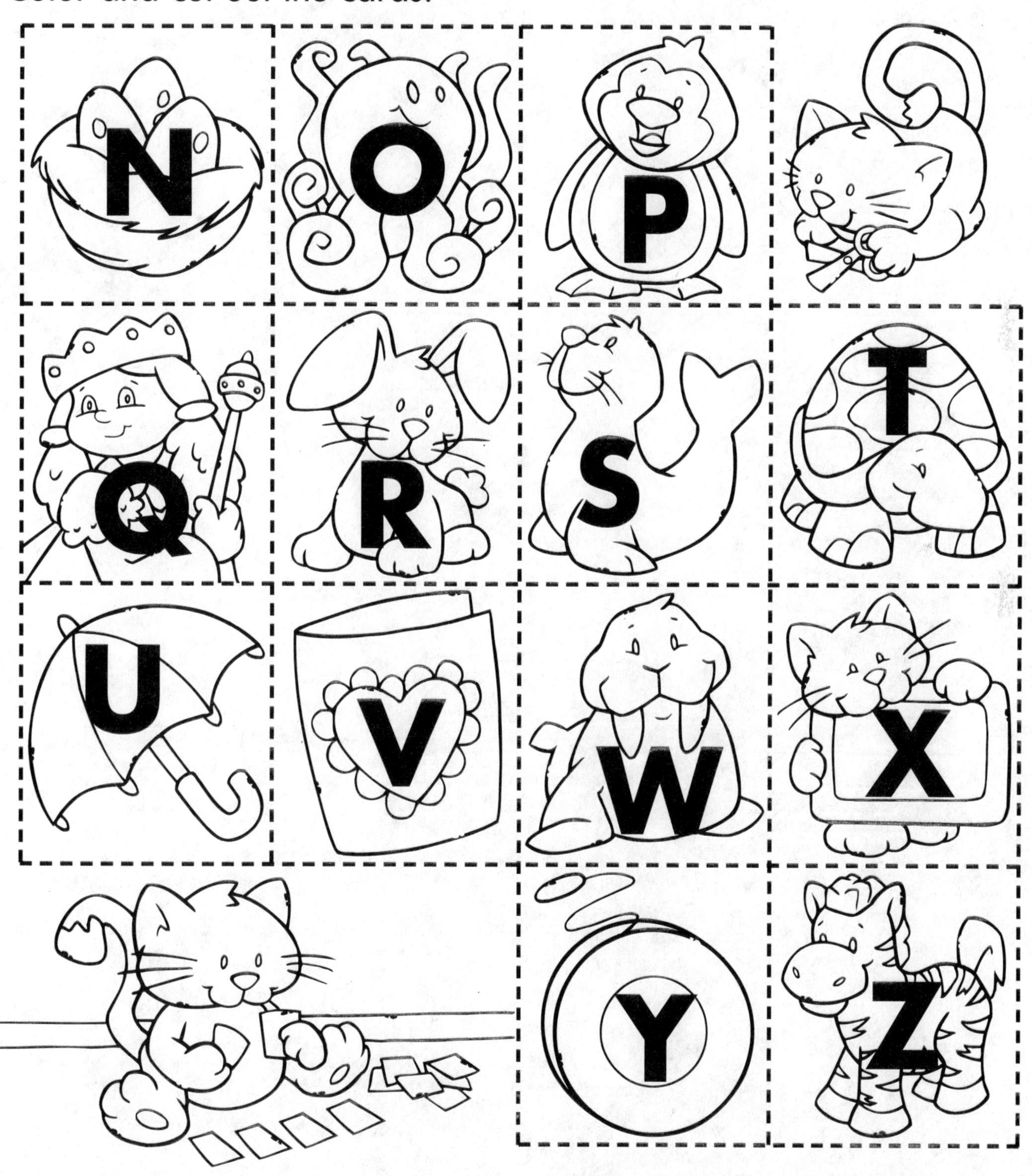

Help the child point to and say each letter. Then have him or her color the pictures and cut along the dashed lines to make alphabet cards. Shuffle the cards and place them on a table. Take turns picking cards from the deck, naming the letters, tracing them with a finger, and matching them with the capital letter cards from page 153.

Alphabet Cards

Color and cut out the cards.

Help the child point to and say each letter. Then have him or her color the pictures and cut along the dashed lines to make alphabet cards. Shuffle the cards and place them on a table. Take turns picking cards from the deck, naming the letters, tracing them with a finger, and matching them with the capital letter cards from page 155.

Alphabet Cards

Color and cut out the cards.

Letters II

Answer Key

As the child completes the pages in this section, review his or her answers. When you take the time to correct the work and explain mistakes, you're showing your child that you feel learning is important.

page 128

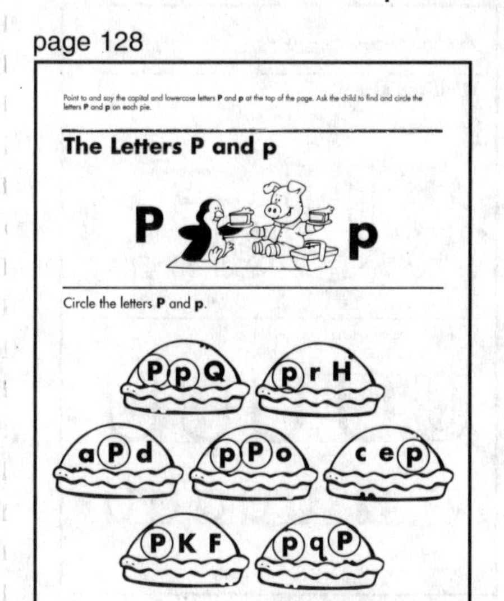

page 129

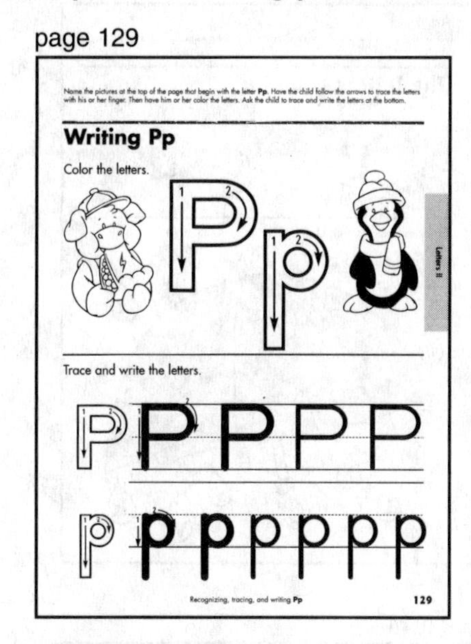

page 130

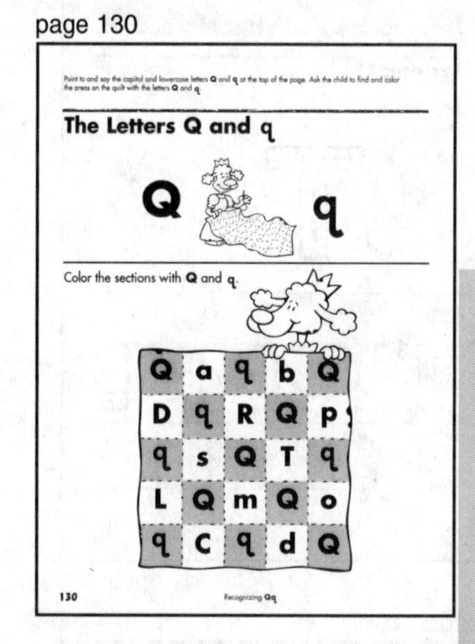

page 131

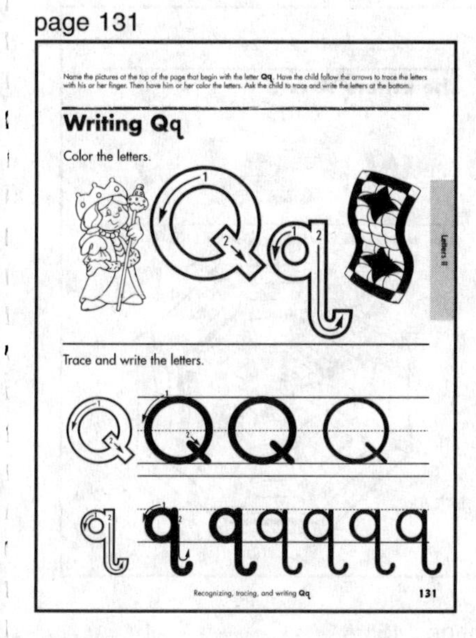

page 132

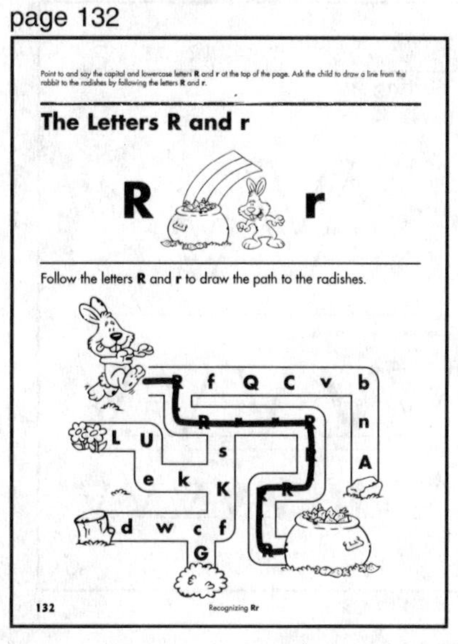

page 133

page 134

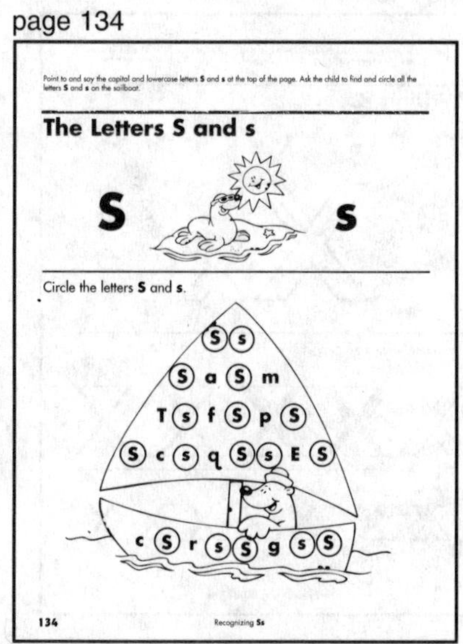

page 135

page 136

Letters II

page 138

page 139

page 140

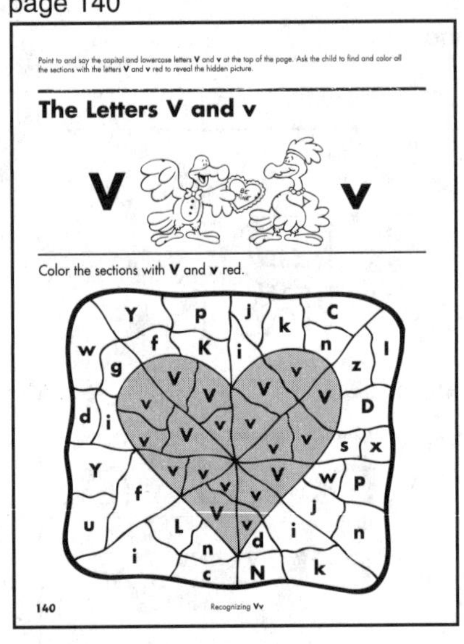

page 141

page 142

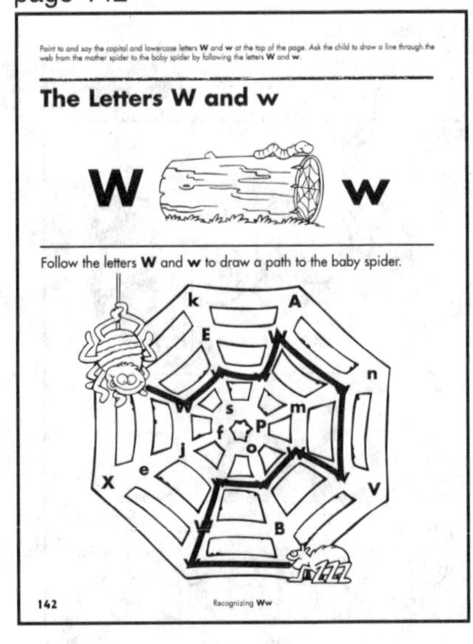

page 143

page 144

page 145

page 146

The Letters Y and y
Circle the letters Y and y.
146
Recognizing Yy

page 147

Writing Yy
Color the letters.
Trace and write the letters.
Recognizing, tracing, and writing Yy
147

page 148

The Letters Z and z
Color the sections with Z and z black.
148
Recognizing Zz

Letters II

page 149

Writing Zz
Color the letters.
Trace and write the letters.
Recognizing, tracing, and writing Zz
149

page 150

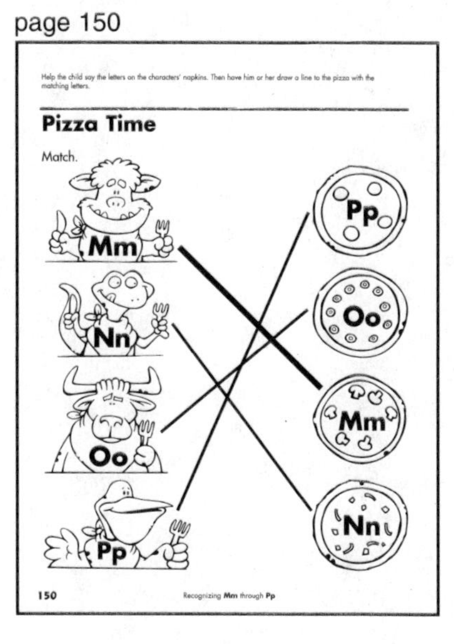
Pizza Time
Match.
Mm
Nn
Oo
Pp
150
Recognizing Mm through Pp

page 151

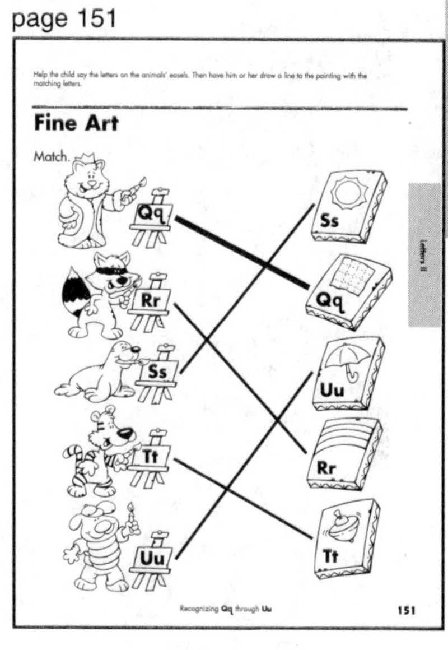
Fine Art
Match.
Qq
Rr
Ss
Tt
Uu
Recognizing Qq through Uu
151

page 152

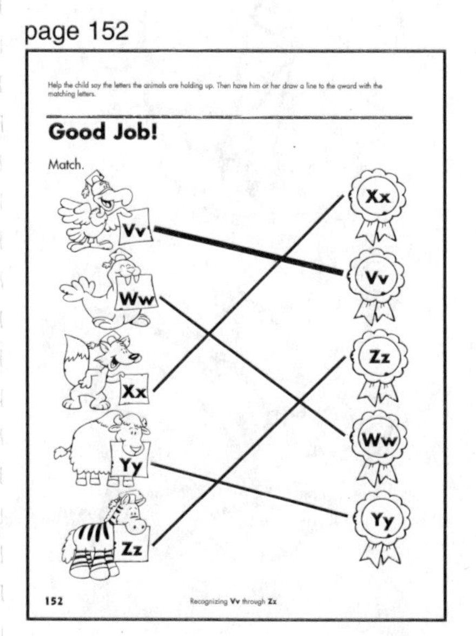
Good Job!
Match.
Vv
Ww
Xx
Yy
Zz
152
Recognizing Vv through Zz

Point to each animal and say its name. Then ask the child to draw a line between the animals that begin with the same sound and color the pictures.

Animal Match

Match. Color the pictures.

Ask the child to say the name of each picture. Then have him or her circle the picture that begins with the same sound as the first picture in each row.

Sounds Like...

Circle the one with the same beginning sound.

Help the child say the name of each picture. Ask him or her to draw a line from the **box** to the other pictures that begin with the same sound. Then have the child do the same for **can** and **pail**.

Put It Away

Draw lines to the ones with the same beginning sounds.

Point to the octopus at the top of the page and say its name. Emphasize the beginning **o** sound. Help the child name the other pictures on the page. Then ask him or her to color the ones with the same beginning sound as **octopus**.

Beginning Sound Oo

Oo

Color the pictures that begin like **octopus**.

Beginning Letter Sounds

Point to the seal at the top of the page and say its name. Emphasize the beginning **s** sound. Help the child name the pictures in the bubbles. Then ask him or her to color the ones with the same beginning sound as **seal**.

Beginning Sound Ss

Color the pictures that begin like **seal**.

Point to the apple at the top of the page and say its name. Emphasize the beginning **a** sound. Help the child name the other pictures on the page. Then ask him or her to color the ones with the same beginning sound as **apple**.

Beginning Sound Aa

Color the pictures that begin like **apple**.

Point to the turtle at the top of the page and say its name. Emphasize the beginning **t** sound. Help the child name the pictures on the turtle's shell. Then ask him or her to color the ones with the same beginning sound as **turtle**.

Beginning Sound Tt

Color the pictures that begin like **turtle**.

Point to the elephant at the top of the page and say its name. Emphasize the beginning **e** sound. Help the child name the other pictures on the page. Then ask him or her to color the ones with the same beginning sound as **elephant**.

Beginning Sound Ee

Color the pictures that begin like **elephant**.

Point to the raccoon at the top of the page and say its name. Emphasize the beginning **r** sound. Help the child name the pictures on the page. Then ask him or her to color the ones in each row with the same beginning sound as **raccoon**.

Beginning Sound Rr

Color the pictures that begin like **raccoon**.

Point to the igloo at the top of the page and say its name. Emphasize the beginning **i** sound. Help the child name the other pictures on the page. Then ask him or her to color the ones with the same beginning sound as **igloo**.

Beginning Sound Ii

Color the pictures that begin like **igloo**.

Point to the nest at the top of the page and say its name. Emphasize the beginning **n** sound. Help the child name the pictures on the page. Then ask him or her to color the ones with the same beginning sound as **nest**.

Beginning Sound Nn

Color the pictures that begin like **nest**.

Point to the umpire at the top of the page and say its name. Emphasize the beginning **u** sound. Help the child name the other pictures on the page. Then ask him or her to circle the ones with the same beginning sound as **umpire**.

Beginning Sound Uu

Circle the pictures that begin like **umpire**.

Point to the lion at the top of the page and say its name. Emphasize the beginning **l** sound. Help the child name the other pictures on the page. Then ask him or her to color the ones with the same beginning sound as **lion**.

Beginning Sound Ll

Color the pictures that begin like **lion**.

Point to the cat at the top of the page and say its name. Emphasize the beginning **c** sound. Help the child name the other pictures on the page. Then ask him or her to color the ones with the same beginning sound as **cat**.

Beginning Sound Cc

Color the pictures that begin like **cat**.

Point to the pig at the top of the page and say its name. Emphasize the beginning **p** sound. Help the child name the other pictures on the page. Then ask him or her to color the ones with the same beginning sound as **pig**.

Beginning Sound Pp

Color the pictures that begin like **pig**.

Point to the monkey at the top of the page and say its name. Emphasize the beginning **m** sound. Help the child name the other pictures on the page. Then ask him or her to color the ones with the same beginning sound as **monkey**.

Beginning Sound Mm

Color the pictures that begin like **monkey**.

Point to the dog at the top of the page and say its name. Emphasize the beginning **d** sound. Help the child name the other pictures on the page. Then ask him or her to color the ones with the same beginning sound as **dog**.

Beginning Sound Dd

Color the pictures that begin like **dog**.

Point to the hippo at the top of the page and say its name. Emphasize the beginning **h** sound. Help the child name the other pictures on the page. Then ask him or her to color the ones with the same beginning sound as **hippo**.

Beginning Sound Hh

Color the pictures that begin like **hippo**.

Point to the bear at the top of the page and say its name. Emphasize the beginning **b** sound. Help the child name the other pictures on the page. Then ask him or her to color the ones with the same beginning sound as **bear**.

Beginning Sound Bb

Color the pictures that begin like **bear**.

Point to the yo-yo at the top of the page and say its name. Emphasize the beginning **y** sound. Help the child name the other pictures on the page. Then ask him or her to circle **yes** if the picture begins like **yo-yo** and **no** if it does not.

Beginning Sound Yy

Circle **yes** if the picture begins like **yo-yo**.
Circle **no** if it does not.

yes **no**

yes **no**

yes **no**

yes **no**

Beginning Letter Sounds

Point to the fox at the top of the page and say its name. Emphasize the beginning **f** sound. Help the child name the pictures in the footprints. Then ask him or her to color the ones with the same beginning sound as **fox**.

Beginning Sound Ff

Color the pictures that begin like **fox**.

Point to the gorilla at the top of the page and say its name. Emphasize the beginning **g** sound. Help the child name the other pictures on the page. Then ask him or her to color the ones with the same beginning sound as **gorilla**.

Beginning Sound Gg

Color the pictures that begin like **gorilla**.

Point to the violin at the top of the page and say its name. Emphasize the beginning **v** sound. Help the child name the other pictures on the page. Then ask him or her to color each section red if the picture has the same beginning sound as **violin**.

Beginning Sound Vv

Color the section red if the word begins like **violin**.

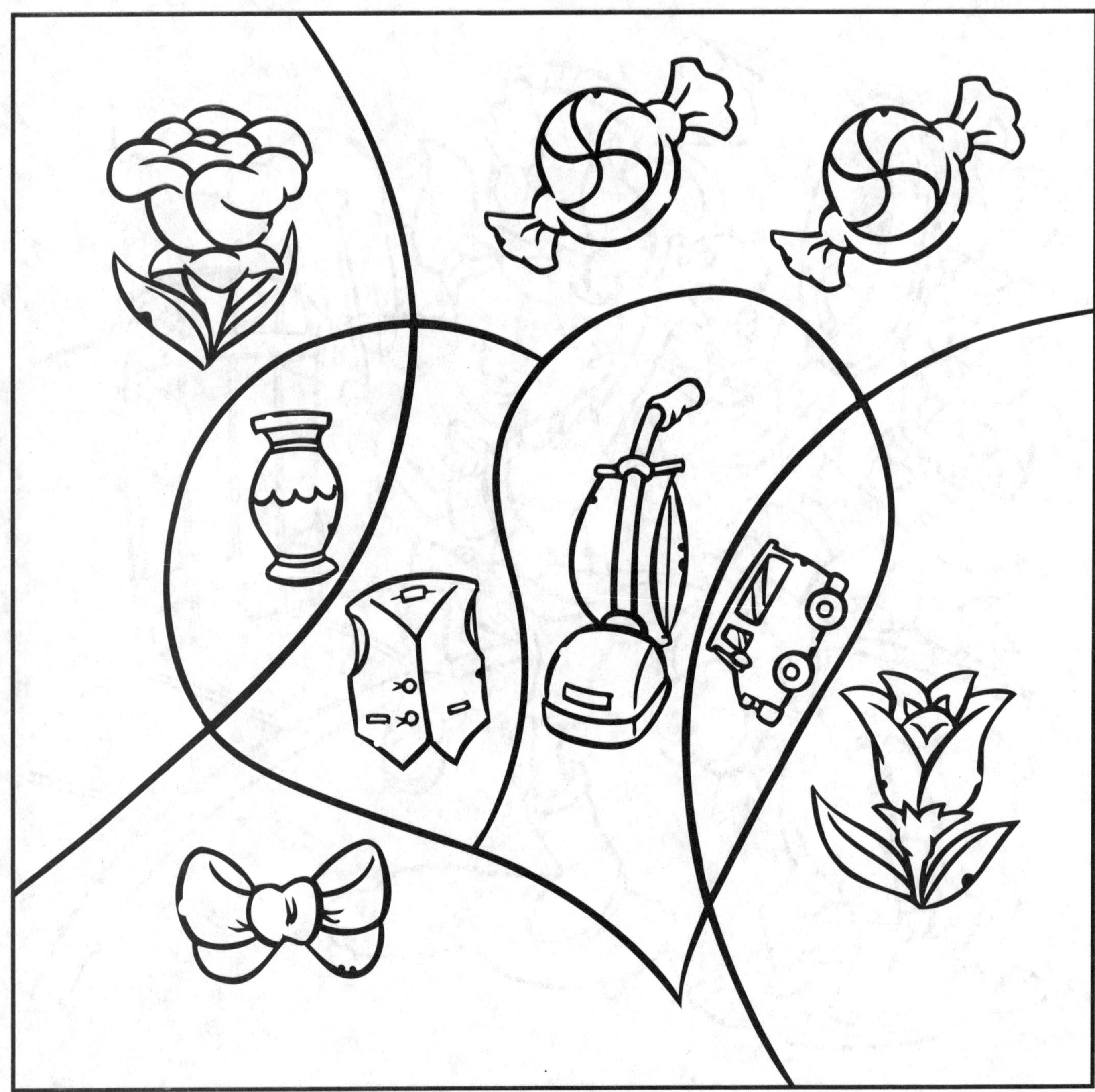

Point to the weasel at the top of the page and say its name. Emphasize the beginning **w** sound. Help the child name the other pictures on the page. Then ask him or her to color the ones with the same beginning sound as **weasel**.

Beginning Sound Ww

Color the pictures that begin like **weasel**.

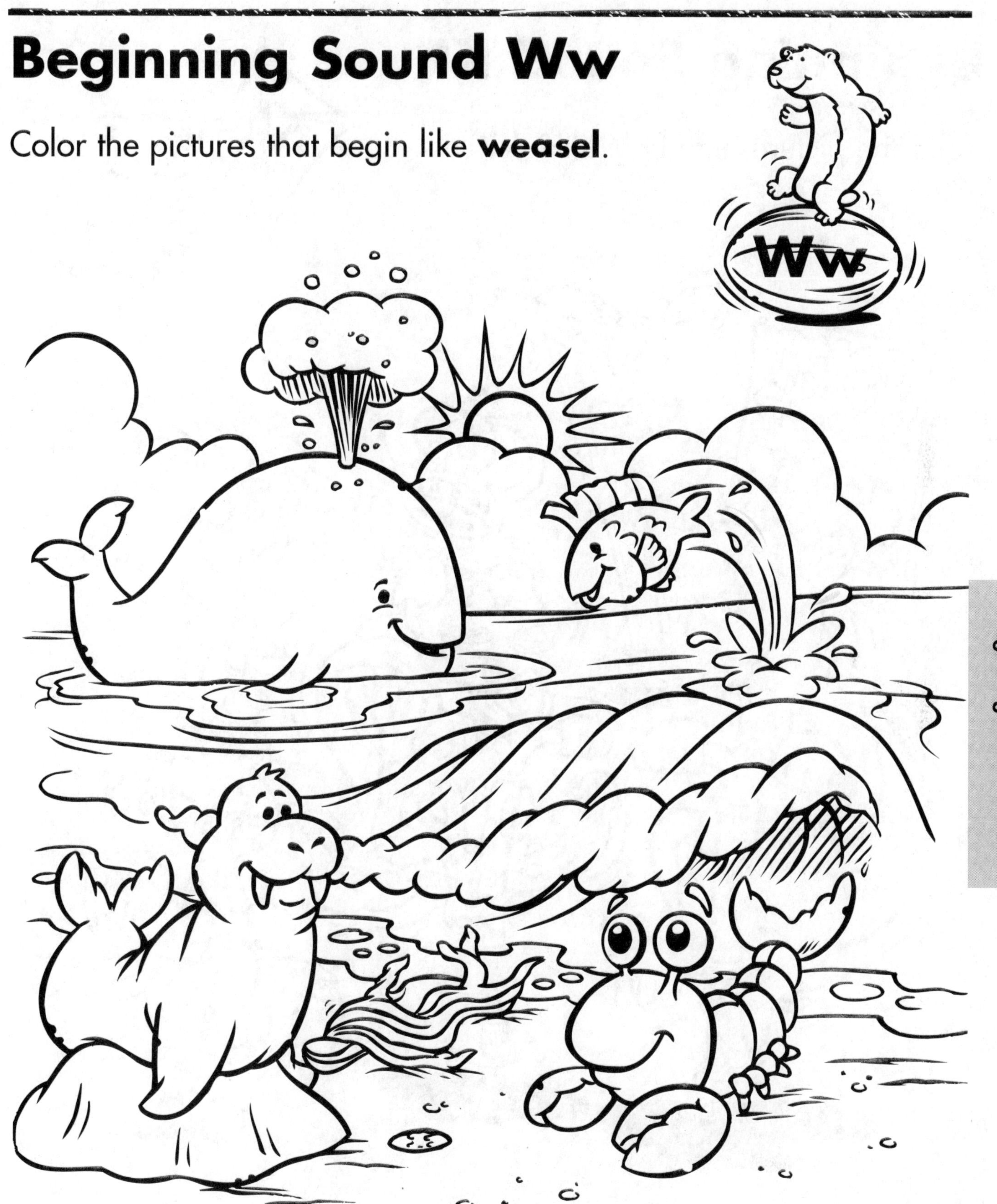

Point to the kite at the top of the page and say its name. Emphasize the beginning **k** sound. Help the child name the other pictures on the page. Then ask him or her to color the ones with the same beginning sound as **kite**.

Beginning Sound Kk

Color the pictures that begin like **kite**.

Point to the zoo at the top of the page and say its name. Emphasize the beginning **z** sound. Help the child name the other pictures on the page. Then ask him or her to color the ones with the same beginning sound as **zoo**.

Beginning Sound Zz

Color the pictures that begin like **zoo**.

Beginning Letter Sounds

Point to the quail at the top of the page and say its name. Emphasize the beginning **q** sound. Help the child name the other pictures on the page. Then ask him or her to color the ones with the same beginning sound as **quail**.

Beginning Sound Qq

Color the pictures that begin like **quail**.

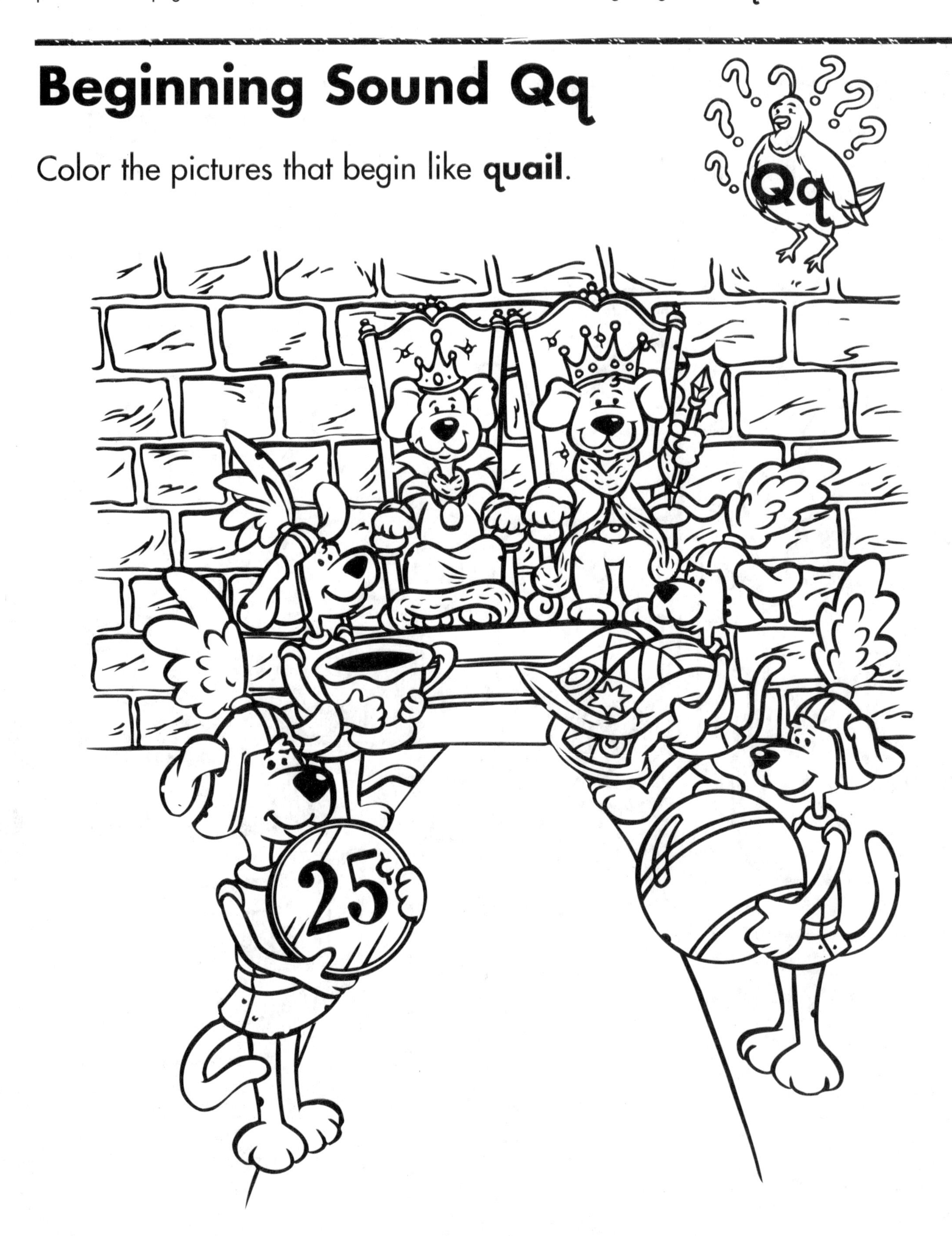

Point to the jack-in-the-box at the top of the page and say its name. Emphasize the beginning **j** sound. Help the child name the other pictures on the page. Then ask him of her to color the ones with the same beginning sound as **jack-in-the-box**.

Beginning Sound Jj

Color the pictures that begin like **jack-in-the-box**.

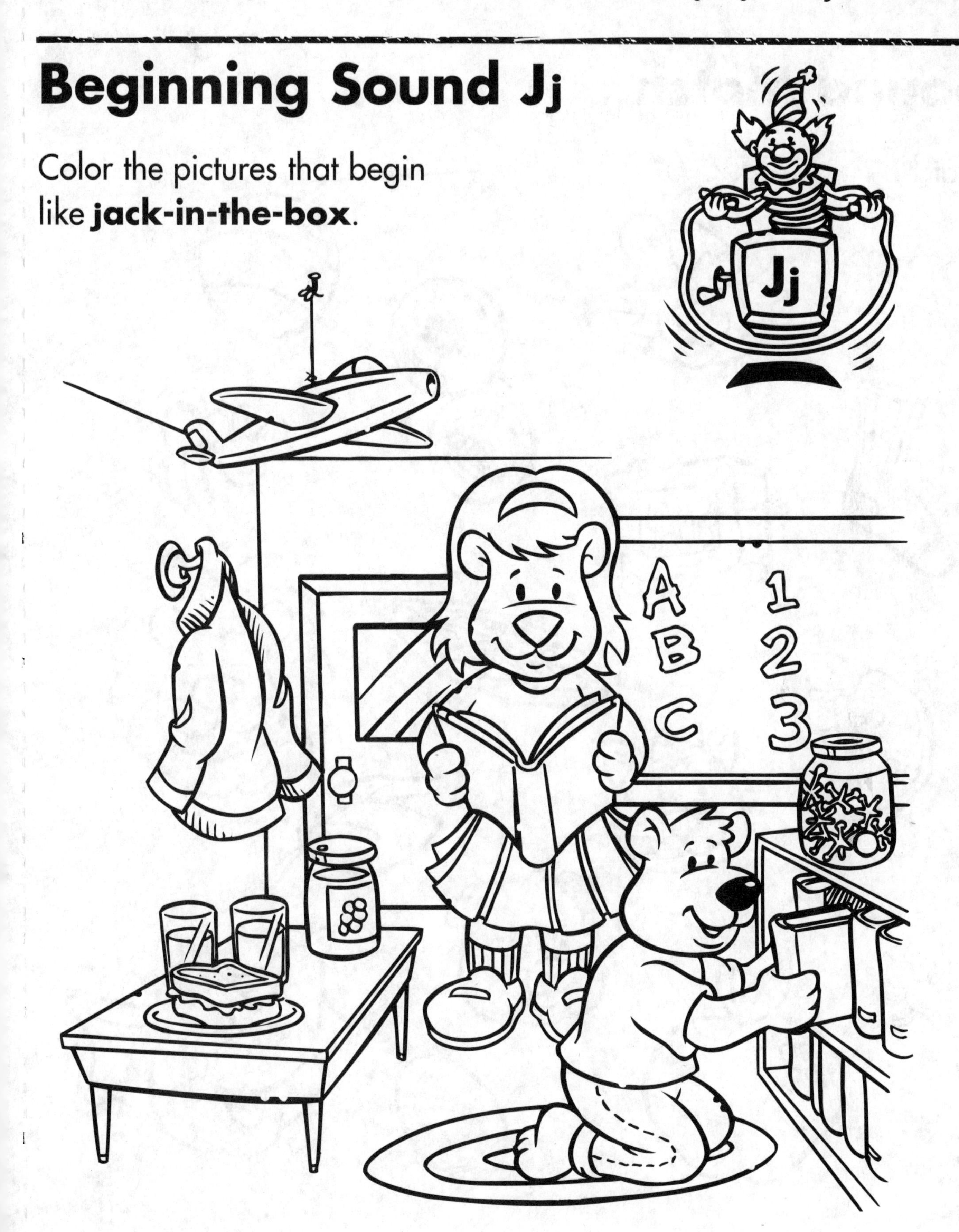

Help the child say the name of each picture. Ask him or her to draw a line between the ones that have the same beginning sound.

Sound Match

Match.

Help the child say the name of each picture. Ask him or her to draw a line between the ones that have the same beginning sound.

More Sound Match

Match.

Answer Key

As the child completes the pages in this section, review his or her answers. When you take the time to correct the work and explain mistakes, you're showing your child that you feel learning is important.

page 164

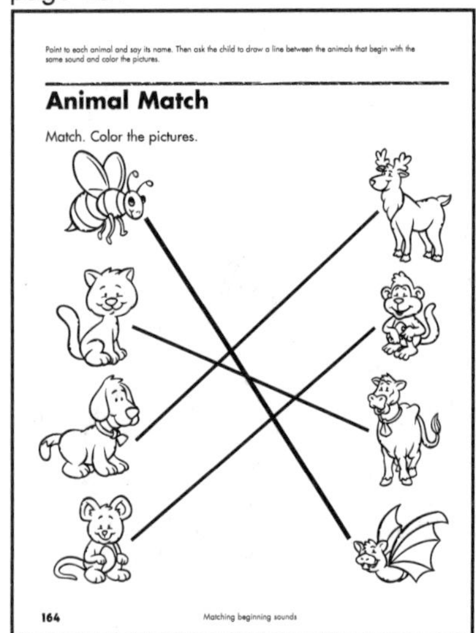
Point to each animal and say its name. Then ask the child to draw a line between the animals that begin with the same sound and color the pictures.

Animal Match

Match. Color the pictures.

164 Matching beginning sounds

page 165

Ask the child to say the name of each picture. Then have him or her circle the picture that begins with the same sound as the first picture in each row.

Sounds Like...

Circle the one with the same beginning sound.

Matching beginning sounds 165

page 166

Help the child say the name of each picture. Ask him or her to draw a line from the **box** to the other pictures that begin with the same sound. Then have the child do the same for **can** and **pail**.

Put It Away

Draw lines to the ones with the same beginning sounds.

166 Identifying beginning consonant sounds

page 167

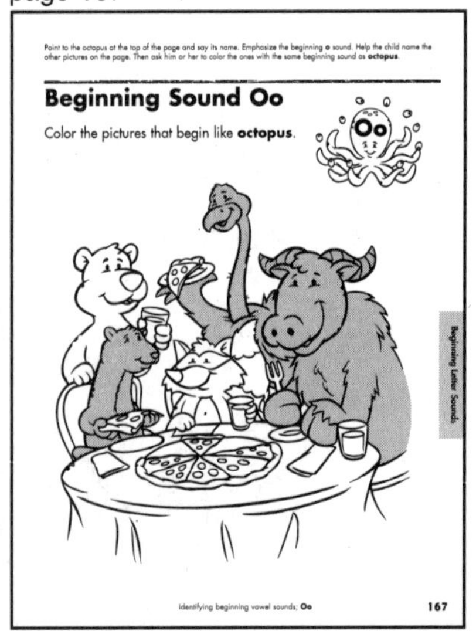
Point to the octopus at the top of the page and say its name. Emphasize the beginning **o** sound. Help the child name the other pictures on the page. Then ask him or her to color the ones with the same beginning sound as **octopus**.

Beginning Sound Oo

Color the pictures that begin like **octopus**.

Identifying beginning vowel sounds; **Oo** 167

page 168

Point to the seal at the top of the page and say its name. Emphasize the beginning **s** sound. Help the child name the pictures in the bubbles. Then ask him or her to color the ones with the same beginning sound as **seal**.

Beginning Sound Ss

Color the pictures that begin like **seal**.

168 Identifying beginning consonant sounds; **Ss**

page 169

Point to the apple at the top of the page and say its name. Emphasize the beginning **a** sound. Help the child name the other pictures on the page. Then ask him or her to color the ones with the same beginning sound as **apple**.

Beginning Sound Aa

Color the pictures that begin like **apple**.

Identifying beginning vowel sounds; **Aa** 169

page 170

Point to the turtle at the top of the page and say its name. Emphasize the beginning **t** sound. Help the child name the pictures on the turtle's shell. Then ask him or her to color the ones with the same beginning sound as **turtle**.

Beginning Sound Tt

Color the pictures that begin like **turtle**.

170 Identifying beginning consonant sounds; **Tt**

page 171

Point to the elephant at the top of the page and say its name. Emphasize the beginning **e** sound. Help the child name the other pictures on the page. Then ask him or her to color the ones with the same beginning sound as **elephant**.

Beginning Sound Ee

Color the pictures that begin like **elephant**.

Identifying beginning vowel sounds; **Ee** 171

page 172

Point to the raccoon at the top of the page and say its name. Emphasize the beginning **r** sound. Help the child name the pictures on the page. Then ask him or her to color the ones in each row with the same beginning sound as **raccoon**.

Beginning Sound Rr

Color the pictures that begin like **raccoon**.

172 Identifying beginning consonant sounds; **Rr**

page 173

Point to the igloo at the top of the page and say its name. Emphasize the beginning i sound. Help the child name the other pictures on the page. Then ask him or her to color the ones with the same beginning sound as **igloo**.

Beginning Sound Ii

Color the pictures that begin like **igloo**.

Identifying beginning vowel sounds; Ii 173

page 174

Point to the nest at the top of the page and say its name. Emphasize the beginning n sound. Help the child name the other pictures on the page. Then ask him or her to color the ones with the same beginning sound as **nest**.

Beginning Sound Nn

Color the pictures that begin like **nest**.

174 Identifying beginning consonant sounds; Nn

page 175

Point to the umpire at the top of the page and say its name. Emphasize the beginning u sound. Help the child name the other pictures on the page. Then ask him or her to circle the ones with the same beginning sound as **umpire**.

Beginning Sound Uu

Circle the pictures that begin like **umpire**.

Identifying beginning vowel sounds; Uu 175

page 176

Point to the lion at the top of the page and say its name. Emphasize the beginning l sound. Help the child name the other pictures on the page. Then ask him or her to color the ones with the same beginning sound as **lion**.

Beginning Sound Ll

Color the pictures that begin like **lion**.

176 Identifying beginning consonant sounds; Ll

page 177

Point to the cat at the top of the page and say its name. Emphasize the beginning c sound. Help the child name the other pictures on the page. Then ask him or her to color the ones with the same beginning sound as **cat**.

Beginning Sound Cc

Color the pictures that begin like **cat**.

Identifying beginning consonant sounds; Cc 177

page 178

Point to the pig at the top of the page and say its name. Emphasize the beginning p sound. Help the child name the other pictures on the page. Then ask him or her to color the ones with the same beginning sound as **pig**.

Beginning Sound Pp

Color the pictures that begin like **pig**.

178 Identifying beginning consonant sounds; Pp

page 179

Point to the monkey at the top of the page and say its name. Emphasize the beginning m sound. Help the child name the other pictures on the page. Then ask him or her to color the ones with the same beginning sound as **monkey**.

Beginning Sound Mm

Color the pictures that begin like **monkey**.

Identifying beginning consonant sounds; Mm 179

page 180

Point to the dog at the top of the page and say its name. Emphasize the beginning d sound. Help the child name the other pictures on the page. Then ask him or her to color the ones with the same beginning sound as **dog**.

Beginning Sound Dd

Color the pictures that begin like **dog**.

180 Identifying beginning consonant sounds; Dd

page 181

Point to the hippo at the top of the page and say its name. Emphasize the beginning h sound. Help the child name the other pictures on the page. Then ask him or her to color the ones with the same beginning sound as **hippo**.

Beginning Sound Hh

Color the pictures that begin like **hippo**.

Identifying beginning consonant sounds; Hh 181

page 182

page 183

page 184

page 185

page 186

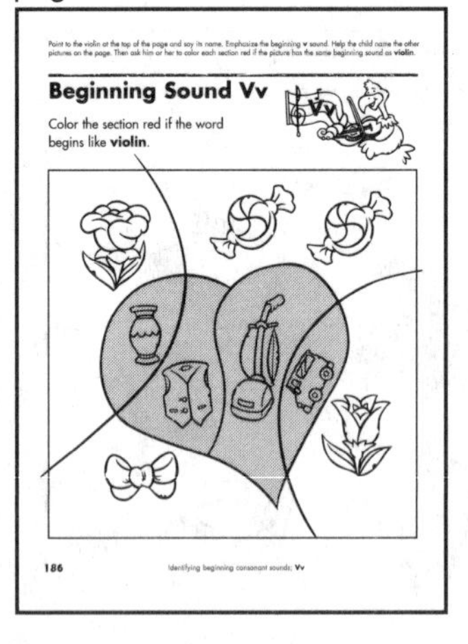

page 187

page 188

page 189

page 190

page 191

page 192

page 193

Ask the child to name each animal. Then have him or her draw a line between the animals that are the same.

Animal Crackers

Match.

Get Ready to Read

Have the child find and color the two animals that are the same in each row.

Look in the Forest

Color the ones that are the same.

Have the child circle the toys that are the same in each group.

At the Toy Store

Circle the ones that are the same.

Ask the child to look closely at the first picture in each row. Then have him or her find and circle the picture that is the same in that row.

Rolling Along

Circle the one that is the same.

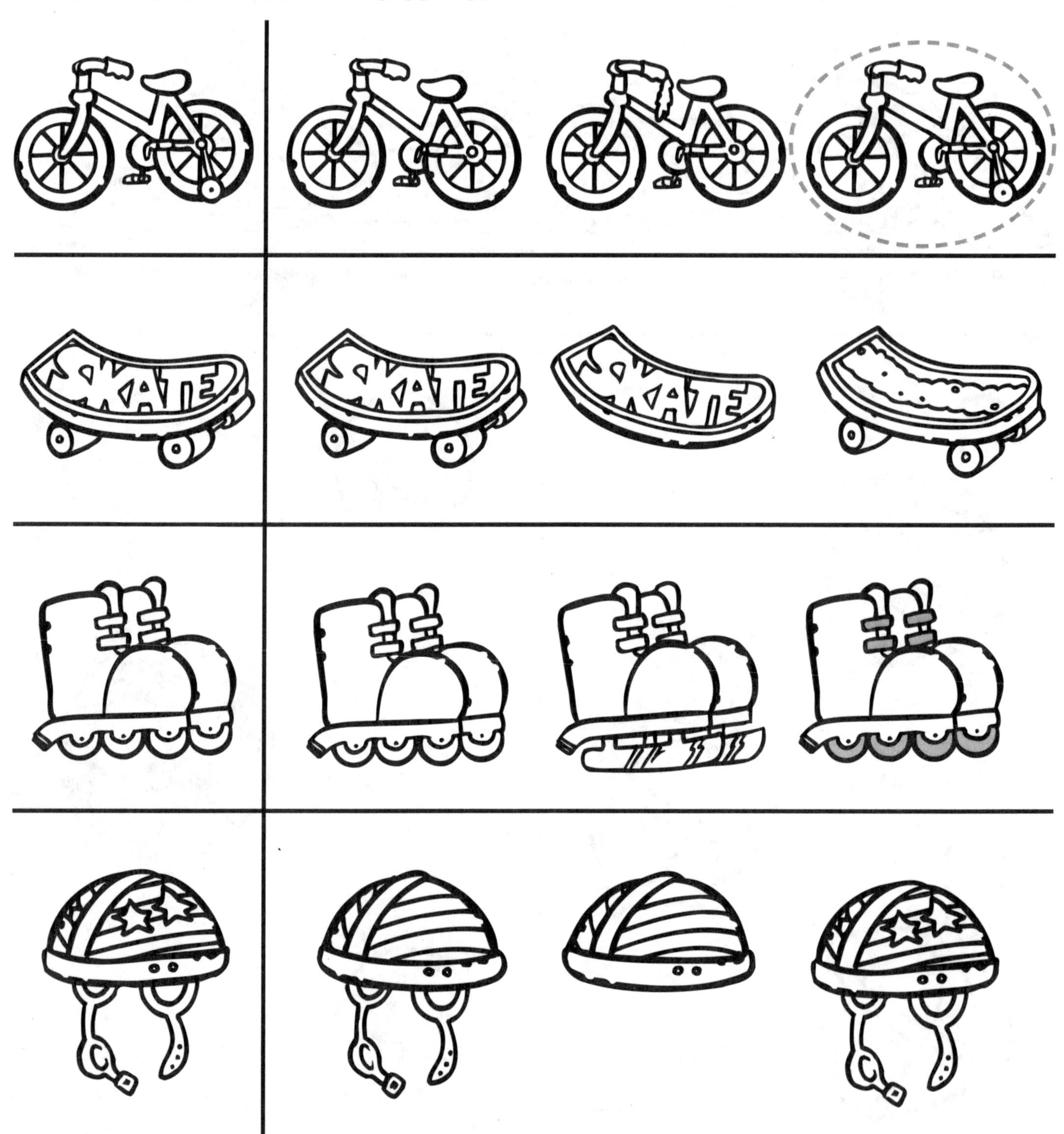

Ask the child to identify the objects. Then have him or her find and color the one that is different in each group.

Fun at the Beach

Color the one that is different.

Ask the child to identify the animals. Then have him or her find and color the one that is different in each group.

Come to the Circus

Color the one that is different.

Ask the child to look closely at the first picture in each row. Then have him or her find and circle the picture that is different in that row.

More Circus Fun

Circle the one that is different.

Get Ready to Read

Help the child identify the objects. Then have him or her find and circle the one that is different in each row.

Time to Plant

Circle the one that is different.

Ask the child to identify the sweet treats. Then have him or her find and circle the one that is different in each row.

Sweet Treats

Circle the one that is different.

Ask the child find and circle the two animals that face the same direction in each row. Then have him or her color them.

Turn-Around on Ice

Circle the ones that face the same way. Color them.

Ask the child find and circle the two insects that face the same direction in each row. Then have him or her color them.

Bugging Out

Circle the ones that face the same way. Color them.

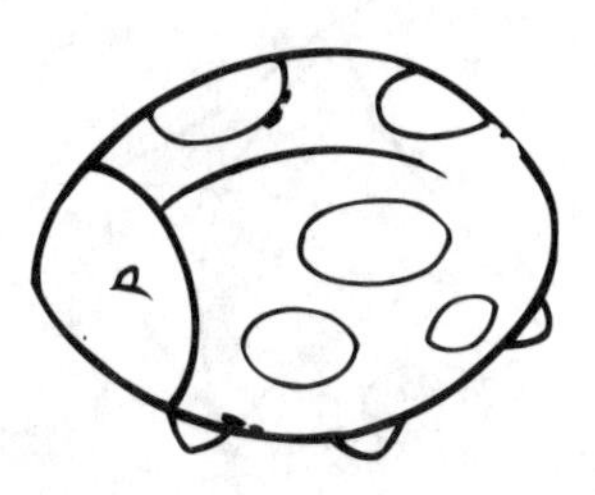 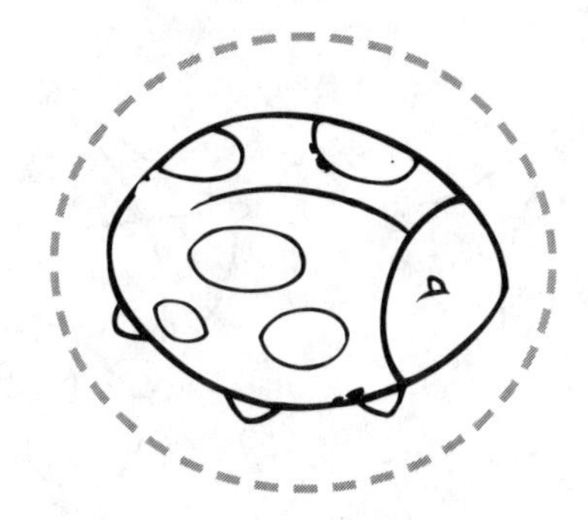 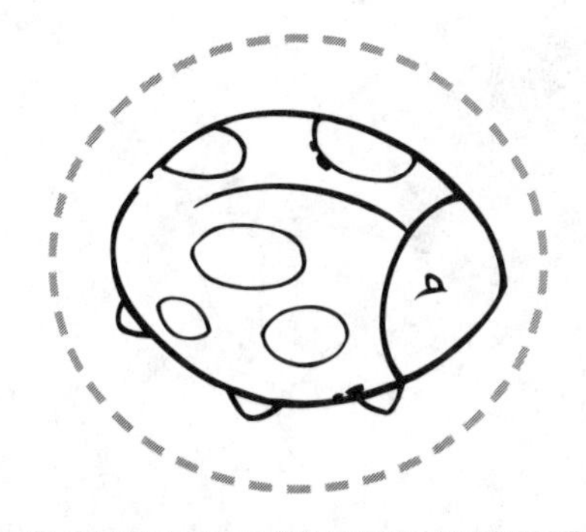

  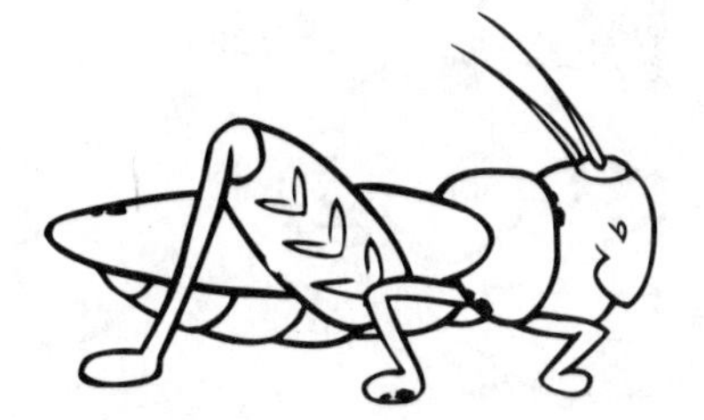

Ask the child to identify these things that fly. Then have him or her find and color the one that faces a different direction in each row.

High in the Sky

Color the one that faces a different way.

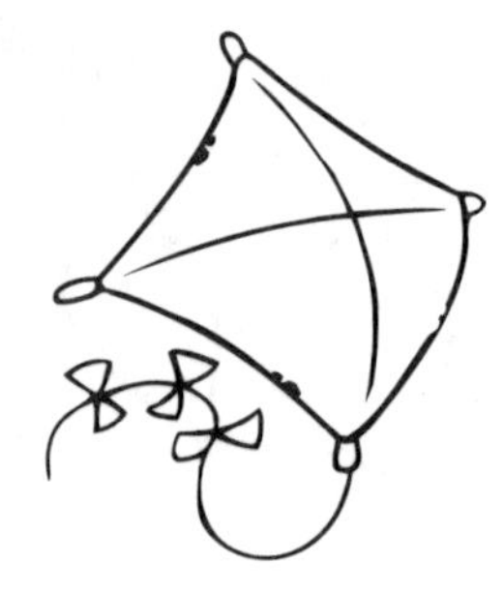 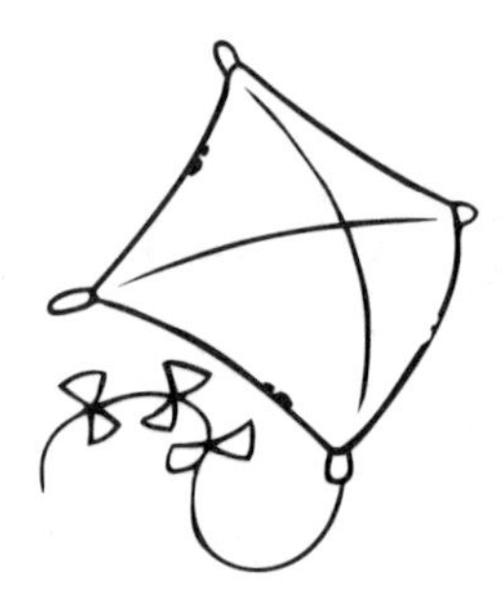 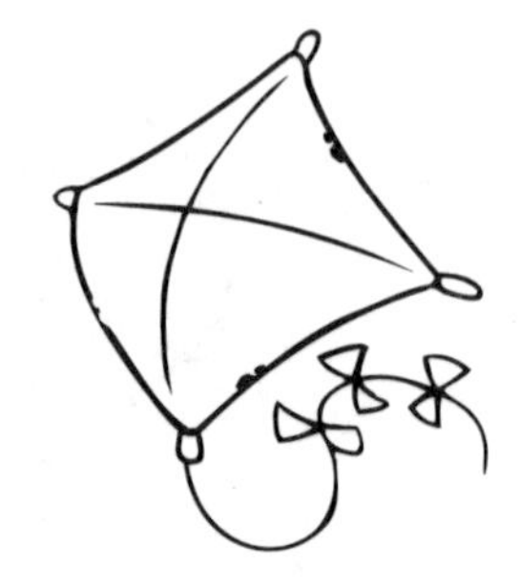 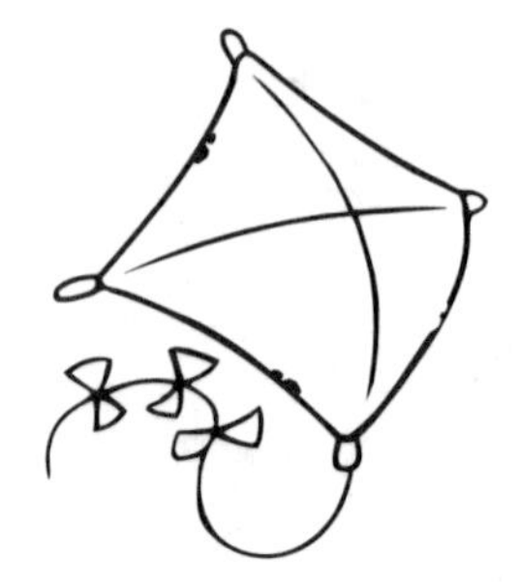

  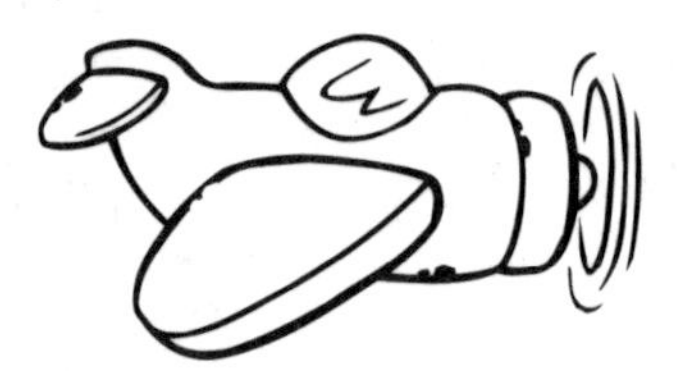 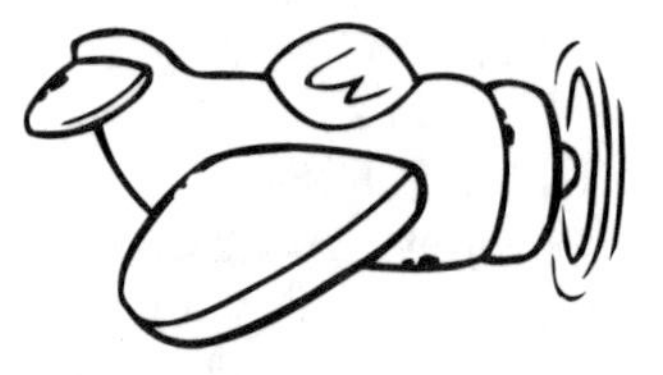

Recognizing differences in direction

Have the child find and color the sea creature that faces a different direction in each row.

Under the Sea

Color the one that faces a different way.

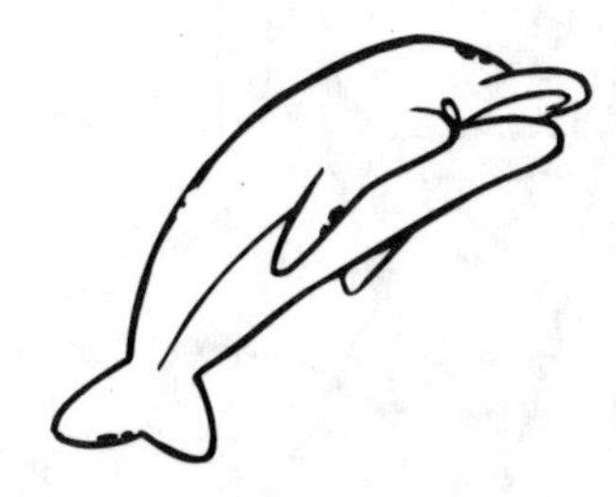

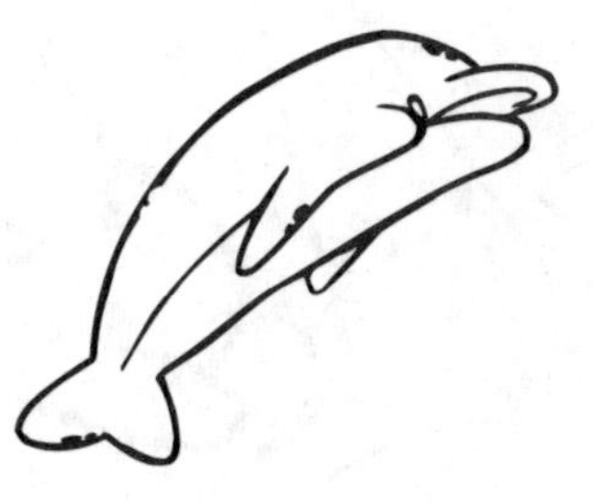

Ask the child to look closely at the picture. Then have him or her find and color four bats.

Going Batty

Color four s.

Ask the child to look closely at the picture. Then have him or her find and color four frogs.

Finding Frogs

Color four  s.

Get Ready to Read

Ask the child to look closely at the picture. Then have him or her find and color five teacups.

Tea for Two

Color five s.

Ask the child to look closely at the picture. Then have him or her find and color five baseball bats.

Batter Up!

Color five 🏏s.

Get Ready to Read

Help the child name each picture on this page. Have him or her color them. Then ask the child to find and color each one in the picture on page 215.

Nursery Rhyme Pictures

Color the pictures. Find and color them on the next page.

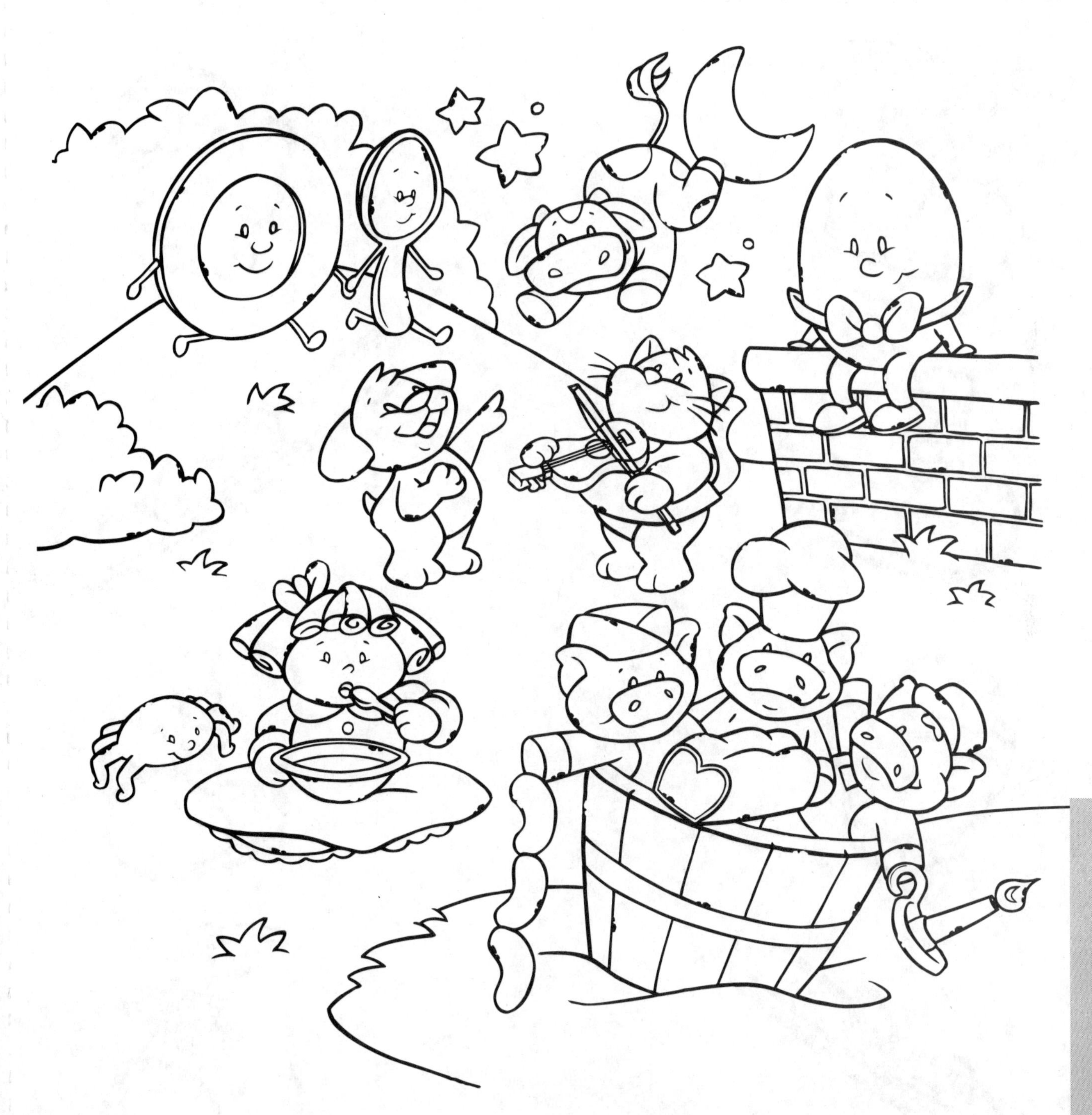

Have the child draw a line between the objects that go together. Then have him or her color the pictures.

Winter Fun

Match. Color the pictures.

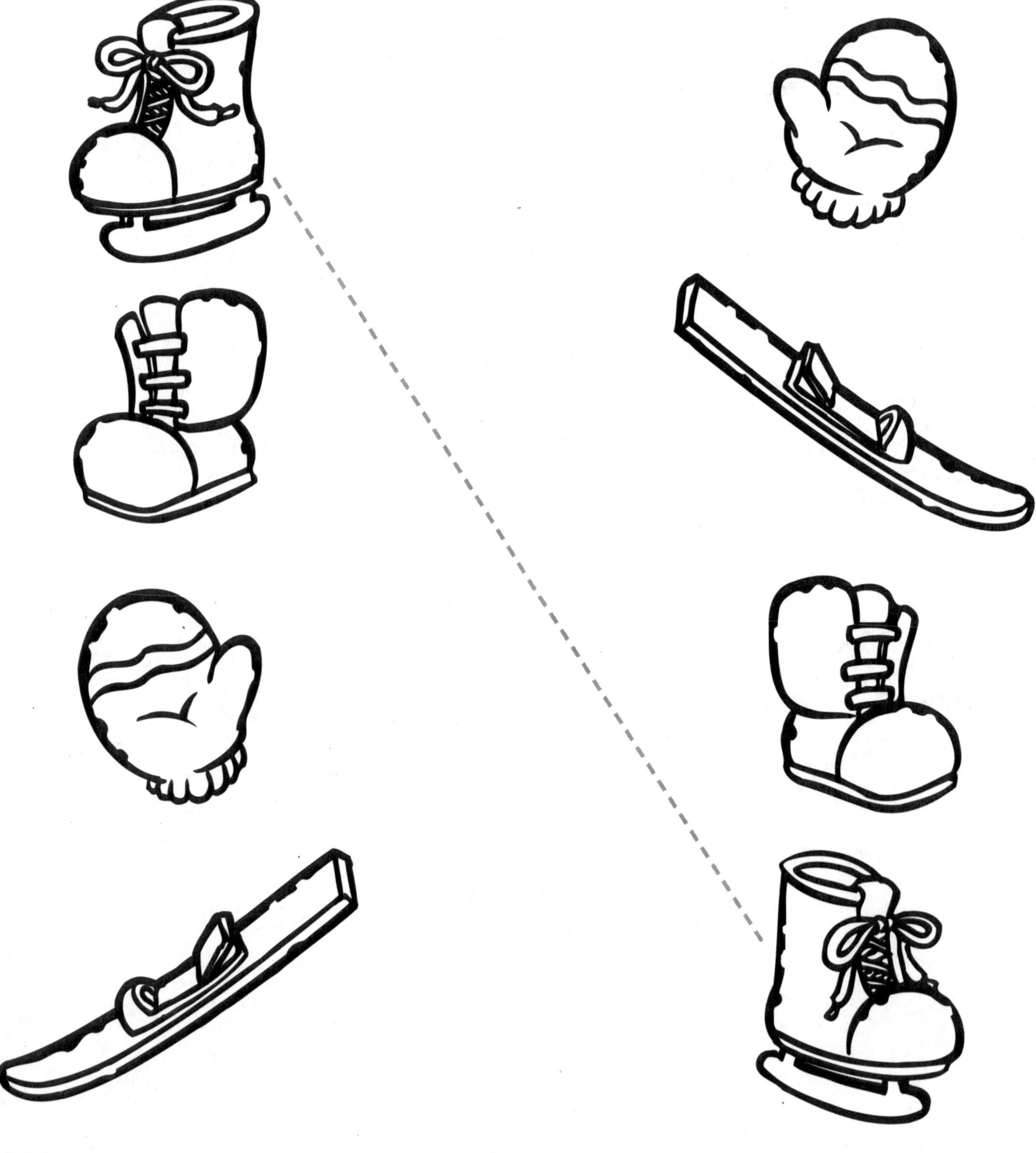

Help the child name the objects in each group on the right and talk about how they are alike. Then help the child identify each object on the left and have him or her draw a line to the group where it belongs.

Which Group?

Match.

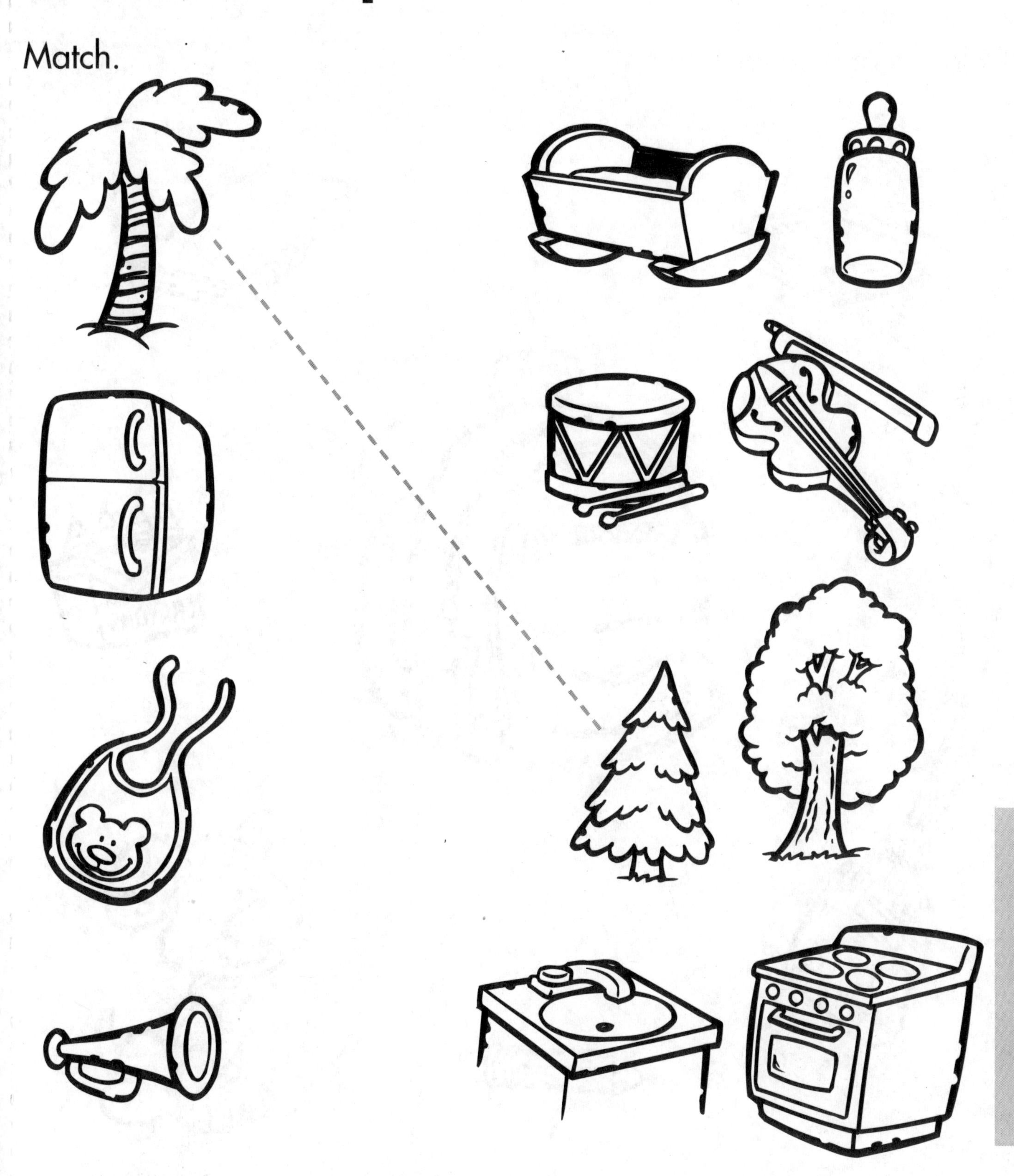

Get Ready to Read

Help the child name the objects. Then have him or her color the ones that belong in the backpack.

Get Ready for School

Color what belongs in the .

Classifying objects; identifying what belongs in a group

Help the child name the objects. Then have him or her color the ones that belong at the playground.

At the Playground

Color what belongs at the playground.

Ask the child to talk about the grocery store and help him or her name the objects. Then have the child circle the objects that do not belong in the grocery store.

The Grocery Store

Circle what does not belong.

Classifying objects; recognizing objects that do not belong

Ask the child to name the pictures. Then have him or her color the one that does not belong in each row.

What Doesn't Belong?

Color what does not belong.

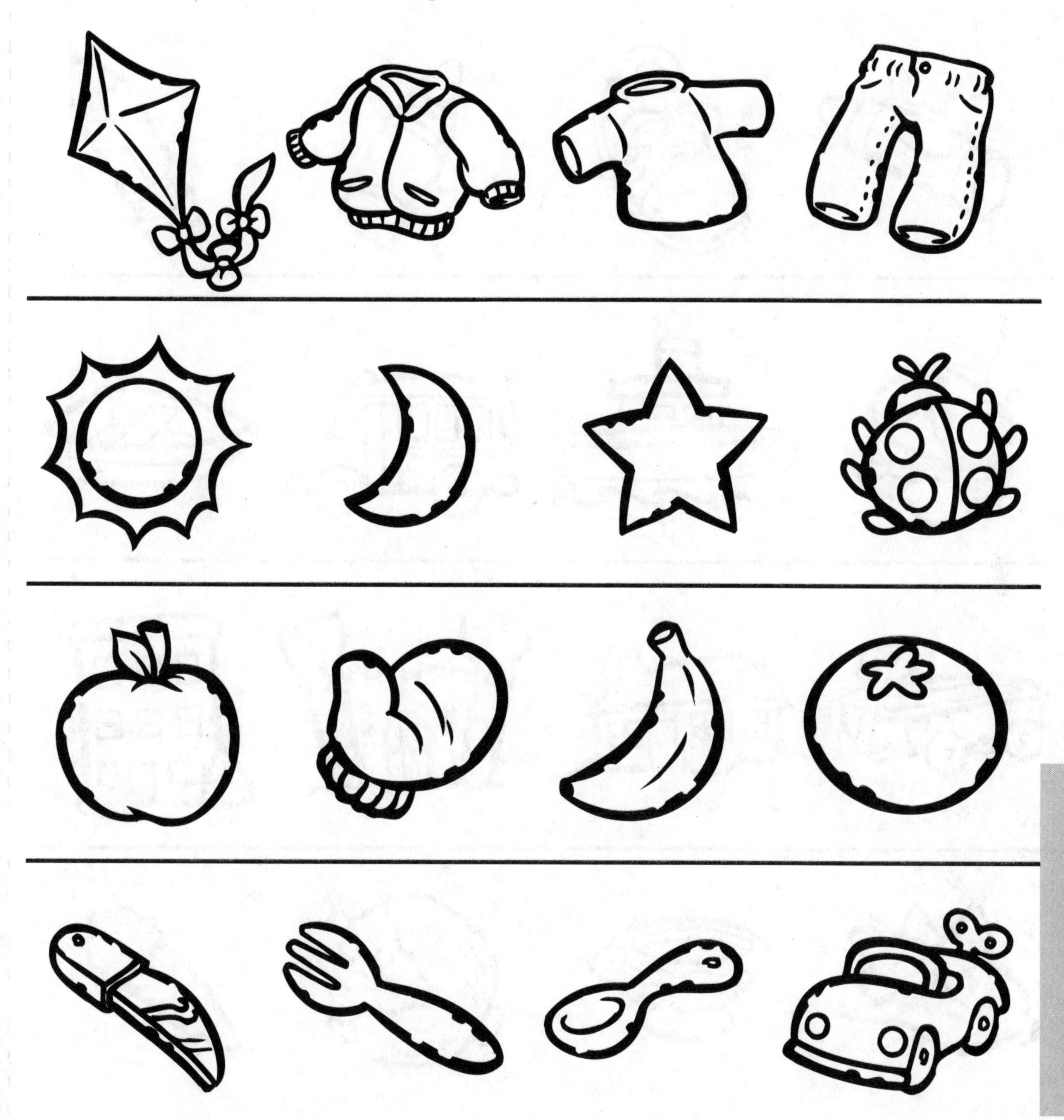

Get Ready to Read

Ask the child to name the objects. Have him or her circle the one that does not belong in each row. Then have the child color the others.

Does It Belong?

Circle what does not belong. Color the others.

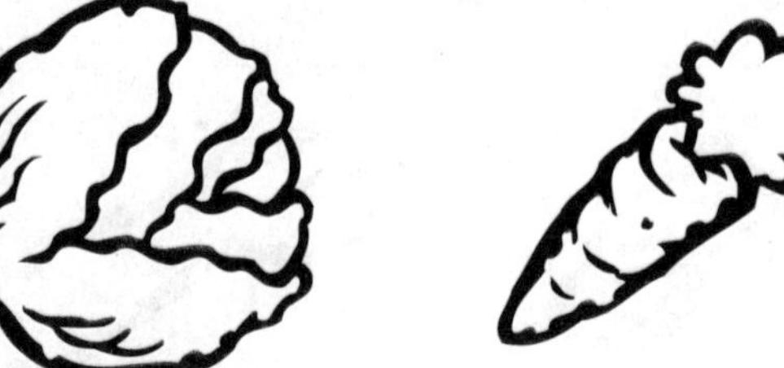

Ask the child to look closely at the first picture in each row. Then have him or her find and circle the picture that goes with it.

We Go Together

Circle what belongs.

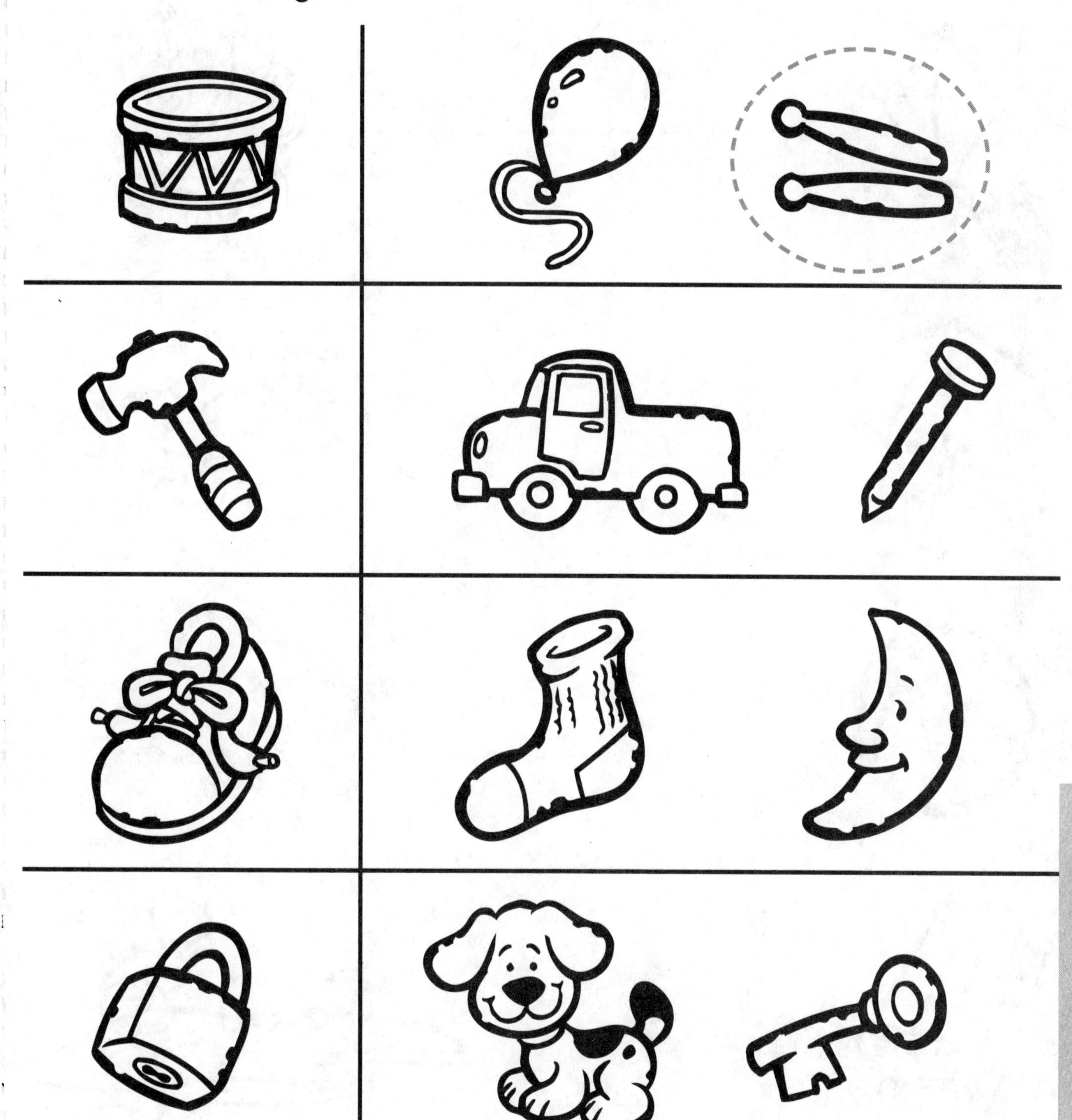

Help the child name the objects on the left and the type of weather in each picture on the right. Then have him or her draw a line between the ones that go together.

Weather Go-Togethers

Match.

Ask the child to name the pictures. Then have him or her color the two that go together in each row.

More Go-Togethers

Color the ones that go together.

Get Ready to Read

Answer Key

As the child completes the pages in this section, review his or her answers. When you take the time to correct the work and explain mistakes, you're showing your child that you feel learning is important.

page 197

page 198

page 199

page 200

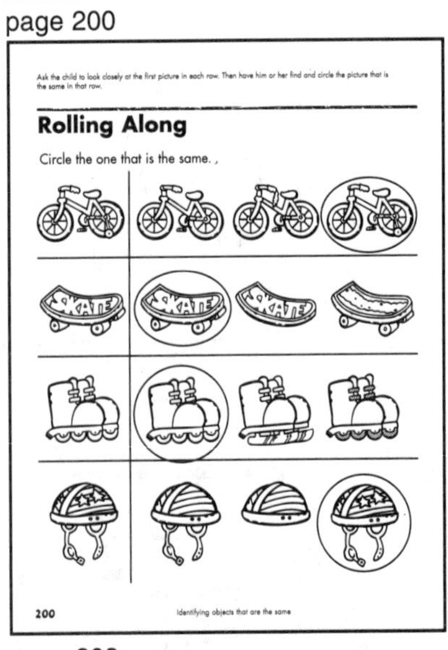

page 201

page 202

page 203

page 204

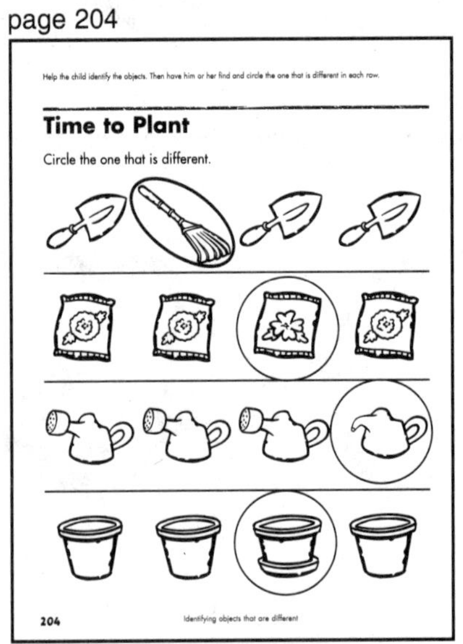

page 205

page 206

Ask the child find and circle the two animals that face the same direction in each row. Then have him or her color them.

Turn-Around on Ice

Circle the ones that face the same way. Color them.

206 Recognizing differences in direction

page 207

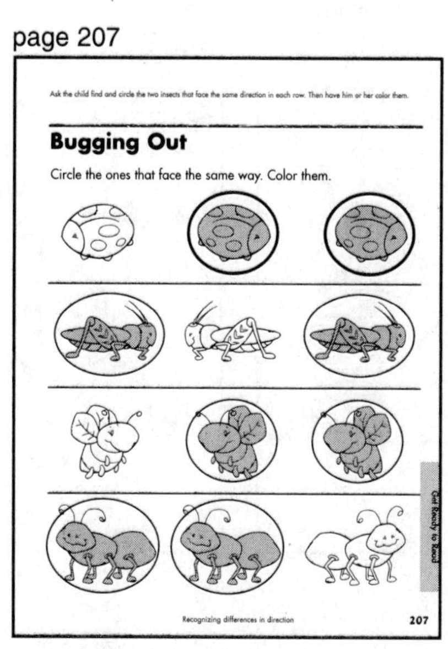
Ask the child find and circle the two insects that face the same direction in each row. Then have him or her color them.

Bugging Out

Circle the ones that face the same way. Color them.

Recognizing differences in direction 207

page 208

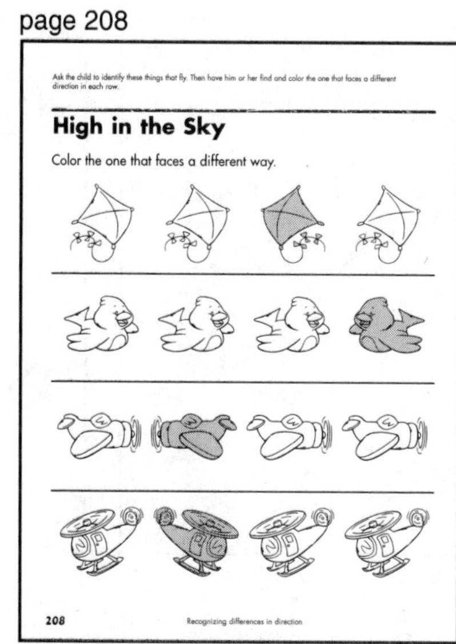
Ask the child to identify these things that fly. Then have him or her find and color the one that faces a different direction in each row.

High in the Sky

Color the one that faces a different way.

208 Recognizing differences in direction

page 209

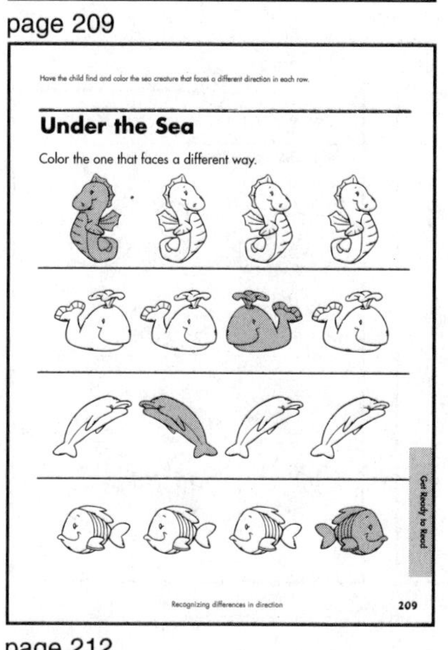
Have the child find and color the sea creature that faces a different direction in each row.

Under the Sea

Color the one that faces a different way.

Recognizing differences in direction 209

page 210

Ask the child to look closely at the picture. Then have him or her find and color four bats.

Going Batty

Color four s.

210 Finding objects in a picture (visual discrimination)

page 211

Ask the child to look closely at the picture. Then have him or her find and color four frogs.

Finding Frogs

Color four s.

Finding objects in a picture (visual discrimination) 211

page 212

Ask the child to look closely at the picture. Then have him or her find and color five teacups.

Tea for Two

Color five s.

212 Finding objects in a picture (visual discrimination)

page 213

Ask the child to look closely at the picture. Then have him or her find and color five baseball bats.

Batter Up!

Color five s.

Finding objects in a picture (visual discrimination) 213

page 215

Finding objects in a picture (visual discrimination) 215

page 216

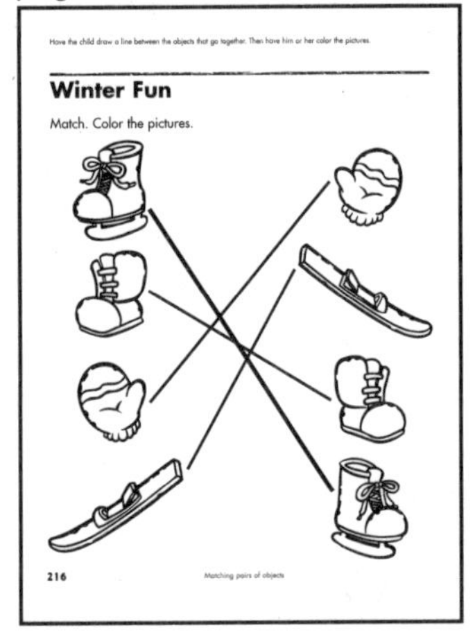
Winter Fun
Match. Color the pictures.

page 217

Which Group?
Match.

page 218

Get Ready for School
Color what belongs in the
CRAYONS

page 219

At the Playground
Color what belongs at the playground.

page 220

The Grocery Store
Circle what does not belong.
MILK
ICE CREAM

page 221

What Doesn't Belong?
Color what does not belong.

page 222

Does It Belong?
Circle what does not belong. Color the others.

page 223

We Go Together
Circle what belongs.

page 224

Weather Go-Togethers
Match.

page 225

More Go-Togethers
Color the ones that go together.

Ask the child to use his or her finger to trace the line from each frog on the left to the lily pad on the right. Then have him or her use a crayon to trace the lines.

Left to Right Frogs

Trace each line from the  to the .

Ask the child to use his or her finger to trace the line from each kitten on the left to the pair of mittens on the right. Then have him or her use a crayon to trace the lines.

Left to Right Kittens

Trace each line from the [kitten] to the [mittens].

Ask the child to use his or her finger to trace the line from each magician on the left to the hat on the right. Then have him or her use a crayon to trace the lines.

Left to Right Magicians

Trace each line from the  to the .

Ask the child to use his or her finger to trace the line from the top of each pole to the bottom. Then have him or her use a crayon to trace the lines.

Top to Bottom Basketball

Trace each line from the **top** to the **bottom**.

Ask the child to use his or her finger to trace the line from the top of each beanstalk to the bottom. Then have him or her use a crayon to trace the lines.

Top to Bottom Beanstalks

Trace each line from the **top** to the **bottom**.

Ask the child to use his or her finger to trace the line across each hotdog from the left to the right. Then have him or her use a red crayon (for ketchup) or a yellow crayon (for mustard) to trace the lines.

Slanted Hotdogs

Trace the line on each .

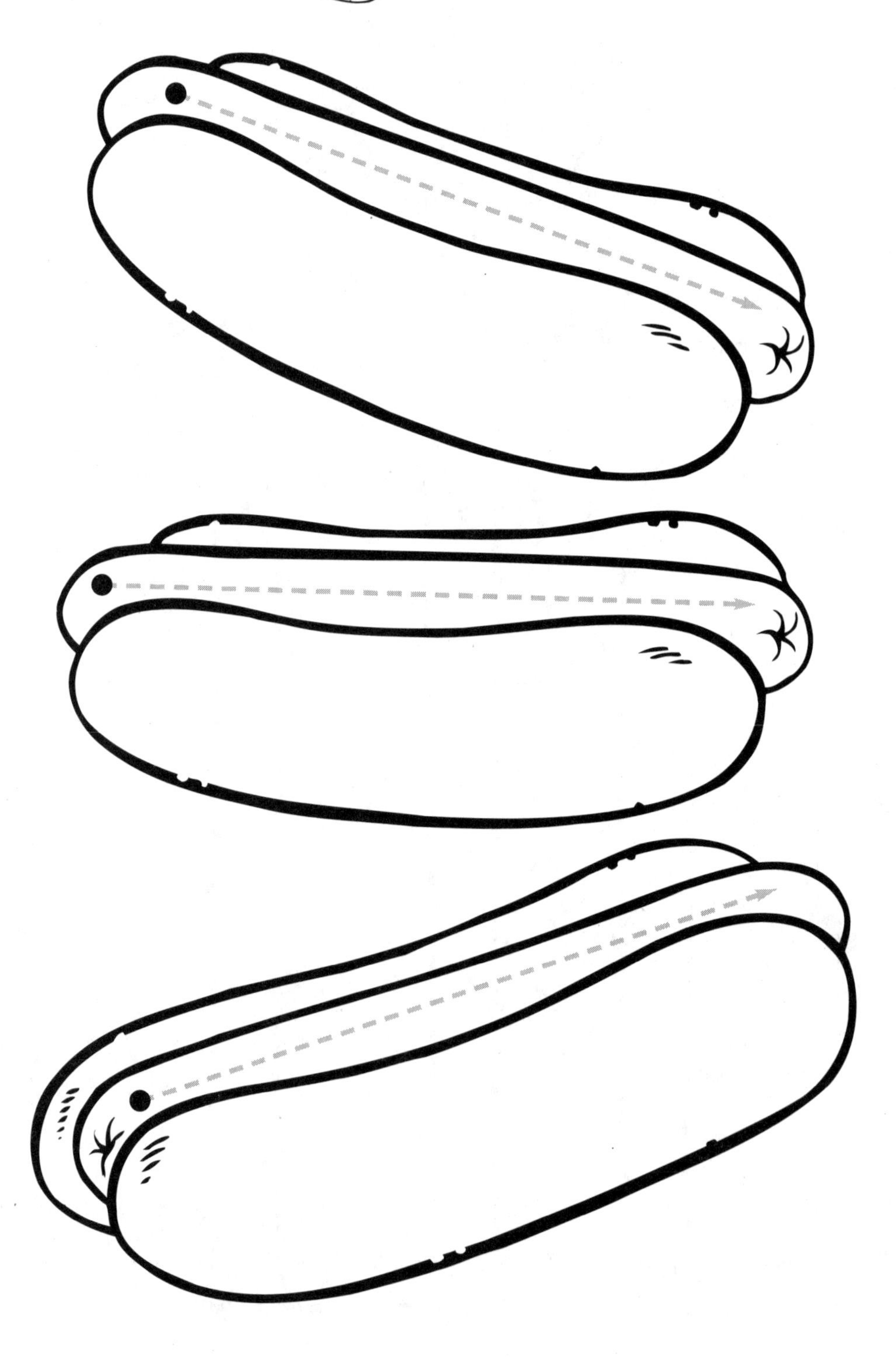

Ask the child to use his or her finger to trace each curved line over the candlestick. Then have him or her use a crayon to trace the lines.

Curved Jumps

Trace each line over the .

Ask the child to use his or her finger to trace the line from each Mother Hubbard on the left to the cupboard on the right. Then have him or her use a crayon to trace the lines.

Paths for Mother Hubbard

Trace each line from the [Mother Hubbard] to the [cupboard].

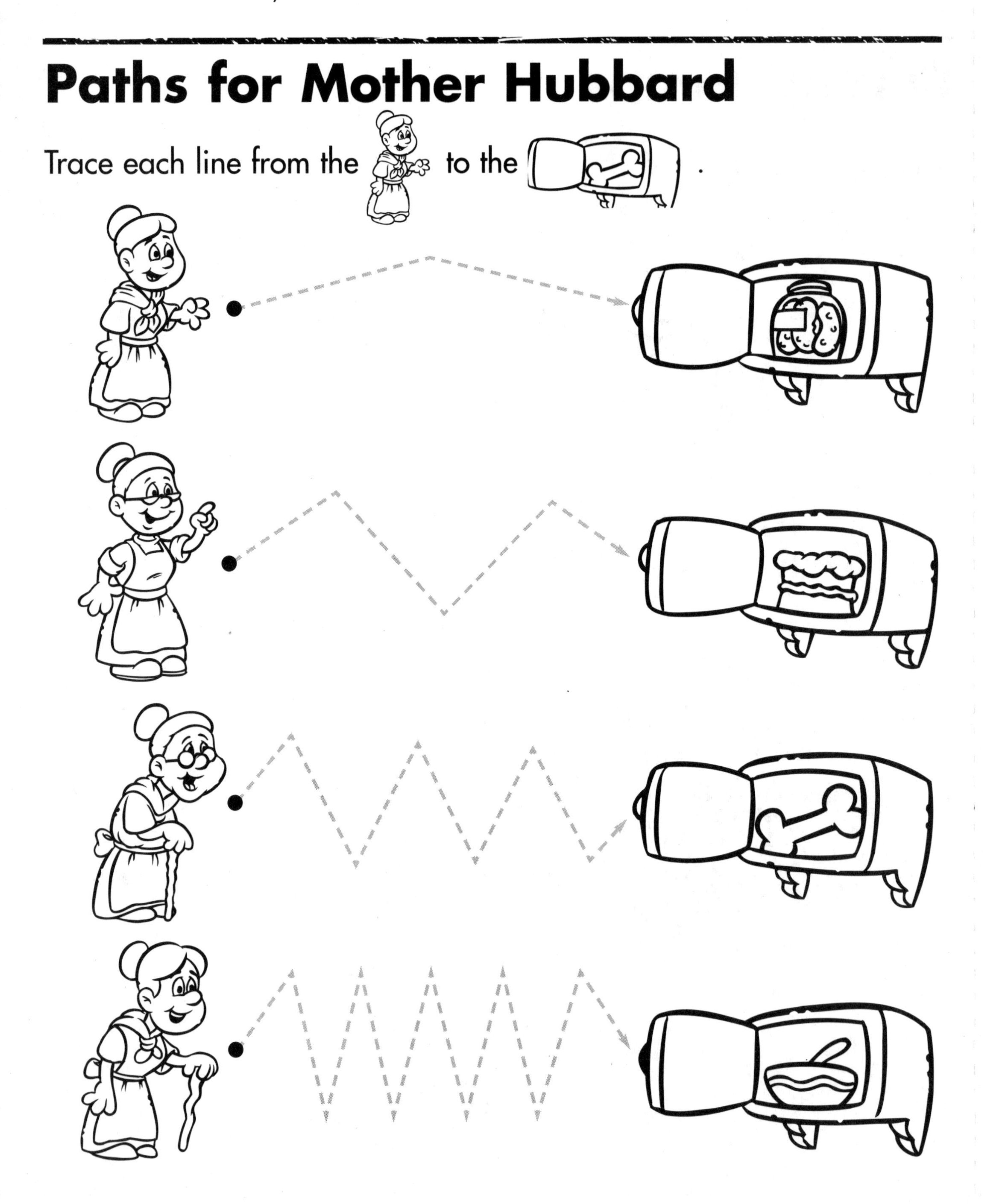

Ask the child to use his or her finger to trace the line from each pig on the left to the picture on the right. Then have him or her use a crayon to trace the lines.

Paths for Little Piggies

Trace each 's path.

Ask the child to use his or her finger to trace the line from each baby animal on the left to its mother on the right. Then have him or her use a crayon to trace the lines.

Paths for Baby Animals

Trace each path.

Ask the child to use his or her finger to trace the dashed lines on the ice cream cone. Have him or her use a crayon to trace the lines. Then ask the child to color the pcture.

Trace a Treat

Trace the lines. Color the picture.

Ask the child to use his or her finger to trace the dashed lines on the boat. Have him or her use a crayon to trace the lines. Then ask the child to color the picture.

Trace a Boat

Trace the lines. Color the picture.

Ask the child to use his or her finger to trace the dashed lines on the monkey. Have him or her use a crayon to trace the lines. Then ask the child to color the picture.

Trace a Funny Face

Trace the lines. Color the picture.

Ask the child to use his or her finger to trace the dashed lines on the valentine. Have him or her use a crayon to trace the lines. Then ask the child to color the picture.

Trace a Valentine

Trace the lines. Color the picture.

Ask the child to use his or her finger to follow the path from the mouse to the cheese. Then have him or her use a pencil or crayon to draw the path.

Hickory Dickory Dock

Draw the path to the cheese.

Ask the child to use his or her finger to follow the path from the dish to the spoon. Then have him or her use a pencil or crayon to draw the path.

Hey Diddle Diddle

Draw the path to the spoon.

Developing fine motor control; drawing a path to complete a maze

Ask the child to use his or her finger to follow the path from the racecar to the finish line. Then have him or her use a pencil or crayon to draw the path.

Race to the Finish

Draw the path to the finish line.

Ask the child to use his or her finger to follow the path of logs from the beaver to the dam. Then have him or her use a pencil or crayon to draw the path.

River Crossing

Draw the path to the dam.

Developing fine motor control; drawing a path to complete a maze

Ask the child to use his or her finger to follow the path of carrots from the mother rabbit to the baby bunny. Then have him or her use a pencil or crayon to draw the path.

Lost Bunny

Draw the path to the baby bunny.

Point to and say the word hen at the top of the page. Have the child repeat it. Ask the child to circle the **-en** ending in the words in the middle of the page. Then have him or her trace the letters **e** and **n** at the end of the words at the bottom.

Words with -en

hen

Circle the **-en** ending.

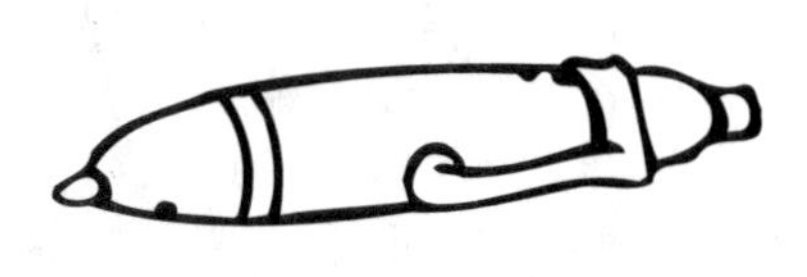

men **pen** **ten**

Trace the letters.

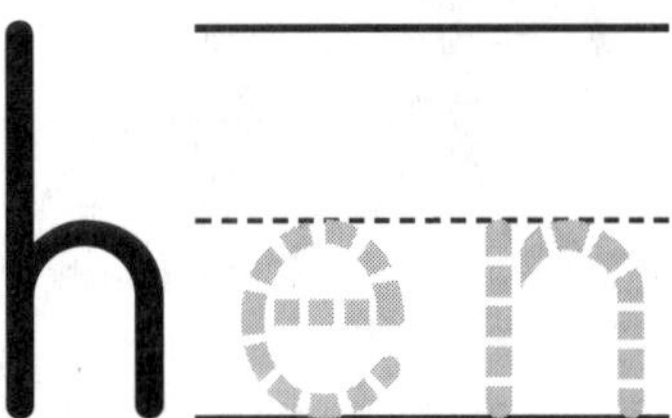

Say the name of each picture. Have the child repeat them. Then ask him or her to trace the letters **a** and **n** at the end of each word.

Words with -an

Trace the letters.

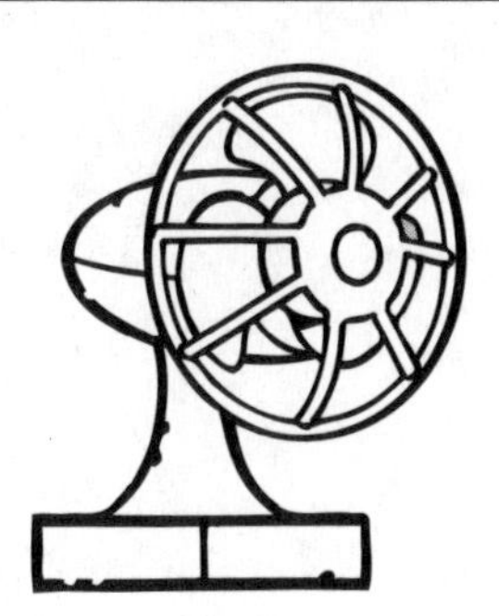

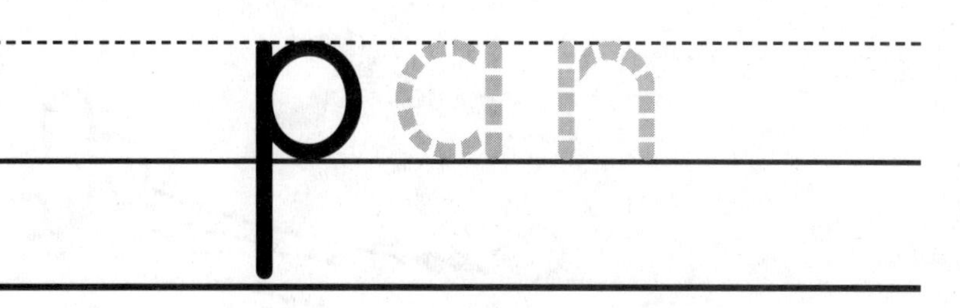

man

Point to and say the word dog at the top of the page. Have the child repeat it. Then ask him or her to trace the letters **o** and **g** at the end of the words at the bottom.

Words with -og

dog

Trace the letters.

Point to and say each word. Have the child repeat them. Ask the child to trace the beginning letter of each word. Then have him or her draw a line to the picture it names on the right.

Words with -ig

Trace the letter. Draw a line to the matching picture.

Point to and say each word. Have the child repeat them. Then ask him or her to trace the letters in each word and color the pictures

Words with -ub

Trace the words. Color the pictures.

Point to and say the words **in** and **out** at the top of the page. Have the child repeat them. Ask the child to trace the letters in each word at the top. Then have him or her trace the words at the bottom to complete each sentence.

A Puppy In and Out

Trace the words.

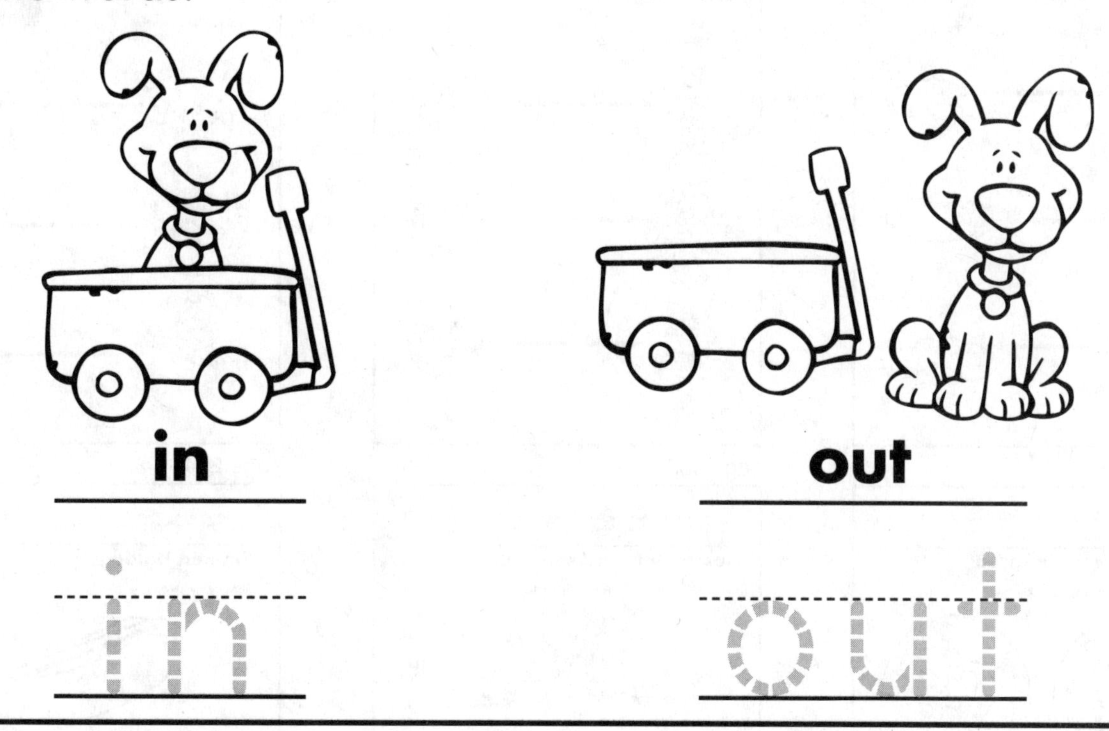

Trace the words.

Answer Key

As the child completes the pages in this section, review his or her answers. When you take the time to correct the work and explain mistakes, you're showing your child that you feel learning is important.

page 229

page 230

page 231

page 232

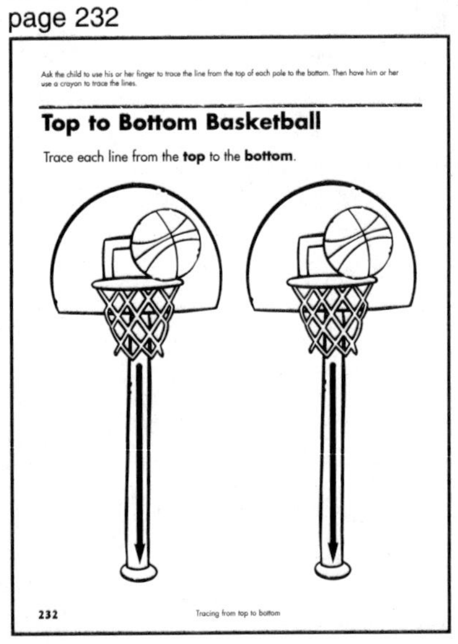

page 233

page 234

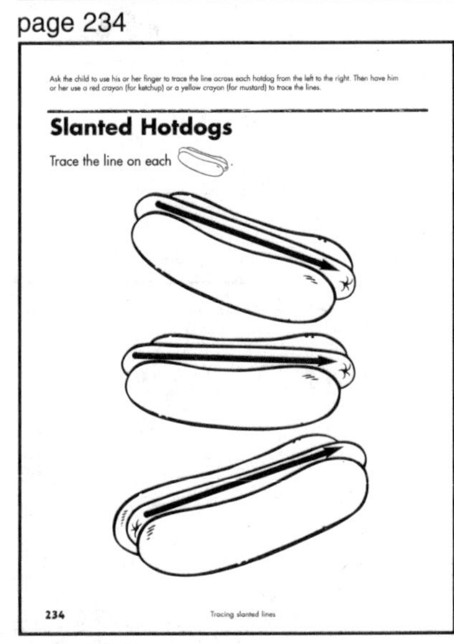

page 235

page 236

page 237

page 238

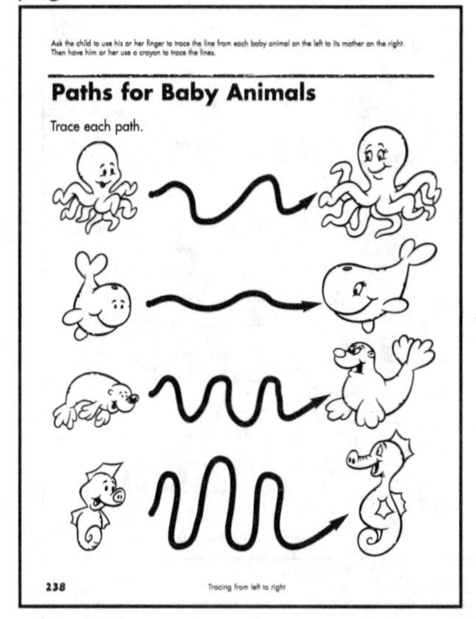

Ask the child to use his or her finger to trace the line from each baby animal on the left to its mother on the right. Then have him or her use a crayon to trace the lines.

Paths for Baby Animals

Trace each path.

238 Tracing from left to right

page 239

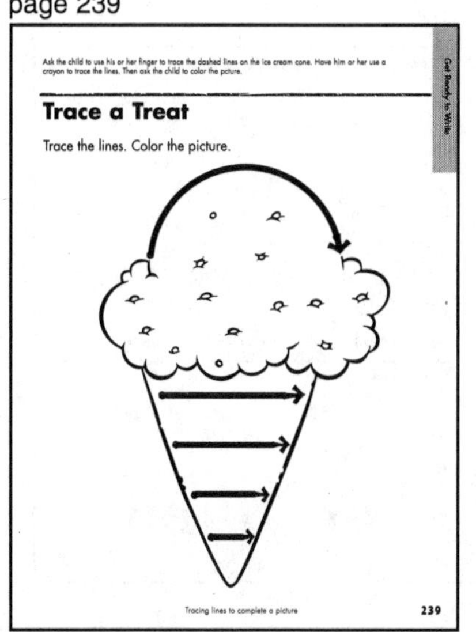

Ask the child to use his or her finger to trace the dashed lines on the ice cream cone. Have him or her use a crayon to trace the lines. Then ask the child to color the pcture.

Trace a Treat

Trace the lines. Color the picture.

Tracing lines to complete a picture 239

page 240

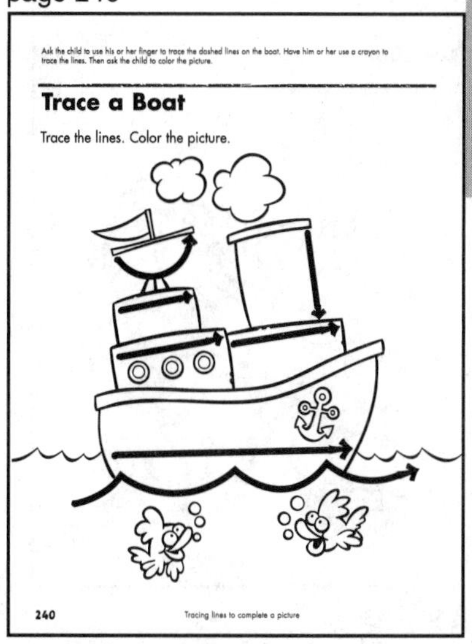

Ask the child to use his or her finger to trace the dashed lines on the boat. Have him or her use a crayon to trace the lines. Then ask the child to color the picture.

Trace a Boat

Trace the lines. Color the picture.

240 Tracing lines to complete a picture

page 241

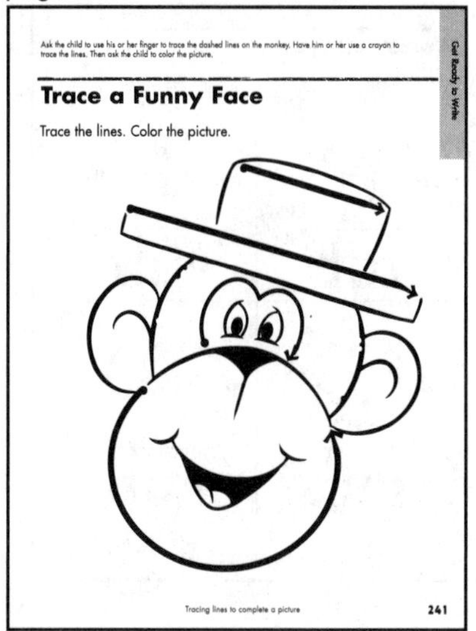

Ask the child to use his or her finger to trace the dashed lines on the monkey. Have him or her use a crayon to trace the lines. Then ask the child to color the picture.

Trace a Funny Face

Trace the lines. Color the picture.

Tracing lines to complete a picture 241

page 242

Ask the child to use his or her finger to trace the dashed lines on the valentine. Have him or her use a crayon to trace the lines. Then ask the child to color the picture.

Trace a Valentine

Trace the lines. Color the picture.

242 Tracing lines to complete a picture

page 243

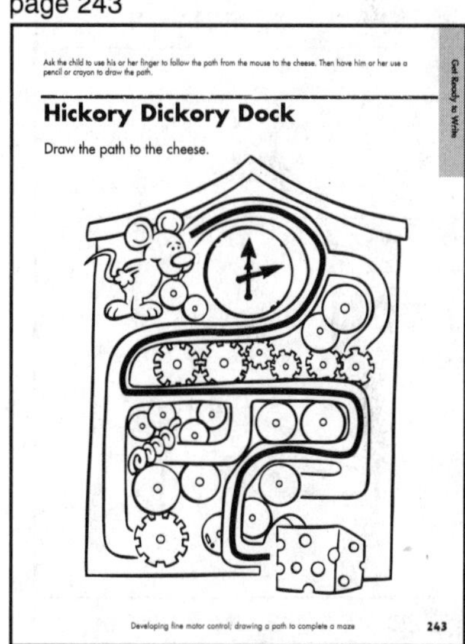

Ask the child to use his or her finger to follow the path from the mouse to the cheese. Then have him or her use a pencil or crayon to draw the path.

Hickory Dickory Dock

Draw the path to the cheese.

Developing fine motor control; drawing a path to complete a maze 243

page 244

Ask the child to use his or her finger to follow the path from the dish to the spoon. Then have him or her use a pencil or crayon to draw the path.

Hey Diddle Diddle

Draw the path to the spoon.

244 Developing fine motor control; drawing a path to complete a maze

page 245

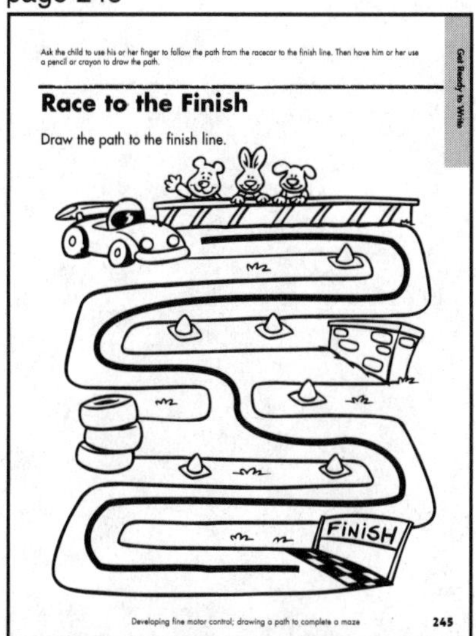

Ask the child to use his or her finger to follow the path from the racecar to the finish line. Then have him or her use a pencil or crayon to draw the path.

Race to the Finish

Draw the path to the finish line.

Developing fine motor control; drawing a path to complete a maze 245

page 246

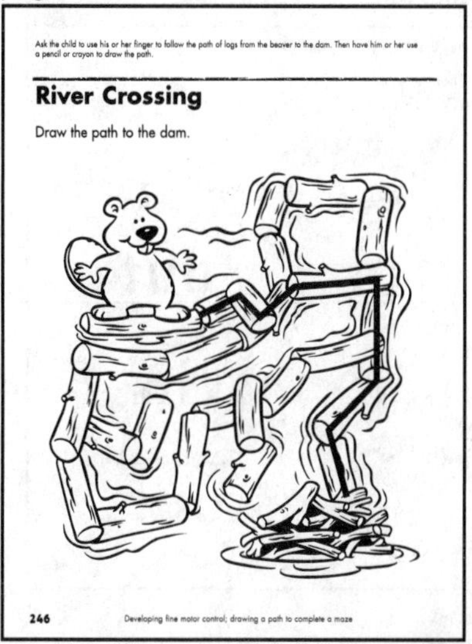

Ask the child to use his or her finger to follow the path of logs from the beaver to the dam. Then have him or her use a pencil or crayon to draw the path.

River Crossing

Draw the path to the dam.

246 Developing fine motor control; drawing a path to complete a maze

page 247

Ask the child to use his or her finger to follow the path of carrots from the mother rabbit to the baby bunny. Then have him or her use a pencil or crayon to draw the path.

Get Ready to Write

Lost Bunny

Draw the path to the baby bunny.

Developing fine motor control; drawing a path to complete a maze 247

page 248

Point to and say the word hen at the top of the page. Have the child repeat it. Ask the child to circle the **-en** ending in the words in the middle of the page. Then have him or her trace the letters **e** and **n** at the end of the words at the bottom.

Words with -en

hen

Circle the **-en** ending.

men pen ten

Trace the letters.

hen ten

248 Tracing letters; identifying words ending with **-en**

page 249

Say the name of each picture. Have the child repeat them. Then ask him or her to trace the letters **a** and **n** at the end of each word.

Get Ready to Write

Words with -an

Trace the letters.

can

fan

pan

man

Tracing letters; identifying words ending with **-an** 249

page 250

Point to and say the word dog at the top of the page. Have the child repeat it. Then ask him or her to trace the letters **o** and **g** at the end of the words at the bottom.

Words with -og

dog

Trace the letters.

dog

log

250 Tracing letters; identifying words ending with **-og**

page 251

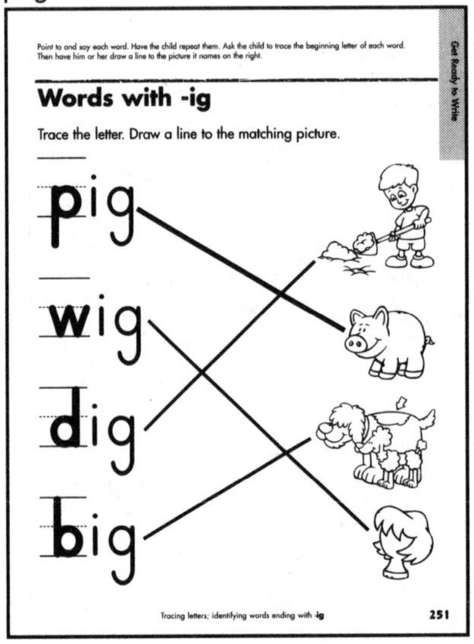

Point to and say each word. Have the child repeat them. Ask the child to trace the beginning letter of each word. Then have him or her draw a line to the picture it names on the right.

Get Ready to Write

Words with -ig

Trace the letter. Draw a line to the matching picture.

pig

wig

dig

big

Tracing letters; identifying words ending with **-ig** 251

page 252

Point to and say each word. Have the child repeat them. Then ask him or her to trace the letters in each word and color the pictures

Words with -ub

Trace the words.

tub sub

tub sub

cub rub

cub rub

252 Tracing letters; identifying words ending with **-ub**

page 253

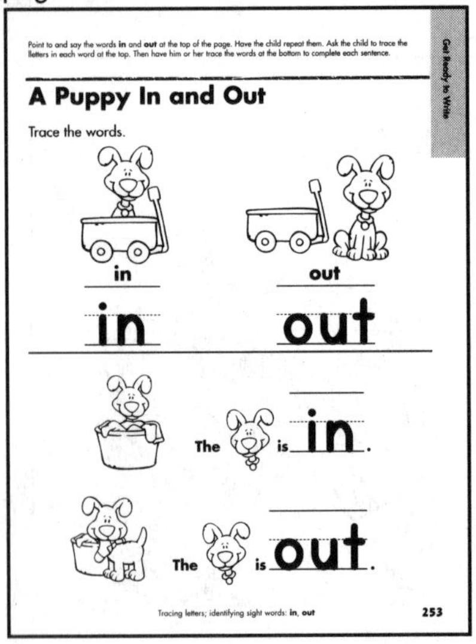

Point to and say the words **in** and **out** at the top of the page. Have the child repeat them. Ask the child to trace the letters in each word at the top. Then have him or her trace the words at the bottom to complete each sentence.

Get Ready to Write

A Puppy In and Out

Trace the words.

in out

in out

The is in.

The is out.

Tracing letters; identifying sight words: **in**, **out** 253

Ask the child to name the pictures on the page. Then have him or her color each one red.

Red

Color the pictures red .

Ask the child to name the pictures on the page. Then have him or her color each one yellow.

Yellow

Color the pictures yellow.

Ask the child to name the pictures on the page. Then have him or her color each one blue.

Blue

Color the pictures blue.

Ask the child to name the pictures on the page. Then have him or her color each one green.

Green

Color the pictures green.

Ask the child to name the pictures on the page. Then have him or her color each one orange.

Orange

Color the pictures orange.

Ask the child to name the pictures on the page. Then have him or her color each one purple.

Purple

Color the pictures (purple).

Ask the child to name the pictures on the page. Then have him or her color each one brown.

Brown

Color the pictures brown.

Ask the child to name the pictures on the page. Then have him or her color each one black.

Black

Color the pictures (black).

Read the directions to the child, identifying each picture and the color word on each crayon. Then ask the child to follow the directions to color the pictures.

Colorful World

Colors

Read the directions to the child, identifying each picture and the color word on each crayon. Ask the child to follow the directions to color the animals. Then have him or her color the pails to match the animals.

Summer Fun

Color the  s 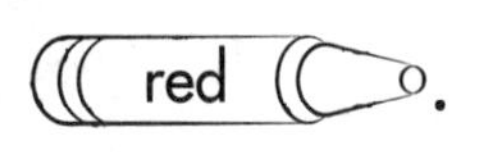

. Color the  s 

.

Color the  s purple. Color the  s to match the animals.

Help the child read the color code, identifying which letter stands for which color. Then ask the child to follow the code to color the clown.

Colorful Clown

Color the clown using the code.

r = red **o** = orange **y** = yellow

b = blue **g** = green

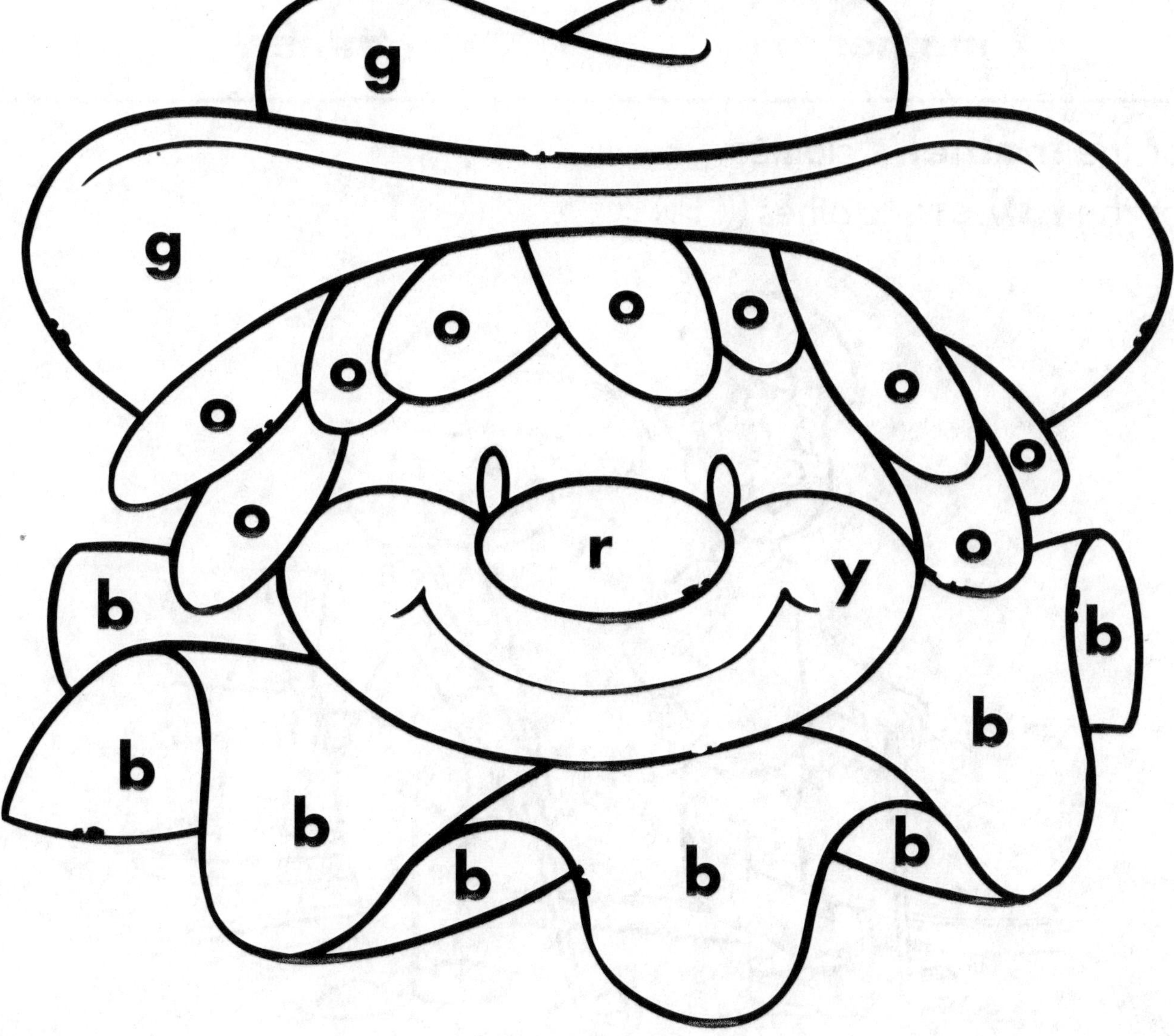

Point to each person at the top of the page and say his or her name. Read the directions to the child, identifying the color of each crayon. Then ask the child to follow the directions to color the picture.

Names for People

mother

father

Color the **mother's** clothes red.
Color the **father's** clothes blue.

Point to each person at the top of the page and say his or her name. Read the directions to the child, identifying the color of each crayon. Then ask the child to follow the directions to color the picture.

More Names for People

sister

brother

Color the **sisters'** clothes green.
Color the **brother's** clothes yellow.

Point to each animal at the top of the page and say its name. Read the directions to the child, identifying the color of each crayon. Then ask the child to follow the directions to color the picture.

Farm Animals

Color the **pig** (pink).
Color the **cow** (brown).

Point to each pet at the top of the page and say its name. Read the directions to the child, identifying the color of each crayon. Then ask the child to follow the directions to color the picture.

Pets

Color the **cat** (yellow).
Color the **dog** (red).

Point to each place at the top of the page and say its name. Read the directions to the child, identifying the color of each crayon. Then ask the child to follow the directions to color the picture.

Names for Places

Color the **house** (blue).

Color the **store** (green).

Color the **fire station** (red).

Point to each place at the top of the page and say its name. Read the directions to the child, identifying the color of each crayon. Then ask the child to follow the directions to color the picture.

More Names for Places

Color the **park** (green).
Color the **zoo** (brown).
Color the **beach** (yellow).

Point to each vegetable at the top of the page and say its name. Read the directions to the child, identifying the color of each crayon. Then ask the child to follow the directions to color the picture.

Names for Things

Color the **carrot** (orange).
Color the **lettuce** (green).
Color the **tomato** (red).

Point to each thing at the top of the page and say its name. Read the directions to the child, identifying the color of each crayon. Then ask the child to follow the directions to color the picture.

More Names for Things

Color the **shell** brown.
Color the **castle** yellow.
Color the **crab** red.

Point to and say the words **long** and **short** at the top of the page. Explain that they are opposites. Read the directions to the child, identifying the color of each crayon. Then ask the child to follow the directions to color the picture.

Long and Short

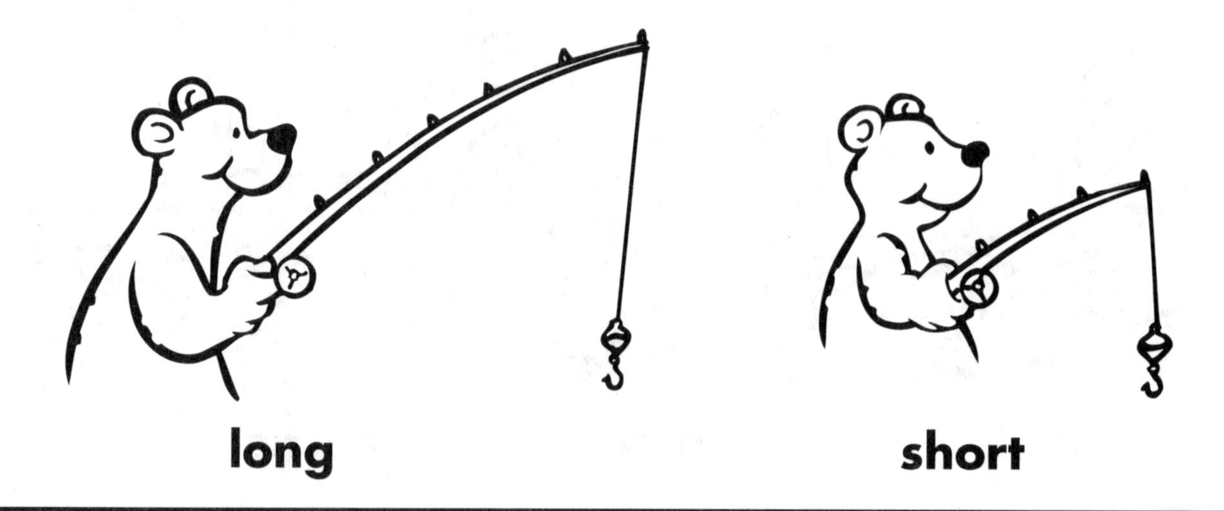

Color the **long** fish blue.
Color the **short** fish orange.
Color the rest of the picture.

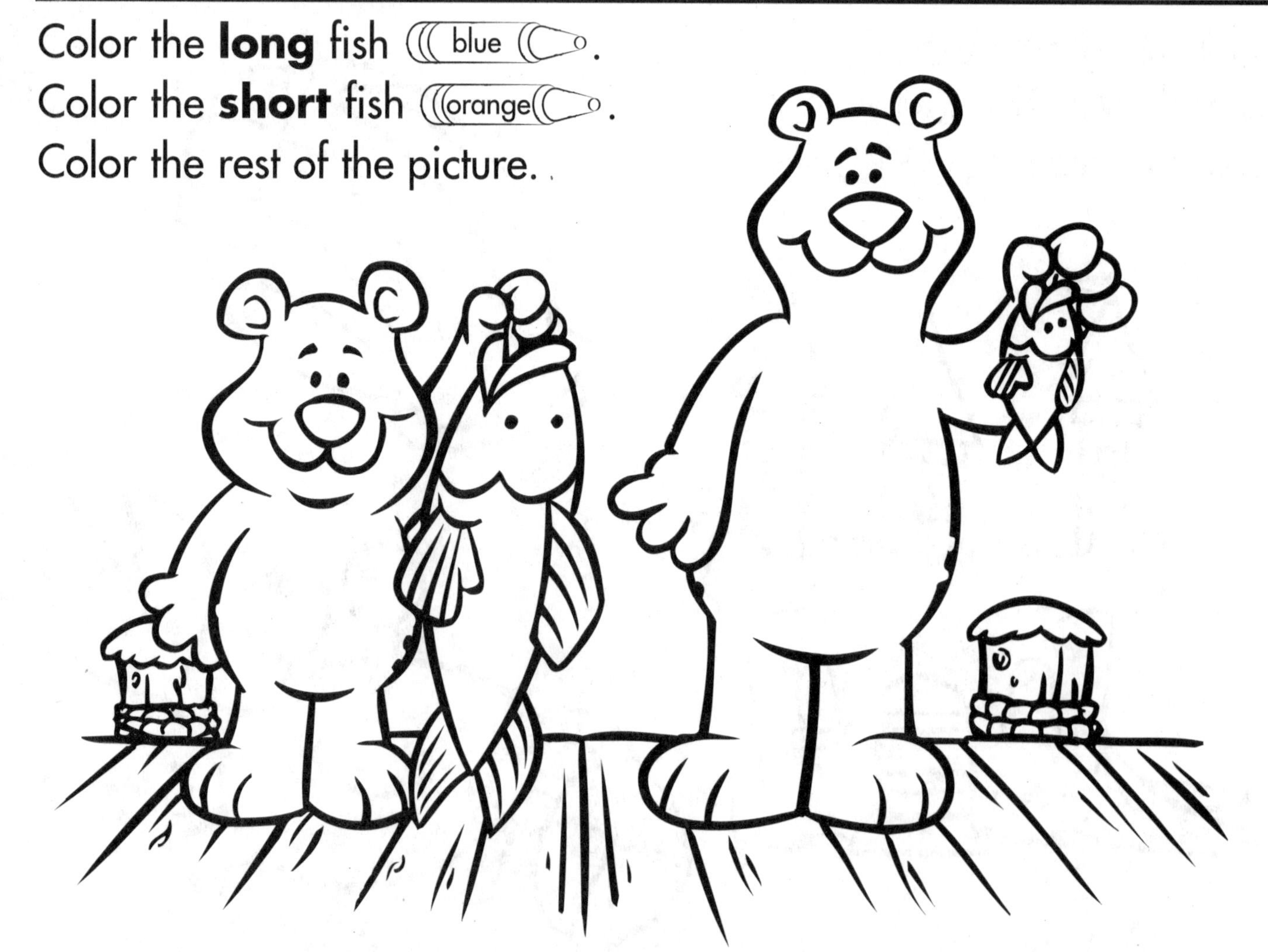

Point to and say the words **hot** and **cold** at the top of the page. Explain that they are opposites. Read the directions to the child, identifying the color of each crayon. Then ask the child to follow the directions to color the picture.

Hot and Cold

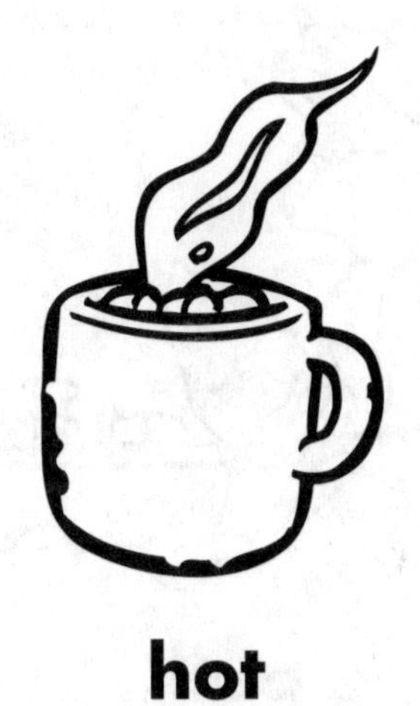

hot

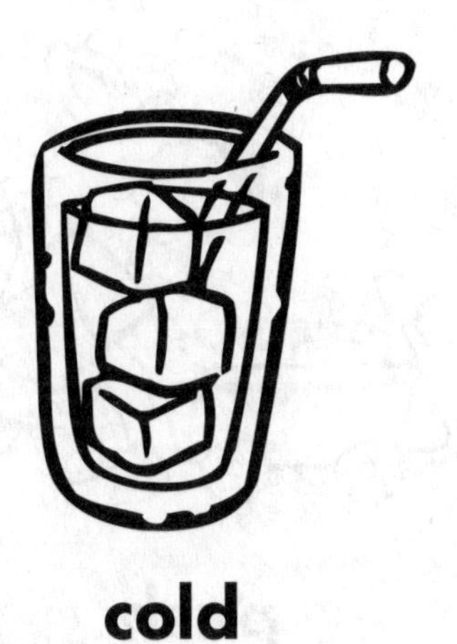

cold

Color the snowman that is **hot** (yellow).
Color the snowman that is **cold** (blue).
Color the rest of the picture.

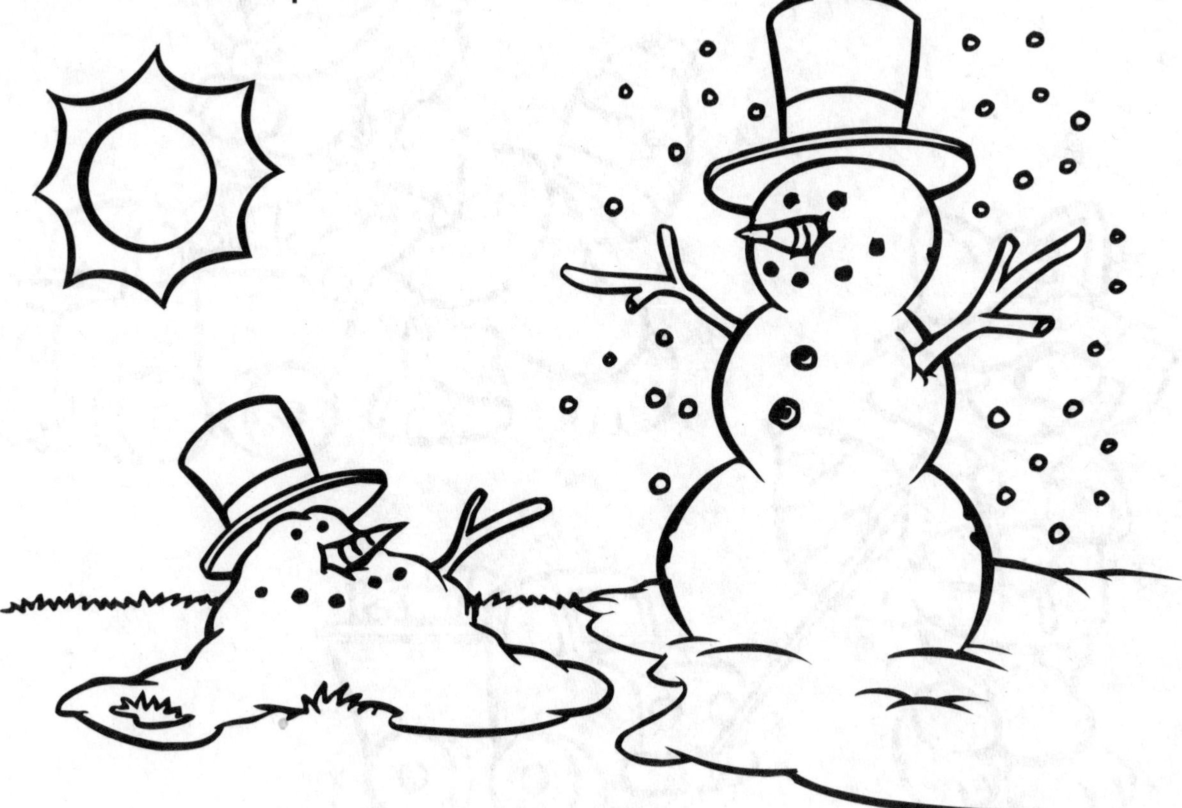

Point to and say the words **push** and **pull** at the top of the page. Explain that they are opposites. Read the directions to the child, identifying the color of each crayon. Then ask the child to follow the directions to color the picture.

Push and Pull

push

pull

Color the truck being **pushed** red.
Color the truck being **pulled** green.
Color the rest of the picture.

Point to and say the words **old** and **new** at the top of the page. Explain that they are opposites. Read the directions to the child, identifying the color of each crayon. Then ask the child to follow the directions to color the picture.

Old and New

old

new

Colors

Color the **old** toy lion green.
Color the **new** toy lion orange.
Color the rest of the picture.

Point to and say the words **clean** and **dirty** at the top of the page. Explain that they are opposites. Read the directions to the child, identifying the color of each crayon. Then ask the child to follow the directions to color the picture.

Clean and Dirty

clean

dirty

Color the **clean** bunny pink.
Color the **dirty** bunny brown.
Color the rest of the picture.

Point to and say the words **day** and **night** at the top of the page. Explain that they are opposites. Read the directions to the child, identifying the color of each crayon. Then ask the child to follow the directions to color the picture.

Day and Night

day

night

Color the penguin that is fishing during the **day** red.
Color the penguin that is fishing at **night** purple.
Color the rest of the picture.

Point to and say the words **top** and **bottom** at the top of the page. Explain that they are opposites. Read the directions to the child, identifying the color of each crayon. Then ask the child to follow the directions to color the picture.

Top and Bottom

top **bottom**

Color the bricks at the **top** red.
Color the bricks at the **bottom** green.
Color the rest of the picture.

Point to and say the words **in** and **out** at the top of the page. Explain that they are opposites. Read the directions to the child, identifying the color of each crayon. Then ask the child to follow the directions to color the picture.

In and Out

Colors

Color the dogs that are **in** brown.
Color the dogs that are **out** yellow.
Color the rest of the picture.

Point to and say the words **on** and **off** at the top of the page. Explain that they are opposites. Read the directions to the child, identifying the color of each crayon. Then ask the child to follow the directions to color the picture.

On and Off

Color the fish that are **on** the pan purple .
Color the fish that are **off** the pan red .
Color the rest of the picture.

Point to and say the words **left** and **right** at the top of the page. Explain that they are opposites. Read the directions to the child, identifying the color of each crayon. Then ask the child to follow the directions to color the picture.

Left and Right

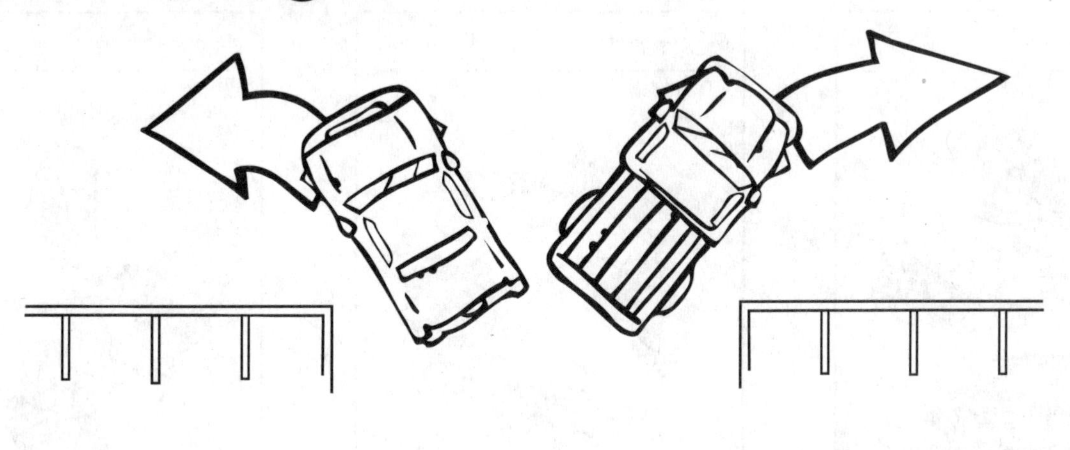

left **right**

Colors

Color the object in the policeman's **left** hand (red crayon).
Color the object in the policemen's **right** hand (green crayon).
Color the rest of the picture.

Answer Key

As the child completes the pages in this section, review his or her answers. When you take the time to correct the work and explain mistakes, you're showing your child that you feel learning is important.

page 257

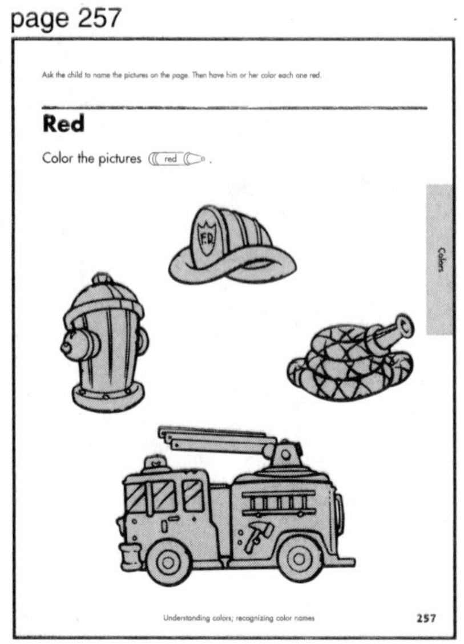

Ask the child to name the pictures on the page. Then have him or her color each one red.

Red

Color the pictures red.

Colors

Understanding colors; recognizing color names 257

page 258

Ask the child to name the pictures on the page. Then have him or her color each one yellow.

Yellow

Color the pictures yellow.

258 Understanding colors; recognizing color names

page 259

Ask the child to name the pictures on the page. Then have him or her color each one blue.

Blue

Color the pictures blue.

Colors

Understanding colors; recognizing color names 259

page 260

Ask the child to name the pictures on the page. Then have him or her color each one green.

Green

Color the pictures green.

260 Understanding colors; recognizing color names

page 261

Ask the child to name the pictures on the page. Then have him or her color each one orange.

Orange

Color the pictures orange.

Colors

Understanding colors; recognizing color names 261

page 262

Ask the child to name the pictures on the page. Then have him or her color each one purple.

Purple

Color the pictures purple.

262 Understanding colors; recognizing color names

page 263

Ask the child to name the pictures on the page. Then have him or her color each one brown.

Brown

Color the pictures brown.

Colors

Understanding colors; recognizing color names 263

page 264

Ask the child to name the pictures on the page. Then have him or her color each one black.

Black

Color the pictures black.

264 Understanding colors; recognizing color names

page 265

Read the directions to the child, identifying each picture and the color word on each crayon. Then ask the child to follow the directions to color the pictures.

Colorful World

Color the yellow. Color the orange.

Color the red. Color the blue.

Colors

Identifying colors; following directions 265

page 266

page 267

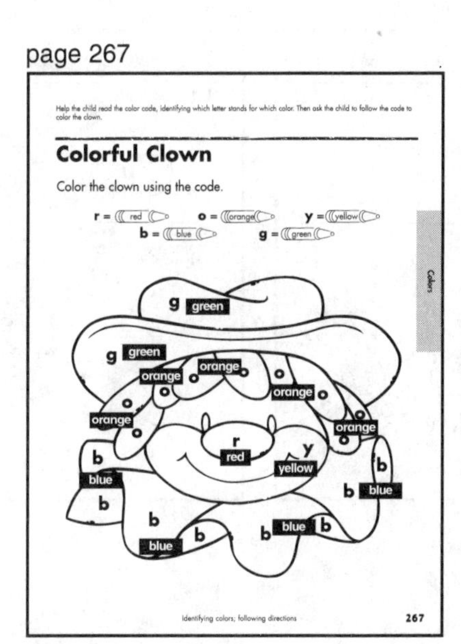

page 268

page 269

page 270

page 271

page 272

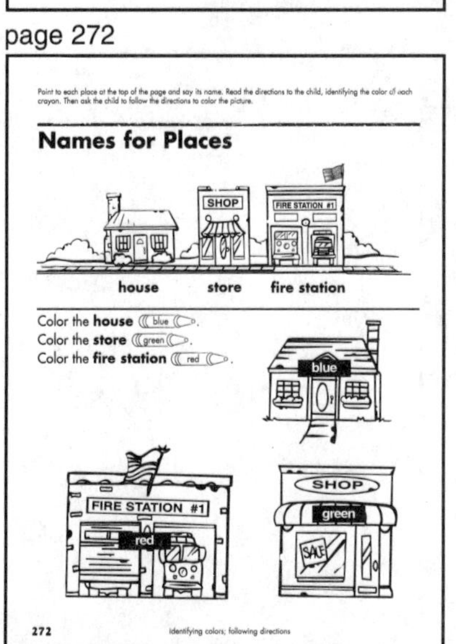

page 273

page 274

Names for Things
carrot
lettuce
tomato
Color the carrot orange.
Color the lettuce green.
Color the tomato red.
orange
red
green
274
Identifying colors; following directions

Colors

page 275

page 276

page 277

page 278

page 279

page 280

page 281

page 282

page 283

page 284

page 285

Point to and say each action word. Ask the child to draw a line between the words that are the same.

You Can Do It!

Match.

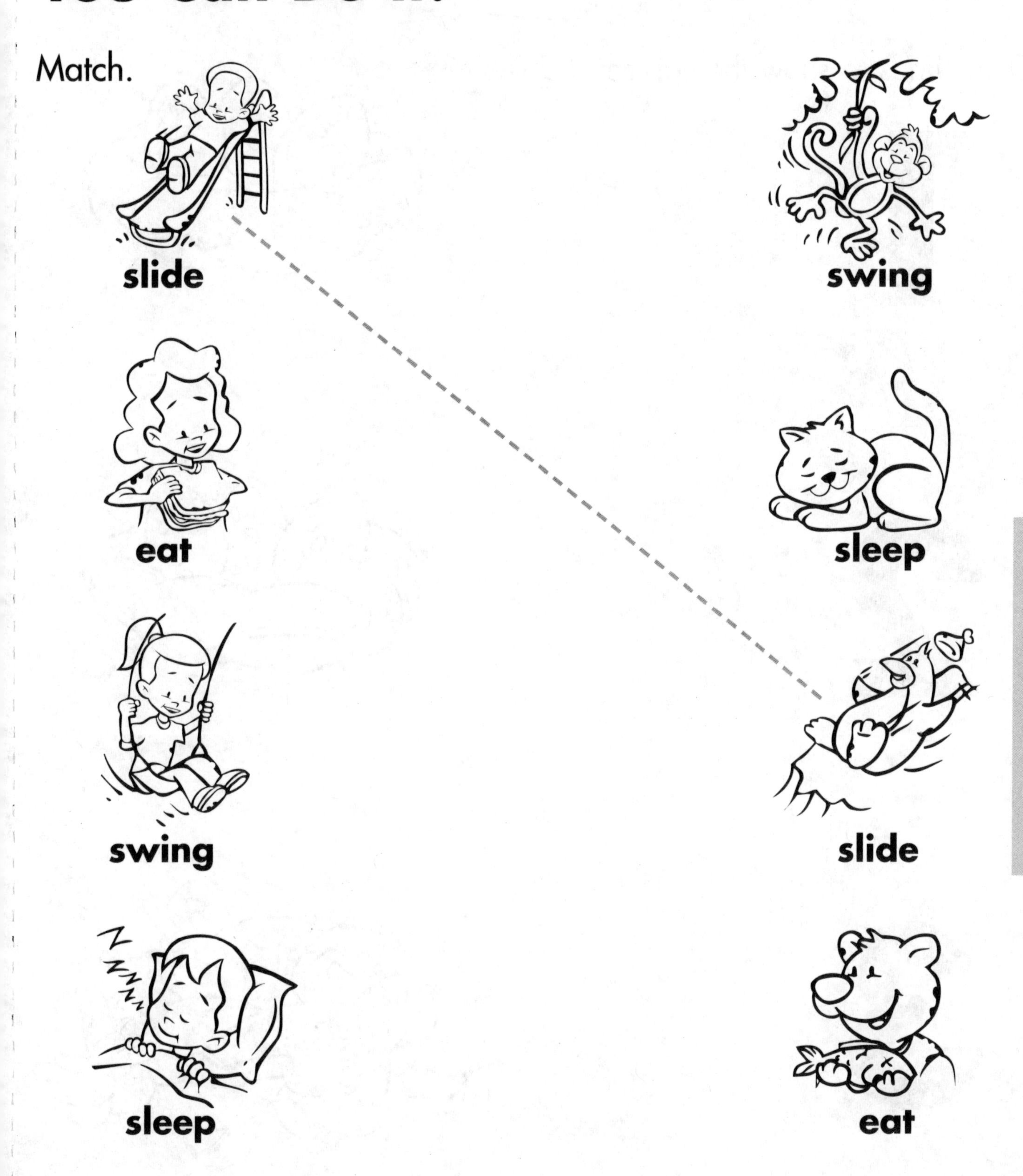

Beginning Reading

Mention to the child that spring is a time of birth and explain that the pictures show three baby robins being born. Then ask the child to draw a line from each number to the picture that shows the correct order of the robins hatching from the eggs.

Robins in Spring

Draw lines to show the correct order.

2

3

Ask the child to draw a line from each number to the picture that shows the correct order of the snowman being built. Then encourage the child to tell a story about the pictures using the words first, next, and last.

Let's Build a Snowman

Draw lines to show the correct order.

Have the child write 1, 2, and 3 in the boxes in each row to show the correct order. Then encourage the child to tell a story about each row of pictures using the words first, next, and last.

Puppy Love

Write **1**, **2**, and **3** to show the order of what happened.

Ask the child to look closely at the picture at the top of the page. Then have him or her color the picture at the bottom that shows what the tigers made.

What Are They Making?

Color what they made.

Ask the child to draw a line from each picture on the left to the one on the right that shows what will happen next.

What Will Happen Next?

Draw a line to what will happen next.

Ask the child to look closely at the first picture in each row. Then have him or her circle the picture in the row that shows what will happen next and color the pictures.

Next, Please!

Circle what will happen next. Color the pictures.

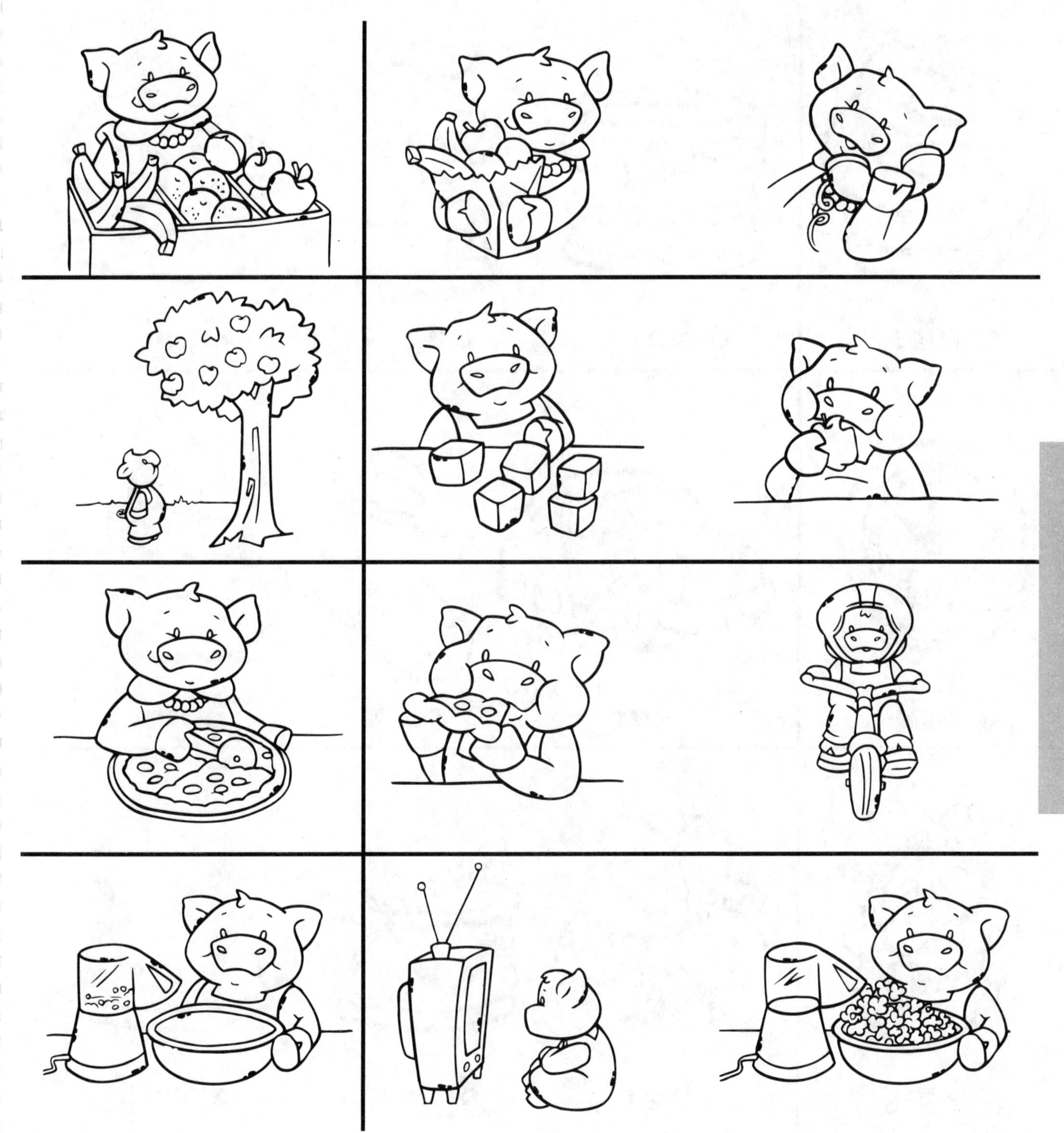

Beginning Reading

Help the child read the word below each picture. Explain that the words **snake** and **cake** in the first row rhyme because they both have the **-ake** sound at the end. Ask the child to circle the cake. Then help him or her find and circle the one that rhymes with the first picture in each of the other rows.

Rows of Rhymes

Circle the one that rhymes with the first picture in each row.

Identifying words that rhyme

Help the child read the word below each picture. Then help him or her find and color the one that rhymes with the first picture in each row.

More Rows of Rhymes

Color the one that rhymes with the first picture in each row.

Help the child read the word below each picture. Then have him or her draw a line between the ones that rhyme.

On-the-Go Rhymes

Match the ones that rhyme.

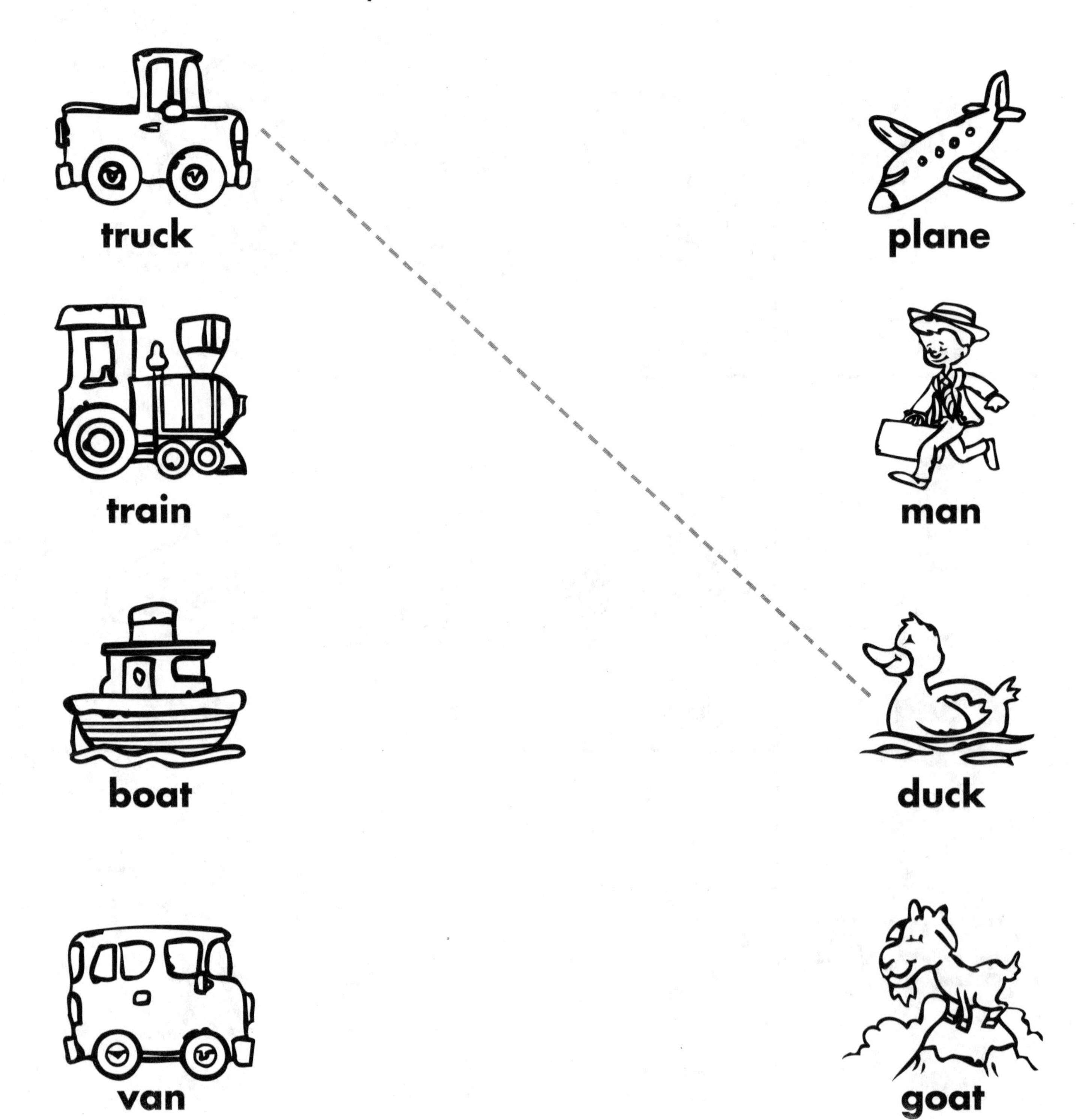

Help the child read the word below each picture. Then have him or her draw a line between the ones that rhyme.

Dress-Up Rhymes

Match the ones that rhyme.

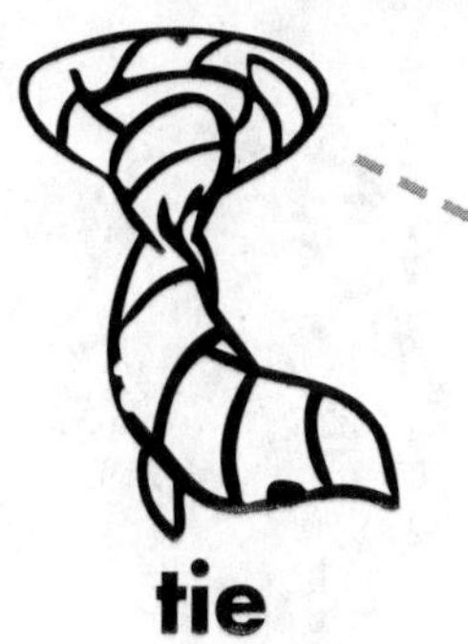

tie

ants

pants

pie

hat

blue

shoe

cat

Help the child read the word below each picture. Then have him or her draw a line between the ones that rhyme.

Art Rhymes

Match the ones that rhyme.

glue

hay

clay

barn

pen

shoe

yarn

hen

Ask the child to look closely at the first word in each row. Then have him or her circle the word in that row that is the same. When the child is finished with all the rows, help him or her read the circled words aloud.

The Cave

Circle the word that is the same in each row.

we	is	we
go	go	am
in	to	in
it	it	do

Ask the child to look closely at the words in each row. Then have him or her circle the words in that row that are the same. When the child is finished with all the rows, help him or her read the circled words aloud.

Cubs In Their Den

Circle the words that are the same in each row.

den	ten	den
mom	mom	mug
rug	hug	hug
cub	tub	cub

Ask the child to say the name of each picture and listen for the beginning sound. Then have him or her complete the word under each picture by choosing and writing the missing letter that stands for the beginning sound. Encourage the child to read the words aloud after he or she completes them.

Make a Word

Write the missing letter to make the word.

d **l**

dog

w **p**

__ig

b **c**

__at

h **p**

__en

Ask the child to say the name of each picture and listen for the beginning sound. Then have him or her complete the word under each picture by writing the letter **b** or **c**. Encourage the child to read the words aloud after he or she completes them.

Make More Words

Write **b** or **c** to make the word.

Ask the child to say the name of each picture and listen for the beginning sound. Then have him or her complete the word under each picture by choosing and writing the missing letter that stands for the beginning sound. Encourage the child to read the words aloud after he or she completes them.

Find a Letter

Write the missing letter to make the word.

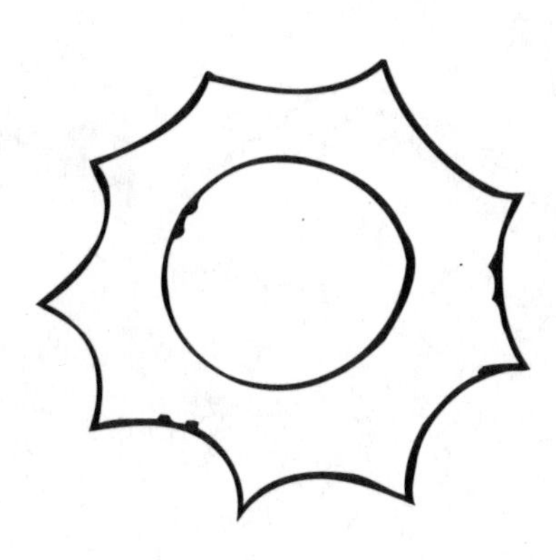

___un

___ap

___en

___ox

Ask the child to name each picture. Then have him or her draw a line from each picture to the word that says what it is. Encourage the child to read the words aloud.

Match Them Up!

Match.

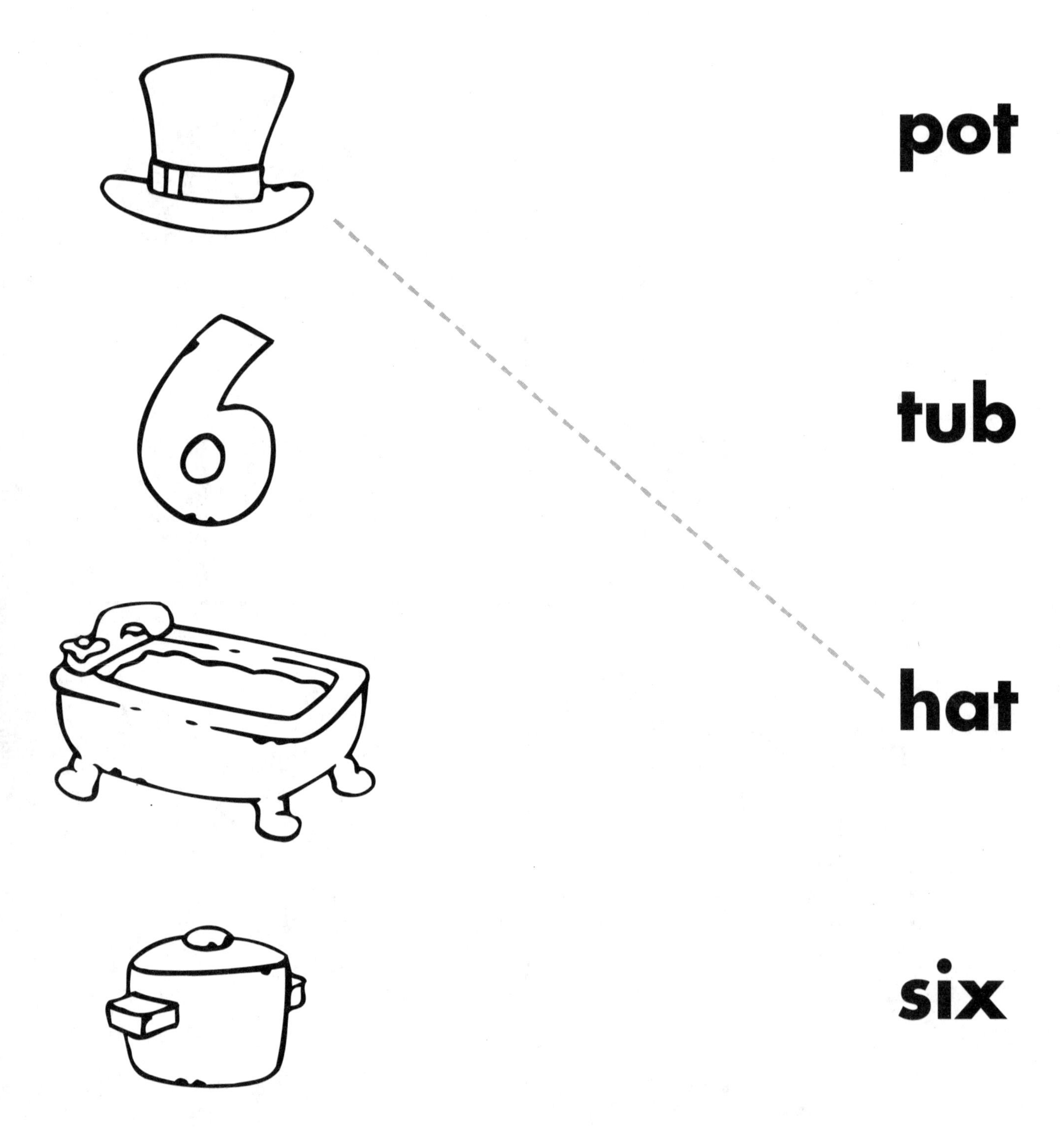

Help the child read each word aloud. Then have him or her draw a line from each word to the picture it names.

More Match-Ups!

Match.

bug

top

net

jam

Point to and say the words **can** and **go** at the top of the page. Ask the child to repeat each word and spell it. Then have him or her trace the words. At the bottom of the page, ask the child to help the tigers get to the finish line by drawing the paths with the words **can** and **go**. Have the child read each word as he or she passes it.

Tigers Can Go!

Read the word. Trace the word.

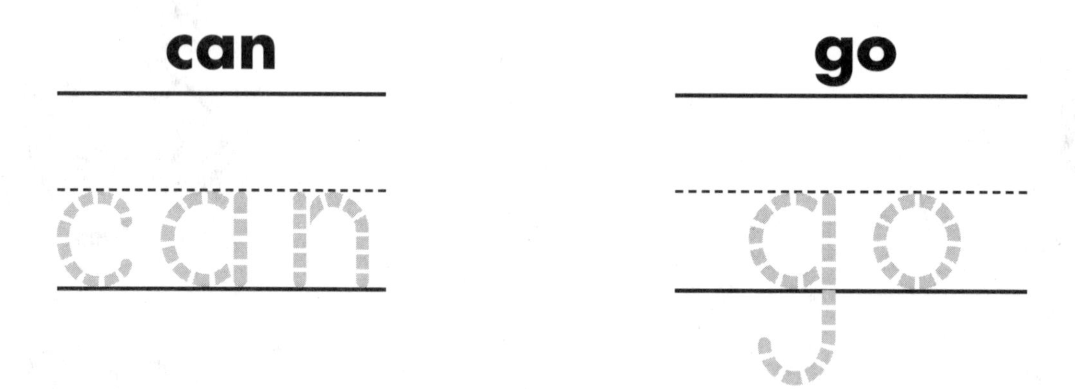

Draw the paths with **can** and **go**.

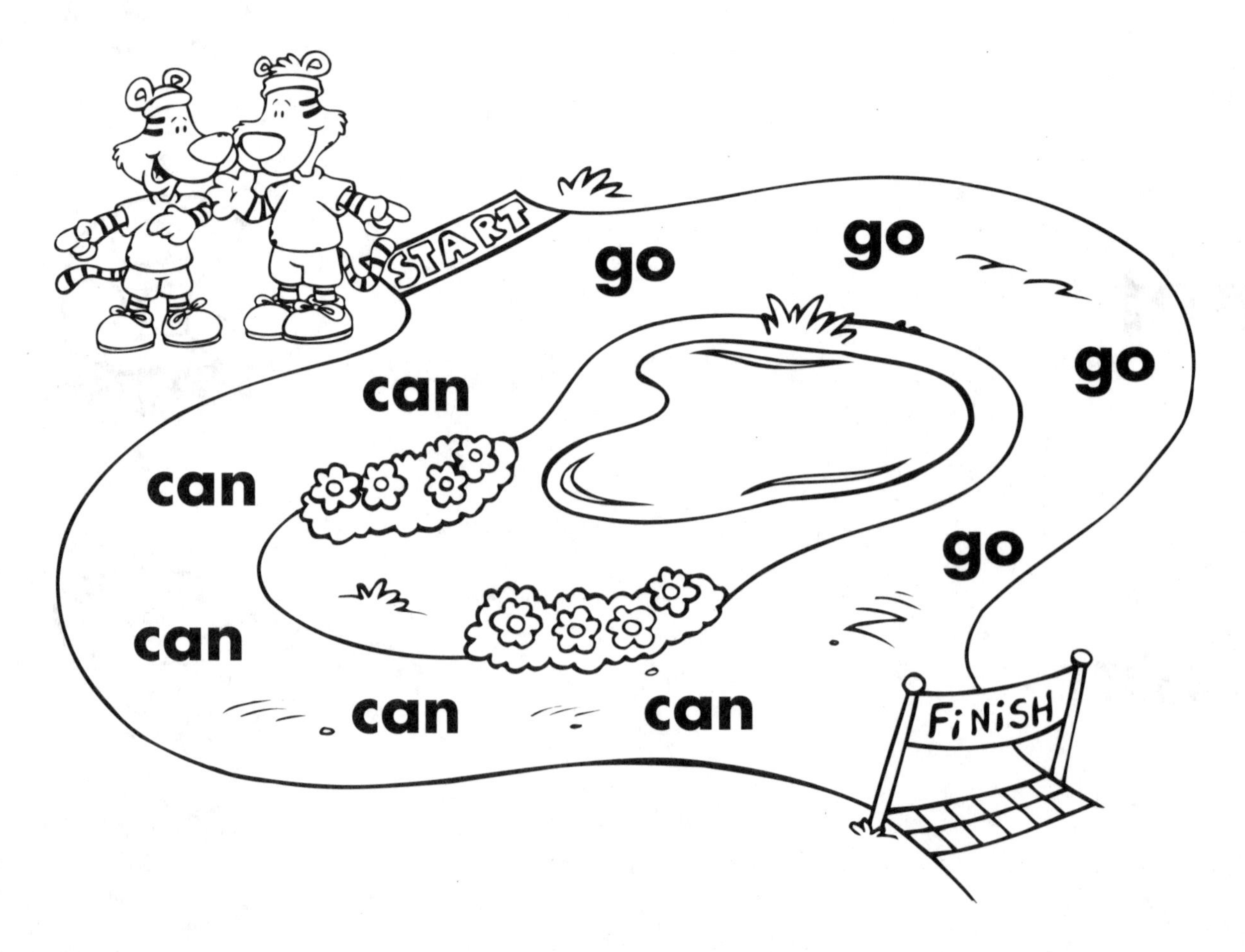

Point to and say the words **yes** and **no** at the top of the page. Ask the child to repeat each word and spell it. Then have him or her trace the words. At the bottom of the page, help the child read each question and circle **yes** or **no** to answer the questions.

Is It A Pet?

Read the word. Trace the word.

yes

yes

no

no

Circle **yes** or **no**.

Is the  **a toy?** **yes** **no**

Is the  **a toy?** **yes** **no**

Is the  **a pet?** **yes** **no**

Is the  **a pet?** **yes** **no**

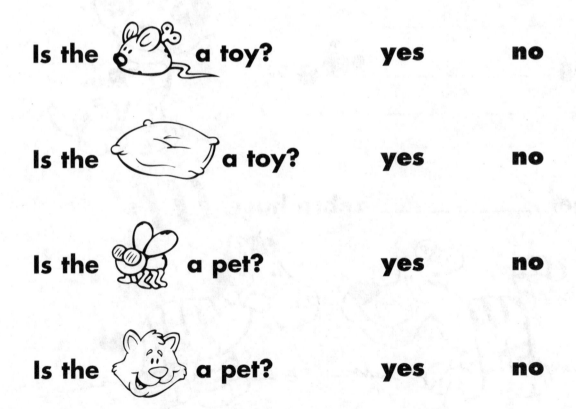

Point to and say the words **has** and **and** at the top of the page. Ask the child to repeat each word and spell it. Then have him or her trace the words. At the bottom of the page, help the child read each sentence and write **has** or **and** to complete it.

Spots and Stripes

Read the word. Trace the word.

has | **and**

has | and

Write **has** or **and** to complete the sentence.

The dog ____________  **s.**

The tiger ____________ **zebra have**  **s.**

Point to and say the word **my** at the top of the page. Ask the child to repeat the word and spell it. Have him or her trace the word. Then have the child write **my** on the blank line. At the bottom of the page, help the child read each sentence and write **my** to complete it. Ask him or her whose ear is in the last sentence. (It's an elephant's ear!)

My, My, My!

Read the word. Trace the word.

My .

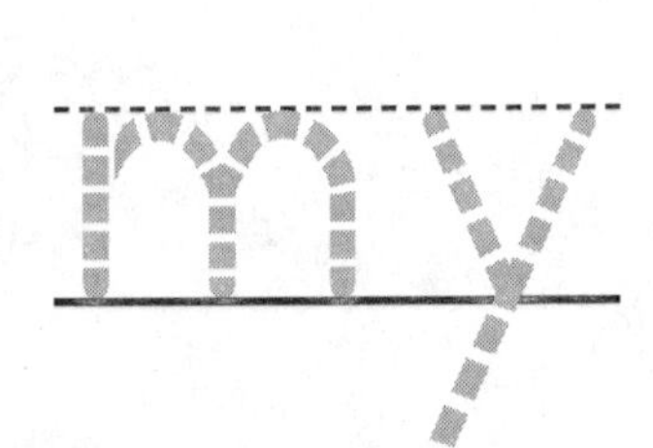

My .

Write **my** to complete the sentence.

That is ______ 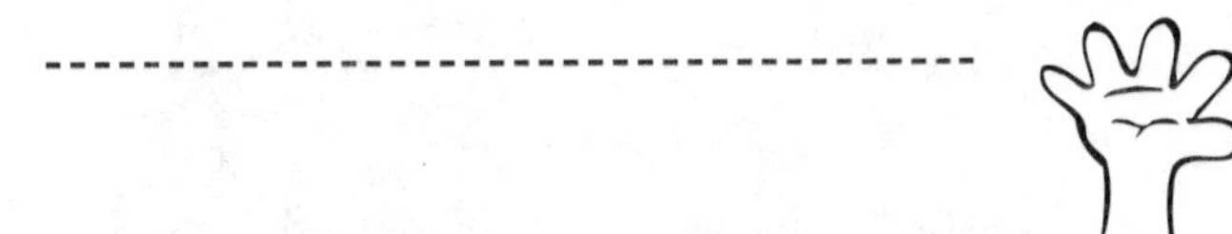.

That is ______.

That is ______ .

That is NOT ______ !

Beginning Reading

Point to and say the words **I** and **we** at the top of the page. Ask the child to repeat each word and spell it. Have him or her trace the words. At the bottom of the page, ask the child to look closely at the pictures and write **I** or **We** to complete each sentence. Help him or her read the sentences.

On the Playground

Read the word. Trace the word.

I **We**

I We

Write **I** or **We** to complete the sentence.

______ **can go on the**  .

______ **can go on the**  !

Ask the child to color the cards. Then help him or her cut them out. Place the cards picture side up on a table and have the child match the pictures with the word cards on page 315.

Picture Cards

Color the cards. Cut out the cards.

Help the child cut out the cards. Place them word side up on a table and have the child match the words with the picture cards on page 313.

Word Cards

Cut out the cards.

mop	van
tub	pen
ham	bag
web	rug

Ask the child to look closely at the pictures at the top of the page. Help him or her identify what is happening in each picture. At the bottom of the page, help the child read each question and circle the answer **yes** or **no**.

I Can! Can You?

Circle **yes** or **no**.

Can a  **hug?**

yes **no**

Can a  **sing?**

yes **no**

Can a  **hop?**

yes **no**

Can a  **run?**

yes **no**

Answer Key

As the child completes the pages in this section, review his or her answers. When you take the time to correct the work and explain mistakes, you're showing your child that you feel learning is important.

page 289

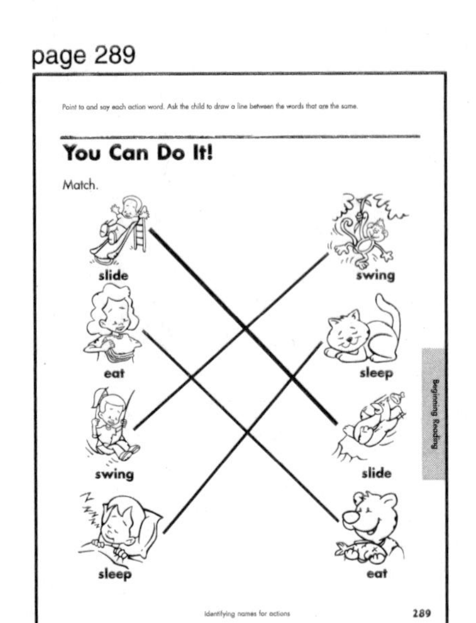

page 290

page 291

page 292

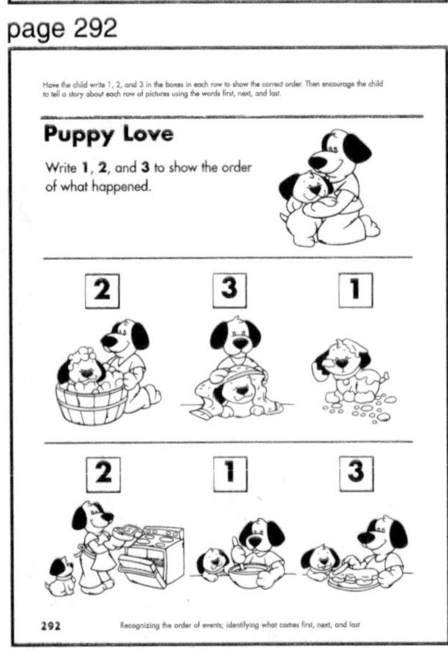

page 293

page 294

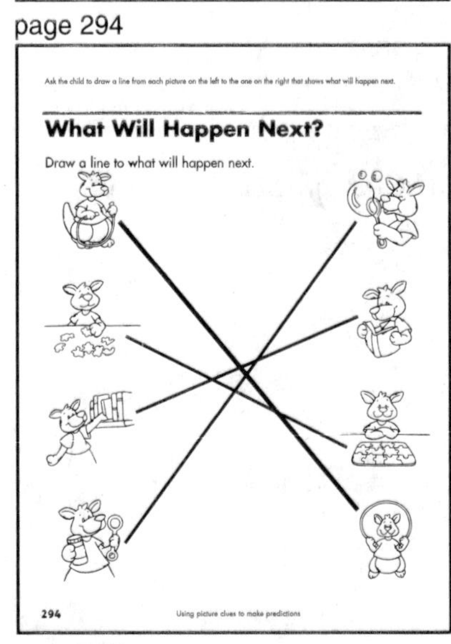

page 295

page 296

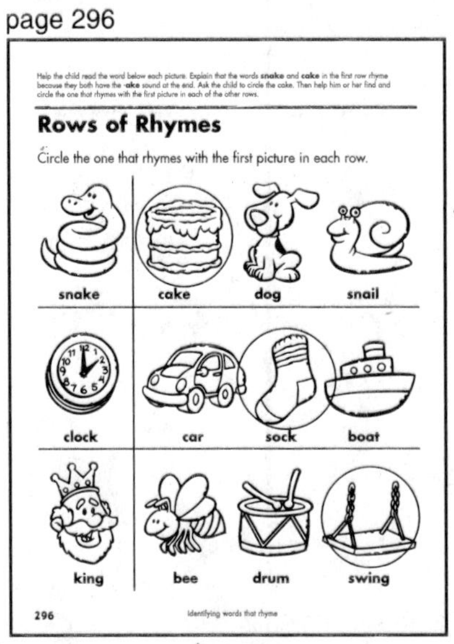

page 297